Cyclic Form
and the English Mystery Plays

» LUDUS «
Medieval and Early Renaissance Theatre and Drama
7

Edited by

Wim Hüsken

Volume 1: English Parish Drama
Volume 2: Civic Ritual and Drama
Volume 3: Between Folk and Liturgy
Volume 4: Carnival and the Carnivalesque
Volume 5: Moving Subjects
Volume 6: Farce and Farcical Elements
Volume 7: Cyclic Form and the English Mystery Plays

Cyclic Form and the English Mystery Plays

A Comparative Study of
the English Biblical Cycles and their
Continental and Iconographic Counterparts

by
Peter Happé

Amsterdam – New York, NY 2004

Cover design: Studio Pollmann

All titles in the Ludus - Medieval and Early Renaissance Theatre and Drama series (from 2002 onwards) are available to download from the Ingenta website http://www.ingenta.com

The paper on which this book is printed meets the requirements of "ISO 9706:1994, Information and documentation - Paper for documents - Requirements for permanence".

Le papier sur lequel le présent ouvrage est imprimé remplit les prescriptions de "ISO 9706:1994, Information et documentation - Papier pour documents - Prescriptions pour la permanence".

ISBN: 90-420-1652-3
©Editions Rodopi B.V., Amsterdam – New York, NY 2004
Printed in The Netherlands

Contents

Preface 7
List of Illustrations 9
Abbreviations 11

1. Cyclic Form (I) 13

2. Cycles and Iconography 67

3. Continental Analogues: A Review of Allied Forms –
   France and Germany 136

4. Continental Analogues: A Review of Allied Forms –
   Italy, The Netherlands and Spain 196

5. English Practice 222

6. Cyclic Form (II) 313

Bibliography 329
Index 346

Preface

A primary interest, even a belief, in the performance qualities of the English mystery cycles has led me to develop ideas in this book on how they might have been revealed during the two centuries or so in which they were originally played. An appreciation of these, much enhanced in the last thirty years by a series of stimulating representations, particularly at York, is a major ingredient of an understanding of cyclic form, my main objective here. I have centred this upon the five extant mystery cycles in England, but I think our appreciation of them can be sharpened by adducing information about the formidable number of cycles generated in neighbouring continental countries during the same period. Beyond this, the qualities of cyclic form inherent in this investigation may also be appreciated by collocation with some aspects of its use in iconography. It is hoped that these continental and iconographic contexts will enhance our reading—and seeing and hearing—of the English plays, by invoking historical perspectives as well as aesthetic or dramatic ones. Such a study may also highlight some notable differences between English practice and that of other places and times.

An undertaking of this kind, which is admittedly selective, involves making use of the work of many specialists in the drama and in iconography, to such an extent that it is impossible to acknowledge my many debts, except in the most general terms. However, it gives me much pleasure to thank the following scholars who have been so generous in supplying suggestions, as well as answers to queries: Richard Beadle, Carla Dauven, Clifford Davidson, Wim Hummelen, Wim Hüsken, Alan Knight, Lynette R. Muir, Roberta Mullini, Nerida Newbigin, Bart Ramakers, Martial Rose, Graham Runnalls, Elsa Strietman and

Meg Twycross. But ultimately it is I who must take responsibility for rummaging about in other people's well-cultivated gardens.

Gundleton (UK), July 2003

List of Illustrations, pages 96 to 102

Fig. 1   Norwich Cathedral Roof Boss (1463+): *Nativity*

Fig. 2   *Biblia Pauperum* (*c.* 1460): Christ Appears to his Disciples, with Joseph reveals himself to his brothers, and the return of the Prodigal Son

Fig. 3   *The Holkham Bible Picture Book* (1325-30): Noah in the Ark with Raven and Dove, British Library, MS Add. 47682, fol. 8r.

Fig. 4   Duccio – Scenes from *Maestà* verso (1311), Cathedral Museum, Siena (detail)

Fig. 5   Giotto – Composite of details from north wall (by 1313), Arena Chapel, Padua

Fig. 6   Memling – *Scenes from the Passion* (1470-1), Sabauda Gallery, Turin

Fig. 7   Tintoretto – *Road to Calvary* (1576-81), Scuola di San Rocco, Venice

Acknowledgements:
(1)   Julia Hedgecoe
(2), (5)   Southampton University
(3)   The British Library
(4), (6), (7) The Syndics of Cambridge University Library

Abbreviations

CD	*Comparative Drama*
EDAM Review	*Early Drama, Art and Music Review*
EETS	*Early English Text Society*
LSE	*Leeds Studies in English*
JEGP	*Journal of English and Germanic Philology*
METh	*Medieval English Theatre*
PL	J.-P. Migne [ed.], *Patrologiae Cursus Completus: Series Latina*, Paris, 1844-64, 221 vols.
REED	*Records of Early English Drama*
RORD	*Research Opportunities in Renaissance Drama*
SATF	*Société des Anciens Textes Français*
STC	W. A. Jackson, F. J. Ferguson, and K. F. Panzer [eds.], *A Short-Title Catalogue of Books printed in England, Scotland and Ireland, and of English Books Printed Abroad*, 3 vols., London, 1976-91 [2nd edition].

Chapter One
Cyclic Form (I)

In this study we shall be concerned with a large number of variables surrounding cyclic form as manifested in the drama of England and continental Europe. As we shall see, its existence can hardly be questioned, but it refuses to conform to a simple definition. In late medieval Europe we can trace dozens, probably more than a hundred large-scale plays based upon a narrative structure drawn from biblical or from other quasi-historical sources. One cannot, however, lay down how large a play had to be in order to become a cycle: the essence of the form lies elsewhere. Criteria arising from performance are as varied as are the texts themselves. Nevertheless we can say that the evidence from the large number of surviving plays suggests that while some early cycle plays can be found in the fourteenth century, or even earlier, the period of greatest growth and popularity is apparently from about 1450 onwards, and that the cycles continued to be of abiding interest throughout the sixteenth century in spite of the coming of new theatrical ideas associated with the Renaissance, and of new religious and philosophical emphases. Such a long period of survival and performance attracts our attention, especially as the cycle plays were performed in so many different ways, and as some seem to have had a fairly stable, even conservative life, while others were rewritten and revised as new ideas and practices were fed into them to such an extent that it might be said that adaptability was one of their hallmarks.

To begin with we shall be concerned to give a general description of the cyclic form, and to describe the contexts, religious, social and theatrical, in which cycle plays evolved, and to give an account of the size and scope which are apparent from the surviving examples. At the same time it cannot be proper to be too exclusive as there are so many analogues to the cycles. These may help to clarify what cyclic form is and also to show what the advantages of it were. We shall suggest some reasons why the form became so popular, or indeed why it came about that so many people with a variety of motives felt it worthwhile to commit enormous resources, financial, artistic and social, to its development. We shall hope to show in Chapter Two that there are a number of important factors to be discerned from the parallel development of visual cycles. In their turn these may have had different motivations and provenances, and they had a longer time span, and yet, considered from an aesthetic point of view, they have a good deal in common with the dramatic examples, and the comparison is mutually illuminating.

In pursuing the cyclic form we shall find examples from a variety of European countries. It will be seen that there are many features which are distinctive to particular locations, and to larger quasi-national groupings. But the position is all the more intriguing because there must have been a great deal of interaction between the way the cycles were conceived in different countries and in local areas. In some places this involved taking over texts from elsewhere, and copying *verbatim*, as well as adaptation to fit differing requirements. On the one hand the appearance of the dramatic cycles comes about at roughly the same time in history, and there are many individual characteristics distributed among them. But on the other hand they fulfilled different functions in different cultural milieux. Moreover they arise from cultural features which transcend national boundaries (themselves unstable and prone to change) since their religious assumptions were part of a faith which was disseminated by similar means through western Europe. It is true too that the Reformation, with its shifts in many aspects of belief did not automatically bring the life of the cycles to an end even though they were conceived under the pervasive influence of medieval Catholicism. There are distinct indications that for some Protestants cyclic form was an opportunity, not least because its origins were distinctly of the old religion. To initiate change to an existing form is in part a recognition of it as an inherent strength.[1] The prolonged 'dialogue' (if that is an adequate word) between Catholics and Protestants lies behind the cycle plays. Some were developed or modified in order to bear upon it, and we shall see that in the case of Chester, at least, Reformation politics are a significant element in what survives today.

Characteristics

Like so many other critical terms, 'cycle' is really an invention of critics and scholars, evolved after the event to which it is retrospectively attached. As far as I am aware it was not used for large scale plays in the middle ages, when the commonest terms were 'Mysteries' (*Mystères*) or 'Passions', and its application to them comes about indirectly by transfer from other cyclic literary forms. When applied to these in English usage the word seems first to have been used to suggest the idea of circularity, of something which returns upon itself (*OED* 3c). To this we may add that although the work has a narrative structure comprising a series of events, this tends to circulate around a core, a central event which attracts the constituent parts to it in some way and constantly invites their appraisal. But the linkage is often very loose, and the term cycle is sometimes pressed into use precisely because no exact relationship between constituent parts can be perceived. Early examples to which the term was applied were poems which were thought to complete Homer's narrative—though his central poems do not seem to have attracted the term until more recent times—and works celebrating the exploits of Charlemagne and King Arthur. It is apparent that some users of the term meant it to be pejorative: to show a lack of unity. This has been traced to Aristotle's comments upon the epic in *The Poetics*.[2] Such a view remains an active part of the critique of cyclic form whether its strength lies in a unity which comprehends the apparent diversity of its parts, or whether individual elements acquire an intense separateness which can be but loosely connected to the whole. At this stage we may therefore suggest that cycles may be both centripetal and centrifugal.

The instances of Charlemagne and Arthur are also remarkable because they are largely concerned with myths and it seems that the power of myth might just have that magnetic force which encourages central reference. Without getting too involved in an interminable metaphor, we might say that a myth, because of the significance it acquires from its high cultural status, may generate other material which reflects back upon it, and that such subordinate material functions as a means of enhancing the central matter, however indirectly.

A further aspect is discernible in the use of the word cycle for the romances about Charlemagne (*OED* 1873). Here we are reminded that the cyclic process may also be one of repetition and high-lighting for which musical form may be a useful analogue. It is perhaps because of this, that we come to the term song cycle or sonnet cycle, where even though there may be an implied narrative, the idea of a cycle seems to pull against the notion of one that is logically developing in favour of a symbolic or iconic process, a series of starts from different points of view. In this form individual items—whether they be songs or sonnets—acquire a poignancy from their very brevity through which larger issues of the work as a whole may be reflected. This process of transcending narrative without dispensing with it may well be one of the most satisfying aspects of cyclic form: it is one which especially gives scope to lyric impulses. This may be the case with Schubert's song cycles (*Die schöne Müllerin* [1823] and *Winterreise* [1827]), whilst in Shakespeare's *Sonnets*, to give another example of the reflexive capacity of cyclic form, we find ourselves contending with an idealization of love (18, 116), a cynical exposure of it (129), and a cool-hearted acceptance of compromise (138).

As the development of the idea of cyclicity was thus separate from the criticism and historiography of the medieval plays it is not surprising that its application to them remains an approximation: but it has also proved a great convenience. Through the implications we have described, the term has been usable to draw attention to important features of the plays, especially the centrality of the birth and death of Christ and the frequency with which different episodes can be shown to echo one another, and to reflect upon these core incidents. The distinguishing factor, however, that this form of cycle was designed for performance adds an extra dimension to a purely literary cycle as such. Among a variety of effects it means that new emphases can be brought to bear, and that the verbal potency of the work can be enhanced by physical aspects visually conceived and received. It enables the semiotics of given details, which are enacted and perceived to point in more than one direction at the same time.

Another effect which the idea of a cycle implies concerns the management of time. Though it may be stretching etymology somewhat, there is a sense attaching to the word 'cycle' which implies an overview of human history. This may arise from the idea of circularity we have already noted. Because narrative is not the only structural ingredient, there is a distancing from it towards a distinctive shape which in itself is a reflection of other purposes. These in their turn may reflect aesthetic, historical, philosophical as well as theological intents by which the narrative material is developed and shaped. It is a process which may be likened to that proposed by Hayden White in his description of the way historians have tended to impose patterns upon the events they seek to present.[3] The critical point about cycles in this connection is that because they comprehend such a large amount of material there is usually a process by which it is arranged and managed reflecting other concerns than those simply associated with the unfolding of a narrative. Once again in the biblical cycles there is perceived the need to interpret the whole of the narrative material—which in itself may be emblematic of the whole of human history even though it does not address every single aspect of it—in relation to the central incidents of the life of Christ. But we shall have to be open to the effect of some other dramatic cycles from the period under consideration which are motivated by different central issues such as the persistent medieval preoccupation with the vengeance of the Lord upon the Jews, or the mission of the Apostles after Pentecost. The occurrence of such work is an important support for the nature and method of the biblical cycles which are the main concern of this study. They make significantly more credible the proposition that the idea of a cycle form of drama did exist at the time and that there was a conscious attempt to make use of it, even though there is apparently no contemporary critical theory to articulate it.

These considerations lead naturally to the question of the size necessary for a cycle to function. Clearly a play dealing only with one episode can hardly be cyclic, and to say that there must be a specific number of episodes or even lines as a minimum would be open to the wrong kind of demarcation dispute. The criterion must rather be that some of the features we have been describing must have room to operate. This means that there must be a facility for different episodes to reflect upon one another, and in doing so to have a bearing upon central issues which dominate the work as a whole. But one cannot assume that there will be uniformity in the size and scope of episodes: indeed there are individual cycles where some episodes are sketched in very briefly whereas others are handled in much greater detail. Thus the dramatic cycles have a narrative sequence, but they also show frequently processes by which events are seen as recapitulating previous occurrences (*analepsis*), or anticipating what is to come (*prolepsis*). This facility to generate cross reference seems fundamental to the dramatic form, and it has analogues with the iconographic material considered in Chapter Two. There we shall find that the interrelationship between the arrangement of pictures and the shape of buildings in which they are placed offers visual interconnection, as in Giotto's work in the Arena Chapel at Padua. Alternatively in Memling's large-scale, single paintings we find that the arrangement of many episodes in one comprehensive picture allows interaction between individual items. The chronological narrative is there counterpointed by painterly decisions about colour, shape and movement, all being essential design features.[4]

The question of authorship of the dramatic cycles is also a consideration, for it is apparent that some surviving cycles are the work of one poet, whereas many others show a variety of hands in their composition, and it may even be suspected that parts have grown up almost as though by the work of a constantly changing committee or by improvisation. However the tendency to expand to very large size is a feature, especially in France, and this may lead to a further enhancement of the form in that individual sections of a very large play spread over many days may allow the development of specific topics or series of ideas. A new day may mean a new start. Beyond this we can also note that on some occasions large sections from one cycle may be added to equally large sections from another.

The information available to us about the occurrence and provenance of cycles prompts a number of generalizations, though all of these need to be treated with some caution since the survival of these early texts must be a matter of chance. Admittedly in France there was the important development by which printing became possible just when the reputation of cyclic plays reached a significant high level in the late fifteenth century.[5] No doubt printing helped to increase their availability. But elsewhere the survival of texts is often a matter of localised convenience, perhaps depending upon the requirements of performance, or upon the presence of antiquarians active enough to preserve material from the past, as at Chester.

The survival of written records, which are so ably being collected and published for Great Britain by the REED project, gives us knowledge of activities in some places based upon the briefest of surviving information, as for example the possibilities of a mystery cycle at Hereford.[6] It is a striking fact that these searches by REED editors have uncovered a large quantity of dramatic and para-dramatic activities and some unknown dramatic texts have also come to light. However, the impact upon what is known about cyclic drama is more limited and specific. Very few new examples have actually been found, suggesting that cycles were developed in only a small number of places. The more popular forms of drama, parish by parish, were rather different. Nevertheless the detailed study of records in some places such as York, Coventry and Chester has made possible a more coherent history of the cycle plays in those places. This work underlines that there is still a great deal about which we are ignorant. Such knowledge as we do have suggests that the cycle plays developed in the fourteenth century under a variety of influences which we shall discuss later, and that there was a large expansion in the fifteenth century.

Here we point to two significant factors which helped this. One was the establishment of the feast of Corpus Christi by Pope Clement V in 1311. Probably the importance of this for the cyclic drama has been overestimated, especially with regard to many Continental examples, but there is no denying that the establishment of a feast which fell outside the narrative embedded in the Church's liturgical year gave rise to a new kind of devotional celebration. The processions which were evolved in support of it, often quasi-dramatic in themselves, had a range of influences upon the development of the cyclic dramas. In some places the cycles became known as Corpus Christi plays: but we must not assume that all plays so named were cycles or that all cycles were performed on that festival.

Secondly, as ideas on a grander scale were developed, the increasing wealth of some cities made available the resources necessary for large-scale performances which required a large space and a good span of time. In such urban circumstances, however, there would have to be some return, and we find that although the cycles undoubtedly had a theological structure designed to promote the devotion of the people, there were also political objectives in the public display of wealth and power by urban corporations, and in some cases the cycles became a political battleground.[7] It is not surprising, therefore, that parts of cycles, if not whole ones, were put on in honour of monarchs and members of ruling houses. In this respect there are links with the royal processions and entries of late medieval Europe and the Renaissance as instruments of authority.

History and Distribution
In the light of the necessity for urban wealth and civic pretensions, it is not surprising that geographically the known cycles are found in areas where there was a collection of prosperous urban centres like north east France, and northern England where Coventry, Chester and York, and almost certainly some other centres like Beverley, Doncaster, Newcastle-upon-Tyne and Durham have left us such a strong heritage.[8] But equally there are plenty of rich urban areas which did not apparently generate cycle plays, and there must have been all sorts of local factors which were instrumental in encouraging their development, rivalry being one. Perhaps in imitation of such urban achievements there are also more isolated survivals in some places, such as Cornwall. This latter is especially interesting because in general the Celtic areas of Europe did not give rise to dramatic cycles.[9] Other limiting factors would be differences in religious orientation. There is not much to be found in the areas influenced by the eastern Orthodox Church, and the Moorish invasion of Spain was also a disincentive, and one which was eventually set aside.

An historical perspective of cycle plays gives us two important precursors. On the one hand the liturgical drama, which by definition was tied to Church services, and was primarily musical, had allowed the development of sequences of incidents surrounding the chief Church feasts at Christmas and more especially at Easter. The survival of the Benediktbeuern Passions from twelfth-century Bavaria illustrates the importance and the degree of artistic complexity of this, and these in turn owed much to precursors in the liturgy which had elaborated items from the Christian narrative like the *Peregrini* and the *Pastores*. Some of these liturgical performances had vernacular elements, but their provenance within Church services, and perhaps their mode of performance, which was primarily for the service and not for an audience, separates them from what was to come for the cycle plays. Nevertheless the impulse to accumulate episodes of liturgical drama around a core should not be overlooked even though a direct link between the liturgical drama and the cycle plays remains problematic. To this we should also add that many cycles incorporated liturgical music as part of performance.

The second significant development was the composition and performance of what might be termed non-dramatic Passions. They represent one important aspect of cyclic plays already noted, the tendency to elaborate the narrative through a long series of events under the pressure of an interpretative strategy. On the one hand these developed into long poems, like the *Northern Passion* which became a kind of encyclopedic source-book for the composers of the dramatic cycles. But there is, in addition, a performative aspect to some of them such as the *Passion des Jongleurs*. This twelfth-century narrative poem contains stage directions in the text which imply that the minstrel-like performers carried out certain actions and movements. The mode of performance remains obscure however, and it is thought that in this case at least, where there was a performance it was more in the nature of a recitation with the performer speaking in several voices. In short while there may have performative embellishment, the purpose of these texts was never theatrical. The poem belongs primarily to the medieval traditions of oral poetry.[10]

Events on an international scale may also have been one of the formative influences on cycle plays. After the period of the Crusades there came a number of important changes in religious beliefs and practices. The impact of the Black Death in the fourteenth century sharpened the sense of mortality as the population of most European towns and cities fell away. It intensified the need for the individual to seek salvation in an uncertain world, and it was accompanied by a decline in prosperity in many places, especially in cities which were dependent upon shifts in trading conditions and the availability of manpower. The growth in popularity and usefulness in the cycle plays in the fifteenth century, and the earlier fourteenth-century preliminaries followed upon and no doubt contributed to intense activity in matters of belief. In England there was incipient dissent and questioning by John Wycliffe, who died in 1384, a movement which anticipated and developed into the Reformation eventually.

But even before this there were changes in religious attitudes and in spirituality, and Wycliffe's critique was by no means the only threat to orthodoxy in the European context. Indeed the mainstream of belief, so to speak, had shown several phases of development. From the twelfth century there was a shift in attitudes to Christ, as there developed a greater concentration upon him as a figure of suffering—the Man of Sorrows—rather than the figure of triumph perceivable in earlier art and theology. The Cross of Victory became the Cross of Salvation and the newly dominant image of Christ as the Man of Sorrows was in part an answer to the question posed by St. Anselm: "Why did God become man?" (*Cur Deus homo?*).[11] A significant contribution was made by the Franciscans who were acknowledged by the papacy as part of the response to the movement known as the Poor of Christ, regarded as heretical in the twelfth century. The proponents of this view had stressed the need for simplicity and rejected the wealthy concerns of many churchmen, turning back to attention upon the poverty and the message of the apostles. The response, which was perhaps epitomised by the work of Innocent III (1198–1216), was not a simple one. He invoked a crusade against the Albigensian heretics in 1208. However he seems to have taken the view that the objections must be contained and not dealt with by confrontation alone and this led to the measures of reform which flowed from the Fourth Lateran Council in 1215. Some of these had been anticipated by its predecessors in 1139 and 1179.

The principal changes in 1215 raised the status of bishops, increasing diocesan activity, and placed greater attention upon the education of priests. The importance of the latter was enhanced by making annual confession by the laity obligatory, and by insistence upon attendance at Easter mass. This revised approach was followed up by a number of events, many after Innocent's death, and also by the production of a significant corpus of written work which in turn fed directly into the theological issues underlying many aspects of the cycle plays. We should note that these were part of general changes in Europe, and that developments in England were reflections of these.

St. Francis had received papal blessing to form his order in 1210, an event which we shall see was later celebrated in the wall paintings in the basilica at Assisi. He received the stigmata in 1224. This pointedly linked him and the legendary narrative of his life with the sufferings of Christ. Bearing the marks of the wounds of Christ, he became a kind of second manifestation of divinity, a second Christ (*alter Christus*), who recalled the suffering of the first. His followers began an extensive missionary development depending heavily upon preaching as the order spread widely. The Dominican friars were recognised in 1216. They were also deeply committed to preaching and often provided a distinctly philosophical dimension to theology. The establishment of houses for Beguines, women withdrawn from the world but not necessarily having taken vows, was accepted in 1235.

In England we can perceive increasing activities by the bishops in the thirteenth century, of which one of the most notable for our purposes was the code issued by Archbishop John Pecham from Lambeth in 1281, known generally by the opening words *Ignorantia sacerdotium* ('The Ignorance of priests ...') of the section called *De informatione simplicium* ('Concerning the information of simple people').[12] The stress is plainly upon attention to the instruction of the laity, and it sets out a number of key items of belief and teaching which were to appear again and again in the instructional literature as well as in the cycle plays: the fourteen articles of faith, the ten commandments of the Old Testament and the two of the Gospel, the seven works of mercy, the seven virtues and seven vices, and the seven sacraments. The importance of this code for the English cycle plays is indicated by its being the basis for the formulation of the instructions for the province of York by Archbishop John Thoresby in 1357 in the form of a catechism. It was translated into English verse by John Gaytrick, a Benedictine monk of St. Mary's Abbey, York, and it became known as *The Lay Folk's Catechism*. Possibly employing verse was intended as a means of encouraging learning by heart, as an indulgence of forty days was offered to those who did.[13]

The intense devotion through the humanising of the story of Christ lead to a number of key texts and the tendency was more and more to produce these in the vernacular, thus making them available to lay readership and devotion. Thus the French text *Le Manuel de Péchés*, written in verse in 1260 was translated into English verse by Robert Manning of Bourne as *Handling Sin* in 1303; and a prose translation, *c.* 1350, called *Of shrift and penance*, is also extant. The French prose *Somme le Roi* prepared by Friar Lorens in 1279 for Philip III of France, and containing much the same material as Pecham's code, with the addition of an *Ars Moriendi* and treatises on the Pater Noster and the seven gifts of the Holy Ghost, was translated by Michael Norgate of St. Augustine's Abbey, Canterbury, in 1340 as *The Ayenbite of Inwit* ('Remorse of Conscience'); and there was another translation, which remains anonymous, as *The Book of Vices and Virtues*, *c.* 1375.[14] We should also notice the work of John Mirk, who was an Augustinian Prior at Lilleshall in Shropshire (*c.* 1400), and whose known works were directed much more towards the need to sustain the parish priests in their normal roles. He produced *Duties of a Parish Priests* in English verse, which followed the general code discussed above and gave advice on how to interrogate penitents at confession, a Latin *Manuale Sacerdotis* in five books, and a collection of sermons arranged for the ecclesiastical year, known as his *Festial*.[15] It is striking that the first information we have about the English cycle plays at York (1375), Beverly (1377), and Coventry (before 1420) follow closely upon this fourteenth-century commitment to the education of the clergy and the laity. We should note too that although some of this material was directed specifically at the priesthood, the ultimate aim recognised that the laity had to be reached, and this perception was stimulated in part by lay initiatives.

The works we have mentioned were further supported by several other compilations which were equally designed to be aids to worship, but also had the specific attraction of providing a conspectus of Christian history. As such they anticipate much that was to be incorporated in the design and the structure of the cycle plays. *The Mirour of Mans Saluacioun* is an anonymous translation of the *Speculum Humanae Salvationis*, which was compiled *c.* 1310-24, and, according to its most recent editor, it has survived in nearly four hundred manuscripts from the fourteenth and fifteenth centuries.[16] Its sources lie in the *Summa Theologica* by Thomas Aquinas († 1274), and Peter Comestor's († 1179) *Historia Scholastica*. For the majority of its forty-five chapters the pattern is to recount an incident of the narrative from the fall of Lucifer to the Last Judgement, though there is no sequential coverage for Old Testament episodes between the fall of Adam and Eve and the Annunciation of St. Anne's conception of the Virgin. This is a structure which we shall see echoed in a number of continental cycle plays, of which Gréban's *Passion* (*c.* 1452) is a significant example. Accompanying each of the narrative elements, however, there are usually three other short references to incidents drawn largely from the Old Testament which are typological parallels. Thus Chapter 18 describes the Betrayal of Christ by Judas, to which Joab killing his brother Amasa, Saul returning David evil for good and Cain's murder of Abel are added. In many of the manuscripts there are also illustrations, which were no doubt meant as aids to devotion and meditation, a practice which anticipates the *Biblia Pauperum*, discussed in Chapter Two below. These juxtapositions enable the present or the future to be interpreted in terms of the past, a characteristic we shall find in the cycle plays.

A text of comparable importance is *The Mirrour of the blessed lyf of Jesu Christ*, Nicholas Love's translation of the thirteenth-century Franciscan text *Meditationes Vitae Christi*, (the attribution to St. Bonaventura, Principal of the order, has not been sustained). This translation was presented to the Archbishop of York, Love being prior of the Carthusian house of Mount Grace at Ingleby, *c*. 1400. It was presumably meant to meet the lay need for access to the Gospel in the vernacular, and perhaps a response to the Lollards. At one point he refers to his omission of the many authorities allegedly cited by Bonaventura as 'inpertynent in grete partye to manye comoun persones and simple soules that this boke in Englische is written to'.[17] The treatment of the many narrative elements here is significant in that a great deal of it is not scriptural, but accumulated over centuries of elaboration of the Gospel narratives. The work is divided into the days of the week. After a brief account of Mary's childhood, the narrative runs from the Annunciation to the Ascension and Pentecost.[18]

Moving further into the documentation of religious experience we can see that there was a strong tradition of mysticism. It can be traced back to St. Anselm in the twelfth century, but it is especially relevant to the cycles in the fourteenth. Among these were the writings of Richard Rolle († 1349), especially his *Emendatio vitae*; Walter Hilton's *The Scale of Perfection* (he died in 1396); *The Revelations of Divine Love* by Dame Julian of Norwich (*c*. 1373); and the *Book of Margery Kemp* which is an account of her spiritual life at the beginning of the fifteenth century. These writings follow different intentions from one another but they are evidence of the significant variety of religious visionaries before the English cycle plays were fully established. In the case of Margery Kemp we get a keen indication of personal identification with the sufferings of Christ, which was a hallmark of the emotionalism embedded in affective piety: 'Hys deth is as fresch to me as he had deyd this same day'. Her approach recalls a remark by Nicholas Love who justifies his inclusion of non-scriptural material as a means of stirring the 'devoute ymaginaciouns' of simple souls.[19] In the cycles there was often scope for both a physical enactment of Christ's agonies, and an elaboration in terms of language and dialogue of Mary's maternal ordeal and of her relationship with her son before and after the crucifixion. Indeed violence is a significant characteristic of many English and continental cycles.

The relevance to the cycle plays of the material discussed here has been pinpointed by Professor Alexandra Johnston in her studies of libraries at York in the fifteenth century. The catalogue of the library of the Augustine Friary composed in 1472 indicates that it was a centre for scholarship at an advanced level. By the time of this compilation there were 646 volumes, but the core was in place in the fourteenth century. She also notes the rhetorical and philosophical texts held in the library of St. Mary's Abbey from a fifteenth-century register, with a strong emphasis upon the works and influence of St. Augustine.[20]

The establishment of Corpus Christi had a profound effect upon many public features of medieval life. Its origins were essentially a manifestation of medieval piety, as distinct from more ancient religious attitudes. At its inception, which was originated by Pope Urban IV in 1264, and confirmed in 1311 by a decree of Clement V, it was unquestionably religious, and yet by its impulse to propagate the image of the Body of Christ the establishment of the feast paved the way for an increasing lay participation in its celebration. The concentration upon the sacrament, which was at the heart of its conception, separated it from the Christian narrative, and this feature is reflected in the date chosen for it. It is a moveable feast tied to the date of Easter, and is celebrated on the Thursday after Trinity Sunday, varying from 21 May to 21 June. In the pattern of the Church's year it occurs when the story of Christ's earthly mission is completed with the Ascension and Pentecost. This theological significance had the great advantage of allowing a retrospective element to be part of the feast, so that events of the Christian narrative from the Creation to Pentecost could be recalled and made relevant to the day itself as required. It was also remarkably convenient that these days of high summer were very long, and they allowed the procession and its concomitant public events to extend from an early dawn to a late nightfall.

The most important contribution made by the inception of the feast of Corpus Christi to the cycle plays was the development of its procession. It was not, in fact, the first day of celebration to have a procession by any means: Palm Sunday processions can be traced much earlier,[21] and there were many local traditions for processions on saints' days, especially for St. John the Baptist at midsummer (June 24), for St. Anne (July 26), for the Assumption of the Blessed Virgin Mary (August 15) and for St. George (April 23). But the separation of Corpus Christi from the Christian narrative, and the special requirement that the Sacrament be central to the feast and to its showing to the laity gave a new impetus. Participation in the procession became a civic as well as a religious obligation, and lying behind the order of events, the arrangements and the financing was the political structure of towns and cities which on this day of celebration was manifested, with the *real presence* of God in the sacrament carried through the streets, as we shall notice in Chapter Three for Künzelsau. It can also be said that such a public demonstration of power would also be likely to bring out tensions and rivalries which the procession might allow to be reconciled, or perhaps even intensified.[22]

The form of the procession was often carefully prescribed and made to reflect the status of participating groups. However there was no uniformity about this. In some places the bulk of the participants were in trade guilds, a factor which emphasises the relationship between economics and political influence. But equally there were other fraternities and religious guilds which took their place in the processions. In some towns there were actually Corpus Christi guilds, and these could be supplemented by guilds having patronal saints, while in others, the contributing and participating elements were often made up by parishes or even streets, as in the performances at Lille. There was thus enormous potential in the interrelationship between the participating elements. In certain areas this led to the development of competition between the contributors.

Within a century of the inception of Corpus Christi some places had developed cycles of plays which were performed on the day itself, but the process by which this change occurred was by no means simple, nor did the move from the subjects of the individual items in the procession to the invention of dramatic forms take place at the same rate throughout Europe. From quite early on scenes from the Christian narrative became the subjects of individual items in the procession. Initially these often took the form of images, perhaps pictorial, or three-dimensional in the form of a show of model figures. A further development was the use of human beings to portray the scenes in the form of dumb-shows or *tableaux vivants.*

One of the most important aspects of any procession is the choice of route. By means of this selection important civic and religious sites could be visited, and in some cases, as at Seville, the procession entered a church. The status of people assembled at individual locations could also be recognised, and there could be a communication, implied or overt, between those in the procession and, behind them, those organising it, with those who received it at the different locations. Moreover it became apparent that at places visited there could also be shows or displays which in some way complemented the subject matter of the items in the procession. This rather theoretical discussion of possibilities actually leads us to the inception of dramatic elements when dialogue is introduced, whether for those taking part in the procession, whilst on the move, as at Draguignan in southern France, or when stopped at the locations.[23] Similarly there could be dialogue provided by those at the places themselves, again complementing what was passing by. The way in which these two states, one stationary and one in motion, could feed off one another is full of dramatic possibilities.

The subject matter of the individual items in the Corpus Christi procession could be very varied indeed, and we need also to recall that these processions were repeated and developed over a many years, so that there was plenty of opportunity for new things to be introduced. An illustration of this comes from Oudenaarde, in the Low Countries, where the earliest surviving information about the Corpus Christi procession dates from 1407, and where the procession continued to take place until 1621. The main topics for the show in its first years were the saints, but at the beginning of the sixteenth century many incidents were introduced so as to cover a large number of items from the Passion. By 1520 shifts in theological orientation tended to discount the saints, and more emphasis appeared upon the Old and New Testaments, perhaps in line with increasing lay interest in the Bible.[24]

Similarly the history of the Corpus Christi procession at Seville shows that its scope surpassed all other existing processions, even royal entries. In 1428 there was immense expenditure and the guilds were involved in the procession, but they also decorated their home bases. Between 1454 and 1498 mobile scenes were enacted by amateurs, taking place on a platform carried by ten or twelve porters. By 1557 these had been enlarged to four-wheeled waggons, but still no text is apparent. At Valencia, however, the items were on waggons from much earlier, but here there were no human "actors" in the fourteenth century. Instead Noah's Ark had fourteen statues inside it. Eventually the statues were replaced by people who sang and played music. In 1425, stopping places or stations had been introduced, and shortly afterwards some dialogue appeared amongst some of those on the waggons, which paused at the stations for only a few minutes for their performance. However the whole procession never amounted to a cycle of plays, and some individual items remained in the form of *tableaux vivants* while others became more adventurous.[25]

In the light of the information discussed here a number of points emerge in relating the feast of Corpus Christi to the cycle plays. There is first the great shift towards the laity, and towards the wealth of the civil authorities. This put the initiative increasingly into the hands of the secular power, and provided a base for the development of the cycle plays, especially as large-scale financial resources and the ability to set up the physical organization of a day's festivities now became available. The evolution of the practice that small groups, whether guilds, confraternities or parishes, could be used to build up a large-scale event by segments was a useful contribution. A very large proportion of the performers were lay people. Though it is necessary to be cautious about the size necessary for cycle plays to be effective, there can be no doubt that this basic requirement was now in place.

As to the content and purpose of Corpus Christi, this is rather problematic, but the fact that many (but by no means all) of the processions did give attention to the Christian narrative must have operated as a precedent. The power to reflect upon the nature and purpose of Christian history was most probably something which the cycles shared with some of those organising the processions. Conversely the doctrine surrounding the Eucharist and its development could also find a place with the cycle plays.[26]

These things may help to show that the evolution of the cycle plays was in all probability much affected by the feast of Corpus Christi. But if this is so, it does not follow that all the references to Corpus Christi plays imply that what was performed was a cycle play. In fact the contrary is true. What Corpus Christi plays have in common is that they were performed for Corpus Christi. Indeed a further complication arises in that although Corpus Christi was widely celebrated by processions in France, in common with much of Europe, the French cycle plays, whether *Passions* or *Mystères*, were not usually performed on the day of the festival. As we shall see, other factors came into play in the dissemination of the French cycles, and these overrode the advantage of this special day.

As to other countries, there is often a strong link between the feast day and the performance of cycles. This occurred extensively in German-speaking countries, but there the cycle plays were more usually Passion plays, rather than cycles extending from Creation to Doomsday. We shall find, in further discussion, that some of these cycles exhibit an unevenness of texture not unlike that noted at Valencia. In Spain the development of dramatic elements came rather later, even though there was a vigorous and long-standing interest in the procession itself. The English practice is somewhat varied, but Corpus Christi was the occasion of the procession and the performance of the cycle at York, until it was felt necessary to separate procession from play by postponing the procession to the following day, Friday. In 1426 it was proposed that the plays, which had become numerous, be done on the preceding day in order to preserve the solemnity of the feast, but in the event the city council had decided by 1476 that it was the procession that should be moved.[27] It is also surprising that even after the abolition of the feast in 1548 by the Reformist administration under Edward VI, York continued to perform the cycle on the traditional day. At Chester there seems to have been a Corpus Christi cycle in the fourteenth century, though its contents are uncertain, and there may not have been an Old Testament component. At some point between 1472 and 1521 it was decided to move the cycle a few days earlier, to the Monday, Tuesday and Wednesday after Pentecost.[28] For the rest of its existence the cycle was normally 'the Whitsun Plays'. The manuscript of the N-Town Cycle which originates in the late fifteenth century was dubbed at the top of its first page 'The plaie called Corpus Christi' by a sixteenth-century hand. The connection of this cycle with the feast is problematic, but the later attribution is symptomatic.

Texts and Performances

Having looked so far at some characteristics of cycle plays and at some aspects of their historical contexts, we shall now review in summary form the variety of the surviving texts and the information available about the complex matter of how they were performed. In this study we are pursuing the idea of cyclicity in two principal types: that which covers the whole of Christian history from Creation to the Last Judgement, and that which concentrates upon the Passion. In the latter the starting point is often the entry into Jerusalem, and the conclusion the Ascension. Though the material covered is somewhat different it seems that the artistic principles governing the two apparently different types are approximately the same, and there seems little doubt that there was much interchange between them. The study may also be supplemented by a limited number of other cycle plays which do not have their chief focus on the life of Christ, the principal examples being the French compilations, *Le mistère du Viel Testament*, *Le Mystère des Actes des Apôtres*, and *Le Mystère de la Vengeance Jhesuchrist* (E. Mercadé), and the Dutch *Bliscapen* (a sequence on the seven joys of Mary). In the last the sense of cyclicity is built up over a period of seven years.

In looking at all the different national groupings, it is apparent that there were many local variations, and, besides this, each surviving cycle has a history of its own in which it may exhibit so many changes that it is necessary to see each one as a dynamic process rather than a static entity. There is also the intriguing question of how much the text actually tells us about performance and whether and how far the text is in fact directly related to a performance at all. In other words some of these texts may be much nearer to being a book for reading than an actual theatrical document. In spite of this, however, the concept of the cycle remains a consistent entity, for it is apparent that just as one author (or authors) may be intending to produce a play, so another may want to compile a book, and yet each may have the objective of taking advantage of cyclic form.

England
In many ways the surviving cycle plays in English exhibit characteristics which make it possible to distinguish an English mode, though we shall see that there are some exceptions. All four of them, York, Chester, Towneley and N-Town, follow a narrative from Creation to Doomsday even though the processes

by which they were created was radically different. This pattern is supported with some consistency by other cycles which are lost or incomplete. These are:

1. *Beverley*: a list of thirty-six plays from the fall of Lucifer to Doomsday, all lost, performed by craft guilds on waggons at six or seven stations;
2. *Hereford*: a list of twenty-seven 'pageants' which may have been plays, from Adam and Eve to the Resurrection, all lost, allocated to craft guilds;
3. *Norwich*: two versions of the Fall, performed by the Grocers, and a list of twelve lost plays from Adam and Eve to Pentecost;
4. *Newcastle*: one text of Noah, performed by the Shipwrights, and a list of eleven other lost plays, from Creation to the Burial of Our Lady, a possible total of twenty-three pageants in all.[29]

As to the custom of performing the cycle on pageant waggons by craft guilds, we can be certain of this only for York, Coventry, Beverley and Chester, with a strong likelihood at Norwich and Newcastle. There are some indications that the Towneley Cycle may have been done in this manner at Wakefield, but if it were, the evidence linking the plays to the guilds is somewhat shaky and rather late, and the dramaturgy of some of the individual plays does not seem to lend itself readily to performance on waggons. At Coventry, from which only two composite plays survive out of a probable ten, there is no doubt that craft guilds performed the plays on waggons, but the presence of Old Testament plays is uncertain.[30] At some time before 1538 John Bale wrote a sequence of plays which centred upon the Passion, introduced by a play dealing with Old Testament figures and extending to the Resurrection: these are discussed at the end of Chapter Five (pp. 291-8). The N-Town text gives no indication at all of guild performance. One may add that there was a Passion play at Leicester, and also at New Romney in Kent where four plays gave rise to fifteen scenes from the Baptism to the Ascension.[31]

Turning to the four complete surviving texts of English-language cycles, it must be noted that the differences between them are remarkable, and we shall see that the generation of these texts has to be carefully differentiated. The appearance of new editions of the the four cycles in recent years by Beadle, Mills and Lumiansky, Cawley and Stevens, and Spector (see Bibliography) has done much to establish local details and circumstances. We do, however, find that they are all written in local dialects and are specific to particular localities. The textual analysis provided by these editions indicates that each of the survivals bears a different relationship to original performances—and we have to add "if any".

For York we have only one manuscript, the Register, comprising forty-eight plays, written at some point in the years 1463-77, about halfway through the presumed life of the cycle.[32] This seems to have been created to provide a central register of already existing texts from which in later years individual plays and players' parts could be copied. Subsequently the Register itself did sterling service as a check on performance for some years into the sixteenth century. It was annotated and marked to show subsequent changes, and, on Corpus Christi, it seems to have been physically present for a number of years, in the possession of the Common Clerk of the city, who was situated before the first station. For the years before this Register was made we have some lists which show that the contents of the plays were altered from time to time, but there is really nothing conclusive about what was actually said on stage before it came into existence.

From Chester, apart from the individual fifteenth-century manuscript of the episode of *Antichrist*, and two fragments from other episodes, there are five extant manuscripts of the cycle which are closely related, but whose most distinguishing feature is that they were all written after 1591. In all probability these texts, which comprise twenty-four plays, go back to a lost exemplar, which itself may have been very close to an actual performance. But its disappearance means that all the texts are somewhat removed from a specific occasion, especially as the last complete performance of the cycle took place in 1575, and this probably had a different configuration from the previous occasions. The history of the Chester Cycle indicates, as we have noted, that it was considerably changed near the beginning of the sixteenth century, and there is very little evidence about what actually went on before that. Though the texts do embody many performance details, the fact that they are all to some extent retrospective, created by an interest that was in some sense antiquarian, means that we cannot be quite sure which text or texts were actually played. These manuscripts may reflect actual productions in an indirect way, but the purpose of the creators of these manuscripts was presumably closer to the making of a book for reading. The surviving records show that Chester also differs from York in that the plays were done at irregular intervals, whereas at York the city council seems routinely to have set out to do the plays nearly every year for most of the sixteenth century, even though they did not always succeed.

The texts of the other two cycles in English do have one thing in common: it is likely that neither was ever actually performed in the way the texts imply that they might have been. Both seem to be compilations drawing upon discrete material. The Towneley manuscript is very ornate, as though it were intended for a presentation for the purpose of reading rather than for acting. The plays are manifestly the work of different authors, the most notable of whom has been called the Wakefield Master, because of his skill as a playwright and poet. Some of the plays are entirely in his style, while others show interpolations which suggest that he revised them. References in his work suggest a strong link with Wakefield. However, six or seven of the plays contain extensive borrowings from plays in the York Cycle, adapted to local requirements. The question of performance has been much debated. It does not seem likely that in the fifteenth century, at least, Wakefield was rich or populous enough to be able to support a cycle of the size presented in the manuscript. Yet the texts of many individual plays do seem to be written with performance in mind, even if there is a shortage of stage directions. Later hands have put the name of a craft guild at the head of five of the plays, but there is very little to back up these ascriptions. There is a possibility that the plays originated in various towns and villages in the Wakefield area, and were pressed into service as components of a cycle. Recent work on the manuscript itself has suggested that it may be as late as the reign of Queen Mary.[33] If this is sustained it raises the possibility that the assembling of the material into cyclic form may have been well into the sixteenth century even though some parts of it are earlier. The process would then have been an imitation of neighbouring practice already well established at York.

The N-Town manuscript is perhaps the most intriguing of all. It is largely in the hand of one scribe, but it appears to have been created over a considerable period of time, and the process of assembling it seems to have involved incorporating sections for the Passion which already had a separate existence. It is written consistently in an East Anglian dialect, but so far no conclusive attribution has been made to any town or city. Indeed the evidence of the language seems to point to a somewhat rural area around Harling in west Norfolk. It is conceived on a large scale, and it is apparent that it was not meant for performance on waggons: nor is there any indication of craft guilds. However a considerable number of the plays have very detailed stage directions about costumes and movement to the extent that it seems highly probable that they are the record of a performance. Moreover the movements about the acting area suggest that the method of production for many of the plays involved the so-called place and scaffold form with fixed locations dedicated to specific characters or localities, rather than a processional mode using waggons. The action consisted partly of the movement between these fixed sites. What emerges from the composite nature of this manuscript is that it looks as though it was deliberately assembled, from whatever material the compiler had at hand, and that in its assembling he was concerned to conform to a pre-existing notion of what went into a cycle of plays. The date, on linguistic evidence, is some point not long before 1500 (the date 1468 appears within the manuscript, but this may refer only to this one particular episode and not the whole codex). At that time the compiler would have been able to assemble his material to comply with the well-known cycles already in existence at York and perhaps Coventry. It should be added that there is some reason to suppose that the Towneley Cycle was assembled in a rather similar way, and again it could have been modelled on existing practice elsewhere.

From Cornwall come two interrelated texts in the Middle Cornish language. *The Ordinalia* was probably composed in the late fourteenth century, and it consists of the *Ordinale de Origine Mundi*, the *Passio Domini Nostri Jhesu Christi* and the *Ordinale de Resurrexione Domini*. The content of these three plays, which were designed for performance in a Cornish round (called a *plen an gwary*, 'playing place') on three successive days, is reminiscent of the selection of plays in the Continental cycles. The actual place of performance is unknown, but a seventeenth-century account suggests that people travelled from far and wide to see the plays, and the Cornish rounds were not necessarily to be found in urban areas. The text of the *Ordinalia* contains three diagrams which indicate the names of the locations for the principal characters. Eight are named for each play and it seems that the same locations were used on each of the three days, with a different designation. The precedent of these plays was sustained by the *Creacion of the World* (also known by the Cornish title *Gwreans an Bys*). This text, which is written in later Cornish typical of the mid-sixteenth century, with English stage directions, is apparently the first day of a cycle, covering from the Creation to Noah. From its conclusion it appears that the second day went on to show the Resurrection. It contains about two hundred lines found in the *Ordinalia*. The presence of detailed stage directions in both these Cornish texts suggests that they were near to the actuality of performance: their scope implies a vigorous independent performing tradition in Cornwall. As we shall see in Chapter Five, this mode of performance makes different demands upon the authors since the scenes have to be planned in different ways from those designed for processional performance.

France
The French cycle plays bulk largest in the genre. There are reputedly over one million lines of text extant, and consequently there are few scholars who have read them all. Here we need to give some outline of what is available for comparison with the cycle plays of other countries, but in the face of such plenitude our account will have to be brief. A good deal of new work has appeared of recent years, especially by Runnalls and Bordier,[34] but it is still felt that a good deal more needs to be done to build up an overview of a very rich culture of composition and performance. Such work would still need to work towards the establishment of text, as well as placing the surviving corpus into contexts by examining local records. In general the French versions are concentrated upon the Passion, and only a few of them cover the whole narrative from Creation to Doom. At their most developed they are far longer than the plays of most other countries, and they often required many days for a complete performance. Whilst many of them show individual originality, much of the extant work is the result of composition by Eustache Mercadé, Arnoul Gréban, and Jean Michel who, in the fifteenth century, between them built up a canon of cycle plays which other entrepreneurs adapted and modified to their own requirements. Because of this it is possible to be precise about the contribution of some known authors, as well as estimating the importance of local adaptation.

The earliest Passions were quite short and as such they hardly require attention as cycles; but they do tell us something about the historical context for the development of the longer plays. Probably the most important forerunners came from Burgundy where the *Passion de Palatinus*, a play of about two thousand lines written *c.* 1300, stands amongst a group of other versions of the Passion and is related to them. It owes something to the *Passion des Jongleurs*, which was not strictly a play but a narrative for recitation perhaps by minstrels, and it has some lines in common with the two extant versions of the *Passion d'Autun*. From this interlaced group there emerged, around the year 1400, the *Passion de Semur*, which has some lines in common and which bears the marks in the manuscript of a complex development and enlargement towards a two-day performance of some 9572 lines.[35]

This may well have been symptomatic of a development in thinking about the cycles, but it has to be remembered that the manuscript upon which the theory of enlargement is based is thought to date from 1488. Well before this there emerged the largest group of full-scale cycle plays, and it remains somewhat problematic whether the Semur enlargement precedes or follows it. The attribution of the *Passion d'Arras* to Eustache Mercadé († 1440) is still somewhat doubted, but he was unquestionably the author of the *Vengeance Jhesuchrist* which has strong links with this *Passion*. Both seem to evidence a significant enlargement in the scope of the cycles. The *Passion* has 25,000 lines and is designed to show the narrative from the Annunciation to the Ascension in four days. The quality of the manuscript, which originates in north west France and had been kept at Arras for many years, suggests that it was written after successful performance. The cycle is thought to have become well-known and there is some evidence that it was used as the basis for performances elsewhere.[36]

However the most influential cycle was the *Passion* of Arnoul Gréban which appeared about 1450 in the Paris area. It has a brief introduction concerning the Fall of Man, and it continues until the Ascension. It is remarkable for its coherence and there is a distinctive sense that this vast sweep of events is seen as a divinely planned entity. It has some 34,400 lines and was intended for performance in four days. Its popularity and influence is evidenced by the fact that there are ten manuscripts extant, not an insignificant fact if one considers the effort necessary to copy such a long text, and also by the number of ways in which it can be shown that its text was adapted by other writers. The most important of these was Jean Michel's rearrangement for a performance at Angers in 1486. He enlarged the second and third days of Gréban's *Passion* into four days (leaving aside the first and fourth). His treatment of the central episodes of the Passion is therefore much more detailed, but he incorporates many of Gréban's lines in his text. The other salient feature of Michel's work is that it was printed at least seventeen times by 1542. This must have increased enormously the possible readership of the play, and it is the only biblical cycle known to have been extensively disseminated by means of printed copies.

From this point on it became the practice in many places in France to enlarge and adapt existing texts. Three examples illustrate this. The surviving manuscript of the *Passion de Troyes* from the last decades of the fifteenth century borrowed heavily from Gréban: of the three days which survive less than a quarter of the lines are not from his known text. Amongst these there is also a passage from *Le Mystère du Viel Testament*. In 1507 the *Passion Cyclique* was printed in Paris, consisting of the four days of Michel, followed by the fourth day of Gréban, covering the Resurrection. The first day of this cycle was partly drawn from Gréban's first day. A few years previously, in 1501, the text of the *Passion* given at Mons was borrowed from Amiens. Most of the text is now lost, but there survives the remarkable working book of the *Régisseur* who planned and controlled the performance, showing how stage business was to be incorporated. The form of this document is to give the first and last line of every speech and to give detailed directions in their proper places. It is now thought that although the text uses much from both Gréban and Michel, the compiler actually went to an edition of the *Passion Cyclique*. If this is so, it implies that there was an earlier version of the latter than the one printed in 1507 noticed above.³⁷ There is an even more complex story for the *Passion en Rime Franchoise*, also called the *Passion de Valenciennes en 20 Journées*, which, though it may predate the Mons *Passion*, exists in a relatively late manuscript dated 1549 and includes material from Gréban-Michel, and four days from the *Actes des Apôtres*.³⁸

Two other Passions stand aside from this network of influences. The *Passion de Nostre Seigneur de la Bibliothèque Sainte-Geneviève*, having some 4,500 lines, is probably too short to exhibit many of the characteristics of cycle plays, and it will not concern us greatly here. Yet it does demonstrate that in the Paris area there was an interest in the Passions before 1400, a date which stands well before the Gréban-Michel expansion. The development of a much larger project in the Auvergne, probably at Montferrand from about 1452, may have been influenced, at least in spirit, by the spread of the Passions in the north, but the conception of this fragmentary cycle and what we can tell of its execution both argue strongly for its independence. The survivals consist of three separate manuscripts and some archive material from Montferrand. Each of the manuscripts comprises a text for a single day, the first, third and fifth of what is thought to be a seven- or eight-day cycle, performed on successive Sundays leading up to Pentecost. These manuscripts come from different times in the life of the cycle, the first from after 1477, the second from 1452 and the third from 1477.³⁹ Elements in the texts and archive show that the cycle was performed in a place-and-scaffold format, and it seems possible, though perhaps surprising, that the performances were separated by twenty-five years. As we shall see in further analysis in Chapter Three, there are many independent features. The most striking, and unique as far as the French canon is concerned, allows that at each of the three days known in detail the action ends with a reunion between Christ and his mother. As in the case of some other French cycles, and all the English ones, the language is distinctly localised.

Cycles in German

Though the extant cyclic material from German-speaking countries is not quite so prolific as that surviving from France, there was undoubtedly a tradition of putting on large-scale plays, albeit in a number of differing ways. Recent work suggests that dramatic activity was spread far more comprehensively over the whole German-speaking area than the extant plays might lead us to suppose.[40] Heavy losses make it difficult to generalise, but there are a number of distinctive tendencies, as we shall see. The surviving plays do, however, indicate that there was much activity from the fourteenth century which built upon a rich liturgical tradition going back for several centuries. A good deal of the earlier material is written in a mixture of Latin and German. The survival of three Latin liturgical plays, one for Christmas and two for the Passion, from the Benedictine monastery at Benediktbeuern in Bavaria (1160-*c*. 1230) may be representative of a strong tradition of church musical drama.[41] In these plays the strict limits of scripture-based ceremony are expanded to include non-scriptural elements, as in the elaborate lamentations of Mary. The early German Passion play is represented by the so-called *St. Gall Passion Play* (named after the monastery at St. Gall in Switzerland) written probably in the fourteenth century in the west of modern-day Germany (1621 lines). Though it is substantially in German, there is a good deal of Latin, especially for music. It contains episodes from the Teachings of Christ to the Resurrection.[42]

It is apparent that in some places, especially at Lucerne, in Switzerland, the tradition of large-scale plays continued into the seventeenth century. Though some links between different examples are discernible, as in the case of Hessen and the South Tyrol, it is not clear that there was such an extensive interlinking, even dominance, as happened in France with the Gréban-Michel group. Nor was there a comparable development of printing the cycles to facilitate their dissemination. Instead we have several examples where local expression and revision show that individual plays were worked over for a large number of years—as at

Frankfurt and Lucerne. One underlying principle noted for the French plays is again found here: plays were made and then remade for individual circumstances and for specific times, so that the state of a cycle was hardly a permanently fixed entity. We are left with a number of glimpses of a long continuing process of performance and adaptation.

Few of the German cycles stretch from Creation to Doomsday. The conventions of liturgical drama had established both Easter and Passion plays, the former centring upon the Resurrection and the latter having a broader scope usually starting with the Calling of the Disciples and extending to the Ascension. Often the Passion plays incorporated the matter of the Easter dramas. As the vernacular drama developed it was sometimes found to be appropriate to prefix episodes showing the Falls of Lucifer and of Adam, but dramatic interest in the detail of the Old Testament was not widespread. These preliminary episodes did however often show that there was to be an overall structure to the cycle which derived from the premisses presented in the early episodes. This particular development does seem reminiscent of the practice noted for Gréban noted above. Similarly, though there are some Christmas plays, the Nativity episodes are rarely linked with the Passion in cyclic form. Both Passions and Christmas plays were normally performed at the time of the relevant church festival.

Though in general there are not so many lines of dialogue in the German cycles as in the French—the Lucerne play is one of the longest at 11,436 lines—several of them were performed over a number of days. Some caution is necessary in estimating the time taken for such performances since there is a considerable amount of music incorporated. Much of it is liturgical in origin and has Latin words, and many of the leading performers were required to sing as well as to speak their extensive roles. The speeches often repeat the sense of the anthems which precede them. Choral singing was also used to point up the emotional and devotional qualities of the performances. At Muri, Frankfurt and Alsfeld the survival of the *Dirigierrolle*, a copy showing cues for movement and for music made for the directors, suggests that there was a high degree of organisation in the presentation, and we can see from these as well as from the stage directions in the texts that elaborate movement and complex management of large casts were features. In considering the duration of a performance, allowance should be made for the time taken by processions during plays.

The most significant texts for our purposes are as follows. The plays are discussed roughly in the order of the earliest date ascertainable, but it is axiomatic that the earliest point from which something survives, be it text or record of performance, is not necessarily the point of origin.

The *Wiener Passionsspiel*, probably form Silesia, dating from 1310-20 and in its fragmentary state consisting of 532 lines, is very selective in its episodes. After presenting the Falls of Lucifer and Adam, it moves on to the worldly life and conversion of Mary Magdalene (a very popular subject in the German dramatic tradition), and then to the institution of the Eucharist.[43] A much longer history is apparent for the plays at Frankfurt. The *Dirigierrolle* survives from 1315-45, and the play can still be found in 1493.[44] From the latter year we have a manuscript of 4408 lines containing a two-day play depicting, on the first day, the Summoning of the Disciples to the Arrest, and, on the second, the Trial before Annas to the Deposition. It is apparent that enormous changes were made between 1313 and 1493 even though some lines survived throughout. The Corpus Christi play of 1391 originating from Thuringia, known as the Innsbruck Play (756 lines), spreading from Creation to Doom, is of particular interest because of its dramatic style.[45] The action is somewhat plain as each speaker introduces his role in the Christian narrative. The bulk of the play shows an alternation between prophets and apostles, most of the prophets singing an anthem. It is framed by an introduction from Adam and Eve and a concluding exhortation by the Pope. There are also speeches by John the Baptist, who sings *Agnus Dei*, and the three Kings.

As already indicated, there is a large amount of material concerning Lucerne plays from 1450 onwards. The span of the later versions of the plays is from Adam to Christ and the Blind Man on the first day, including Jacob, Joseph, Moses, David, the Nativity, John Baptist and Mary Magdalene. The second day runs from Lazarus to Christ's Appearances to the Disciples, one text going to the Ascension.[46] This cycle was performed in Easter week, and differing texts survive for the performances in 1545, 1571, 1583, 1597 and 1616, as well as background archive material from 1538. From 1583 Renward Cysart, the Town Clerk, became responsible for the plays, and the detailed diagram, which had been made earlier, and which he used and annotated for some years afterwards, for the two days of performance still survives.[47] It shows that the place of performance, the "Weinmarkt", was set out with a large variety of acting locations, some of which had elaborate settings or structures, but it is clear that the idea of processions of different kinds between these locations was a significant part of the dramatic experience. The whole of Cysart's work is characterised by meticulous, even obsessive attention to detail.

From 1470 at Donaueschingen (Baden) there is a text of a two-day Passion Play of some 4177 lines, the range of episodes being from Mary Magdalene's worldly life to Judas on the first day, and up to the Visitation to the Tomb on the second. For this play there is also a ground plan showing that the performance took place in a church.[48] By contrast the *Künzelsau Fronleichnamspiel* (Hessen) is a Corpus Christi play, and the manuscript of 1479 contains a text of 5872 lines covering many episodes from the Creation to Doomsday, including several from the Old Testament.[49] The actual management of this cycle is somewhat problematic. It appears that there were three stations, and the key figure in the presentation was the *Rector Processionis*. He begins at the first station with an act of worship to the Sacrament and then addresses the people. The procession then passes by the other two stations, where there may have been musical items. The full performance of the dramatic text in the manuscript probably came as a final act in the market place where the *Rector* introduced each item.⁵⁰

The Eger text, also called a Corpus Christi play, dates from *c.* 1480 (though it may have evolved much earlier), and it is notable for the extensive spread of episodes and for the frequency of musical items which are numbered up to 194 in a rubricated manuscript of 8312 lines.⁵¹ The first day, which contains both Falls and Old Testament material including Cain, Noah, Abraham, Moses, David and Solomon, goes up to Christ and the Doctors. The second day comprises the Calling of the Disciples to the Condemnation of Christ, and the third shows the Carrying of the Cross to the Appearances to the Disciples. The stage directions are in Latin (in black ink contrasting with the red musical cues), and they make it clear that the presentation was for an open space or square with fixed locations, including Paradise and Hell and movement between them.

The Passion from Bozen, whose text has been dated between 1495 and the second half of the sixteenth century, is one of a group from the South Tyrol also evident at Brixen (1551), Hall (1514) and Sterzing (text from 1486 to *c.* 1550).⁵² This became a seven-day event, but the days chosen for performance stretched from Palm Sunday to Ascension Day. The performances are known only at irregular intervals (1476, 1489, 1495, 1512, 1514) and they took place inside a church. The surviving manuscripts cover only three days, the narrative running from the Last Supper to the Resurrection. The performances at Sterzing were also in a church, occurring every seven years between 1455 and 1503. Later in the sixteenth century the interval was reduced to three years up to 1580.

The Alsfeld Passion (Hessen) perhaps rivals Lucerne for the detail which it leaves us, and in its closeness to the circumstances of performance. It is unique in that its *Dirigierrolle* corresponds with the extant text of 8095 lines, though this in itself is a document which served for the 1501 performance and was subsequently modified, in different hands, for performances in 1511 and 1517. The *Dirigierrolle* is in the same hand as the additions for 1517. Among the surviving fragments are individual parts for John, the Merchant, Synagoga and Lucifer.[53] The musical content is again large, there being cues for over three hundred items. The work is arranged for three days, but the structure is interesting in that it does not use any pre-Passion material, other than an elaborate devil scene which sets up the main antagonism of the whole cycle. The action begins with Lucifer climbing onto a barrel to summon his followers. It continues by incorporating many interventions by devils throughout. Though the plays were done in the market place at Alsfeld it seems that there were not many large structures, and that barrels were used repeatedly, as, for instance, for the pinnacle of the Temple. There are other important features in the role of the Proclamator, and in the extended dispute between Synagoga, representing the Jews, and Ecclesia, representing Christ's new religion.

Finally the *Heidelberger Passionsspiel* (6125 lines) survives in a manuscript dated 1514.[54] Once again there is a large musical element, there being four hundred and fifty-three scripture cues which were almost certainly sung. This cycle may be somewhat older than the date of the manuscript suggests, partly because it is specifically related to a procession, and partly because of its structure. This shows a remarkable feature, reminiscent of the alternation of prophets and apostles in the Innsbruck (Thuringia) play. Of the fifty episodes those from n° 25 to n° 35 (the Woman of Samaria to the Entombment), each stage of the life and death of Christ is preceded by what is specifically designated a 'Prefigura' from the Old Testament. Many of these, such as the carrying of the wood for sacrifice by Isaac and the carrying of the cross (n°s 33A and 33), are found in patristic literature. The size of the episodes varies considerably: the Calling of Matthew has only six lines, whereas the Crucifixion has 376.

This corpus of German plays, from which those detailed here are but a sample, gives rise to a number of significant implications for the study of cyclic drama. One is that the rationale of the cycle may vary, especially in the light of the antagonisms set up within the action of the plays. Another is the place of interpreter figures such as the Proclamator or the *Rector Processionis*. The link with Corpus Christi is also a shaping influence mostly in terms of the scope of the dramatic episodes and the importance of processions. The differences in arrangements for performance are also valuable. Some plays were presented in the market squares, but there were also performances arranged around processions which presumably had civic importance as in Lille and in places in England. It is also especially interesting that in German-speaking countries the tradition of performing cyclic plays within churches manifestly continued. These may reflect earlier, but still continuing traditions of liturgical drama. This link may also be significant in the way the large numbers of musical items are integrated into the performance. But the latter happens in performances outside the churches as well as inside them. Indeed the importance of music is underlined by the initial direction of the Frankfurt *Dirigierrolle*:

> First then the characters are solemnly led out to their locations accompanied by musical instruments and the clangour of trumpets.
> [Translated from Latin.]

Other Countries

In Italy, the Netherlands and Spain the occurrence of cyclic plays was apparently somewhat rarer, and it can be dealt with here more briefly. Italy had many biblical plays in the vernacular, but the mode of performance was usually for short, unrelated episodes which were associated with processions and with presentation in churches. The first known reference to the 'laudesi' who performed poetic and musical religious items, eventually becoming dramatic, is 1183. In 1220 St. Francis petitioned the Pope for permission to stage a play on the Nativity, thus marking an interest in drama which was much developed by his followers as they realised the missionary power of plays.[55] At Perugia in 1259 the mystic fervour of Ranieri Fasani set up the movement of the

Flagellanti which rapidly spread throughout Italy and beyond. Processions of penitents beating themselves became the focus of religious ceremonies and these in turn became dramatic as dialogue was added. The close link with procession remained a factor for many years, and it is not surprising that the plays which emerged, the *sacra rappresentazioni*, preserved the link with processional ceremony.

The continuity and multiplicity of episodes associated with cycles appeared in a few places. But the approach to cyclicity is sometimes questionable, though nonetheless illuminating. The twelfth-century Passion in Latin at Montecassino is a peak of the liturgical drama, and at Cividale in Friuli the clergy performed a Latin cycle on Whitsunday in 1298 and 1303.[56] At Perugia a narrative sequence in Italian was presented on significant days for religious observance from the first Sunday in Advent until Pentecost, the first showing Lucifer and the Antichrist, and the last the descent of tongues upon the Apostles. In Lent there was a play for every one of the forty days, and in Holy Week the story of the Passion was shown from Christ with the Disciples on Palm Sunday, to the Harrowing on Holy Saturday and the Resurrection on Easter Day with the Appearances to the Virgin, Mary Magdalene and the disciples.[57] Thus the continuity of the narrative was present and the fact that at times the plays pressed upon one another day after day is important. The collection made in 1405 at Orvieto by Tramo di Leonardo of the plays performed by three Confraternities may of itself approximate to cyclicity since it covers a selection of events from the Creation to the Appearances, but many of the conventional episodes are missing, and evidence of performance as a cycle is lacking even though it is known that complex scenery and elaborate music were provided.[58]

At Florence there was a vigorous dramatic tradition, but probably the most significant record for our purpose is that by Marco Palmieri for the procession for St. John's festival on 22 June 1454. He lists twenty-two items in a procession of which the majority (sixteen) form a sequence from the War in Heaven to

Judgement Day. These were not plays, even though there is strong evidence that plays were given in Florence at a variety of locations at this period. Though there are a considerable number of extant play texts, it is not clear that any single one actually fits this occasion, and there is no indication of speeches in Palmieri's account, apart from one comic intervention. If the idea of a cycle is the basis for the procession, the question of whether there was a spoken component is unresolved. Palmieri notes, however, that the episodes of the Passion and the Burial of Christ were not included because they were not suitable for a festive occasion, a comment which perhaps indicates an underlying motive for some processions, even though those of the *Flagellanti* noted above pointed in another direction. An account by Bishop Abraham of Suzdal, a Russian visitor in 1439, indicates that the show for the Ascension at S. Maria del Carmine definitely had words, but the episode was apparently isolated.[59]

Texts of dramatic performances of two-day plays in Florence on the subjects of Santa Uliva and Queen Rosana also survive.[60] A substantial number of plays survive in manuscripts. One of the oldest was copied by Lorenzo di Ser Niccolaio di Diedi (fl. 1465-79). It contained twelve plays of which six are concerned with biblical narrative, but, there is no suggestion of continuity between these texts: prologues and epilogues offer no links to other parts.[61] The manuscript Magliabechiano VII, 760, however, presents us with a more coherent undertaking, though it is not possible to identify a place or a process of performance. It has been held to be a genuine example of cyclic form by D'Ancona and others, and Neri's description of the codex suggests that this may well be so, even though the heading suggests diversity:

> Here begin some Mysteries [plural] of the Death, Passion, Resurrection and Miracles of the Saviour of the World.

The episodes portrayed, which comprise some 15,000 lines, run from the Annunciation through the Appearances to some of the acts of the Apostles. Neri notices that the texts contain elements from other shorter plays, and indeed he describes the relationship between this manuscript and others, and also with some printed texts, as a labyrinth. He considers it independent of the plays performed in the Colosseum, which we mention below, but notes that it may well have been influenced by it.[62]

Against this background, however, there are three cycles which will command our attention in Chapter Four, all noted in the second half of the fifteenth century. From Bologna, where a Confraternity was active before 1417, there survives a collection of *sacra rappresentazioni* in cyclic form copied by T. L. Bononiensis in the second half of the century. The collection amounts to 1760 lines, and runs from Adam to Christ and the Thief, and there is a fragmentary Judgement. These texts were shown on a series of 'edifizi', supported by carts. At some point after 1486 there was a representation of the Passion in the Colosseum at Rome on Good Friday, also on 'edifizi'. The extant fragmentary texts, amounting to 1009 lines, run from Peter's Denial to the Appearance to Cleophas and Luke.[63] These two examples seem to have had very similar scope with regard to the size of the episodes. *La Passione de Revello*, however, was on a much grander scale, being arranged for three-day performance. The manuscript was completed on 15 July 1490, and it is thought that the play was given at Revello in 1492. The first and longest day (7717 lines) comprises the Nativity, beginning with the Magi, and runs though Baptism of Christ and the Calling of the Disciples to the Arrest and Trial before Caiaphas. The second day (2412 lines) concentrates upon the events of the Passion up to the Trial before Pilate. The third day (2385 lines) gives the incidents from the Condemnation to the Appearances to the Virgin and Mary Magdalene. No explanation has been offered for the uneven length of the three days. It is apparent that many specified locations in the form of scaffolds were used in the acting area, including Calvary, and that there were crowd scenes and stage directions requiring specific movements from place to place. The scope of this text as well as the type of performance suggest that it was much influenced by the French Passions, Revello being situated in Piedmont, contiguous to France. Its most recent editor, however, has indicated that the language is Tuscan.[64]

To these three examples we must add one further brief reference because it echoes some cycles from elsewhere in Europe (notably *La Passion d'Auvergne*). De Bartholomaeis prints a *Rappresentazione delle Passione* form Abbruzzo comprising about 2300 lines in six-line stanzas. It covers the narrative from the Conspiracy to the Tomb, and it has the distinctive feature of a dominating role for the Virgin. Christ tells her that he must die to free mankind.[65] She remains a presence throughout most of the episodes, reacting to them and addressing the Jews. She begs the cross to let her touch Christ, and touches the crown of thorns, the lance and the sponge (instruments of the Passion). Her role fulfills a poetic function and does much to unify this play.

In the Low Countries the narrative of scriptural history is found in the so-called *Maastricht Passion* of the early fourteenth century. It is a relic of older poetry, the extant fragment having 1500 lines, and its genre may well incline rather to pious story telling than performed drama. The languages of the text are somewhat mixed. It is largely in Ripuarian, a West Frankish dialect, originating from near Aachen, but there are Middle Dutch interpolations, mainly the episode of Mary Magdalen. It begins with the Fall of Lucifer and the Temptation, and after brief anticipatory episodes, it moves to the Annunciation, the Nativity, with Shepherds and Kings, and presents the Passion as far as the Betrayal.[66]

However, much of the surviving material from the Low Countries points emphatically to the close link between processions and cycle plays. The vigorous tradition of processional performance is well documented in many places. In 1553, for example, there was a procession and a play performed by fifteen guilds on St. Anne's day (July 26) at Zwolle. Though no text survives, the subject matter gave some emphasis to the Old Testament, and included David and Goliath, and the Golden Calf, as well as the

Seven Sybils. These were part of a long sequence which began with the Fall of Man and concluded with the Pilgrims at Emmaus.[67] At Oudenaarde the procession usually contained *tableaux vivants* showing episodes of saints' lives or of the scriptural narrative. Ramakers has shown that for about fifty years after 1500 the Passion sequence became the core of these *tableaux* as they moved through the city. Later in the century, however, with a shift in religious attitudes, the concentration was less upon the sufferings of Christ and more upon the use of the scriptures for exemplary purposes. Associated with the procession were fixed stages along the route at which various groups, drawn from such entities as the Rhetoricians' Chambers and neighbourhood companies, also presented shows. Besides these there were also waggon plays which could be done after the procession was over, at a fixed location.[68] An example of this type of play from Antwerp is also found in the quasi-dramatic text of *Mariken van Nieumeghen* which contains a performance of such a waggon play within its action, performed in the "Grote Markt" at Nijmegen.[69] The situation at Oudenaarde is made the more intriguing by the evidence of a lost Passion play which was performed there at Easter from 1504 at intervals of from four to seven years. This application of cycles over a longer period may indeed be a matter of economics, but it emphasises that the idea of a cycle had great persistence.

So it appears also at Brussels with the partially extant *Bliscapen*, which dealt in seven parts with the Joys of Mary. This procession and play is first recorded in 1448—elsewhere in Europe a significant period for the evolution of cycles—and it continued at least until 1566. The pattern of performance worked in a seven-year routine, each of the seven Joys being celebrated annually in turn. The origin of the celebration goes back to 1348 when a miraculous statue of the Holy Virgin was brought into the city, and it was subsequently celebrated by a sumptuous procession (*Ommeganc*) organised by the Guild of Crossbowmen at Pentecost. The practice of showing one of the Joys as a stage play is noted in a decision by the magistrate on 18 February 1448 about the *Eerste Bliscap* (First Joy). Thus the celebration developed two parts: a procession in the morning with waggons showing scenes from the life of Mary, and implying the scriptural narrative, and in the afternoon a performance of one of the seven episodes of the Joys.

In 1549 Juan Christoval de Estrella, a Spanish eyewitness visiting the city, gave an account of the procession of the Fourth Joy on June 2.[70] He records thirteen waggons with the following subjects: Mary's Birth and Childhood; Mary and the Infant Jesus; the Presentation in the Temple; the Annunciation; the Birth in the stable; Shepherds; Circumcision; Kings; Purification; Christ's Resurrection and Appearance to his mother; the Ascension; Pentecost; and the Assumption. The account stresses the beautiful appearance of all the young girls who impersonated Mary, and it mentions music and some of the actions of the performers and indeed the animals. These delightful details, which no doubt had iconic impetus, show that the organizers had a cycle in mind, and that the effect was to bring out the beauty and charm of the occasion. Though this event was a procession, it appears that there was a distinctly mimetic element. The description of the waggon showing the Shepherds contains the following:

> The mother of God, represented by a beautiful girl, lay in bed with her Child, while holy Joseph carried out his carpenter's trade. From time to time he stopped his work, as though delighted by the gladness of the heavenly concert of angels and the song of the shepherds.
> (Translated from Leendertz [1907], 494)

The texts of the *Eerste* and *Sevenste Bliscapen* (First and Seventh Joys) have survived in manuscripts which show signs of having been used for performances before being returned to the archives.[71] On the afternoon of Pentecost, the performances were given in the "Grote Markt", and the acting area is described, somewhat cryptically, as being in the form of a Colosseum. It is apparent from the texts that there was an elevated place used for heaven, and this suggests that scaffolds were constructed. As the

Rhetoricians' tradition suggests a linear stage with subdivisions and an elevated section, the allusion to the Colosseum is rather surprising, but it may be occasioned by the large number of people assembled in the square for the spectacle. The subject matter of the two extant plays shows that the treatment of the Joys probably varied considerably, and the plot may well have been designed to suggest individual items without a specifically chronological concern. Thus the *Eerste* comprises the Fall of Adam, a petition for God's mercy by Mary, details of Mary's conception, birth and childhood, her marriage, including the story of Joseph's rod, and it finishes with the Annunciation. The *Sevenste* concentrates first on St. John's care for her in contrast to the conspiracy of the Jews against her, and God's intervention calling her into heaven.

The study of Spanish plays has recently begun to reveal that there were significant examples of cyclic material.[72] We may begin by noting that the celebration of Corpus Christi began early in Toledo (1280), Seville (1282 or 1311), Gerona (early fourteenth century), Barcelona (1320), and Valencia (1355). Perhaps the most striking development was at Seville where there was immense expenditure in 1428 on the procession, in which guilds had become involved. The scale of the event is said to have surpassed even the extravagance of royal entries. The scenes presented included the Creation, the Fall, The Incarnation, the Passion, the Ascension and the Last Judgement. Again we find that there is an interaction between the procession itself and individual sites along the way. The guilds, it appears, decorated their home bases on the day of the procession. By 1454 (and again in 1496) human actors had appeared to present mobile scenes performed on platforms carried by ten or twelve porters. However spoken scenes emerged relatively late, between 1550 and 1551, a phenomenon which is perhaps paralleled elsewhere in Spain. The procession at Seville would last for several hours, but the performances at individual stopping places lasted for only a few minutes. These developments were on an amateur basis, but in 1554 the guilds gave up their financial commitment towards producing the shows. The city took over and professional performers were introduced. After the Council of Trent (1545-64) the dramatic elements were excluded from entering the cathedral, but support continued for the religious representations in general, providing that the text was approved.[73] It is apparent that the context of the Corpus Christi celebrations created an environment in which the drama could evolve, and that once this had happened it became a resource for the Church to enrich the faith.

Less distinctly cyclic were the procession and plays at Toledo where performers were paid in 1493, and where Alonso del Campo, a cleric who was responsible for the Corpus Christi celebrations in the years 1481-99, is known to have written plays, including a now fragmentary Passion of 591 lines.[74] The guilds concerned with presentation also paid professional playwrights at this time. Information has been published showing that in the years 1493-1510 many subjects were shown, including Adam fourteen times, the Resurrection six times and the Ascension five.[75] These seem to have been rather irregular, and it is not clear what triggered the choice on each occasion. We have seen elsewhere that the notion of a cycle could be extended over quite long periods, even years, but here it is more problematic. It is apparent that, in spite of rather sketchy archival evidence, there was also production of plays at Corpus Christi in other places, including Murcia, Málaga and Orviedo.[76]

From the kingdom of Catalonia, whose boundaries lay across the present French-Spanish frontier, there survive fragments of a Passion cycle, perhaps influenced by French practice, from the years 1534-45. Here the performance was on several days in Holy Week: the Entry to Jerusalem and the Trial on Palm Sunday, Limbo, the Laments of Mary and John, and the Deposition on Good Friday and Holy Saturday.[77] More controversial is the fourteenth-century Passion of 2370 lines in the Didot manuscript which was identified as Provençale by Shephard in 1928. Recent work led by Catalan scholars has made it more likely that this was primarily from Catalonia.[78]

Conclusion

Taken chronologically the cycles reviewed in this chapter appear to have developed in a primary phase through a number of dramatic and non-dramatic routes. The initial impulse in religious terms is to be found in the spiritual changes beginning in the twelfth century and developing through the changes we have referred to in the following centuries. The challenges to orthodoxy had to be met and the cycle plays were no doubt part of this process, as well as being concerned with the establishment of new spirituality, and also with civic and social aspects. But the aesthetic features of cyclic form, such as structure, anticipation, recollection, and cross reference can also be seen in the iconography of the period. We shall look at this in Chapter Two, noting that the cycles in this form had a much longer history than that found in the dramatic form. This will be followed by a more detailed discussion of the continental cyclic drama in Chapters Three and Four, and of the English counterparts in Chapter Five. Finally we return to cyclic form itself in Chapter Six. The changes which took place in England, France and German-speaking countries in the fifteenth century established the idea of the cycle as a large-scale form. This was more fully realised in the first half of the sixteenth century. The changes in belief at the Reformation eventually altered the nature of the cycles, but these plays proved inherently adaptable and their success continued, albeit intermittently, through the century.

Notes

1. See my 'John Bale's Lost Mystery Cycle', *Cahiers Elisabéthains* 60 (2001), pp. 1-12.
2. See David Staines, 'The Medieval Cycle: Mapping a Trope', in: Sara Sturm-Maddox & Donald Maddox [eds.], *Transtextualities: Of Cycles and Cyclicity in Medieval French Literature*, Binghamton, 1996, p. 22.
3. Hayden White, *Metahistory: The Historical Imagination in Nineteenth-Century Europe*, Baltimore, 1973, pp. 5-8 and 11-3.

4. Wolfgang Kemp, *The Narratives of Gothic Stained Glass*, [trans.] Caroline Dobson Saltzwedel, Cambridge, 1997, pp. 22-5, offers an important distinction in the arrangement of visual cycles. He notes that the narrative may be arranged in loose sequences or in highly structured systems, and he also points out that the selection of items may be directed towards outstanding themes, or to progressive, even causal exposition.
5. Graham A. Runnalls, *Les mystères français imprimés: Une étude sur les rapports entre le théâtre religieux et l'imprimerie à la fin du moyen âge français, suivi d'un répertoire complet des mystères français imprimés (ouvrages, éditions, exemplaires), 1484–1630*, Paris, 1999.
6. The REED (*Records of Early English Drama*) project is collecting drama and musical records up to 1642. For Hereford, see David N. Klausner [ed.], *REED: Herefordshire, Worcestershire*, Toronto, 1996, pp. 10 and 105-6.
7. In the case of the York Cycle it has been suggested that the development of cyclic form contributed to the development of the craft guilds as well as being dependent upon them; see P. J. P. Goldberg, 'Craft Guilds in the Corpus Christi Play and Civic Government', in: *Society, Politics and Culture*, Cambridge, 1986, pp. 16-47, and R. B. Dobson, 'Craft Guilds and City: The Historical Origins of the York Mystery Plays Reassessed', in: Alan E. Knight [ed.], *The Stage as Mirror: Civic Theatre in Late Medieval Europe*, Cambridge, 1997, pp. 91-105.
8. For continental conurbations see Lynette R. Muir, *The Biblical Drama of Medieval Europe*, Cambridge, 1995, pp. xxi-xxiii.
9. The Breton Passion, printed in 1530, is comparatively late, and was influenced by the work of Gréban: see *Le grand mystère de Jésus, passion et resurrection, drame breton du moyen âge, avec une étude sur le théatre chez les nations celtiques*, [ed. and trans.] Théodore Hersart, vicomte de La Villemarqué, Paris, 1865, pp. iv-vi. Brittany is also notable for its churchyard sculptures (*calvaires*) on the life of Christ, and there were considerable cultural links between Brittany and Cornwall. See E. Royer, *Nouveau guide des calvaires bretons*, Rennes, 1985.
10. Anne J. A. Perry [ed.], *La passion des jongleurs: Texte établi d'après la bible des sept estaz du monde de Geufroi de Paris*, Paris, 1981 [*Textes, dossiers, documents*, 4], p. 25.
11. For links with the Eucharist and devotional images see R. N. Swanson, 'Passion and Practice: The Social and Ecclesiastical Implications of Passion Devotion in the Late Middle Ages', in: A[lasdair] A. MacDonald, H. N. B. Ridderbos & R. M. Schlusemann [eds.], *The Broken Body: Passion Devotion in Late Medieval Culture*, Groningen, 1998 [*Mediaevalia groningana*, 21], pp. 1-30. See also Herbert Grundmann, *Religious Movements in the Middle Ages: The Historical Links between*

Heresy, the Mendicant Orders, and the Women's Religious Movement in the Twelfth and Thirteenth Century, with the Historical Foundation of German Mysticism, [trans.] Steven Rowan, Notre Dame, 1995; and for a summary as well as a critique of this perspective, David Aers, 'Humanity of Christ: Reflections on Orthodox Late Medieval Representations', in: David Aers & Lynn Stanley, *The Powers of the Holy: Religion, Politics and Gender in Late Medieval English Culture*, University Park, 1996, pp. 15-43.
12. W. A. Pantin, *The English Church in the Fourteenth Century*, Cambridge, 1955, pp. 193-4; Eamon Duffy, *The Stripping of the Altars: Traditional Religion in England, c. 1400 – c. 1580*, New Haven-London, 1992, pp. 53-4.
13. Pantin, *The English Church in the Fourteenth Century*, p. 212.
14. *Ibidem*, pp. 224-6.
15. For editions of *The Lay Folk's Catechism, Handlyng Synne, The Ayenbite of Inwyt, The Book of Vices and Virtues, Mirk's Duties of a Parish Priest*, and *Mirk's Festial*, see: Bibliography.
16. Avril Henry [ed.], *The Mirour of Mans Saluacioun[e]: A Middle English Translation of Speculum Humanae Salvationis, a critical edition of the fifteenth-century manuscript illustrated from Der Spiegel der Menschen Behältnis*, Speyer, Drach, c. 1475, Aldershot, 1986, p. 10.
17. Lawrence F. Powell [ed.], *The Mirrour of the Blessed Lyf of Jesu Christ ... made before the year 1410 by Nicholas Love*, Oxford, 1908, p. 158. I read 'persones' to mean 'priests'. See also Duffy, *The Stripping of the Altars*, pp. 62 and 79.
18. Elizabeth Zeeman, 'Nicholas Love — A Fifteenth-Century Translator', *Review of English Studies* n. s. 6 (1955), pp. 113-27.
19. Sanford Brown Meech & Hope Emily Allen [eds.], *The Book of Margery Kempe: The text from the unique ms. owned by Colonel W. Butler-Bowden*, London, 1940 [EETS, 212], p. 148/13-14; Powell [ed.], *The Mirrour of the Blessed Lyf of Jesu Christ*, p. 9.
20. Alexandra F. Johnston, '*The Word made Flesh*: Augustinian Elements in the York Cycle', in: Robert A. Taylor *et al.* [eds.], *The Centre and its Compass: Studies in Medieval Literature in Honor of Professor John Leyerle*, Kalamazoo, 1993, pp. 225-46; *Idem*, 'The York Cycle and the Libraries of York', in: Caroline M. Barron & Jenny Stratford [eds.], *The Church and Learning in Later Medieval Society: Essays in Honour of R. B. Dobson*, Donnington, 2002, pp. 355-70.
21. 1070-80 is suggested by Miri Rubin, *Corpus Christi: The Eucharist in Late Medieval Culture*, Cambridge, 1991, p. 246.
22. *Ibidem*, pp. 263-7.

23. [Louis] Petit de Julleville, *Les Mystères*, 2 vols., Paris, 1880, vol. I, pp. 208-10.
24. B. A. M. Ramakers, *Spelen en figuren: Toneelkunst en processiecultuur in Oudenaarde tussen Middeleeuwen en Moderne Tijd*, Amsterdam, 1996, pp. 298-302, 314-50.
25. Jean Sentaurens, *Séville et le théâtre de la fin du moyen âge à la fin du XVIIe siècle*, 2 vols., Talence-Lille, 1984, vol. I, pp. 37-57.
26. V. A. Kolve, *The Play Called Corpus Christi*, London, 1966, pp. 154 and 165; Sarah Beckwith, *Signifying God: Social Relation and Symbolic Act in the York Corpus Christi Plays*, Chicago, 2001, passim.
27. Alexandra F. Johnston & Margaret Rogerson [eds.], *REED: York*, 2 vols., Toronto, 1979, vol. I, pp. 43 and 109. It has been pointed out that although the principal religious guilds in York each had its own dramatic activity they did not have any responsibility for the Cycle: David J. F. Crouch, *Piety, Fraternity, and Power: Religious Gilds in Late Medieval Yorkshire, 1389–1547*, Woodbridge-Rochester, NY, 2000, p. 142.
28. David Mills, *Recycling the Cycle: The City of Chester and its Whitsun Plays*, Toronto, 1998, p. 112.
29. E. K. Chambers, *The Mediaeval Stage*, 2 vols., Oxford, 1903, vol. II, pp. 338-41, and Diana Wyatt, 'The Pageant Waggon: Beverley', *METh* 1 (1979), pp. 55-60; Klausner [ed.], *REED: Herefordshire, Worcestershire*, pp. 10 and 105-6; Chambers, *Mediaeval Stage*, vol. II, pp. 425-6 and 424-5.
30. Hardin Craig [ed.], *Two Coventry Corpus Christi Plays [...] re-edited from the manuscript of Robert Croo, 1534*, London, 1957 [2nd ed.] [EETS ES 87], pp. xviii-xix. See also Pamela M. King & Clifford Davidson [eds.], *The Coventry Corpus Christi Plays*, Kalamazoo, 2000, pp. 3-4.
31. Chambers, *Mediaeval Stage*, vol. II, p. 376; James M. Gibson, '"Interludium Passionis Domini": Parish Drama in Medieval New Romney', in: Alexandra F. Johnston & Wim Hüsken [eds.], *English Parish Drama*, Amsterdam, 1996, pp. 140-4.
32. Richard Beadle [ed.], *The York Plays*, London, 1982, numbers up to forty-seven, but he amalgamates two plays which share material. Two further plays are known but lost.
33. Barbara D. Palmer, 'Recycling "The Wakefield Cycle": The Records', *RORD* 41 (2002), p. 110, note 6, and p. 96.
34. The most important comprehensive studies of the corpus are Petit de Julleville, *Les Mystères*, Graham A. Runnalls, 'Les mystères de la passion en langue française: Tentative de classement', *Romania* 114 (1996), pp. 468-516, and Jean-Pierre Bordier, *Le jeu de la passion: Le message chrétien et le théâtre français (XIIIe–XVIe s.)*, Paris, 1998, especially

pp. 21-48.
35. Graham A. Runnalls, 'The Evolution of a Passion Play: *La passion de Semur*', *Le Moyen Français* 19 (1986), pp. 163-202.
36. Bordier, *Le jeu de la passion*, p. 44.
37. Runnalls, 'Tentative de classement', p. 495. For the Mons text see Gustave Cohen [ed.], *Le livre de conduite du régisseur et le compte des dépenses pour le mystère de la passion, joué à Mons en 1501*, Paris, 1925.
38. See Runnalls, 'Tentative de classement', pp. 497-504.
39. The piecing together of these fragments is traced in: John R. Elliott & Graham A. Runnalls [eds.], *The Baptism and Temptation of Christ: The First Day of a Medieval French Passion Play*, New Haven, 1978, and Graham A. Runnalls [ed.], *La passion d'Auvergne: Une édition du manuscrit nouvelle acquisition française 462 de la Bibliothèque Nationale de Paris*, Genève, 1982.
40. See Hansjürgen Linke, 'A Survey of Medieval Drama and Theater in Germany', *CD* 27 (1993), pp. 17-53. He points out that the archival work of Bernd Neumann has established this, including his *Geistliches Schauspiel im Zeugnis der Zeit*, München-Zürich, 1987. For example there was a performance in 1498 of a lost play of biblical history from Adam and Eve to the Passion at Calw in the Black Forest (see Neumann, *Geistliches Schauspiel*, pp. 258-9). It should be noted that plays in German do not necessarily come from the geographical/political area of modern Germany: Lucerne in German-speaking Switzerland is the most notable exception considered here.
41. David Bevington [ed.], *Medieval Drama*, Boston, 1975, pp. 178-223.
42. Text in: Rudolf Schützeichel [ed.], *Das mittelrheinische Passionsspiel der St. Galler Handschrift 919*, Tübingen, 1978. See also Larry E. West [ed. and trans.], *The Saint Gall Passion Play*, Brookline, Mass., 1976 [*Medieval classics, texts and studies*, 6].
43. Ursula Hennig [ed.], *Das Wiener Passionsspiel: Cod. 12887 (Suppl. 561) der Österreichische Nationalbibliothek zu Wien*, Göppingen, 1986.
44. Texts of both are in: Richard Froning [ed], *Das Drama des Mittelalters: Die lateinischen Osterfeiern und ihre Entwicklung in Deutschland*, Darmstadt, 1964 [rpt.], pp. 340-73 and 379-532. See also Johannes Janota [ed.], *Die hessische Passionsspielgruppe: Edition im Paralleldruck*, I: *Frankfurter Dirigierrolle—Frankfurter Passionsspiel*, Tübingen, 1997.
45. Franz Joseph Mone [ed.], *Altteutsche Schauspiele*, Quedlinburg-Leipzig, 1841, pp. 145-64.

46. Heinz Wyss [ed.], *Das Luzerner Osterspiel*, Berne, 1967, 3 vols. For commentary see Marshall Blakemore Evans, *The Passion Play of Lucerne: An Historical and Critical Introduction*, New York, 1943.
47. Peter Meredith & John E. Tailby, *The Staging of Religious Drama in Europe in the Later Middle Ages: Texts and Documents in English Translation*, Kalamazoo, 1983 [*Early Drama, Art and Music Monograph Series*, 4], pp. 8 and 283.
48. Antonius H. Touber [ed.], *Das Donaueschinger Passionsspiel*, Stuttgart, 1985.
49. Peter K. Liebenow [ed.], *Das Künzelsauer Fronleichnamspiel*, Berlin, 1969.
50. For more details see below, p. 178-81 and my 'Procession and the Cycle Drama in England and Europe: Some Dramatic Possibilities', *European Medieval Drama* 6 (2002), pp. 31-47.
51. Gustav Milchsack [ed.], *Egerer Fronleichnamsspiel*, Tübingen, 1881.
52. Linke, 'Survey', pp. 25-6. For the Bolzano text, see Bruno Klammer [ed.], *Bozner Passion 1495: Die Spielhandschriften A und B*, Berne-Frankfurt, 1986. See also extensive records in: Neumann, *Geistliches Schauspiel*, pp. 130-246, and William Tydeman [ed.], *The Medieval European Stage, 500–1550*, Cambridge, 2001, pp. 370-7.
53. Neumann, *Geistliches Schauspiel*, pp. 105-6. For the play text, see Froning, *Drama des Mittelalters*, pp. 562-860, and Larry E. West [ed. and trans.], *The Alsfeld Passion Play*, Lampeter, 1997; and for the *Dirigierrolle* see Cristoph Treutwein [ed.], *Das Alsfelder Passionsspiel: Untersuchungen zu Überlieferung und Sprache*, Heidelberg, 1987, pp. 280-365.
54. Gustav Milchsack [ed.], *Heidelberger Passionsspiel*, Tübingen, 1880.
55. David L. Jeffrey, 'Franciscan Spirituality and the Rise of Early English Drama', *Mosaic* 8 (1975), pp. 17-46; Ronald E. Surtz, 'The Franciscan Connection in the Early Castilian Theater', *Bulletin of the Comediantes* 35 (1983), pp. 141-52.
56. Robert Edwards, *The Montecassino Passion and the Poetics of Medieval Drama*, Berkeley, 1977; Karl Young, *The Drama of the Medieval Church*, 2 vols., Oxford, 1933, vol. II, p. 540. For documentation relating to the Cividale and Friuli performances, and to early (lost) vernacular plays at Avignon (1400) and London, at the Skinners Wells (1390-1409), see Tydeman [ed.], *Medieval European Stage*, pp. 147-57.
57. Vincenzo de Bartholomaeis [ed.], *Laude drammatiche e rappresentazioni sacre*, 3 vols., Firenze, 1942 [rpt. 1967], vol. I, pp. 32-3.
58. *Ibidem*, vol. II, pp. 337-473.
59. Nerida Newbigin, *Feste d'Oltrarno: Plays in Churches in Fifteenth-

Century Florence, 2 vols., Firenze, 1996, vol. I, pp. 60-3. For Palmieri's list and a discussion of the possibilities of a spoken element, see Nerida Newbigin, *Nuovo corpus di sacre rappresentazioni fiorentine del quattrocento*, edite e inedite tratte da manoscritti coevi o ricontrollate su di essi, Bologna, 1983, pp. xxviii-xxxii. For documentation about theatre spectacles in Florence, see Tydeman [ed.], *Medieval European Stage*, pp. 450-66.

60. De Bartholomaeis, *Laude drammatiche*, vol. III, pp. 3-165.
61. This Florentine codex (MS Conventi Soppressi F.3.488) has the following topics in order, with plays on other topics interspersed: Creation, Abraham, Judgement, Nativity, Purification, Decolation of St. John. This means that the compiler, unlike the one for N-Town, was not closely following a set pattern, and it may well be that this manuscript is a collection of essentially unrelated items. For discussion of this MS, see Newbigin, *Sacre rappresentazioni*, pp. xi-xiii.
62. Further details of the episodes and a critical commentary are in F. Neri, 'La "Passione"', *Pallante* 8 (1929), pp. 9-73. See also Alessandro D'Ancona, *Origini del teatro italiano, libri tre, con due appendice sulla rappresentazione dramatica del contado toscano e sul teatre mantovano nel sec. XVI*, 2 vols., Torino, 1891 [2nd ed.], vol. I, pp. 465-6.
63. De Bartholomaeis, *Laude drammatiche*, vol. III, pp. 191-291 and II, pp. 154-96.
64. Anna Cornagliotti, *La passione di Revello: Sacra rappresentazione quattrocentesca*, Torino, 1976, p. lxxii.
65. Vincenzo de Bartholomaeis [ed.], *Il teatro abruzzese del Medio Evo*, Bologna, 1924, pp. LV and 48-9.
66. The text is edited by Julius Zacher, 'Mittelniederländisches Osterspiel', *Zeitschrift für deutsches Alterthum* 2 (1842), pp. 302-50. I am grateful to Carla Dauven for comments on the dialects in a private communication.
67. J. A. Worp, *Geschiedenis van het Drama en van het Tooneel in Nederland*, 2 vols., Groningen, 1904, vol. I, p. 45.
68. B. A. M. Ramakers, 'The Oudenaarde Corpus Christi Tableaux and Late Medieval Drama', in: Francesc Massip [ed.], *Formes teatrals de la Tradició Medieval*, Barcelona, 1995, pp. 195-207.
69. Dirk Coigneau [ed.], *Mariken van Nieumeghen*, Den Haag, 1982, ll. 708-892.
70. *El Felicissimo Viaje d'el Muy Alto y Muy Poderoso Principe Don Phelippe*, [Antwerp], 1552, sig. VIIv and pp. 74-8. This was edited and translated into Dutch by P. Leendertz [ed.], *Middelnederlandsche dramatische poëzie*, Leiden, 1907, pp. 493-4, but he mistakenly gives the year as 1556.

71. W. H. Beuken [ed.], *Die Eerste Bliscap van Maria en Die Sevenste Bliscap van Onser Vrouwen*, Culemborg, 1973.
72. See Tydeman [ed.], *Medieval European Stage*, p. 559.
73. Sentaurens, *Séville*, pp. 36-30, 47-58, 164-5.
74. Text in Ronald E. Surtz [ed.], *Teatro castellano de la Edad Media*, Madrid, 1992, pp. 103-25. See also the introduction, pp. 33-7, which suggests that del Campo may have deliberately avoided the cruellest parts of the Passion.
75. Carmen Torroja Menéndez & María Rivas Palá, *Teatro en Toledo en el siglo XV: 'Auto de la pasión' de Alonso del Campo*, Madrid, 1977, pp. 45-7.
76. Ronald E. Surtz, 'Spain: Catalan and Castilian Drama', in: Eckehard Simon [ed.], *The Theatre of Medieval Europe: New Research in Early Drama*, Cambridge, 1991, pp. 189-206 (196-8), and Charlotte Stern, *The Medieval Theater in Castile*, Binghamton, 1996.
77. Agustí Durán i Sanpere & Eulàlia Durán [eds.], *La passió de Cervera, misteri del segle XVI*, Barcelona, 1984.
78. William P. Shephard [ed.], *La passion provençale du manuscrit Didot: mystère du XIVe siècle*, Paris, 1928 [*SATF*], p. xxxiii; Aileen Ann Macdonald [ed.], *Passion catalane-occitane*, Genève, 1999, p. 44.

Chapter Two
Cycles and Iconography

The main purpose of this chapter is to show that visual cycles have a number of close links with dramatic ones in overall design and in the functioning of individual episodes. The familiar processes of cross referencing, whether analeptic or proleptic, are to be found in both forms, and so is the process by which one episode or item may be linked causally, symbolically or figuratively with another. The networking of items, characteristic of cyclic form, is also manifest, together with the selective use of repetition and overlap. This may amount to an overall rationalising approach whereby all the elements are seen as subject to a grand design or comprehensive thematic consistency as in Memling's *Advent and Triumph of Christ.* However, this is something which is facilitated by cyclic form but not essential to it. Underlying both visual and dramatic forms there is also the common function of embodying religious experience as well as of setting out deliberately to instruct. There is a kind of creative tension between reiterating what is familiar and giving information or advice, which may be new. It is a recurrent theme in consideration of dramatic cycles that they offer experience of the enacted scenes to the audience. The didactic element may never be entirely dispensed with, but we ought not to come to either visual or dramatic cycles with a disposition to see them as entirely instructive. The experiential aspect in both forms centres round emotional experiences portrayed, and, much more difficult to be sure about, the emotional impact the cycles might have had upon contemporary audiences and viewers. There is also the presence of devotional activity, prayer and intercession especially, which is embodied in both forms. Audiences and observers are invited to participate in acts of worship in the plays, and in the iconographical material there is often, as in the Books of Hours, for example, a purposeful stimulation of penitence, worship, and meditation. The sense of design and interrelationship found in cyclic form could be mobilized to make effective use of these. Beyond this there is also the structuring of ideas which, once constituted, are conveniently transmitted by cycles. It is apparent that dramatic cycles could have deliberate ideological or polemical intentions, and the same occurs, though more rarely in the iconographical versions.

The consideration of the two forms side by side points strongly to one particular aspect of cycles which needs further comment. The historical perspective on iconography suggests that large-scale connected Christian narrative goes back to the fifth century at least, as in the mosaics in the nave of S. Maria Maggiore in Rome. With this as our earliest example we shall range over a thousand years and more of iconography to Tintoretto's paintings in the Scuola di San Rocco in Venice, dating from late in the sixteenth century. By contrast the chronological spread of the cycle plays available for us to consider is more restricted in time. Most of the latter are generated from the thirteenth century onwards, and there is very little which allows us to suppose its existence is much older, apart from some features of the liturgical drama. Indeed there seem to be significant historical points in the history of dramatic cycles like the evolution of the York pageant-waggon method by 1415, the dissemination of Gréban's *Passion* after 1450, and the impact of printing late in the fifteenth century, which made Michel's *Passion* widely available. There is a long-standing controversy about the interaction between iconography and drama, originating largely with E. Mâle.[1] The view which is sustained in this study is that cyclic form seems to have developed earlier in iconography than in the drama: but that does not necessarily mean that we can deduce a one-way traffic from iconography to drama. The truth is more likely to be in a process of interaction over a long period. It is also worth noting that the religious and aesthetic purposes underlying the two forms of cycles would be substantially the same at the same period. But there is a qualification to this in that theological emphasis, developing and shifting over the thousand years of iconographic arts, might have carried forward concepts which had become archaic by the epoch of the dramatic cycles. Nevertheless there remains the understanding that both visual and dramatic forms played a large part in the lives of the faithful, and that they were likely to have reached an unimaginably large number of them as they were promoted under the patronage of the Church.

In the following pages we shall attempt a historical survey of both the dates and also the variety of examples of iconographic material which may enhance our study of dramatic cycles; this will be followed by studies of some individual works holding special significance for the use of cyclic form. In view of the enormous complexity of surviving iconography, the method of working must necessarily be selective. The criteria for inclusion are partly matters of date, and partly the need to select from the variety of material which may have a bearing. We shall deal first with paintings and other forms of architectural decoration, and then with illustrations in books.

I

The survival of iconographic material, as with the plays, is subject to chance and accident, and we should perhaps not place too much emphasis upon the early date of the mosaics at S. Maria Maggiore in Rome and S. Vitale at Ravenna. Such a medium was designed to last. The arrangement of the pictorial scenes at S. Maria brings in at once the importance of the location of items within the structure of a church and we shall find that this continues to be a recurring aspect within individual church buildings. Here the left side of the nave has Old Testament incidents concerning Melchisadek and the story of Abraham, Jacob and Esau, while the right side has fifteen episodes covering the story of Moses and Joshua. The fifth-century apse contains further mosaics from the thirteenth century showing the Coronation of the

Virgin, a work which is supplemented by paintings of the fifteenth and sixteenth centuries concerning the Life of Christ as reflected in the Joys of Mary in the nave above the Old Testament mosaics. These items, coming as they do from different periods in the life of this church, show a concern with the continuity of narrative and also bring out the early importance of the Old Testament episodes for the devotional life.[2]

The art of the painter may well have supplemented mosaics in this particular church, but later in the medieval period it took on a more independent role. This is seen in the extensive use of murals for the purpose of constructing a narrative, and also in the creation of individual paintings which stand alone and yet enrich the devotional atmosphere of churches by their exploitation of cyclicity. We begin to be aware of these works in the twelfth century, and in the two subsequent centuries there is much to notice. In fact there is evidence to suggest that in Rome old St. Peter's had Old and New Testament cycles as well as a cycle devoted to the life of St. Peter, as early as the seventh century.[3] In quite small parish churches there was an interest in presenting a narrative of the life of Christ in the twelfth century in the diocese of Bourges in France. This is to be found in a number of churches, which are the subject of Marcia Kupfer's study. Particularly at Brinay and Chalivoy-Milon there are significant examples of a cycle of the life of Christ, but Kupfer additionally makes the case that such work may have been more widely disseminated in this region. She also notes that through a process of memory and anticipation incidents in the continuous narrative may have a function in establishing 'collective identity' and in furthering current values. The political aspects of her thesis suggest that the selection of specific incidents, as well as their location at key points in a church may have had more than a purely religious function. At Chalivoy-Milon, for instance, she identifies a core register of four scenes in the barrel vault above the quire: the Raising of Lazarus, the Entry into Jerusalem, the Cleansing of the Temple, and the Paying of Judas. These may well reflect concerns, as she suggests, about wealth and avarice in the community, especially in terms of defining the roles of the clergy and the laity.[4] At a lower register, the wall paintings in this church have a sequence from the Nativity to the Massacre of the Innocents on the north wall. The Passion begins on the south wall near the chancel and its chronology back down the nave shows the Last Supper and continues to Christ before Pilate. In the chancel itself we find the Crucifixion and, above the altar, Christ in Majesty. The emphasis upon New Testament scenes is sustained elsewhere in this part of France, and Kupfer's evidence points to a different position from Mâle's noted earlier.

The pictorial narrative at St. Aignan, Brinay, is rather more detailed, and it concentrates on the earlier part of the New Testament sequence. The walls and the east end are arranged in two tiers. The upper level of the north wall begins the sequence with the Annunciation through to the Journey of the Magi, with the lower tier continuing from the Magi before Herod to their Return. The east wall shows the crisis of Herod's intervention through his command for the Massacre of the Innocents and the Massacre itself. This is on the upper tier above the altar, a dominating position which may well be a deliberate substitution for the Crucifixion on typological grounds: a 'Crucifixion' obliquely suggested. It is counterbalanced by the lower tier which shows the Presentation of Christ in the Temple, Joseph's Dream and the Flight into Egypt, the latter being typologically linked with the Resurrection. The south wall, also in two tiers carries the narrative of the Baptism, and the Temptation and the Wedding at Cana, one of the commonest themes in the portrayal of the Ministry because of its significance as a point where the New Law of the Church was substituted for the Old Law of the Synagogue.[5] Another scene in this sequence is the Falling of the Idols, which epitomises the strength of the coming of Christ. The whole of the mural scheme depends upon a narrative sequence, but its locating in relation to the building itself is clearly intended to be meaningful and coherent. The absence of Passion scenes is striking in the light of the implications of what has been chosen.

The analysis by Marilyn Aronberg Lavin of the arrangement of the mosaics during the 1340s in the Baptistery of San Marco in Venice suggests that for mosaics as well as for paintings there was scope for the exploitation of architectural features in support of the importance of locating narrative elements. The position is made more complex here because of the interaction of Byzantine architectural forms with western visual art.[6] One of the main effects of her work is to bring out the importance of linking devices between individual scenes and to show that the sequences between individual sections of extended narratives became more and more sophisticated. This was especially the case where the narrative worked in several tiers and also where it included the ceiling.

The focus of the scenes in the Baptistery is the Crucifixion above the altar at the east end, with the figures of Mark and the Virgin on one side and the Baptist and St. John the Evangelist on the other. The sequences on either side combine the life of John the Baptist with that of Christ. Hence the narrative begins near the altar with the Annunciation to Zachariah, and originally it ran along the south wall to the Birth of John. At the end opposite to the altar, the Life of Christ begins with the Magi speaking to Herod, and it continues on to the north wall where incidents from the two lives are intermingled. The Baptism of Christ and John's Preaching to the Pharisees point up the interrelationship of the two narratives. After the portrayal of her dance, Salome is seen, in the last lunette, close to the Crucifixion again, with the head of the Baptist. But the last scene of all, closest to the Crucifixion, is the burial of the Baptist's headless body. At the top of the main cupola of the Baptistery, Christ exhorts the Apostles to baptise and preach to the world, and he is surrounded in this dome by a series of scenes showing them carrying out his command. The thematic connection between the selected narrative items in this part of San Marco cannot be missed, and there are distinct elements here which point to the working of cyclicity as a means of bringing the two narratives into contact with one another.

The complexity of the architecture of San Marco in its Byzantine style means that there are many interesting and usable interrelationships between surfaces, and the mosaic designers made much of the opportunities these afforded. In the principal nave, for example, the cupolas devoted to the Ascension and Pentecost are divided by a vault showing central events in the Passion. In this dominating position the sequence running from the Kiss of Judas, and continuing with the Condemnation by Pilate, the Crucifixion, the Women at the Tomb, the Descent to Limbo, the Appearance to the Women to the Appearance to St. Thomas hangs over the nave. At its extremities it reaches down towards ground level, now in a perpendicular orientation, the Kiss at one end and the Appearance to St. Thomas at the other being the items closest to the level of the human spectator. One of the most striking features of this configuration of spaces is the way the height of the cupolas is exploited for the Ascension and Pentecost, two scenes which particularly benefit from a vertical dimension. It is indeed the case here in the huge space of San Marco that the spectator or worshipper is drawn into a three-dimensional world, and that the mosaics themselves are made to interact through vertical and horizontal planes, and there is much exploitation of the rounded effects of such features as arches and cupolas.

The evidence of these mural decorations in central France and Venice suggests an interest in using cyclic form within differing architectural structures. The fact that such architecture has wider political, religious and social significance means that cyclic form can be made to serve these as well. One of the most important buildings to influence the development of the idea of the cycle may well have been the Basilica of St. Francis at Assisi. There are a number of factors working here together. The development of the Basilica itself in the thirteenth century after the death of the saint (1182-1228) meant that there was a cultural centre at which one set of ideas could play upon another. The Basilica itself was consecrated in 1253 and within the next century a complex of cyclic paintings was developed. In the lower church the north transept has frescoes on the Passion by Pietro Lorenzetti and his pupils (1315-19), and in the Magdalen Chapel there are scenes from the life of Mary Magdalen painted by the pupils of Giotto before 1309. The major contributor was perhaps Cimabue who painted the Crucifixion in the north transept of the Upper Church, and eight scenes from the Life of the Virgin in the apse end, ranging from the Annunciation of her Birth to Joachim through to her Assumption and Triumph. He also had a hand a series of episodes from Revelations.[7] Besides Cimabue, it is apparent that Giotto also made a significant contribution. He painted two scenes from the Old Testament showing Isaac blessing Jacob, and Isaac rejecting Esau, and he is thought to have influenced a further series from both Testaments, including the Death of Abel, Joseph in the Pit, Joseph and his Brothers, Christ and the Doctors, the Baptism of Christ, the Lamentation, the Resurrection, the Ascension and Pentecost. One of the most significant features of these is that they are at least partially interlocked with twenty-eight paintings on the Life of St. Francis. Although these are not entirely by Giotto, the connection between the life of Christ and that of St. Francis is of some moment. It is presumably the product of an intense and persisting body of Franciscan thinking and devotion, which sought to elaborate a series of parallels between the two lives and to see St. Francis as a second Christ (*alter Christus*). The correspondences could be very rich indeed in such scenes as St. Francis preaching, driving out devils, healing the sick, his ecstasy, his death and ascension, his receiving the stigmata, and St. Clare lamenting his death. In the Upper Church at Assisi the Confirmation of the Rule of St. Francis is placed below Isaac blessing Jacob, and the Death and Ascension of St. Francis is below the Crucifixion. It is interesting, however, that such correspondences are not apparently pursued obsessively: they seem rather opportunist than systematic.

What seems to be a most significant aspect of this accumulation of narrative sequences is that they are the work of a number of different artists, whether maestri or pupils, and that one design feeds off another. There is not one clear narrative line which takes in all the episodes and integrates them, but there is the characteristic cyclic feature of cross reference and of the presentation of detailed aspects in individual episodes which may have wider significance. It also seems important from the point of view of the cyclic drama that all this rich development happened in the thirteenth and fourteenth centuries. The growth of the Franciscan order was no doubt an important means for the dissemination of iconography, and it is clear that the order was responsible for a considerable number of commissions of narrative paintings elsewhere.[8] It is also notable that the Franciscans, following their founder himself, had an abiding interest in drama as part of their missionary duty.[9] There was no doubt a theological basis for this in the concern to make Christianity a more human religion, close to the lives of its practitioners, and it is not too far a cry to see cyclic forms playing a part in this. Giotto, in particular, in his detailed studies of human beings and their emotions seems to have been laying the basis for his own more extended work in the Arena Chapel to which we shall return later in this chapter. Hans Belting has suggested that the work by Giotto at Assisi is mostly determined by documentary realism, and that there is a shift of emphasis in the Arena Chapel at Padua towards psychological realism and the expression of moods and personalities. Admittedly such generalisations may be subjective, but there does seem to be some weight in the emotional concentration we shall find at Padua.[10] The occurrence of this development of cyclic form in painting seems particularly apposite to the coming of the dramatic cycles later in the fourteenth century. Even in England, where cycle drama is relatively early, there is little doubt of the influence of Franciscan thinking from an early date.[11]

At this point we should take particular notice of two examples of three-dimensional work which operate at least in part through their physical location in churches. They both involve some use of cyclic form, but in different ways. They are the bas-reliefs at Chartres Cathedral, and the stone roof bosses in England, of which the prime examples are those in Norwich cathedral. For the most part the narrative element is rather limited at Chartres but the technique of juxtaposition is evident in the west tympana where the central image of Christ in Majesty is flanked by the Ascension on one side and the Incarnation on the other.[12] The façade was originally constructed in the eleventh century, but these figures were added in 1145-55. The tympana of the transepts followed in the years 1205-35, and the designs are more complex. For the north door Christ and Mary are central with subordinate scenes of Mary's Death, Resurrection and Triumph. The Incarnation appears on one side and the Judgement of Solomon on the other.[13] For the south, the subject is the Last Judgement, showing figures of the Virgin and St. John interceding on either side of Christ, who displays his wounded hands and sides. Beneath these large figures the souls are divided, those on Christ's left being received by devils.

Roof bosses are by nature single scenes of quite small dimensions. The artist was constrained to economise on space, as in the Norwich depiction of the Last Supper, where there are only six disciples, plus Judas and Christ. Cyclic effects are thus found rather in the arrangement of the bosses in sequences, and occasionally in the reappearance of figures of characters from one scene to another. In their recent work Rose and Hedgecoe have indicated that the installation of the bosses in Norwich took place through a series of initiatives stretching from about 1300 to the first decades of the sixteenth century.[14] Such an observation supports the notion we find elsewhere that cyclic form can be sustained and added to, and it may not be fully envisaged by those who initiate it. The new cloisters, built between 1297 and 1450, following a fire, have some four hundred bosses. Before it was decided to construct sequences some of the earliest were of flowers, foliage, hybrids and grotesques. These may have come from similar decoration to be found in Psalters.[15] Nevertheless a Passion sequence of six central bosses was put in place along the north end of the east side of the cloister, from the Flagellation to the Harrowing. Even at this early stage it was also perceived that the central sequence could be supported by allusive bosses on connected ribs related to it, and such a perception undoubtedly enhanced the cyclic potentialities, perhaps in a way unique to this form of decorative art. It created the possibility of a kind of web of allusion, and of a means of focussing and refocussing.

The next important step in the evolution of cyclic material came with the decision in about 1422 to insert a sequence of bosses picturing key aspects of the Book of Revelation along the south and west sides of the cloister. The main symbolic and devotional importance of this sequence is carried by the central boss in each bay, but it is again clear from the discussion of each by Martial Rose that there were connections with other bosses in each bay of a subordinate nature to the main intention.[16] The last cyclic sequence in the cloisters came on the north side where a narrative of post-crucifixion episodes was inserted. These start at the east end with the Sealing of the Tomb, picking up from the Harrowing, which ends the narrative of the Passion in the east side of the cloister; and they continue through Emmaus, the Ascension, Pentecost, and the Coronation of the Virgin. Once again the main narrative is embellished by cross-referencing in the subordinate bosses.

This technique was further extended in the next phase in the insertion of narrative roof bosses. In 1463 another fire destroyed the wooden vaulting over the nave, and Bishop Lyhart inaugurated a stone replacement, fitted with roof bosses. Though it was, and is much more difficult to see these bosses than those in the cloister because of the greater height of the nave vaulting, the overall plan was very ambitious. There are fourteen bays and the design accepted was to represent in outline the history of the world, with seven bays for the Old Testament, and seven for the New. The scheme started at the crossing with the large central boss showing the Temptation of Adam and Eve. The narrative then proceeds back down the nave towards the west window with the central bosses showing the Ark, Abraham about to sacrifice

Isaac, Jacob's sheep, Joseph in the pit, Pharaoh drowned in the Red Sea and David enthroned. Through lineal descent from David, the story passes on to the Life of Christ. The New Testament sections contain the Nativity, the Baptism of Christ, the Last Supper, Christ before Pilate, the Crucifixion, the Ascension and Christ enthroned in Judgement, a match for the enthroned David. This boss of the Last Judgement, in bay 14, can illustrate the astonishing simplicity and directness of much of this work. There are only five figures. Christ is uppermost, his hands aloft to display his wounds. On each side of him an angel blows his trumpet. At Christ's feet the moon lies on its back, and below it a crowned, naked king looks hopefully upwards while a naked pope, his tiara on his head, looks guiltily over his shoulder. Within each bay the main picture is enhanced by supplementary material. The Last Judgement is elaborated by the surrounding subordinate bosses, several of which show three naked souls looking towards the central act of judgement. Some are damned and some not. The story of Joseph is filled out in bay 5, and the Crucifixion in bay 12 is extended by bosses showing the Trial before the High Priest, the Nailing, the Dicing, the Entombment, and the Harrowing.

The sense of narrative in these bosses shows itself in a slightly different form in the bosses which were added to the two transepts by Bishop Nikke after yet another fire in 1509. Since the nave had outlined the whole of history comprehensively, he chose to attend in more detail to some aspects from within it. For the north transept the theme was the infancy of Christ, and for the south the interest was in the Ministry. In their analysis of the details of these, Rose and Hedgecoe make it clear that the appearance of the same episode, such as the Presentation in the Temple, several times in different contexts is functional to the detail of these narratives.[17] There is also a special interest in the life of the Baptist in both transepts. The process of elaborating a web of references seems even more complex here. For example in bay 3 of the south transept, the central boss shows the marriage feast at Cana. Of the seventeen associated bosses, three are directly related to it, one shows Christ's baptism and the remaining thirteen are about the Baptist himself. Some of these concentrate on Herod's feast with its grim outcome, in contrast with the joy of the miracle at Cana.

It is difficult to do justice to the extraordinary visual impact, and indeed the sheer quantity of the Norwich bosses, especially as we can now see them in modern photographs. The scenes present us with dramatic details and moments of high emotion. The detached ear of Malchus is stuck on the front side of Peter's sword, and behind it the face of Malchus in profile is distorted with horror and pain. The manipulation of space within designs allows striking emphases and also it can have more than one centre. Thus for the meal at Bethany the table is tapered. Above it Martha offers wine to Christ, while below Mary, with streaming hair, embraces his feet. On the other hand the wonderful simplicity, often symmetrical within the circularity of the boss, shows itself in the Nativity where Mary and Joseph sit on either side of the naked baby and above it the ox and the ass look on (Fig. 1). At the Washing of the Feet, the principal disciple, having taken off his shoes, will be for ever struggling to remove his red fifteenth-century boot.

After Nikke's initiative the interest in the bosses declined, partly, no doubt, because of the shift to Protestant emphases in the sixteenth century, but for the purposes of the use and development of the cyclic form the accumulation at Norwich is remarkable evidence. It illustrates a number of ways in which the form can be exploited, and it is especially interesting in respect of the transepts where the concept of expansion and elaboration is clearly manifested. It shows a sustained interest in maintaining and developing this material over a long period. There has been speculation about possible connections between the bosses and the lost Norwich Corpus Christi cycle of plays. It remains a possibility, but one difficult to substantiate. However Rose and Hedgecoe have pointed out that the craftsmen making the bosses would have belonged to the Guild of Saint Luke's, and it was this Guild which petitioned the city authorities to be relieved of its long-standing burden of providing for processions and pageants in 1527. The earliest narrative bosses in the cloister were probably begun before the dramatic cycle came into existence, but those in the nave and the transepts were made in the period when we can reasonably suppose that a dramatic cycle was being performed on Corpus Christi. Though the earlier history of the plays at Norwich is sketchy, there is a very strong indication in the *Paston Letters* of a performance in 1478.[18] The N-Town Plays were also compiled in Norfolk, not far from Norwich, during this period, though their performance remains problematic.

From the very large amount of surviving medieval stained glass which might have a bearing on the exploration of cyclic form it is possible to mention only two here. They share with the other media we have been discussing the practice of utilising the architectural shape of the buildings in which they were placed. The two examples used here are relatively late in the period under consideration, both of the sixteenth century, but they provide a useful contrast in the way cyclic effects are achieved: they are the windows at the church of St. Mary, Fairford, Gloucestershire, and those of King's College Chapel in Cambridge.[19]

The principal difference in the cyclic material is that at Fairford the emphasis is upon placing a rather straightforward progressive narrative around the church, and allowing it to co-exist with other non-cyclic windows; whilst at King's the narrative is virtually all-embracing, but it is supplemented by an elaborate and sustained interest in showing a relationship between the Gospel material and its prefiguration, together with some extension beyond into the deeds of the apostles. In both sets there is a distinct narrative, so that this aspect of cyclicity is sustained. The design at Fairford turns upon the selection of the Crucifixion for the east end, behind the altar, and the Last Judgement for the west.[20] The narrow vertical shape of the perpendicular type windows means that the design was usually constrained to a high vertical dimension and a narrow horizontal one. This was overcome at the east window by devoting the five lower lights, from left to right to the Entry, the Agony, Christ before Pilate, the Flagellation, and Carrying the Cross. All five lights in the upper range, however, are combined into one scene for the Crucifixion. The outermost lights show mounted soldiers with lances, a suitably vertical configuration, and then the repentant thief, Christ himself, and the unrepentant thief fill the middle three lights on elevated crosses with mounted and standing figures at their bases.

This grasp of the vertical dimension is also manifested for the Last Judgement, but in this case it was again decided to bring together the individual lights into one composition, disregarding the stonework between them. In the drama cycles the theatrical problem of the Last Judgement is that it does not have much of a plot, and yet thematically it has great potency. In the Fairford arrangement, as in other visual versions, there can be a range of individual situations, which are really going on simultaneously, and which, taken together make up the emotional and didactic impact. The symbolic effect is striking because the upper half of this, the largest window, is devoted to heaven, where Christ sits in judgement surrounded by concentric circles of seraphim, cherubim and angels bearing the instruments of the Passion, in different colours, and with a rainbow at his feet. Mary and John intercede, and from Christ's mouth proceeds the sword, as in Revelations 1:16.[21] The lower half of the window shows earth and hell. At the lowest level the souls rise from their graves, and in the centre Michael in armour weighs a soul. To his right St. Peter receives the blessed, while to his left the devils are at work receiving and tormenting the damned. The management of the light is notable, because the area concerned with hell and damnation is dark with reds and blues, while the upper ranges are much brighter. This powerful window is supported by two others in the same plane at the west end: on its south side there is the judgement of David on the Amalekite, and on the north the judgement of Solomon. Though there has been some loss from storm damage to the glass the two scenes are apparently similar in design. Wayment points out that the association of these three scenes of Judgement derives from the same page of the *Biblia Pauperum*.[22]

This group of windows in the west is separated from the main narrative surrounding the east window of the Passion by a series of individual portrayals of prophets in the windows of the north aisle, and of disciples on the south aisle. The narrative itself begins in the north aisle, level with the crossing. It comprises four windows on the north side, which deal broadly with the life of the Virgin, and four on the south side with the events after the Crucifixion. The first of the north windows anticipates incidents in the Virgin's life by Old Testament prefigurations, including the Temptation of Eve and the Queen of Sheba before Solomon.[23] The sequence runs through the Annunciation and the Nativity, and it reaches the Lady Chapel whose east window comprises the Flight into Egypt, the Innocents and the Doctors; but it is interrupted by a central light showing the Assumption. The narrative on the south side of the Crucifixion is carried through the Appearances, Emmaus, the Ascension and Pentecost, but it too is interrupted in a key window on the east wall, in the Chapel of Corpus Christi, showing the Transfiguration. Like the Assumption, this occupies an emphatic place in relation to the continuing narrative and it is located symmetrically with it, as far as the architecture of the east end of the church will allow.

The design of the windows in King's College Chapel encompasses virtually the whole of its rectangular shape. The convention for the direction of the narrative adopted here for twenty-four of the windows of four lights each is to read from left to right. The lower pair in each window forms the narrative, which begins at the west end of the north side with the Meeting at the Golden Gate, the first episode in the Life of the Virgin. It continues until the Crown of Thorns at the east extremity. The east window itself has six lights, reading first along the lower three, *Ecce Homo*, Pilate washes his hands, and Carrying the Cross, and then to the upper three, the Nailing, the Crucifixion, and the Deposition. Thus the Crucifixion is in the central position in the upper register. The narrative then continues with twelve lower lights in the south side, from The Entombment to Pentecost; whereupon it turns to episodes containing apostles, primarily Paul, and ends with the Assumption and Coronation of the Virgin. The centrality of the Crucifixion is thus sustained by the narrative detailed before it and by the one after it. However we need to add to this account details of the upper range of each of the twenty-four windows, in the two long walls. These consist of a typological system, derived again from works like the *Biblia Pauperum*, whereby each of the upper lights shows a prefiguring of the event in the narrative sequence below. Thus window 9 on the north side has Finding the Manna above the Last Supper on the left and the Fall of the Angels above the Agony in the Garden on the right; and window 20 on the south side has the Translation of Elijah above the Ascension on the left and Moses with Tables of the Law above Pentecost on the right. This arrangement undoubtedly brings an extra dimension into the cycle, but it follows inevitably that while the narrative in the lower windows pursues a more or less chronological sequence, the upper windows have no such structure since their places are determined solely by the figure each is to present from the Old Testament and its relation to the lower sequence. Thus the effect of this arrangement is to include many episodes from the bible and associated accounts, but to present them with much cross-referencing. Attention and contemplation, controlled by the lower narrative, spring into a rich variety of non-chronological connections.

The developments and variations upon cyclic form we have been discussing give evidence for the exploitation of architectural space and the way in which a whole church, or significantly large parts of one, could be enriched for worship and instruction by means of murals and other decorative schemes. However there are many other visual media in which cyclic form could have effect and could be used to manipulate external objectives. Some individual paintings, for example, are relatively small in surface area and could be placed as a unit almost anywhere in a church, or indeed elsewhere and still bring to bear some of the characteristic cyclic effects. Later in this chapter we shall be looking in some detail at the cyclic aspects of Duccio's *Maestà*, a work which was brought into the Duomo at Sienna on 9 June 1311 and hung at the crossing under the dome, above the high altar.[24] Not all such paintings are cyclic: many altar pieces, for example, juxtapose a series of figures around the central figure of Christ or the Virgin, and in this way make an impact without direct use of narrative. Even so there may still be a tendency for narrative to be evoked by the very appearance of figures like the Baptist or Mary Magdalene in such juxtapositions.

With regard to cycles there are two conventional patterns, which were of significance, and there is evidence that the Franciscans were interested in both. The first to be considered here is the dossal or altarpiece which has episodes from the Passion grouped on either side of the central picture of the Madonna and Child. In one rather limited example from the Convento dei Frati Minori del Farneto (1285-90), the Child is not a baby, but a small standing man, dressed in a long robe, which may well be a (Franciscan?) habit. On the left there are pictures of the Kiss of Judas, and Christ standing before the Cross; and on the right there is the Deposition and the Entombment. A more extended example from S. Maria dei Candeli, Florence (1280-90), has six scenes on each side painted by one artist, comprising a narrative from the Last Supper to *Noli me tangere*, and a central Madonna and Child with two angels painted by another.[25] In this example there is an important variation in the narrative showing Christ mounting the Cross by a ladder, a motif which appealed to the Franciscans because it embodied his willingness to accept the sacrifice. The layout of this kind of dossal puts together the two most closely felt periods in the life of Christ: his birth and his passion.[26] The relationship between the figure of the Madonna and Child at the centre and the episodes of the narrative is a potentially fruitful one, and it was much exploited in iconography.

In anticipation of the discussion below of the cycle of paintings by Tintoretto at the Scuola Grande di San Rocco in Venice, we should note here that a significant tradition of cyclic paintings of the type we have been discussing appeared in the city from the fourteenth century. Paolo Veneziano's polyptych of 1350 shows the Virgin in the centre with the Nativity, Baptism, Last Supper and Betrayal on the left, and Carrying the Cross, the Crucifixion, the Resurrection and the Ascension on the right.[27] There also survive four scenes from eighteen of a cycle of Old and New Testament paintings from the main hall of the Scuola di S. Giovanni Evangelista (1421-40); and six from the Life of the Virgin at the Scuola di S. Maria degli Albanese (1494-1500).[28]

A second type of painting which associated a figure with narrative scenes is the historiated cross. Garrison's catalogue shows that this way of portraying the Crucifixion was most popular in the years 1150-1300: from these years he cites twenty-five examples. The episodes are grouped, usually symmetrically, on either side of the upright of the cross, in an area known as the 'apron'. But there is also scope for small illustrated panels at the top of the cross, at its left and right extremities, and at its base. The effect of the cyclic material is to elaborate key moments in the Passion, rather than to give the contrast we have noticed in the dossals. However the posture of the central figure Christ may have a significant effect on the work as a whole and there is some evidence that in the early years of the thirteenth century the triumphant figure on the cross was replaced by one whose posture indicated suffering: *Christus triumphans* became *Christus patiens*.[29] In some of these, Christ is portrayed as dead, and in others he is alive. Such variations must have had considerable emotional impact, and they indicate the range of effects which might be achieved. The choice of incidents to be shown in the illustrated sections would also have a marked effect, chiefly towards intensifying the impact of suffering. The selection concentrates mainly upon the mocking and tormenting of Christ. Frequently there are scenes showing breaking the legs of the two Thieves; Peter's denial appears at the foot and the Ascension at the head. The terminals of the cross-piece may carry illustrations of the Last Supper and the Washing of the Feet, and sometimes individual figures of the Three Marys and St. John the Evangelist. The effect of this material on the Crucifixion as a whole could be to give a strong thematic element as a means of controlling individual scenes and the responses to them. These painted crucifixions could be accommodated at a number of places within a church, and it is clear that conventional forces worked towards settling the locations, and also enabled individual artists to draw upon the traditions which had been set up. This illustrates the point made earlier that each iconographical form did not only work within a cyclic frame: it also embodied conventional assumptions about design and the selection of contents.

II

We now turn to books which in their different ways reflect cyclic form, even if it is not a major concern in all of them. In doing so we need to bear in mind the conditions of medieval literacy, which varied somewhat at different periods and between different social levels, and also to observe that in these books a great deal of their function is embodied in visual material as well as in words. Implicit in these matters there are questions about the kinds of readers for which they were intended, and also the use to which such readers might have put them. It is also needful to have regard to the nature of the text and whether it can be regarded as definitive. For the purposes of this study I have chosen to look at three Psalters, some Books of Hours, the *Biblia Pauperum,* and *The Holkham Bible Picture Book.*

With the exception of the last, these are all somewhat Protean in as much as they are types of books and it is not possible to identify an essential specimen, or a prototype. All three were produced over quite extensive periods and for readers from a variety of social classes, and presumably with varied degrees of literacy and theological expertise. In the absence of a definitive and defining specimen of each we shall nevertheless try to identify some of the ways cycle material may have contributed to each genre. From the point of view of the present study we shall find that cyclic techniques work in ways which are parallel to the cyclic drama. It should also be noted that for the most part these three genres antedate the development of the cyclic drama in much the same way as the decorative schemes we have discussed in relation to church interiors: they are also contemporary with it however. All three kinds form an invaluable insight into the nature of medieval piety. They remind us that contemplation and meditation were essential parts of religious life, and that these iconographical works are facing up to the same spiritual concerns and problems as the dramatic cycles. They are usable for the same process of reinforcement of what is already known and believed: it is not simply a matter of filling up empty, 'leued' minds. At the same time, caught in the circumstances of their own inception, they had to answer to non-religious aspects of the societies in which they were generated. These may be difficult to interpret, especially as both the plays and the iconographic material are the object of very considerable expenditure, and to some extent we need to be aware of the perennial intertwining of devotion and conspicuous consumption. In the case of the books we may add to this the requirements and practices of the book trade, and this applies notably to the three genres to be considered here. Within each genre there is manifestly a growth of conventions of expression which might have been accessible to practitioners.

I shall begin with Psalters because they seem to be the earliest of the three types to take shape. The examples here are *The Winchester Psalter*, *The De Lisle Psalter*, and *Queen Mary's Psalter*. Saying or reading the Psalms was part of both private and public devotion, but the likelihood is that most Psalters were meant for the former, and they were often made to order. *The Winchester Psalter* is probably the earliest of those considered here: it is thought to have been in existence before 1161. In the introduction to her edition, Kristine Edmondson Haney makes it clear that its creator, who had associations with the Benedictine priory of St. Swithun's at Winchester, as well as with the Abbey at Bury St. Edmunds, was familiar with a range of earlier material of a similar nature, some of it going back to Anglo-Saxon works, and some of it directly attributable to Bury. She indicates that he was adept and learned enough in this to combine these in a personal and individualistic way, possibly in response to the requirements of the patron, as well as reflecting a particular set of attitudes. He may have been following well-established forms, but he found considerable scope for originality. The principal designer's selection of topics for illustration gives important status to the Virgin. Some of this Haney attributes to earlier values which now needed reassertion in view of the contemporary interest in the Immaculate Conception.[30]

The constituents of a Psalter follow a general pattern. In the Winchester example, the first section is a comprehensive set of illustrations. After this there follows the text, comprising the calendar, two versions of the Psalms, the Canticles, some prayers, the Apostles Creed, and the Litany. One of the motives in constructing Psalters was apparently to provide a comprehensive aid to the Christian life. Haney quotes two passages from different examples which underline the relationship between the comprehensive narrative and the spiritual benefit to be gained from this in connection with the Psalms themselves.[31] Possibly a folio is lost at the beginning of the illustrations in the *Winchester Psalter*, the subject being conjecturally the Creation and Fall. The extant series runs from the Expulsion from Paradise, through the life and death of Adam and a group of Old Testament figures, Noah, Abraham, Moses, Jacob, Joseph, and David, and on to the Life of the Virgin, the Annunciation, the Nativity, Lazarus, the Crucifixion, the Resurrection, the Triumph of the Virgin and the Last Judgement. In all, there are thirty-eight pages of illustrations, and they present a formidable collection of visual effects at the beginning of this manuscript. The artist has shown considerable ingenuity in the variety of ways he has set out the pages. He also shows the cyclic technique of expanding and contracting episodes to suit his own preoccupations. Thus, besides the space given to the Virgin, as noted above, he devotes four pictures on two pages to David (fols. 6-7), a not uncommon practice in Psalters because David was thought of as the composer of the Psalms. Here the pictures show his triumph over Goliath, his life as a shepherd, and his anointing by Samuel. In fact there are further subdivisions in three of these scenes, which are indeed characteristic of the visual compression notable throughout this Psalter. In the encounter with Goliath, for example, he can be seen beheading the giant on the right of the picture, and presenting the severed head to King Saul on the left. For the Last Judgement there are nine pages, some of which are static portraits of Apostles. In this section he includes two pictures of the Saved, two of the Damned and two of the Torments of Hell (fol. 38), together with one of the Angels who is locking up the Damned into hell forever (fol. 39).

The compiler of the *Winchester Psalter* does not seem to have been very interested in Types and Antitypes. The main thrust of his illustrations, apart from the groupings we have been discussing, point towards very distinctive characterisation, especially for the range of grotesque and hideous devils, who appear differently conceived in several episodes, and in the powerful visual actions encapsulated in many of the scenes, such as the Massacre of the Innocents. The visual effect of many of these illustrations is to freeze a sensational moment—there are many telling gestures by hands and arms—and in these still moments the intensity of the gaze of many of the participants makes a notable effect, and one likely to promote the meditation for which the book was intended. On the other hand the cruelty in the faces and actions of those who are responsible for the evil actions portrayed may have prompted a sense of human corruption which was essential to the promotion of penitence.

The *De Lisle Psalter* approaches the management of illustrations differently. The state of the manuscript is less secure than that of the *Winchester Psalter* and there is some dispute about the order of pages.[32] There is no Old Testament material: the concentration is upon the Infancy and the Passion. The book contains several pages of diagrams and other material, some of it cosmological, and pictures of the Annunciation, the Visitation, and the Virgin are inserted into some of these. But the main effort is in nine pages of illustrations distributed in different ways. Three of these have six scenes and they seem to be conceived in a unified way, concentrating on specific sequences featuring selectively the rejoicing at the Nativity (p. 11), the Ministry to the Betrayal (p. 12) and the suffering at the Passion (p. 13). The cross-referencing between these groups is no doubt complex, as Sandler suggests (p. 21). Taking the second of them for a closer look, we find the top pair of scenes contrasts the Murder of the Innocents and the Wedding at Cana, the second pair is Lazarus and the Entry to Jerusalem, and the third offers another contrast between the Last Supper and the Betrayal. Within this page there is the horror of the first and last incidents, and between them episodes of spiritual reassurance, which demonstrate Christ's authority. The selection is notable for the many incidents of Christ's life that it leaves out, as well as for the emotional contrast with the other two pages of similar layout on either side of it, the one mainly rejoicing about birth and the other mainly despairing about death.

After this group of three pages there follow two pages with four illustrations: the first, with the Harrowing, the Deposition, the Entombment and the Watch, shows the momentous impact of the death of Christ (p. 18); and the second, with the Resurrection, the Marys, *Noli me tangere*, and Emmaus shows his emerging in triumph (p. 19). These are followed by four whole-page illustrations of the Ascension, Pentecost, the Coronation of the Virgin and Christ in Majesty (pp. 20-3), all of which celebrate the triumphant ending of the Incarnation. In the light of this it is perhaps significant that there is no Last Judgement in this manuscript. We should also note that the editor makes it clear that it contains the work of two anonymous artists, whose contributions may be twenty years apart.[33] Nevertheless there is consistency in costume, including hats and haloes, from scene to scene. After a certain point St. Peter consistently appears tonsured, a traditional device.

The arrangement of visual material in *Queen Mary's Psalter* is rather closer to the *Winchester Psalter*. The work dates from the beginning of the fourteenth century, and the provenance is probably the Benedictine St. Augustine's Abbey at Canterbury. However the editor points out that by this time the production of Psalters was no longer exclusively the work of scriptoria in the regular houses, and that there were by now many laymen who were able to benefit by participating in their production.[34] The volume begins with an extensive Old Testament sequence from the Fall of Lucifer to the Death of Solomon, some 223 pen and ink drawings, often two to a page (fols. 1v-66). The illustrations are accompanied by brief descriptions on page in Anglo-Norman French, some of them rhymed; but there are, additionally, some of these passages on separate pages with no illustrations. The incidents chosen are mainly biblical, but many are apocryphal. The episodes dealing with Moses, for example, portray incidents from his childhood at the court of Pharaoh (fol. 23). The last of the five pictures for Noah shows him receiving the dove back into the ark, and the commentary describes the events illustrated in this way:

> And Noah at its entering the ship cries 'Benedicite', where he sits at the helm. And the devil flees through the bottom of the ship, and the serpent thrusts his tail into the hole. (fol. 7 [Warner's translation].)

There follows a Calendar, illustrated by entirely non-religious pictures, and then the texts of the Psalms containing within them miniatures of varying sizes portraying the Life of Christ in chronological order (fols. 85-294). The first of these is a full-page portrayal of the Annunciation, which faces the beginning of Psalm 1, itself illustrated by the Nativity. By the end of the Psalms the narrative has reached the Entombment, and it continues through the next part of the volume, the Canticles, where the story progresses through the triumphant last episodes, featuring the Assumption of the Virgin, Christ enthroned, and finally the Trinity. The Litany then begins with a picture of the Last Judgement, but, the narrative now being complete, this part of the book is illustrated by many static pictures of patriarchs, prophets and saints.

For the Life of Christ the illustrations are in full colour. Many are grouped in fours, especially for the Passion sequence, where these are made up of closely related incidents, as for the two sets of four at Gethsemane. This is somewhat reminiscent of the practice in the *De Lisle Psalter* but it appears less complex, though it is graphically more sophisticated. On some pages the narrative is also carried forward by illuminated initials placed below the fours, at the beginning of individual Psalms. The locating of such incidents of the narrative in relation to the individual psalms may be thematically determined. For example there are two pictures of Christ with the Doctors. The first is above the illuminated capital D which begins the first words of Psalm 52 (Vulgate) (fol. 150v). These are *Dixit insipiens* ('The Fool says ...'). The illumination within the 'D' shows King David with a fool carrying a bauble and a bladder, and the viewer is presumably being invited to see the connection with the Doctors.

These examples are drawn somewhat arbitrarily from a large extant corpus of Psalters. They indicate that these books could deal with a very long narrative sequence, and that the unfolding of such narratives could be managed to bring about a variety of emphases, which themselves could contribute to the experience of devotion. Because many of them were produced to the order of patrons, or could be sold in response to demand, it is apparent that this form of religious activity was widespread, and the purchase of such books was in itself part of religious participation or aspiration.

The Books of Hours offer a further insight into devotional practices which most likely influenced the way in which cycles were conceived and experienced. They are part of a broadening of literacy, whereby the laity began to worship in private, but also in imitation of the clergy. Though there were many rich patrons of these books during the period of their greatest popularity, which lasted from the late thirteenth century to the first decades of the sixteenth, many were created for and used by bourgeois society, and also there was extensive use by women. Their invention may well have been associated with the evolution of portable bibles, and they exhibit persistent interest in the role of the Virgin, whose cult was dominant in this period. Indeed they must have contributed to it in some measure. As with the Psalters, many of the Books of Hours were bespoke and were designed to meet the requirements of individual patrons, whether aristocratic or not. This period of popularity is perhaps significant in relation to the development of cyclic drama. It does appear that the books were conceived before the coming of the cycles with which we have been concerned, and that they were in widespread use during the centuries of performance. Geographically about two thirds of the surviving copies were made in France, and in the fifteenth century extensive production also developed in the Low Countries. From these regions there was an export trade into England, where there was also production, notably at Oxford, the place where the de Brailes Hours were made *c.* 1240.[35] Before the invention of printing the methods of production of manuscripts were highly organised to meet strong demand, and these were intensified once the printing trade came into the market. It is apparent that the products of this trade, whether manuscripts or printed books, was so extensive that even today when only a fraction of the original flood survives, it is still difficult to grasp comprehensively the large amount of material available.

Commonly there were eight parts designed to sustain worship every day in each book. Of these the Hours of the Virgin and the Hours of the Cross are the most relevant sections to this study since to some degree they make use of scriptural narrative which is located in the devotional context, the former rather more than the latter. The Hours of the Virgin followed the eight periods of daily worship, the canonical hours, already established for the regular clergy of both kinds, and they formed the central part of the book. The texts were drawn from the bible, especially the Psalms, and from a variety of other devotional material. It is the illustrations, however, which hold the major interest for this study because they portray in sequence events centred on the life of the Virgin and upon the Passion, in a mode which is highly reminiscent of the other visual cycles under consideration in this chapter. These pictures no doubt encouraged contemplation and they were provided in a variety of ways to make them bear upon the verbal content of the devotions.

One of the factors we need to be aware of is that though there was scope for variety in the content of the Hours of the Virgin, both verbal and visual, there was also a conventional pattern of organisation which was popular and commonly adhered to. Substantially this divided the narrative of the life of the Virgin into segments, which were deemed appropriate to the worship planned for each of the times of the day as shown in the following scheme:

MATINS	Annunciation
LAUDS	Visitation to Elisabeth
PRIME	Nativity
TERCE	Annunciation to Shepherds
SEXT	Adoration of Magi
NONE	Presentation in the Temple
VESPERS	Flight into Egypt
COMPLINE	Coronation of the Virgin

Commonly there was a picture of each of these episodes at the beginning of each Hour. In a considerable proportion of cases, however, the individual Hours were linked with eight episodes from the Passion cycle, episodes appearing in this order:

The Agony in the Garden
The Betrayal by the kiss of Judas
Christ before Pilate
The Flagellation
Carrying of the Cross
Crucifixion

Deposition
Entombment

In most cases, whichever of these narratives is chosen, the chronological order is adhered to, but the significant aspect pointing to cyclic form lies in the various ways in which these narratives are embellished by means of additional material. For example the two cycles of the Life of the Virgin and the Passion could be visually interrelated as in the Book of Hours by the painter of Gold Scrolls, working in what is now Belgium, c. 1440. In this case the artist has chosen to make the Passion the main illustration, and the cycle of the Virgin is interwoven by putting an episode from it inside an historiated initial on the same page: The Agony in the Garden, with the Annunciation beneath, and so on.[36] The emotional effect of such juxtapositions must have been considerable, especially as the tone of the Life of the Virgin is essentially triumphant, in spite of her sorrows, whilst the Passion is progressively more sombre, yet potentially triumphant in a different way. Similarly in the Hours by the Master of Ghent Privileges, c. 1440, the Passion appears in full page miniatures with large historiated initials on each facing page: the Entombment, for Compline, is matched with the Massacre of the Innocents.[37] This possibility of linking could be extended to prefiguration. In the Rouen Book of Hours, c. 1480, the scenes from the Life of the Virgin concerning the infancy of Christ are at the foot of the page and the Old Testament prefiguration is the main feature above them.[38] These relationships have implications for cyclic form, and the occurrence, albeit in a limited number of Hours, suggests that a process of cross-referencing similar to that in the dramatic cycles is taking place. During the meditation, which the Hours were meant to engender, the movement between different layers of significance must have been profoundly moving. A further kind of embellishment is found in the provision of subsidiary narrative elements which enlarge the impact of the conventional main images. This technique is reminiscent of the way the narrative is handled for the roof bosses in the nave of Norwich cathedral.

Fig. 1
Norwich Cathedral Roof Boss (1463+): *Nativity*

Fig. 2
Biblia Pauperum (*c.* 1460): Christ Appears to his Disciples, with Joseph reveals himself to his brothers, and the return of the Prodigal Son

Fig. 3
The Holkham Bible Picture Book (1325-30): Noah in the Ark with Raven and Dove (British Library, MS Add. 47682, fol. 8r.)

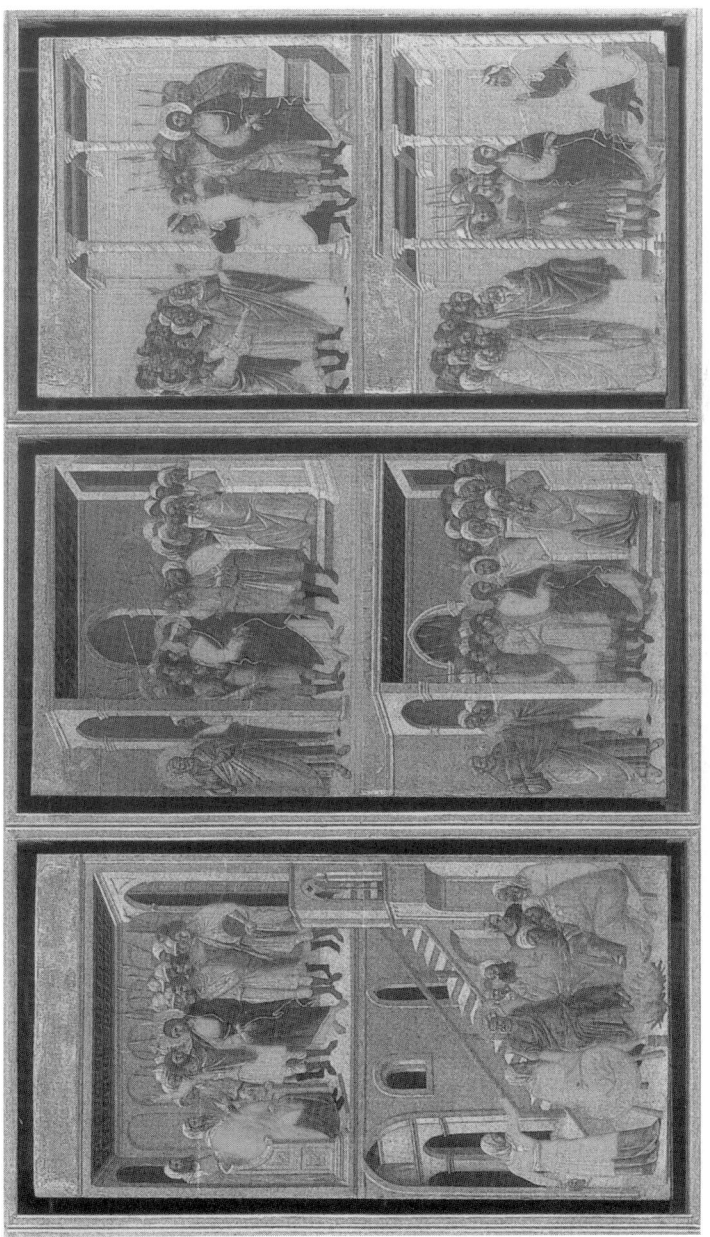

Fig. 4
Duccio – Scenes from *Maestà* verso (1311) (Cathedral Museum, Siena [detail])

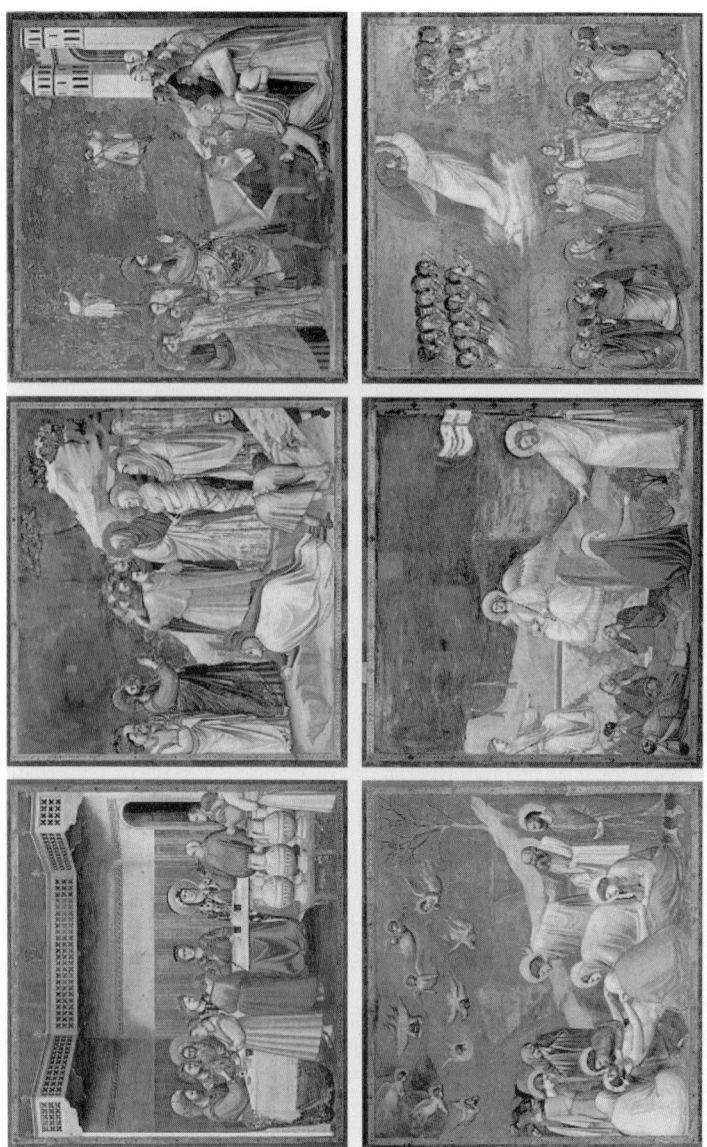

Fig. 5
Giotto – Composite of details from north wall (by 1313) Arena Chapel, Padua

Cycles and Iconography

Fig. 6
Memling – *Scenes from the Passion* (1470-1) Sabauda Gallery, Turin

Fig. 7
Tintoretto – *Road to Calvary* (1576-81)
Scuola di San Rocco, Venice

The *Biblia Pauperum* has survived in very considerable numbers, though once again what we have is but a small fraction of what was probably produced originally. Because of the variations in page layout in different copies, in the number of illustrations per page, and in the varieties of sequence in the images, it has to be regarded as a type capable of variation within certain limits. The discussion here is based upon the example edited by Avril Henry, which is a blockbook printed *c*. 1460, but the earliest manuscript versions go back to the mid-thirteenth century, and there is a fragment from *c*. 1300.[39] The essential technique is to juxtapose images which are related as Type and Antitype, and to elaborate this with subordinate images and with verbal quotations which bring out a variety of connections between them. The process works further because each opening can be arranged so that the facing sets of images are related in some way. Some of the manuscript examples have a potentially more complex interrelationship with two main pictures and their surroundings per page, so that one opening may be offering four sets of pictures and generating the relationship between them. The central illustrations on each page are from the New Testament, and in the copy under consideration there are thirty-six of these, running from the Annunciation to the Ascension. These are known as Antitypes, and they are each flanked in this version by two Old Testament images. Thus the design of the book is substantially chronological, but, as we have noticed in some earlier examples such as the windows at King's, the presence of Types which embellish them means that the chronological structure is subject to counteraction which is not in itself chronological, but thematic, forming instead a network of reference. Once this sequence is complete the four last sets of images are concerned with the Last Judgement, the Damned entering Hell, Christ gathering the Blessed, and Christ giving the crown of life. It should be added that the layout of all the pages in the facsimile by Henry follows the same pattern (except that the decorative framework of the left-hand pages differs consistently from those on the right) and this is undoubtedly a prompt to cross reading from one page to another. In spite of the chronological sequence noted above, it is apparent that the book may be read and thought about in many different directions.

The use of typology is complex here because the verbal elements on each page sometimes point directly to the central image or its subordinates; but equally the words may lead to more remote relationships. Their function is no doubt based upon the concept that everything in creation is the work of God and that therefore there is a network of signs by which this may be comprehended. This is especially important in connection with the widely held supposition that the way the Old Testament prefigured the New was the result of divine inspiration.[40] In practice one senses that some of the relationships are much more obscure than others, their source being almost always written exegeses by the Fathers of the Church and other theological authorities. The simplest form of relationship between Type and Antitype is a direct parallel, as when Joseph revealing himself to his brothers is placed next to Christ's Appearance to the Disciples, a sort of anticipation. But the other Type on this page is the return of the Prodigal Son, and it seems that to equate Christ with the repentant sinner is rather a strain (Fig. 2).[41] This suggests that part of the meditative process, which the book is designed to promote, is partly a search for the way in which the various elements might be manifested. One may look on it as a kind of holy puzzle, which is inherently challenging to interpretation and has within it a strong element of ingenuity. If this is so, it reminds us that the forms we have been discussing, as well as the cyclic drama itself, are accessible at different levels. The putative "man in the street" watching the mystery cycles may have had access to only part of what he was watching, yet in a sense it was all before him, with the potential of discovery. The complexity of the relationship between reader/viewer and book is made all the greater because the verbal elements mentioned above are in Latin. This suggests that a good deal of the potential meaning would be inaccessible to many. Yet the *Biblia Pauperum*, in its turn, seems to have been influential with artists working in other visual media, including stained glass.

Another aspect of the *Biblia Pauperum* attracting our attention is that we are again dealing with a highly selective process regarding the choice of incidents. To some extent the selection of supporting images, the Types, were determined by authorities which might be accessible to the compiler, but Henry's commentary makes it clear that convention is the basis for variation, and the same principle appears to be operating with the cycle plays. The fact that versions were continually being re-invented suggests that the form of the *Biblia Pauperum* was valued for this very capacity of adaptability.

The Holkham Bible Picture Book has been dated 1325-30.[42] It may have had some relationship to illustrated bibles and Psalters, but we can regard it as substantially an independent work, by one artist, who drew with fine quills. Another artist, working with brushes, added colour to the drawings. Many pages are divided horizontally in the middle, giving substantially two pictures, but the artist varies this by adding many smaller scenes, sometimes involving only one or two people. There are five miracles from Christ's infancy on one page (fol. 16). As we shall see, the artist also uses whole pages for some principal scenes. The work is characterised by very detailed and carefully drawn figures and scenes, and there is a strong sense that the artist has generated his own visual idiom. There is a written commentary which names the incidents portrayed and describes details. Because this is in Norman French it has been suggested by Hassall that the work was made for upper class laity, possibly women. The subject matter draws upon a range of biblical and apocryphal material and its selection and arrangement show some distinctive features. An important source has been found to be Peter Comestor's *Historia Scholastica*, the twelfth-century harmonisation of sacred history.[43]

The book falls into three sections, which are physically distinct, but some themes and ideas cross these boundaries. The first deals with the Creation and Fall and follows scriptural history to the end of Noah (fols. 2-9). It begins with a series of pictures showing God carrying out the Creation at various stages. The first of these is a full page showing him with a pair of compasses describing a great orb, with angels at the top and a grotesque at the foot (prematurely suggesting hell mouth?) (fol. 2). The next page shows creation of the plants and animals, and the third, which is divided, shows the creation of Adam, and of Eve, drawn from out of his side. This sense of the wonder of creation is disturbed, however, by the subsequent portrayal of the sins of men and women, through Adam, Eve, Cain, Cain's children and the contemporaries of Noah, who are sensationally overwhelmed by the Flood. Noah's survival ends the Old Testament sequence, and the concentration upon sin and the need for the Redemption could hardly be more apparent (Fig. 3). His outstretched arms with the dove in his right hand and the raven in his left anticipates Christ on the cross, between the good and bad thieves (fol. 8). The tree of knowledge appears in two full-page pictures. In the first, the prohibition by God, a pelican at the top of it is plucking blood from its breast for its brood. This is a link with the tree of the Cross, which has three appearances, also in full-page in the second section. At the second of these Adam, naked at the foot of the Cross, collects Christ's blood from the wounded side in a cup (fol. 32v). This linking of Tree and Cross we shall encounter in dramatic cycles, especially the Cornish. In this book it is strengthened by the two versions of the Tree of Jesse, which open the second section dealing with the Life of Christ (fols. 10r-v). These Jesse Trees are useful because they summarize the whole of history from Noah to the Incarnation. They are thus linked with the other two Trees, and also with the overriding sense of divine history suggested by God at the Creation, as noted above. Nevertheless the artist has decided to leave out a great deal of detail from the Old Testament: its function is strictly limited here.

The middle section of the book deals with the Life of Christ as far as the Appearances and the Ascension. It begins with a scene showing a devil asserting to Christ that he will remain in charge of all souls until a virgin conceives. This suggests that the designer was aware of the motif of Christ's deception of the devil, and that he intended his work to have a comprehensive structure. The selection of material is unusual, but it is a feature of Warner's commentary that he has been able to find analogues or sources for many apparently unusual items. This extends to details of Christ's life while he is in exile, and his obedient behaviour to his parents while he is a child. It seems as though one of the motives is to suggest the happy family in contrast to Herod's. The latter kills his own sons, falls sick and commits suicide (fols. 16v-17).[44] These events often hover between a rather realistic mode of presentation, and the use of more symbolic situations. After the Resurrection, when Christ appears to the Disciples by Lake Tiberias, one is seen to be blowing the coals to grill fish for him (fol. 37). In one incident while the holy family is on the way to Egypt they are stopped by a robber and his son. When the latter sees the face of Christ he prevents his father from doing any harm. A marginal comment reveals that this boy grows up to be the good thief who is crucified on Christ's right hand (fol. 14). These items all suggest that there is a strong anecdotal stratum in this collection. Nevertheless the cruelty of the Passion is presented in great detail, and there are several scenes showing the naked body of Christ tormented and bleeding, suggesting that the author—and perhaps his intended readership—might be moved by such strong emotional material. On the cross Christ is naked at first and then Mary covers him (fols. 32 and 32v). This aspect of *The Holkham Bible Picture Book* may well be related to the increasing emphasis upon the sufferings of Christ traceable in Germany and the Netherlands in the years before 1450. In much devotional literature, both in manuscripts and incunabula, narratives increasingly included scenes of terror and pathos. The increase has been associated firstly with Franciscan interest in the Passion, and also with the so-called *Devotio Moderna*. Some of it was derived from Psalm 21 and Isaiah, but also from non-biblical sources. There is an interesting link here with the sense of divine inspiration for the bible, which gave rise to elaborate re-interpretation.[45]

The Passion ends with a full-page Ascension, followed by a blank in the manuscript. The last section is the Last Things, leading up to the Last Judgement. The penultimate scene is the return of Christ in glory, a scene hinted at in the York Last Judgement, and the Judgement itself follows with Christ, accompanied by angels carrying instruments of the Passion, dividing the souls. Among the damned is an ale-wife, a convention which re-appears in Chester. These final scenes are preceded by the fifteen signs of judgement, attributed by Warner to St. Jerome. These show symbolic elements like the darkening of the sky, the destruction of Jerusalem and there is an especially graphic page showing the great and the small fighting among themselves (fol. 40).

III

In this section I shall look at four examples of painting which seem to me to have the concept of a cycle deeply embedded in them, and which use cyclic form and techniques consistently. Each of the four I have chosen has something to show in relation to the way cyclic form may be used. It must be admitted that other cycle paintings might well have been offered here instead, but these four, which differ in a number of ways, should serve as a basis for comparison. Nevertheless the paintings considered here may stand as culminations of much of the iconography we have been observing. Admittedly they are all highly canonical, blessed (or cursed) by receiving the status of high art through several centuries. Yet it is possible that these artists have been able to show us how effectively cyclic form may be used by those resourceful enough to exploit it extensively.

These works are all conceived as a whole, though the process by which they were evolved was not necessarily similar, and in three of them there is some matter extraneous to cyclic form. They are the work of known painters whose other painting forms a context for the individual works discussed here. Two of them were completed early in the fourteenth century before cycle plays, as we shall describe them, can be fully identified. Duccio's painting, the *Maestà*, was put in place in the Duomo in Siena in 1311.[46] On the back of it there is an extensive Passion sequence. Giotto, having worked at Assisi and other places, painted the walls and ceiling of the Arena Chapel in Padua after its consecration in 1305, probably completing the project by 1313.[47] This was a comprehensive design filling almost the whole of the available space (with the exception of the lowest tier, which is an allegorical series in grisaille) with a cycle showing a narrative from the Expulsion of Joachim from the Temple to the Last Judgement. There is a possibility that Giotto had a hand in the architecture of the Chapel as well: certainly his work fits it like a glove. Memling's *Scenes from the Passion of Christ*, painted in 1470-1, cover the events from the Entry to Jerusalem to the Appearance by the Sea of Galilee. This was conceived as one complete painting, and given a number of unifying characteristics. However it does not contain the Ascension. This subject was incorporated into *Scenes from the Advent and Triumph of Christ*, which concentrated on the Joys of Mary, and was painted in 1480, in many ways complementary to the earlier Passion.[48] Finally Tintoretto's paintings on the walls and ceilings of three rooms in the Scuola di San Rocco in Venice were painted between 1564 and 1588. This work has much that is a characteristic of a cycle, but it is apparent from the contractual arrangements that Tintoretto's conception developed over a number of years.[49] To some extent we must look at what he painted here in the light of the shape and structure of the rooms he worked upon, but we have also to consider aesthetic features which promote his version of cyclic form.

From these brief comments we can see that we are dealing with two kinds of cycle as discussed earlier in this chapter: one which works by a sequence related to the configuration of walls and ceilings, and one which works on single and ultimately transportable surfaces, either episodically separated, as in the *Maestà*, or seen as one complete design with episodes fitted into one another, as with the Memlings.

Duccio (fl. 1278-1318)
Duccio's *Maestà* is the work of an artist well versed in traditional forms of religious paintings, and it was created towards the end of a career lasting at least thirty years. Its installation above the high altar of the Duomo in Siena on 9 June 1311 was the occasion for some rejoicing perhaps because it was a work planned on such a grand scale: it is large in size (468 x 499 cm. approximately) and rich in the elaboration of details. Its nucleus was on the front face of this two-sided work, portraying the Virgin and Child enthroned, flanked by angels and saints. Though this part is rather large, it is a clear development of many other works embodying the subject. What is of prime interest for this study is the very large number, the complexity and the variety of the many smaller paintings on the life of Christ and the Passion which are here associated with this traditional subject. These are placed below it on the predella and, more plentifully, on the reverse of the main painting as well. The original work remained *in situ* until 1506, when it was taken down and some parts of it were distributed, and some lost. The original design has had to be reconstructed in a theoretical exercise in modern times.[50] Over fifty scenes can now be accounted for. There is some evidence that a number of painters collaborated with Duccio in many scenes, but there is little doubt that he remained the overseeing influence and a major contributor to these paintings.[51]

Most of the cycle is on the back, and its design must have been associated, at least in part, with the role of the Virgin as intercessor, as is established by her portrayal on the front. There is a strong contrast between the static glory of the Virgin and Child on the front and the vigorous and dramatic scenes embodied in the cycle on the reverse. The cycle centres visually upon the Crucifixion, which is one of the double panels and is centrally placed in the Passion sequence. The narration is distributed into groups of related episodes. The principal one containing the Crucifixion begins with the Entry to Jerusalem, also a double panel, and it works from left to right in vertical pairs with twenty-six episodes as far as the Road to Emmaus. Above the Crucifixion is a sequence of seven episodes about Christ after the Resurrection, and it includes the Appearances, the Ascension and Pentecost. Beneath the main sections on the Passion the events of the Ministry are shown on the predella, from the Baptism of Christ to Lazarus, taking up nine panels. On the front of the work the predella covers the Childhood of Christ from the Annunciation to the Doctors in seven scenes, all of them closely associated with the Virgin. In this section prophets are interspersed between the narrative scenes, giving Old Testament prefigurations of the gospels. Above the main picture of the Virgin, the last events in her life are presented in seven panels, from the Annunciation of her Death to her Burial, including the Assumption and Coronation. As this is at the top it invites comparison with the events of Christ's life on the verso. The whole scheme thus comprises notionally fifty-eight panels, some being missing, and as such it must be considered one of the most comprehensively detailed of all cyclic sequences.[52]

Some cross-reference is present in addition to the prophets sequence just noted. If we read up the central column of pictures on the back we find that the following is the order: the Wedding at Cana, the Agony in the Garden, the Kiss of Judas, the Crucifixion, and the Ascension. Indeed it is the network of links which encourages us to see it as a cycle. There is a consistency of characters throughout both sides, emphasized by colour and costume. Thus the static portrayal of ten apostles above the Virgin on the front is taken up by their costumes and their colours as they participate in the scenes on the verso. Christ's costume as an adult is self-consistent, with the significant exception that after the Resurrection it changes to white and gold. This happens within the main Passion sequence and then it is sustained through the Appearances, thus tying this uppermost sequence to the main work. Duccio also developed a keen impression of place by his use of buildings, and also by natural scenery. In the examinations before Annas, Caiaphas, Herod and Pilate consistency is maintained, and this is made continuous from the group of panels on the lower right through to those on the upper left. John White shows in some detail how, in his efforts to sustain a consistent sense of place, Duccio is forced at times to alter some architectural features under the pressure of design problems as he had to fit in large numbers of spectators for these public scenes. In doing so he made covert adaptations to the buildings, even omitting parts, but still preserving a consistent impression.[53]

The exploitation of linking can be illustrated further in the four scenes concerning Peter's Denials (Fig. 4). The first shows Peter by the fire, challenged by the Maid. Behind him a staircase rises to the upper level, in the next panel above, where Christ is examined by Annas. The Second Denial is on the lower panel to the right of this, but this time Peter is outside the threshold of the chamber in which Christ is questioned by Caiaphas, who tears his garments as in scripture (Mark 14:63). For the Third Denial, in the panel immediately above, Peter is in a similar position, still outside on the threshold, but this time Christ within is blindfolded and beaten with rods as Caiaphas looks on. As the cock is now crowing on a perch directly above Peter's head there is no doubt that this is meant to be the Third Denial, following Christ's forewarning. This small subgroup of paintings shows that Duccio was prepared both to condense and expand incidents as he combined the gospel narratives. But it also invites an intensely visual interpretation. As the eye moves from one panel to another we see that the figures of Christ and Peter are actually brought closer together, so that by the third occasion Peter is only a few steps from the derided and blindfolded Christ, with the questioning Maid now standing in the doorway between them. Each of the scenes is powerful enough in itself, but the juxtaposition intensifies the ironic significance of the denials taken as a whole. It is especially poignant that for the third scene Christ is blindfolded.

We can develop the perception of the comprehensive overall organisation of the work by an extraordinary variety of devices, large and small. Their scope encourages us continually to pass from the narrative backwards and forwards across the designs, and it does so by means of many different kinds of association. When he is shown healing the blind man, on the back of the predella, Christ touches his eyes. There is however a double take as the blind man is also seen with his back to his original self, now looking upwards towards the right-hand edge of the picture. If one follows the line of his new gaze it points directly to the top of the next picture, which shows the Transfiguration, with Christ standing at the top of a mountain. In another device, the Annunciation of Christ's Birth to Mary appears at the left-hand extremity of the front of the predella. It is echoed at the top of this side by another Annunciation, that of Mary's Death, which begins the sequence containing her Assumption and Coronation. On the obverse a small but disturbing feature appears in the Agony and the Arrest, the two scenes below the Crucifixion. In each there is a group of three trees in the background: even though there are others present, this seems a deliberate anticipation of the three crosses in the panel above them to which there is a direct visual link.

A much broader feature can be observed in the main Passion panels. As I have said, the main direction of the narrative is across and upwards. But this narrative movement is supported and sustained by an upward visual effect, as it were towards the spiritual apotheosis at the topmost level. Many of the pictures have a strong diagonal component in their composition which is emphatically initiated at the Entry panel, where Christ on the ass are to the lower left on their way upwards to the gate on the right where a crowd awaits him. The low left high right diagonal is echoed elsewhere in the shaping of the rocks in the Agony and the Betrayal, in the stairs at the First Denial of Peter, in the ladder of the Deposition, and on to the rocks in Limbo, *Noli me tangere*, the Entombment, the Marys at the tomb, and the road to Emmaus, where, as in the Entry, the road seems to point upwards to the right.

The features of the *Maestà* emphasize Duccio's overall preoccupations, which are partly religious and partly artistic. Cyclic form makes possible the network of references of interpretative importance through the visual process of looking at the work, back and front. Even though the narrative has a distinctive direction, it is still a function of the web of visual activity, which ranged backwards and forwards over the two sides of the painting. Originally one had to move from front to back, and vice versa, to appreciate this. But now that the work is documented and reproduced in book form, we can perceive the process more systematically in the study.

Some of the features which play such a strong part in establishing our sense of cyclicity here in the *Maestà* are also to be found in Giotto's work in the Arena Chapel. These include consistency of characters and their costuming, the incorporation of architectural and natural features in the backgrounds, giving a sense of place, these also linking scenes with one another.

Giotto (1267-1337)
The most striking thing about Giotto's thirty-nine paintings in the Arena Chapel from the cyclic point of view is the highly organised and even way in which the pictures are presented. The narrative begins at the uppermost of the four tiers with twelve episodes in the Life of the Virgin up to her marriage. The Life of Christ fills the third and second tiers running through twenty-two episodes from the Nativity to Pentecost. In addition to these thirty-four paintings, the east end has the Annunciation presented in two parts symmetrically over the arch, Gabriel on one side, Mary on the other. Above this God sends the Angel on the mission to Mary. Below it on the left we see Judas receiving payment, with a bestial black devil behind him, and on the right the Visit to Elizabeth. All the episodes are more or less the same size and there is an immediate sense from their uniformity that one scene leads directly to another. One may note also the effect of the unifying decorative framework into which the pictures are set. Some of these frames contain miniatures on subjects from the Old Testament which are placed next to the main pictures. Thus the Creation of

Adam is appropriately next to Lazarus, Elijah in the chariot of fire next to the Ascension and St. Michael fights Satan next to the Cleansing of the Temple.

The uniformity of design within the pictures shows itself in the frequency of motifs within them and in the management of a whole range of visual characteristics. These include colour of the background (blue predominates for sky and distance), architectural and natural features within the paintings, colours of costumes which are generally consistent through many individual paintings, and, perhaps most striking of all gestures and body postures. In spite of the pressure of narrative in these paintings, from the Expulsion of Joachim to the Last Judgement, which itself fills the whole west wall, we are constantly being invited to transfer our attention from one picture to another across the narrative. This often involves moving up and down the walls, against the horizontal narratives, and also crossing from one side wall to its opposite. Among these are some which are packed with emotional and spiritual emphasis. Examples are the visual echo between the Flight into Egypt and the Entry to Jerusalem showing Mary and Christ on asses arranged in a similar configuration, but set upon opposite sides of the chapel. There is also Christ's gesture of blessing which is repeated in the Marriage at Cana, Lazarus, the Entry, and the Washing of the Feet. Although these particular incidents have different functions in the narrative, the presence of the divine blessing given by Christ in all of them is a distinctly cyclic feature (Fig. 5).

We can say much the same about several paintings which focus two heads in close proximity at the heart of individual paintings. The most portentous is the kiss of Judas, but the motif also appears at the Golden Gate (when Mary is conceived), Mary bending over the infant at the Nativity, and her tearful embrace of Christ's body at the Lamentation. In the last two it is not just a matter of heads; her bodily postures and the angle for the embrace are closely similar. Sometimes such links by way of similarity are suddenly changed. Through most of the incidents of the Ministry and the beginning of the Passion, Christ is seen in profile looking towards the right edge of the picture, even in the very active scene when he drives out the merchants from the temple. But a dramatic change comes at the pitiful moment of his mockery before Caiaphas. At this point he turns his face fully towards the viewer and this continues in all subsequent scenes except the Lamentation. It seems as though this is an invitation to share his feelings, an aspect indeed of affective piety. But even if we do see this facial image repeated in these two schemes, there is a special change at the Crucifixion, for there the face is bowed and it is smaller, less beautiful and the hair is roughened and the beard shorter: he is hardly recognisable as himself, as Mary says in Gréban's *Passion*.[54]

The visual experience is deeply involved in echo and contrast. We are offered all sorts of links between the individual pictures, and this interplay which is both anticipation and retrospect, also involves a *circularity of observation and feeling*. It is enhanced by the arrangement of the pictures around the whole chapel and the crucial experience that there is no one place from which the whole can be or should be viewed. It is true that the Last Judgement is a dominating feature and that within the paintings on each main wall the predominating light flows from that end of chapel, casting shadows away from the west. This feature was perhaps linked to the penitential nature of the chapel as a whole. Charles Harrison has suggested that the idea of usury as a mortal sin is part of the ideological thrust of the Chapel, and it may have special point in that the donor was concerned that his father had been a usurer.[55] But it is impossible to find a place within the chapel where one can actually see everything. Instead the experience is one of resonance and echo, an essential aspect of cyclic form. It has an effect here of embracing the viewer with a multiplicity of sights which themselves react upon one another. We have already considered a number of other examples in which the interior decoration has a strongly cumulative and embracing effect, but in the peculiar intimacy of the Arena Chapel this is very remarkable.

The design of the individual pictures is intriguingly managed to give a kind of uniformity of depth and proportion. The human figures are often arranged in a kind of decorative unity: usually they are the same size in each painting. But perhaps the most dramatic aspect is the variety and intensity of facial expression. This works partly because the same faces are recognisable from one painting to another and that these similar appearances, supported by consistency of costuming, encompass a variety of moods: John, the beloved disciple, sleeps in Christ's lap at the Last Supper, and he stands over Christ's body with his arms thrown back, contorted with grief at the Lamentation. It is the same face and the same costume. Some of the most appealing detail is provided by the angels, who are usually of miniature size. Five of them cluster over the stable in adoring attitudes, while the shepherds and their sheep watch the Child. One hovers over Joseph's head, perhaps recalling the warning in a dream, and another is above Simeon in the Presentation in the Temple. But their vocabulary of horror and grief is most clearly seen as ten of these beautiful but sad figures cluster around the arms of the cross, and another ten fly over the Lamentation, their sorrowful gestures more dramatic and disturbed than those of the people beneath them (Fig. 5).

The architectural simplicity of the scenes is an important resource. A strong sense of place is suggested within the frame of each picture by simple shapes of buildings. For example we never see the whole of the Temple, but we are aware that it is the same building in half a dozen scenes through differing perspectives. The gate of Jerusalem appears in the Entry as well as being the departure point for the road to Calvary in ironic contrast. In some scenes this topographical aspect is conveyed by a natural background of rocks, as in the Baptism. It cannot and should not be argued that these details influenced or were influenced by stage sets far away in time and space on pageant carts at York, but the confluence of ideas is still worth remarking upon. There must be a setting for the Passion. It has to touch actuality in some way, and yet the focus is upon the emotional tension and the suffering. From this there can be no distraction.

In discussing the management and relationship of wall paintings we have noticed that these can be part of a cyclic effect, as at Assisi. Here the suggestions are rich, but it is also true that it is hard to perceive one overriding impulse. Instead we are provided with juxtapositions which seem suggestive. Since the direction of the narrative is from left to right on the three tiers of each wall, these relationships have to work principally in a vertical dimension. Thus the Birth of the Virgin has beneath it Christ and the Doctors, and below that the Way to Calvary: two joyful scenes with a grim one at the lowest. This configuration occurs in other verticals, as with Mary on the steps of the Temple with the Baptism and then the Crucifixion beneath it. It is perhaps material to note at this point that in some painted narratives there is a tendency to read up from the bottom, rather than or as well as from left to right. This happens in the pairs of scenes in the *Maestà*. It is especially interesting that the culminating scenes of the Passion are all at the lowest level—nearest to the eye level of the viewer standing on the floor of the Arena Chapel, but still above it. It is these scenes of suffering which Giotto has contrived to bring closest to the viewer.[56]

In Chapter One it was suggested that one of the features of cyclic form was its capacity to accommodate a series of starts from differing points of view. The works by Duccio and Giotto we have been considering seem peculiarly well adapted to this notion since the individual scenes are separate and conceived as individual wholes. Yet the extent to which we are induced to identify exchange between them and the variety of response which they invite does seem very close to the individual initiation proposed. The accumulations of scenes are especially effective since they work through both visual devices and though interpretative mechanisms such as irony.

Memling (c. 1440-94)
In considering Memling's *Scenes from the Passion of Christ* (1470-1) and its associate, *Scenes from the Advent and*

Triumph of Christ (1480), it is apparent that although he was a highly innovative painter, with a capacity to develop cyclic form for his own purposes, there was a vocabulary of narrative paintings in German countries and the Netherlands upon which he could draw.[57] The existence of such a tradition is a reminder that the idea of cyclicity is likely to have been widespread. In Memling's case we are dealing with two comprehensive paintings which use cyclic method, and they are each conceived as unified works, their aesthetic priorities and features pointing up the spiritual truths to be pursued. The two works are highly selective both in overriding significance and in the choice of incidents—of which many possible ones are omitted. Here we shall concentrate upon the *Passion* but the *Advent and Triumph* has some relevant individual aspects in addition.

The overall impact of the *Passion* is that it is crammed with detail as the events are played out in the city of Jerusalem, and in its environs (Fig. 6). The city plays a large part in the painting, its towers, pinnacles, gateways, courtyards, alleyways, windows, gables and the embracing outer wall filling most of the frame. This is one of the ways by which this painting, so full of individual, separated incidents which can be viewed simultaneously, is made into a whole. Even the episodes outside the walls, the Entry, Gethsemane and the Arrest, the Crucifixion, the Entombment, the Resurrection and Emmaus are all perceived as being in a physical relationship with the city. In the main part of the picture, the cruelty to Christ in the heart of the city, and the long procession which finds its way out towards Calvary, the people involved are much larger than the rest. The largest figure of all is probably Christ, who carries the cross in the right foreground. At this point, for the first time he looks directly at the viewer.

The lighting of the piece also makes for unity and helps to direct our attention. The source is the upper right distance and it floods over the centre of the city where the torture takes place, fading into darkness at the lower left where the Agony and the Betrayal are shown. In the darker parts of the picture torches give an intermittent light, and some tiny scenes, like the Conspiracy and the Last Supper, shine brightly in a dark framework. Though the brightest area is in the remote distance upper right, it is partly overshadowed by the heavy clouds over Calvary. Memling's use of light naturally guides our progress through the painting, but it is also significant because it embraces and comprehends so many detailed scenes, which are by nature sequential, and involve the same people in different circumstances. It is true, however, that although the main flow of light is from upper right to lower left, many incidents in the brilliantly lit torture sequence in the centre of the picture throw shadows across it.

The scope of the painting runs for twenty-three scenes, from Christ's farewell to the Virgin before the Entry in one continuous narrative line through Cleansing the Temple and the Passion up to the departure for Calvary, where we see the Crucifixion to the Entombment, and then, on the right of the painting, the Harrowing, the Resurrection, *Noli me tangere*, and Emmaus. This narrative does not show the Ascension. The scenes are arranged across the painting, starting at the upper left, with the scenes of torment within Jerusalem in the centre and lower front. The Crucifixion is far away in the distance at the top of the painting, and the events after Christ's death are arranged in a vertical line upwards, disappearing in the remote distance towards Emmaus. The picture is very densely filled, and although there are many cross-currents, as we shall see, the narrative sinuously threads its way through.[58]

There is much careful attention to both the physical consistency of the characters and to their clothing. Christ wears the same dark blue robe through all the incidents up to the Flagellation, where it lies at his feet. For a time he wears the white fool's robe and the purple cloak after this, but when he sets off for Calvary, he again wears the original blue, in accordance with the intent that he should appear the same to the public at his execution as he had during life (a point made by Gréban). He is stripped for the Nailing, but the blue robe again lies conspicuously at his side. After his death he wears the red robe of triumph and carries the vexilla. Pilate is dressed in a conspicuous black and gold floral design, but it is not distinctively Roman. Like the soldiers and officials he wears fifteenth-century costume. Such details, and many other minute items, such as the axe used to shape the cross, all show forth Memling's own time, bringing the past into the present, and turning Jerusalem into the city of Bruges where Memling lived and worked.

In fact there is an intriguing tension between this meticulous contemporary realism and the iconic dimension of what we see. The selective process in the narrative—there is no Barabas or Herod, for example—is complementary to this. Instead several of the incidents are subtly touched with suggestive symbolism. The nude statues of Adam and Eve stand in niches over the doorway where Peter denies Christ; between them a cock crows. Above Pilate's seat of judgement there is a bass relief in the arch showing the Judgement of Solomon. A third example is more difficult to interpret, though we are justified in entertaining our suspicions. This is over the largest arch, virtually the centre of the whole picture, where Christ is beaten by the torturers. On the left of the arch is a figure with a jawbone, perhaps Cain, and on the right a figure with a bow and arrow, perhaps Lamech.[59] These last two scenes, the Judgement and the Flagellation, stand side by side, under two contiguous arches, and in fact this arrangement of arches and niches is quite unrealistic from an architectural point of view. Their function is to provide a series of frameworks for the iconic scenes set out below them. Other unrealistic figures suggesting interpretative motifs are the peacock on the city wall by the scene of the Agony, and the monkey on the rooftop close to the distant perspective of Pilate returning from Calvary.[60]

These items, while they may have allegorical meaning, also point to Memling's grasp of cyclic form. It seems that he was using individual scenes for differing emotional effects, and yet the accumulation of them all creates a comprehensive icon, which is full of meditative possibilities. The painting is packed with vigorous activities, comings and goings, but it invites us to stand back from our emotional involvement and take part in an active contemplation which is full of the cross-references and individual variations we have observed elsewhere in cyclic form. Even though, from our own contemporary viewpoint, we can still see that he was drawing upon a range of iconic traditions in creating his own comprehensive vision here, it is apparent that his use of what were familiar iconic details is more than a little mysterious. His originality lies in the exploitation of a tradition and a combination of many of its parts.

The view can be sustained if we look at his later cycle painting, the *Advent and Triumph*. Here the selection of events is different; so enigmatic, indeed, that there has been some uncertainty about an appropriate title. The alternative has been *The Seven Joys of Mary*, while another focused upon the Three Kings.[61] This actually reveals a truth about this large painting (roughly 1 x 2 m.): that it ingeniously related three different narratives. The Virgin is present in practically all the scenes which show the principal events: the Annunciation, the Nativity, the Adoration, the Flight with its miracles, the Resurrection, Christ's Appearance to her, the Ascension, Pentecost, where she is the central figure, and her Death and Assumption. But this narrative pointedly omits the Passion. After the Adoration and the Flight, it jumps to events after Christ's Death. This significant alteration to the usual narrative turns upon another interpolation. The story of the Magi, from their first astrological observations, through the meeting with Herod and their Adoration is emphatically ended by their return, as they bypass Herod on the way to their waiting ships.

There is no doubt that the management of this highly familiar material is strikingly original, and it is given a number of significant visual emphases. The focus of the work is the Adoration by the Magi in the centre foreground followed by their dramatic departure as they are seen travelling right up the middle of the picture to their ships at the top of the frame. Effectively they divide the painting in two: on the left the story up to the Adoration; on the right the post-Passion episodes. But the lower edge of the painting also foregrounds from left to right: the Nativity, the Adoration, the Resurrection, and Pentecost—four triumphant episodes which force themselves upon the viewer's attention by their prominent locations at the front of the painting. This device of juxtaposition is echoed by a number of other features. If we examine the top of the picture we find it offers a panoramic view (in sharp contrast to the detailed intimacy of the Nativity and Adoration) with three mountain peaks and the rising sun. On each of these mountains one of the kings is examining the star, which sends a beam down to the Adoration at the front of the picture, cutting directly across the meandering narrative. The direction of the narrative is that the kings, having each observed the star, set out to follow it, and they can be seen meeting at a bridge outside the city. But the top of the painting also shows on the right the Ascension of Christ, and not far beyond, Mary's Assumption takes place in parallel: both figures rising in golden clouds.

In one other schematic device we see that the Annunciation, with Gabriel and Mary, near the upper left margin, is visually balanced by Christ Appearing to the Virgin on the right extremity. These scenes take place in small buildings with the participants facing one another past a pillar in each case. This symmetry is a counteraction to the vertical division of the painting mentioned earlier. Apart from the Murder of the Innocents and the Death of the Virgin, all the scenes in this cycle are directed towards joy and celebration, and it has to be recognised as a work of great optimism in contrast to the cruelty and suffering of the Passion. The reality of these scenes is enhanced by fascinating details. One of the shepherds is playing his bagpipes as he approaches the stable. Each of the kings has an individually coloured standard and standard bearer which can be identified throughout their journeys. As they depart in their ships one of their horses, which are also colour coded, can be seen being winched up from a tender. However because of the panoramic world here presented, with its extremes of vast distances and close intimacy, Memling seems concerned to show the cosmic dimension of these events, an effect which is emphasised in both paintings by his device of beginning the narrative in the top left and laying it out through the middle of the pictures, leading to the conclusion in the top right. In the *Advent and Triumph* there is again a strong sense of unity and he controls the many incidents in such a way as to suggest an organised, if mysterious, universe.

Tintoretto (1518-94)

Tintoretto's long working life as a painter was spent almost entirely in Venice. He was prolific and redoubtably hardworking, but he seems to have turned to cyclic painting on biblical subjects only once in his life even though, as we have noted, there was a strong Venetian tradition for it.[62] He worked on a large number of individual biblical scenes, and revisited some episodes, like the *Last Supper* and the *Crucifixion*, several times.[63] Some of these can help us to view his work in the three rooms of the Scuola di San Rocco, which were painted between 1564 and 1588. During these twenty-four years, at the summit of his career, he evolved his own approach to cyclicity, even though, with characteristic energy, he continued work on other paintings elsewhere, some on a large scale. What he has left us comes from late in the sixteenth century, when the impulse towards cyclic form was still discernible, but when many of the contextual features we have been describing were beginning to change irremediably. One of these was the unified vision of medieval Catholicism, and it seems that Tintoretto was an orthodox believer, who sought to reaffirm old ways and to confirm the old faith. Giandomenico Romanelli suggests that his sense of the contemporaneity of scriptural events, not historical events so much as present and real experiences, still alive and living, accorded with Tridentine doctrine.[64] Yet his independence as a painter was unrivalled, and he was given a free hand and adequate resources by the authorities of the Scuola to express and develop his work.[65] The result is that the cycle does not seem to be overtly dogmatic or polemical. He follows a high proportion of the scenes traditional in cycles, from the Temptation of Adam to the Ascension, and some cross-referencing between scenes follows well-established links. One cannot but be impressed, however, that as a painter he sought to re-think ways of presenting these scenes, and the result was original in design and extraordinarily powerful in its emotional and dramatic aspects. Perhaps this profound aesthetic reconsideration should be seen as a manifestation of his religious belief.

Tintoretto worked in three phases, one for each of the rooms in the Scuola. In the beginning he won a competition against three other painters to paint the ceiling of the Sala dell'Albergo, the smallest and innermost space. Having won he painted the *Crucifixion*, one of his largest paintings, measuring 534 x 1224 cm., and then he added three other scenes in the same room: *Christ before Pilate*, the *Way to Calvary*, and the *Crown of Thorns*. Though these are related as being close to the central events of the Passion, the other paintings in this room were unrelated, and most of them were allegorical subjects. Nevertheless this work, completed between 1564 and 1567, must have led to the idea of elaborating from it as central sequence. There followed first in 1576-81 his paintings in the Great Hall (Sala Grande), and then the Lower Hall (Sala Inferiore) in 1582-7. The former was a huge undertaking for which he had a contract with the Scuola, where he had by now been admitted to membership. His choice of subjects, for which he may well have had learned, clerical advice, was partly influenced by the status of St. Roch whose special significance was his help against the three bodily enemies of mankind, sickness, thirst and hunger.[66] This led to the first three large paintings on the ceiling concerned with the story of Moses: the *Erection of the bronze serpent*, *Moses striking water from the rock* and *The Gathering of Manna*. These works were also an expression of the charitable concerns of the Scuola di San Rocco. Their execution is closely associated with the decision to support Tintoretto in carrying out further decorative work. He added ten murals on the Life of Christ, and on the ceiling a further eighteen from the Old Testament.

The scheme he was setting up was complex, but one way of reaching it is to follow the scenes which show the strength and triumph of Christ against growing difficulties. Thus the narrative runs *Shepherds*, *Baptism* on one side, crosses to *Temptation* and *Curing the Paralytic* on the other. On the same side at the opposite end we find *Distributing the Loaves and Fishes*, with *Lazarus* next to it, and then we cross back to the first side for the *Last Supper* and the *Agony in the Garden*. These bring us to the two central paintings on each wall, the *Resurrection* and the *Ascension*, which face each other across the Hall. The episodes on the ceiling are particularly linked to the principal paintings about Moses, and bring out the ways in which the bodily enemies were overcome.

In the Lower Hall there are eight paintings which are close to a Marian cycle. They show events in the Life of the Virgin from the *Annunciation* to the *Assumption*, but the structure is varied by pictures of *Mary Magdalene* and *Mary of Egypt*, who were linked as both doing penance in the desert. Apart from the cruelty of the *Slaughter of the Innocents*, most of these paintings have a joyful connotation. The decision to concentrate in the Lower Hall on Mary in contrast to the focus on Christ's life seen in relation to events in the Old Testament is one which can be paralleled elsewhere. Indeed we have noted how cycles in many places tend to polarize the Passion and the Life of Mary.

From this description it is apparent that a highly selective process was at work, and that Tintoretto was searching for some spectacular effects, especially in the strong interface between the *Resurrection* and the *Ascension* in the Sala Grande. As these paintings are not in a church different principles of deployment are in use here. But one of the most emphatic aspects of his use of cyclic form was the intense preoccupation with the designs within individual scenes. Sometimes we can find links and correspondences in visual terms with other episodes, but it is apparent from a design point of view that scenes are primarily conceived as separately integrated units. There are some figures which are present in more than one scene, but in general this aspect is less in evidence than we have noticed in Duccio and Giotto.

We might here look at some general features of Tintoretto's designs and at some paintings individually. There is a strong possibility that one of his leading motives was to find ways of concentrating attention upon the human figure. This has an effect upon the ways figures are shown. For example there are some moments of foreshortening, as in the case of the thief whose cross is being raised on the left side of *The Crucifixion*, in the sleeping disciples in the *Agony*, and in one of the angels at the *Resurrection*. In several paintings the key figures are floating or supported aloft, most strikingly in the *Resurrection* where Christ leaves the tomb far below him. This facilitates a view of the whole body from head to toe. There is a skilful art too here in the manipulation of the viewpoint, for often we are being invited to look up at the figure above our eye line. This happens in the *Resurrection*, the *Agony*, the *Loaves and Fishes*, *Lazarus*, and the *Ascension*. Notably in all but one of these it is Christ who is the elevated figure. The exception is Lazarus placed high in the centre of the picture, while Christ, dignified and quiet, is located in the lower right. Sometimes this concentration is achieved by means of diagonals, as in the *Way to Calvary* (Fig. 7). Here Tintoretto has remembered that Calvary was a hill, and he shows the two thieves labouring upwards from left to right, their figures dominated by the two uprights of their enormous crosses on their backs. Then halfway up the painting the diagonal switches as Christ, also burdened with a similar cross, is led upward from right to left. In *Christ before Pilate*, Christ, clad in the white fool's robe given by Herod, stands perfectly erect and very tall (anatomically slightly stretched for this effect) before a seated Pilate, whose figure is shortened by lateral movement as he washes his hands.

One might elaborate further on the ways in which Tintoretto pursued this concentration on the human form, but it is probably more urgent to note that it has an ideological impact which shows itself in the intensely human and realistic settings of his paintings.[67] The point seems to be to communicate a very real sense of the here and now. There are haloes in some paintings, it is true, but more often than not the presence of the supernatural and the numinous is implied by the very reality and tangibility of what we see before us. The actuality is palpable, but the supernatural is more often than not implied rather than emphasized. This understatement of the spiritual is potent.

Nevertheless the dramatic, even sensational design of the individual pictures is often an important means of setting this up. Not only does Tintoretto re-think the traditional iconographic shapes, he also seems to want to choose particularly striking moments when vigorous action is going on, but when the painting freezes it momentarily. This can be pinpointed in the *Last Supper.* Instead of having Christ in the middle of the table, surrounded by his disciples, Tintoretto has foreshortened the table itself, and we look across one corner in the foreground. The disciples are in disarray, presumably because they have been told of the coming betrayal. Christ himself is at the far end of the table in profile (with a glow of light profiling his head and distinguishing him from the haloed disciples). His is the smallest figure at the table. The foreground is dominated by the agitated group of disciples, who are superimposed upon one another. A dog below points his nose directly at this centre of disturbance, but the normality of the scene is established by five figures, servants or attendants, who are placed naturalistically at intervals at the front and rear of the action, on the periphery.[68]

There are two ways of arranging the contents of the paintings which seem to have appealed to Tintoretto and which he used more than once in the Scuola. One is to divide the frame into upper and lower sections, as we have already observed in the *Way to Calvary*. This is also done in the *Loaves and Fishes*, where Christ is blessing in the upper half and people are being comforted in the lower; in the *Temptation of Christ* where Satan offers the stones from below; and in the *Nativity* where the holy family is in the upper storey of the stable, while the Shepherds offer from below. The other device is the exploitation of the distant background, which gives great depth to the rather intimate scenes. This is especially interesting because for some subjects outside this cycle, Tintoretto worked with an enormous perspective, as for the *Paradiso* in the Palazzo Ducale (700 x 2200 cm.). At the *Baptism*, John baptizes Christ in the foreground, and behind them stretching far into the distance are crowds of people, perhaps the baptized or just listeners to John's preaching. Their outlines are emphasized by white highlights which catch the glow from above. The glow is perhaps the heavenly approval, as in Scripture, but no heavenly Father is apparent. Similarly at the *Agony*, where Christ is high up on the mountain and the disciples sleep in the foreground, a numberless crowd of soldiers, led by Judas, is approaching, again highlighted in white; and at the *Adoration* the Magi's entourage cluster outside the stable in the distance.

Tintoretto challenges expectation in many ways, and often this turns upon a brilliantly realised individual figure. In the *Slaughter of the Innocents* there are, surprisingly, not many babies to be seen. Most of the action is a vigorous conflict between mothers and soldiers, which also stretches as far as the eye can see into the distance. But centrally, one mother leans down from a ledge, her arm stretched vertically down the painting in an attempt to drag her naked son by his hand up towards her. This movement is completely isolated visually, and lit dazzlingly. At the *Temptation of Christ* Satan, holding up the stones, is a beautiful naked human figure. Though male, his physique is hermaphroditic and sensual, and it is surely meant to recall the seductive figure of Eve as she holds out the apple in the picture on the ceiling not far away. It is possible to see both from the same position.

The challenge extends to the San Rocco *Crucifixion*, one of the first paintings Tintoretto did in the cycle, perhaps as he began to see the possibilities of the form. Because he has chosen a wide painting he can offer a panoramic view, but he eschewed the familiar sight of the three crosses in parallel next to one another. To the left and right extremes there are large gatherings of onlookers, some mounted. Instead of showing the three victims together in the traditional way (as followed by Duccio: see above p. 102), Tintoretto has constructed a (frozen) action scene in which the central vertical cross, with Christ already hanging on it, divides the picture from top to bottom. To the left one thief, just fixed to his cross, is agonisingly raised by struggling executioners into a diagonal which extends directly to Christ's head at the top centre. On the right the other thief is bending his back to lie down on his cross: his torment is still to come. The central figure of Christ is lonely, desolate and visually isolated by the device of having nothing behind it in the distance. The light on his head and face is subdued.[69] The agony is not explicit here, but the emotional charge is enhanced by the confused heap of sympathisers around Mary who has fainted directly below the vertical of the cross in the foreground. There is no sign of Adam.

In the light of these features Tintoretto's use of cyclic form appears highly individualistic. It enabled him to do many things which he did in his other biblical works, but to concentrate here on seeing anew the individual scenes. He found it apparently rewarding to point up the vigorous action of the scenes and to force the viewer to observe from new perspectives. He could exploit light and distance to expose a series of intimate scenes, some of which fill up the canvas entirely simply by being magnified. But in spite of the astonishing versatility of his designs, there is a consistency in his own attitude which seeks to illustrate the dramatic intensity of many events in this cycle.

The range of material discussed in this chapter and the many different decisions taken by individual artists help us to see that these visual cycles share with the dramatic ones many opportunities and techniques. The versatility of cyclic form gave a remarkable opportunity to depict and support the religious life, and we now turn to the realisation of cyclic form in the drama, concentrating first upon the continental forms.

Notes
1. Emile Mâle, *The Gothic Image: Religious Art in France of the Thirteenth Century*, [trans.] Dora Nussey, New York, 1972 [rpt. from the 1913 ed.].
2. Mâle, *The Gothic Image*, pp. 177-9, notes that in French churches there is a preponderance of Old Testament material.
3. William Tronzo, 'The Prestige of Saint Peter's: Observations on the Function of Monumental Narrative Cycles in Italy', in: Herbert L. Kessler & Marianna Shreve Simpson [eds.], *Pictorial Narrative in Antiquity and the Middle Ages*, Washington, D.C., 1985 [*Studies in the History of Art*, 16], p. 105.
4. Marcia Kupfer, *Romanesque Wall Painting in Central France: The Politics of Narrative*, New Haven and London, 1993, pp. 2, 80-96.
5. Mâle, *The Gothic Image*, pp. 188-9.
6. Marilyn Aronberg Lavin, *The Place of Narrative: Mural Decoration in Italian Churches, 431-1600*, Chicago-London, 1990, pp. 78-81.
7. Maria Chiellini, *Cimabue*, Firenze, 1988, pp. 41-5. The dating is conjectural: *c.* 1280.
8. Charles Harrison, 'Giotto and "the rise of painting"', in: Diana Norman [ed.], *Siena, Florence, and Padua: Art, Society, and Religion, 1280-1400*, 2 vols., New Haven-London, 1995, vol. I, pp. 88-90. Edward B. Garrison, *Italian Romanesque Panel Painting: An Illustrated Index*, Florence, 1949, nºs 371, 394, 402, 405 and 408-10, notes some works centring on St. Francis with associated scenes.
9. See David L. Jeffrey, 'Franciscan Spirituality and the Rise of Early English Drama', *Mosaic* 8 (1975), pp. 17-46.
10. Hans Belting, 'The New Role of Narrative in Public Painting of the Trecento', in: Kessler & Simpson [eds.], *Pictorial Narrative*, p. 152.
11. On the combination of worldly and supernatural elements by Giotto in the Franciscan cycle at Santa Croce in Florence see Michael St. John, *Chaucer's Dream Visions: Courtliness and Individual Identity*, Aldershot, 2000, pp. 99-102. There is a strong impression that the period of the development of pictorial cycles at Assisi coincided with important features of the development of painting. Harrison, 'Giotto and "the rise of painting"', p. 88, writes: 'Around 1300 the potential status of painting

131

was thus considerably advanced in the distribution of powers and priorities between words and images, the literary and the pictorial, which any civilized society must manage according to its own ends'.
12. Adolf E. M. Katzenellenbogen, *The Sculptural Programs of Chartres Cathedral: Christ, Mary, Ecclesia*, New York, 1959, figs. 27, 25 and 9. See also Wolfgang Kemp, *The Narratives of Gothic Stained Glass*, Cambridge, 1997, pp. 22-51.
13. Katzenellenbogen, figs. 47, 53 and 58.
14. Martial Rose & Julia Hedgecoe, *Stories in Stone: The Medieval Roof Carvings of Norwich Cathedral*, London, 1997, p. 8. I acknowledge a considerable debt to this valuable recent research. For information about bosses elsewhere, especially the fourteenth-century sequence of fourteen on the life of Christ at Tewkesbury Abbey, see Charles J. P. Cave, *Roof Bosses in Medieval Churches: An Aspect of Gothic Sculpture*, Cambridge, 1948.
15. Rose & Hedgecoe, *Stories in Stone*, pp. 30-1.
16. Martial Rose, *The Norwich Apocalypse: The Cycle of Vault Carvings in the Cloisters of Norwich Cathedral*, Norwich, 1999, p. 221.
17. Rose & Hedgecoe, *Stories in Stone*, pp. 114-5.
18. *Ibidem*, pp. 123 and 130.
19. The studies used here are by Hilary Wayment, *The Stained Glass of the Church of St. Mary, Fairford, Gloucestershire*, London, 1984, and Idem, *The Windows of King's College Chapel, Cambridge: A Description and Commentary*, London, 1972 [*Corpus Vitrearum Medii Aevi: Great Britain.* Supplementary Volume 1].
20. Wayment, *Fairford,* plates VII and XXII.
21. At Fairford the point is towards Christ's mouth, a tradition followed in John Bale, *The Image of Both Churches: After the Reuelacion of Saynt Iohan the Euangelyst*, [Antwerp?, 1545?], [*STC* 1296.5], sig. cvi. In the 1550 edition [*STC* 1298] it points away, sig. cv.
22. Wayment, *Fairford*, p. 57-8. See Avril Henry [ed.], *Biblia Pauperum*, Aldershot, 1987, p.120, and below pp. 103-5.
23. These are associated with the Annunciation and the Adoration of the Magi in the *Biblia Pauperum*, pp. 48 and 52.
24. Luciano Bellosi, *Duccio: La Maestà*, Milano, 1998, p. 11.
25. Both these are illustrated by Anne Derbes, *Picturing the Passion in Late Medieval Italy: Narrative Painting, Franciscan Ideologies, and the Levant*, Cambridge, 1996, figs. 3 and 4, p. 44. See also Garrison, *Italian Romanesque Panel Painting*, n° 422 and n° 367.
26. For other examples, see Garrison, *Italian Romanesque Panel Painting*, n°s 381, 382 and 385.

27. This is illustrated in Giovanna Nepi Sciré, *The Accademia Galleries in Venice*, Milan, 1998, plate 2. Subordinate figures indicate a Franciscan origin. See the Accademia catalogue n° 21, and for further examples n°s 23 and 26 from the first half of the fourteenth century.
28. Patricia Fortini Brown, *Venetian Narrative Painting in the Age of Carpaccio*, New Haven-London, 1988, Catalogue n°s VII and XVIII.
29. Derbes, *Picturing the Passion*, p. 5. For further examples see Ferdinando Bologna, *Early Italian Painting: Romanesque and Early Medieval Art*, London, 1964, figs. 20, 21 (twelfth century) and 22, 41, 69 (thirteenth).
30. Kristine Edmondson Haney, *The Winchester Psalter: An Iconographic Study*, Leicester, 1986, pp. 71-3. The title is a matter of convenience and it is not original. The manuscript is British Library MS Cotton Nero C.IV.
31. 'Receive ... this prayer for the psalms which I, a sinner and unworthy, presume to sing in commemoration of the Nativity, Passion, Resurrection, Ascension and Second Coming or our Lord Jesus Christ.' (British Library, MS Arundel 155); 'In the Psalter alone ... you may find the prophets, the Gospel and the apostles ... you will find there the first and second coming of the Lord prophesied, and also the Lord's Incarnation, Passion, Resurrection and Ascension ... and by the grace of God you will come to the healing of intimate understanding.' (Cotton Tiberius C.VI). Quoted and translated by Haney, *The Winchester Psalter*, pp. 50-1.
32. Lucy Freeman Sandler, *The Psalter of Robert De Lisle in the British Library*, Oxford, 1983, pp. 11, 28. The shelf mark is MS Arundel 83 II.
33. Sandler, *Psalter of Robert De Lisle*, p. 13. The manuscript is dated November 25, 1339 (see p. 11).
34. *Queen Mary's Psalter: Miniatures and Drawings by An English Artist of the 14th Century, Reproduced from Royal MS. 2 B VII in the British Museum*, [intro.] George Warner, London, 1912, pp. 3-6. The title derives from the history of the manuscript, which was presented to Queen Mary in the sixteenth century.
35. Claire Donovan, *The de Brailes Hours: Shaping the Book of Hours in Thirteenth-Century Oxford*, Toronto-Buffalo, 1991, p. 23; Janet Backhouse, *Books of Hours*, London, 1985, pp. 4-6.
36. See Roger S. Wieck, *Time Sanctified: The Book of Hours in Medieval Art and Life*, New York-Baltimore, 2001 [rpt. from the 1988 ed.], fig. 45.
37. Wieck, *Time Sanctified*, p. 71 and plate 27.
38. Wieck, *Time Sanctified*, fig. 52.
39. Avril Henry [ed.], *Biblia Pauperum*, Aldershot, 1987, p. 4.

40. *Ibidem*, p. 9. Henry also suggests that the twelfth-century resurgence of theological scholarship may have been the basis for the development of the typology inherent in the *Biblia Pauperum*. Typology undoubtedly goes back to written sources (p. 10).
41. *Ibidem*, p. 109. Henry suggests that Christ shares with the Prodigal the idea of that which was lost is now found (p. 111).
42. W. O. Hassall [ed.], *The Holkham Bible Picture Book*, London, 1954, p. 27. The shelf mark is British Library MS Add. 47682.
43. Hassall links this work with a number of manuscripts including *Queen Mary's Psalter* (p. 26), and he sees a parallel with the bible cycles usually prefixed to Psalters (p. 44).
44. Patrick J. Collins, *The N-town Plays and Medieval Picture Cycles*, Kalamazoo, 1979, pp. 36-8, has worked out some interesting parallels in the treatment of Herod and the Magi between N-Town, *Queen Mary's Psalter*, and *The Holkam Bible Picture Book*.
45. James H. Marrow, *Passion Iconography in Northern European Art of the Late Middle Ages and Early Renaissance: A Study of the Transformation of Sacred Metaphor into Descriptive Narrative*, Kortrijk, 1979 [*Ars Neerlandica*, 1], pp. 18-24 and 195-8.
46. Bellosi, *Duccio: La Maestà*, p. 11.
47. Luciano Bellosi, *Giotto: The Complete Works*, Florence, 1981, p. 31.
48. Dirk de Vos, *Hans Memling: The Complete Works*, London, 1994, catalogue n°s 11 and 38.
49. See Carlo Bernari & Piero De Vecchi, *L'opera completa del Tintoretto*, Milano, 1970, pp. 116-7.
50. See John White, *Duccio: Tuscan Art and the Medieval Workshop*, London, 1979.
51. Diana Norman, '"A noble panel": Duccio's *Maestà*', in: Norman [ed.], *Siena, Florence, and Padua*, vol. II, p. 466.
52. This view is endorsed by White, *Duccio*, p. 102.
53. See the discussion of Pilate washes his Hands: White, *Duccio*, p. 112, fig. 77.
54. Marrow, *Passion Iconography*, pp. 54-61, discusses the motif of Christ's disfigurement.
55. Harrison, 'Giotto and "the rise of painting"', in: Norman [ed.], *Siena, Florence, and Padua*, vol. II, pp. 91-2.
56. Michel Alpatoff, 'The Parallelism of Giotto's Paduan Frescoes', *The Art Bulletin* 29 (1947), pp.148-54, made an important exposition of vertical aspects of the life of Christ here, but he saw the life of the Virgin as separated from it.
57. For examples of this tradition see De Vos, *Memling*, p. 20.

58. Memling repeated the techniques of simultaneous narratives, and the effect of a narrative which runs across the paintings from left to right in his Passion Triptych (Greverade Triptych) of 1491; see De Vos, *Memling*, catalogue n° 90. In this work the Crucifixion is much more prominent than in the other two considered here.
59. De Vos, *Memling*, p. 105, notes the allegorical trend, but does not identify these two figures.
60. The former may suggest eternal renewal, and the latter the Devil (De Vos, *Memling*, p. 109, note 4, and p. 107). On the other hand, as Christ rises from the tomb, past the sleeping soldiers, an anonymous father, son and their dog walk on the riverside path opposite, looking casually at them.
61. *Ibidem*, p. 38 and note 1.
62. He did paint six episodes on the life of St. Catherine for her patronal church in 1590-2.
63. Giandomenico Romanelli, *Tintoretto: La Scuola Grande di San Rocco*, Milano, 1994, p. 9.
64. *Ibidem*, p. 37.
65. Hans Tietze, *Tintoretto: The Paintings and Drawings*, New York, 1948, p. 47.
66. Bernari & De Vecchi, *L'opera completa del Tintoretto*, p. 116.
67. Romanelli, *Tintoretto*, p. 33, notes an emphasis upon the humanity of Christ at the expense of iconographical reference. See also for the 'human' meaning: Virgil Mocanu, *Tintoretto*, [trans.] Carlos Kormos, London, 1977, p. 19.
68. A dog appears again in another of Tintoretto's paintings of the *Last Supper*, at the church of San Stephano: here in almost the same attitude he points directly at Christ who is at the front of the picture (See Bernari & De Vecchi, *Tintoretto*, p. 124).
69. Bruce Robb, 'Tintoretto's San Rocco *Crucifixion*', in: C. Weight [ed.], *Painters on Paintings*, London, 1969, p. 24.

Chapter Three
Continental Analogues: A Review of Allied Forms – France and Germany

France

Our brief introductory survey in Chapter One has indicated that the surviving corpus of French cycles is the largest in Europe and it is not surprising that it shows a wide variety of approaches to cyclic form. This underlines a basic premise which concerns the flexibility of this genre, and its adaptability to different requirements, both of performance, and, if it can be considered separately, of text itself. Here we shall be concerned to present a number of perspectives on the surviving French examples, and to consider in some detail the particular nature of two of them. Such a process is admittedly selective, and is constrained by space, but it does illustrate that in France there was a rich culture of composition, performance and dissemination centred on the cycles. The perspectives we shall pursue are concerned with historical development, regional interest, codicological and manuscript aspects, and the performance culture which was evolved around the genre. After looking at examples of cycle form based on the biblical narrative of salvation we shall also notice a few which lie outside this primary concern in pursuit of our description of the nature and scope of the genre.

The historical perspective indicates that there were early versions of continuous Passion narratives before the fourteenth century. The *Passion des Jongleurs*, essentially a narrative poem which may have been performed, is thought to have influenced some early dramatic forms, some of them composed in regional speech.[1] Most of these are relatively short, and thus give little scope for the characteristics of cyclic form in England. It is in the fifteenth century that major steps were taken, apparently by a number of identifiable individuals who made significant contributions to the genre by enormously enlarging its length and the variety of incident they chose to include. Since the surviving material is bound to be only a partial sample we need to bear in mind the possibility that many further specimens may have been lost. This is made manifest in the discussion by Runnalls of the fragmentary Passion from north-east France, whose existence could hardly have been guessed.[2] As we shall see in addressing regional aspects, there were a number of important strands in the development of large-scale cycles. It is striking, however, that unlike the circumstances in England, Spain and Germany there was little or no close link with the feast of Corpus Christi in France. As the size of the cycles increased, it became a common practice to spread the performance over a large number of days, sometimes up to twenty-five, not necessarily continuous. Nor was it the widespread practice to present a narrative from Creation to Doomsday. The majority of the survivals deal with the Passion, often starting with John the Baptist and concluding with the Resurrection.

In Chapter One we noted the early date of the *Passion Sainte-Geneviève*. This relatively short work has some linguistic indications which link it to the north or the east of Paris, perhaps to Troyes.[3] The manuscript is part of a codex which also contains plays on the Nativity, the Three Kings, and the Resurrection, but these are not apparently connected with the *Passion*, and their inclusion offers no direct evidence about an interest in cyclic form. The latter is itself an independent work and though attempts have been made to link it with other cycles these have proved inconclusive. But a case can be made for its continuing popularity since the existing manuscript and a related fragment were copied in the mid-fifteenth century, while the original text preserved with them has linguistic features going back to the fourteenth century.[4] This argues a persistent interest in this *Passion* independent of others. The early date itself, and the apparent continuity suggested by the copying of the manuscripts suggests the possibility that by its very existence for this crucial period of development it may in itself be an influence on those who were to develop the full-scale cycles, should they have been aware of it. The narrative here runs from the visit to Simon at Bethany to Christ's Appearances after the Harrowing of Hell. The Prologue gives an outline of the content in advance, though there is no mention of earlier episodes in the biblical story.

The development of scale began in the fifteenth century with the *Passion d'Arras*, attributed to Eustache Mercadé before 1440. This work, which survives in manuscript form, comprising 24,945 lines, covers a narrative from the Annunciation to the Nativity (Day 1); the Baptism of Christ to the Despair of Judas (Day 2); the Trial before Pilate to the Deposition (Day 3); and the Watch on the Sepulchre to Pentecost (Day 4). However the whole cycle is framed by the *Procès de Paradis* which seems to have been Mercadé's innovation, perhaps stimulated by his concern over the origins of Man.[5] This comprises the Debate of the Four Daughters of God over the predicament of Man and his guilt, and the problem of the Incarnation. The issue goes back to Anselm's *Cur Deus Homo*.[6] At odds at the beginning, the Daughters, Miséricorde, Justice, Paix and Verité, appear several times in the cycle and are finally able to achieve reconciliation after the narrative is complete and Man has been redeemed. This didactic structure is supported by several sermons in the course of events expressing the author's concern for the need to teach his audience. Mercadé's sense of the conflict between Christ and the Jews was a significant structural thread, and he linked the Jews with devils whom he introduced into the Passion for the first time.[7] It was Mercadé who also wrote *La Vengeance Jhesuchrist* conceived for a four-day performance. We shall return to this in dealing with non-scriptural cycles later on, but it is significant that this cycle which was one of many versions of a very popular subject was intended as a continuation of the conventional biblical narrative. It deals with events after the Ascension, and shows how Christ's vengeance was wreaked on the Jews for the crucifixion in the capture of Jerusalem by the Roman legions. It also showed the terrible fate of Pilate when he was brought to book for his offences against Christ. Both the *Passion* and the *Vengeance* were performed in tandem at Metz in 1537, requiring a total of eight days.

Historically this long sequence of composite material occurs at the beginning of a period of development in the French cycles in the fifteenth century during which a more ambitious method of production involving huge resources of manpower and wealth was adopted. It is to be found in arrangements for performance of this kind, but it also has considerable importance in the history of the genre in as much as it became the practice to assemble texts *ad hoc* when performances were envisaged. In the case of the next two important authors of cycles, their work became a flexible resource for performance and for the compilation of composite texts associated with them. However, these composite texts may not always have been directly tailored for performance so much as to be a book for reading and devotion. In either case it is remarkable that the impulse towards cyclic form was a significant motive.

The work of Arnoul Gréban and Jean Michel is central to the development of the idea of the cycle in France, though, as we shall see, there was a significant number of other manifestations which lie quite outside the large group of plays which they influenced and which were derived from the cycles which they each composed. Gréban's *Passion* appeared in about 1450 and it has come down to us in a considerable number of manuscripts copied within a few years of that date.[8] Gréban worked closely with scripture, and yet he was skillful in the development of dialogue in many complex scenes, and he showed a remarkable ability in his manipulation of theatrical space in terms of the complexity of time and place he was able to present. This was supplemented by his clever use of processions between the physical centres of interest as the complex narrative of Christ's arrest and trial was enacted. His sense of the cyclic form showed itself markedly in his presentation of spectacle with a sense of the divine order of the universe underlying it. In his four-day structure Gréban was also interested in a narrative from the Fall of Lucifer to the Appearance to Thomas, followed by the reconciliation of the Four Daughters of God. This longer perspective came to be of some importance in the compilation of later cycles for performance and publication since the narrative of parts of the Old Testament as well as of Christ's upbringing could be used to introduce or prefigure the central treatments of the Passion itself. His dramatic realisation of the origins of Man in more detail gave greater emphasis to the idea that God had foreseen the Fall.[9] He made a specific point in separating the sin of Lucifer from that of Adam: a special note on one manuscript says that Gréban made this Creation to show the difference, the sin of Man having been put right, that of the Devil not.[10] The role of the devils was of importance to Gréban. He elaborated Satan's function as a messenger, having him report on the life of Christ to the other devils in hell, and showing increasing anxiety about the threat posed by him.[11] Within a short time the process of adapting one cycle by incorporating another is found at Troyes, first known in 1482. In this manuscript the first, second and fourth days of Gréban were linked with episodes from *Le Mistère du Viel Testament*.

However, in his close adaptation of Gréban's work Jean Michel's *Passion* took a remarkable direction away from this longer perspective. Instead he concentrated upon Days 2 and 3 of Gréban's play which covered the narrative from the Baptist to the Deposition and expanded these into four days, making extensive use of many of Gréban's lines, but expanding them in a different direction. He attended much more closely to the Gospel and the Ministry of Christ, and omitted a good deal of the legendary and exegetical material which played a part in Gréban's dramatisation. He did not, as Mazouer points out, deal with original sin, the Four Daughters, the Incarnation and the Resurrection.[12] Such selectivity may indeed remind us of that we have observed in the Cornish *Ordinalia*. Michel's concern with the salvation of the individual Christian led him to develop scenes portraying the worldly life, spiritual suffering and conversion of Madeleine (Mary Magdalene) and Lazarus. In the case of Madeleine, he develops Day 2 of his cycle extensively to portray her worldly life of dalliance (*mondanité*), for which he used material from contemporary love songs, and developed her dialogue with a marked eroticism (ll. 8469-8644). Even the apostles are presented as worldly men requiring conversion. The laments of Peter and other apostles for the ways they fail Christ at critical moments intensify the human side of the story. It has been shown that he was especially interested in the idea of penitence, and this can be related to his concern for individual salvation noted above.[13] This appears in the way John the Baptist is used in Day One. Michel begins by creating a sermon for him in which he says, 'I am a voice in the desert crying penitence' (ll. 950-1), and he returns to his theme repeatedly (as at ll. 1061, 1169). This first day also brings out the importance of the Baptist by showing the beheading and ending with his burial. Michel also added four sermons for Christ in which he makes direct address to the audience about their own spiritual state.

Because the period covered by his narrative is much shorter than Gréban's, Michel employs a number of devices which develop the sense of cyclic drama. In the Prologue he does not recount the story of creation and the origin of the world, but he makes a series of references to Adam and Eve, the Fall of Lucifer and the Annunciation, and he also anticipates the Passion and the Judgement. All these are put within the framework of preparing for the coming of Christ. Besides the passage revealing the worldliness of Madeleine, he develops extensive retrospects for Pilate and Lazarus containing details of their past lives which are indeed not scriptural. At the beginning of Day 2 the heading says, 'And to begin with the apostles make a recapitulation of the deeds of Jesus treated in the first day'.[14] These measures are somewhat different to those taken by Gréban to be explored in more detail below. One further point is that the ending of Michel's *Passion* is rather abrupt, and the Prologue Final refers to having completed the Passion in short order. The next move was perhaps to go on to the Resurrection which Gréban had already done on his fourth day.

Michel's *Passion* was performed in the Place des Halles at Angers in August 1486. By this time the custom of large-scale presentation of cycles had become well established, though we find that in most places the performances did not occur with the frequency and regularity observable, for example, at York. In France there is usually a sense that each performance was conceived in its own right and had to be specially set up by the authorities. This may have occurred because the scope of many of these cycles, together with the enormous administrative problems in mounting the elaborate performances, meant that the undertaking could not be made lightly. However the performance of Michel's play was soon followed by a development of great importance in that the text was printed, the first edition being at Poitiers before 1490. At least sixteen further editions were issued before 1542, and the cycle is unique in receiving such attention from printers which led to dissemination and use through much of France.[15] Consequently this *Passion* acquired a unique position in the development and exploitation of cyclic form in France. It became the central episode in a number of cyclic performances which also comprised some of Day 1 from Gréban's *Passion* as a beginning and his Day 4 covering the Resurrection as a conclusion. This was the form adopted for performances at Amiens in 1500 and Mons in 1501.[16]

It was not only a matter of combining for performance, however, for there survives a printed edition from Paris in 1507 to which modern editors have given the name *La Passion Cyclique*. Here the text was modified to establish links between the different elements, and the title page and colophon were made to emphasize the continuity of the narrative, suggesting that the impulse towards cyclic form was very conscious. This conflated text was probably used again in Paris by the Confrérie de la Passion for a performance in 1539 in the presence of François I, and it was followed by *Les Actes des Apôtres* in 1541 and *Le Mistère du Viel Testament* in 1542.[17] Subsequently other composite volumes were made up comprising the same elements by Gréban and Michel , but in all the other known cases the attempt to integrate is less complete. In the British Library copy, for instance, the two parts by Gréban were printed in 1541 and 1542, and it is difficult to tell when the three parts were combined— possibly some time later than the actual printing.[18] Nevertheless the frequency of such combinations argues strongly for the conception of cyclic form, however pragmatically achieved.

Besides the strongly influential Gréban-Michel group, the independent *Passion d'Auvergne* provides us with further valuable evidence of the nature of the cyclic form in the fifteenth century. Before examining it in some detail, however, we shall consider several different regional manifestations, drawing attention to the extent of the distribution of cyclic plays throughout France. At this point we shall not take much account of the many variations in size and scope since the main point to establish is the widespread interest in the dramatisation of the biblical narrative and the variety of approaches to it.

Apart from the Gréban-Michel group which originated in the Paris area in the mid-fifteenth century, but had influence at Angers, as well as the region of Mons and Valenciennes in the north east, a significant group of texts has come down to us from Burgundy. The *Passion du Palatinus*, the *Passion d'Autun* and the *Passion de Semur* all owe something to the narrative poem of 3894 lines, noted above, originating in the late twelfth century or shortly after, now known as the *Passion des Jongleurs*. This influential text was almost certainly the work of a clerical author writing for spoken performance, which, though not a play, had some dramatic features. It comprises events in the biblical narrative from Christ's visit to Bethany to the arrival of the three Marys, Magdalene, Salome and Jacobi, at the tomb. The clerical origin of the text is authenticated by the range of exegetical material which has been found to be amongst its sources. The lan-

143

guage has been described as a mixture of ecclesiastical and courtly registers. The text is divided into sections with headings, such as 'This tells how the wife forged the three nails to crucify Christ' (l. 1525). Though the main method is to narrate the events, there is a good deal of dialogue, usually introduced by such phrases as 'one of them said this...' (l. 1528). The most likely method of presentation would be to use one performer who would change his voice for different speakers. There is also the possibility that the narrative may have been accompanied by mime.[19] Besides the influence in Burgundy, parts of the *Passion des Jongleurs* appeared in the English *Northern Passion*, one of the sources for English cycles.

The earliest of the Burgundian plays, the *Passion du Palatinus*, is thought to date from about 1300, and in 1996 lines it covers events from the point when Christ sends Peter and John to Bethany to his Appearances on Easter morning. It repeats a number of lines directly from the *Passion des Jongleurs*, and in turn parts of it are followed by the *Passion d'Autun*. The latter survives in a copy by Philippe Biard and another by Antoine Roman, both made in about 1470. After a prologue recalling Adam's sin and the Incarnation, the former (2117 lines) represents the preparations for the Last Supper to the Appearance to Mary Magdalene. It ends with a retrospective sermon, and then Christ's speech from the cross, even though out of sequence (ll. 2012-2117). Roman's version (937 lines) has many lines in common and covers the narrative from the same preparations up to Joseph and Nicodemus and the Deposition. There is another fragment of eighty-seven lines from Sion dealing with the Descent into Hell. Although the position is made more complex because parts of *Autun* are drawn directly from the *Passion des Jongleurs* independently of *Palatinus*, there is no doubt that these texts point to a continuing interest in the Burgundy area. The processes by which one is adapted from another, and the implication that repeated attempts were made to alter the texts for new requirements all point to the practice which can be discerned in the transmission of the Gréban-Michel corpus. If the dating of *Autun* is correct, these copies were made after Gréban's work had begun to make an impact in northern France. The process of adaptation is a reminder that essentially these plays do not necessarily have a definitive form, but their existence always implied the possibility of development. Of the two versions of *Autun* the one presented by Roman is a distinctly dramatic work, while that of Biard is dramatic in origin but, as it now stands, it is a poem partly in dialogue and partly in narrative adapted for reading.[20] In this respect Biard's text is closer to *Palatinus*.

These plays are relatively short, but in the surviving version of the *Passion de Semur* we come to a text which, in the manuscript copied in 1488, was arranged for a performance over two days. It is now thought that the play comes from Semur-en-Auxois, about 35 miles north of Autun. The analysis of the manuscript by Runnalls reveals a complex development which touches many of the points under consideration here. Working through the prosody and some aspects of layout, he uncovers a number of ways in which the extant text gives indications of revision and proposes five phases of development. He thinks the origins lie close to the narrative poems noted above, and indeed there is a considerable number of lines which are in common with the *Passion des Jongleurs*.[21] The first or earlier stage, corresponding roughly to the second half of the manuscript (not quite the same as the later point of division between the two days), is similar to *Palatinus* and the *Passion Sainte-Geneviève* in showing episodes from the Baptism of Christ to the Appearances. To these were added, probably in independent stages, the Old Testament section, containing Creation, Cain and Abel, the Oil of Mercy, Noah, Abraham, and Moses, together with New Testament subjects including the Annunciation and the Nativity. This makes *Semur* one of the rare examples in France to present a comprehensive biblical narrative. The later stages involved the addition of comic and vulgar Rusticus episodes, not in itself a unique process even though inventive here; the division of the text into two days, together with the provision of appropriate Prologues and Episodes which feature separately, out of their proper place, in the manuscript; and finally the making of the fair copy by Jehan Floichot in 1488. As this whole evolution, in the view of both Runnalls and Bordier, was spread over more than a century, it sustains our sense of the continuity in the life of the cycle plays, as well as the readiness to revise and to incorporate both new and old material. The addition of the events before the Baptism uses a good deal of apocryphal material, as does the suicide of Judas and the Dream of Pilate's Wife. Some of it is unique, including the sacrifice of a lamb by the Jews just before they strike the bargain with Judas (ll. 5831-5904).

A number of other independent Passions are known, which contribute to our sense of the distribution and variety of cyclic form. There was a Passion play of eighteen days at Châteaudun to the south west of Paris which shared its now lost text with Amboise on the Loire.[22] The so-called Leiden *Passion* is thought to have originated in the thirteenth century in western France or Normandy. A number of aspects of the fragmentary *Passion*, described and edited by Runnalls, gives an insight into both provenance and status of the survivals. He shows that linguistically the two parts come from Picardy in the north east of France or the adjacent part of Belgium (in the Walloon dialect). Of the two fragments, totalling 261 lines, one deals with the Presentation in the Temple, and the other gives the speech of the angel at the tomb. These passages are long enough to indicate that they are independent of the Gréban-Michel group even though they may well come from an area in which the latter was well known, and even though they can be dated *c.* 1480, the very time of its expansion. Runnalls makes the point that the *Passion* of which these fragments are part would not otherwise have been known, and whether there was an extensive development is a matter of speculation. He does raise the possibility of a connection with the lost seven-day *Passion* from Hainault. There is one notable aspect which links specifically with cyclic form. The fourteen-year-old

Christ seated on the tomb, in a unique speech, recounts his past and future life, from the Nativity to the Crucifixion.[23]

In the Breton *Passion*, printed in 1530, the traditional events are divided into two, perhaps reflecting a two-day structure. In the first the narrative runs from Bethany to the Deposition, while the second gives the Appearances. There are strong dramatic features in this text, especially the prolonged interchange between Christ and his mother. Her appeal to him opposes the love of mother-son to that for humanity and justice. His terrible death is foretold, and when she begs for her own death he explains that she must not die before Christ has redeemed mankind because her purity means she must go direct to heaven and not be placed in limbo with the other virtuous humans. As we shall see, this material is similar to Gréban.

In the south there is evidence for Passions at Arles and Nîmes, but the most important surviving texts in southern dialects are the *Passion* in the Didot manuscript and the *Mystères Rouergats*. The former, dating from the mid-fourteenth century, is now thought to be primarily of Catalan origin, or perhaps from the area of Perpignan.[24] Now called the *Passion Catalane-Occitane*, it is the earliest known Passion in an Occitan, or southern dialect (the *langue d'oc*). It is distinct in its treatment of the Passion from its contemporary in the language of northern France (the *langue d'oïl*), the *Passion de Palatinus*, which is equally the first surviving version. Apart from some associated fragments the Occitan text has 2372 lines and is roughly divided into the *Passion*, beginning with the miracle of the Blind Man, and the Resurrection, with the Lament of the Virgin in between. The role of Maria Magdalena is much developed, and her passion for Christ after the discovery of the empty tomb is almost physical. As it happens her emotional speech has a number of lines in sequence with the corresponding passage in the *Mystères Rouergats*.[25] The *Passion Catalane-Occitane* contains a version of the early life of Judas which is given in a soliloquy before he complains about the ointment. It recounts how he was sent away as a baby by his mother at the time of the Massacre of the Innocents and how he unknowingly killed his father and entered an incestuous relationship with her (ll. 433-594).

The *Mystères Rouergats* are a collection of plays from near Toulouse running to 9000 lines, plus two fragments. The codex was written out at some point after 1481, and consists of ten episodes of different lengths. The order of these in the manuscript is not conventional, and presumably bears no chronological relationship to a performance either completed or proposed. The order is Creation and Fall; the Woman of Samaria; the Resurrection of the Dead; the Judgement of Jesus; Hymn to the Virgin; the Resurrection of Lazarus; the Meal at the House of Simon; the Resurrection; Joseph of Arimathea; and the General Judgement. In the manuscript there are also two tables which themselves differ, but they both list the Passion as well as a number of other episodes in common whose texts do not now appear.

To some extent the irregular order has been explained by the desire to fill up spaces in the manuscript. As there is also reference to another (lost) copy ('lo libre'), this might have been a more coherent version, and one which followed more closely the traditional cyclic order. There is no doubt that the presentation of the plays was different in style and concept from other French cycles. The Judgement of Jesus is distinctly unusual, not only because the episode is rare in France, but also because of the mode of performance. Some of the stage directions have been modified as though following a performance, and some show a great deal of detail. The setting for the General Judgement is particularly elaborate and distinctive. It includes the instruments of the Passion, St. Peter in a papal tiara, emperors and kings with their consorts, Death on his own scaffold, as well as gatherings of the Jews, of unbelievers, and of religious orders. There are many aspects which are unusual in this episode. The Jews are condemned for the crucifixion, but the judgement also bears upon non-human characters. Lucifer on his scaffold sends Beelzebub to plead for mercy from Notre Dame. Accepting the petition, she goes from her place to Paradise, accompanied by angels, and pleads before Our Lord for all sinners including Lucifer (ll. 6444-6585). Death and Life are both tried before the Judge. After being condemned, each of the Deadly Sins is punished by a devil in hell: naturally Lucifer is the tormentor of Pride. Altogether this manuscript is a remarkable adjunct to our study of the cycle form in that it is not apparently in conformity with other cycles, yet the idea of the cycle is palpably present.

The work of Jacques Chocheyras on survivals from Savoie and Dauphiné has given us further evidence of a number of performances of Passions. Though texts and much other information are often wanting, it is clear that there was a Passion lasting at least nine days at Vienne in 1510 which extended from the Annunciation to the Ascension. The text is lost, but Chocheyras suggests that it might have been the *Passion Cyclique* noted above. At Grenoble in 1535 he observes that a Passion was copied—implying that an existing text, perhaps Michel's, was brought into use, and that rehearsals lasted five months. The performance took place, or started on May 14, a great press of people being present, but it is not known how long the performance lasted. On this occasion Pierre Buchiert, a Doctor of Laws, played Christ, and a woman called Françoise Buatier played Notre Dame.[26] *Lou Mysteri de Rampans* is written in the Embrunnais dialect and the text was kept for a while in Grenoble. It consists of 2753 lines, is dated 1531 and dramatizes the Passion narrative from the Entry to Jerusalem to the pact between Judas and Satan, followed by a scene in which Christ consoles his mother. For our purposes it is interesting because it has been shown that the narrative follows closely that of Michel, but at the same time it contains a number of sequences not found there, including some opposition from the disciples over Christ's intention to enter Jerusalem. No information has come to light about the performance, but the epilogue of the Messenger speaks of further episodes including the arrest of the thieves and the sufferings of the Virgin.[27]

Having reviewed the distribution of the cycle plays in many different regions of France, and also the general background in which the genre developed, we can now turn to two individual texts to identify some of the ways in which the form was exploited. We shall look at a selection of aspects from the work of Gréban, and at the *Passion d'Auvergne*.

One of the ways in which the design of Gréban's cycle is sustained may be perceived by looking at the role of the Virgin. As we have noted the cycle does not present the Old Testament episodes except for some events surrounding Adam. It is apparent from a Prologue, which contains dramatisation of the Fall, the crime of Cain, Seth's journey to the earthly Paradise, and the deaths of Adam and Eve, that a deliberate decision was made to leave out Abraham, Isaac and Jacob (ll. 1498-1501). The Acteur explains that the main concern is to show the reparation of the sin of the first parents. This suggests that Gréban could have included these and other Old Testament episodes, perhaps following rare precedents in France, and that instead he had a deliberate and specific objective in this focus. The first day then begins with the discomfort of the souls in limbo, and the first to speak is Adam who laments his fault and its consequences, and looks forward to the Messiah. These two sequences set up the chief issue of the cycle which is how to put right all that follows from Adam's sin. They are followed by the *Procès de Paradis* in which the daughters of God dispute how the difficulty shall be overcome. The upshot is the insistence by Justice that the sins must be paid for. In response to Misericorde's question about who is suitable for such a sacrifice, Sapience's response, in the midst of a dialogue which is full of complex argument, is a dramatic speech consisting of two words: 'Le Filz' ('The Son', l. 3121). Sapience further explains that the Son will join human nature to his divinity (ll. 3217-22). God the Father hopes that there must be some other way, but Justice is inexorable, and it is this conflict between the inexorability of Justice which links the *Procès* to the Virgin. The main purpose of this solution is to restore humanity to primary virtue, and the heavenly ones sing a song to celebrate this as Gabriel is despatched to make the Annunciation. This begins at line 3425, about one-third into the first day, so that we see these important thematic issues are set up early on and relatively quickly. There is no mistaking that this cycle is built upon a selective procedure towards a specific end. There is a distinct sense that the Incarnation and what follows is in the logic of history. Nevertheless the Father's rather human feelings for his Son are not confined to this initial *Procès*. No doubt the staging arrangements contained a heavenly scaffold and God could well have been visually present for the audience throughout the cycle. He intervenes from time to time and though these interventions often coincide with scriptural events, some of them sustain his fatherly concern for his Son. At the Mount of Olives for instance, God says he hears the pitiful eloquence of his Son. He says it is right that he hears them as a father hears a beloved son who expects to receive tenderness (ll. 18775-7). Nevertheless this speech heralds a reprise of the *Procès*. It also, to an extent, puts God in a state similar to that experienced by Mary, whose maternal feelings conflict with necessity.

Mary obediently and joyfully accepts the news of the Incarnation, but later in the cycle she reflects the tension between sympathy for Christ and the necessity of Justice found in the *Procès*. One sign of this is the insistence by the young Christ in the Temple that there are things concerning the 'magnificence' of his Father with which he must be concerned in spite of her anxiety. Nevertheless the tension persists because he also asserts his obedience to his earthly parents. This scene has been much expanded from its limited scriptural prototype. It occupies an important strategic position at the end of Day 1 (ll. 9841-80). Mary's special role is even more emphatic at the approach to the Crucifixion, where her maternal sufferings become an important motif directly related to the issues initiated in the *Procès*. Indeed her feelings are in conflict with its conclusions, which she is constrained to accept. These sufferings are only relieved at the Resurrection.

After the Raising of Lazarus when Christ is about to enter Jerusalem she pleads with him to beware of the threat presented by the evil Jews. He knows of the threat but asserts that the Scriptures will be fulfilled. Divine justice has proposed and ordered that his body will suffer, for that was the reason he was born (ll. 15396-403). He will leave Mary Magdalene and Martha to comfort her. She can do nothing but obey, but her unhappiness is a mark of the continuing stress in her role. In her following scene at Bethany (ll. 16396-599) her intervention is more sustained. Initially she weeps in anticipation of his death and fear of what he will encounter at the hands of the Pharisees. But Christ replies that he must do as Scripture demands, and repeats the earlier point that it was to endure pain that his flesh was formed in her womb (ll. 16422-7). It is a feature of this cycle that both Christ, and God the Father respond to a necessity identified with the Scriptures and the words of the Prophets (ll. 12165-7, 26008-12, 28901-8, and 33961-90). Mary admits that she cannot impede such a high purpose, but begs to make four petitions. These are that the deliverance of humanity be achieved by some other means than his death; that if he must die, he die without pain; that she be allowed to die before him; and that she be insensible of his death. All these, in different ways, reflect her love as a mother, but as Christ responds to each of them in turn he brings in other powerful necessities. Scripture demands his death; the huge quantity of human sins demands his pain; she cannot die before him because being without sin she must not go to limbo but directly into heaven; and finally that she must feel compassion for him. The only consolation he offers is that eventually her sorrow will turn to joy at his resurrection, and he leaves for Jerusalem, promising that he will soon return. Mary kisses him as he departs for the Last Supper. Alongside the structural function of Mary's role the episodes we have been considering contain many examples of how the comprehensive narrative of salvation is constantly referred to and made accessible to the audience. Even though other dramatic purposes are evident, the cyclic anticipation and recapitulation persist.

Before the Crucifixion, as St. John approaches Mary with news recalling the details of the arrest, which the audience has just witnessed, she has no recourse but to pray. She again asks for a different solution for the salvation of humanity, which divine grace has power to bring. Her Son, she says, will not defend himself because of his obedience. This plea does relate to the recurring idea that Christ's was a willing submission, but it also sustains the pervading sense of her agony. Gabriel replies that she has heard Christ himself say that he must yield himself to death in order to deliver mankind, and thus her plea cannot be met. However Gabriel promises to be with her in her grief. At the last moments on the cross the scriptural detail gives Christ's final words, but the dramatist, working upon a tradition traceable in drama and iconography, interweaves the sufferings of Mary, comforted at times by St. John and Mary Magdalene. After Christ's words *Consummatum est* which he himself glosses as 'It is finished!', he adds that this fulfils all the Scriptures, and that 'Now this mystery (*mistere*) of the passion is completed whose purpose was directed at the redemption of humanity' (ll. 25828-34). Mary, grieving, asks why he has left her alone, and as Christ dies, she faints. Griffon, one of the tormentors, admits that he has pity on her.

In her subsequent lamentations over the body of Christ as the *Mater dolorosa*, she impugns 'false Death' for having the audacity to take her son without killing her at the same time: 'Faulse Mort, / comment as eu le hardement / de prendre mon filz seulement / sans moy tuer conjoinctement!' (ll. 26917-20). Her lamentations continue to complain about her predicament: she asks the True God why he ever gave her a son, 'whom I had never asked you for' ('qui point ne te le demandoye', l. 27019), if the result was that she should feel such grief.

During Gréban's fourth day, Mary's rejoicing at the Resurrection extends over several scenes. When she meets Christ she seems to acknowledge the close interweaving of grief and hope: 'En mes plainctes vous actendoye' ('I awaited you in my lamentations', ll. 29015). Her last words are a short lyric in praise of the Trinity at the Descent of the Holy Spirit (ll. 33755-66). She does not appear in the final episode of the cycle which in the text is headed 'Final Morality', but the substance of it refers to her sufferings and joy, in much the same way as at the beginning. There is a good deal of recapitulation including references to Adam and to Christ's suffering, and the action of the cycle ends with the kiss of reconciliation between the Four Daughters marking the completion of salvation. The Final Prologue apologises for mistakes, asking for kind correction and leads into the singing of *Te Deum laudamus* ('We praise thee, O God').

In the following discussion about performance I shall concentrate upon the third day of the Gréban *Passion* comprising Christ's examination by Caiaphas to the setting of the watch. We should not assume that there was necessarily only one layout: the proliferation of texts implies many different possibilities. But the text requires specific locations in or at which action took place, and which also facilitated the important process of moving between them, of leaving and approaching. These locations may have been in a straight line, or a curve, but there is also the possibility of staging in the round. Thus the Pharisees frequent the Temple; Pilate has a palace with a throne room, a separate courtroom, and a bedroom for his wife. Lucifer is confined to hell, probably chained, while Satan and other devils spend time on earth, moving back to their base in hell to report, consult, and be punished. Limbo, the prison for human souls, is near to or probably an integral part of hell, and it has gates, which Christ breaks open. As we have noticed, God remains in heaven throughout.

There are at least two kinds of dramatic movements, one exploiting a fluid use of space and one based upon a single location around which a number of episodes are constructed. About half of Gréban's third day is concerned with the scriptural narrative following Christ's arrest as he is examined in turn by Caiaphas, Pilate and Herod. This culminates in the procession to Calvary, which is one of the pivotal staging moments of the day. From then the action is centred upon the site of the crucifixion, centripetally conceived. Gréban's dramatic sense works differently for the two types.

In the first there is a deliberate exploitation of short interventions and a marked interest in switching between locations. Sometimes attention is closely centred upon processions, but there are also times when the movement is purely functional. These features can be illustrated by two sequences in Gréban. After a preliminary examination during which Christ remains silent, Caiaphas tears his clothing and orders him a beating, but he finds it only entertainment, and wants it instead to be fatal. Persuading the other Jews that the matter must be taken to Pilate, he arranges the order of the journey to Pilate's palace, naming the twelve advisors who are to accompany him, and instructing his servants to place Christ in the procession (ll. 21039-44). Before leaving he sends Maucourant to fetch Annas to join him at Pilate's in support. As Caiaphas and his group process, we see Maucourant reach Annas, who is more than willing to join in. When Annas sets out, attention switches to Judas who, in an unspecified place, decides to return the accursed money he has received. The result is noted by a stage direction functioning as a further shift in attention: *Icy va Judas pour reporter l'argent. Item vient Saint Jehan a Nostre Dame* (Here Judas goes to give back the money; next St. John comes to Our Lady, l. 21138sd). John gives an account of the arrest and of Caiaphas' intentions to Mary. Supported by the three Marys, she decides to go to Pilate herself (ll. 21257-8). Three groups are now converging upon Pilate, while Judas, in wretched isolation, seeks the Pharisees.

In the second illustration, Pilate is unwilling to condemn Christ, and the dramatist is keen to show his vacillation. After a designated Pause, Pilate shows the beaten Christ to the world (*Ecce homo*) and speaks movingly in sympathy (ll. 23019-21). The following sequence cleverly uses different locations. Pilate shares his anxiety with the Jews, goes back to Christ, and again back to the Jews. At this point there is a Pause and Pilate has a seven-line apostrophe to Christ followed by another Pause, after which he tells the Jews he will pronounce 'la sentence finable' ('the final judgement', l. 23138). Immediately there comes a call from Adam and Eve in limbo longing for deliverance. God sends Michael to limbo where the subsequent rejoicing disturbs Lucifer in hell. Whereupon Lucifer blames the devils for their misunderstanding, but Satan, 'in the world' (ll. 23341sd, in Paris and Raynaud only), rejoices at Christ's condemnation and returns to hell with what he considers joyful news. Lucifer, fearing a loss of power, sends him to persuade Pilate's Wife to stop the condemnation. Back goes Satan to her bedroom where he warns her in a frightening dream. She sends to Pilate who listens, but is unable to alter the sentence, and so he washes his hands as in Scripture. By such use of the staging space, events can be made to press hard upon one another, and tension increased by short but pointed interpolations of different kinds of dramatic material. Thus Pilate's *Ecce homo* speech (ll. 22969-94) broadens the emotional range of events since he cannot really be expected to sympathize with Christ.

Some of Gréban's verbal effects are intimately related to visual aspects, or to movement about the stage. Probably the largest category is the use of patterned rhyme schemes and variations in line lengths. Thus in a climactic moment there are two eight-line passages at the beginning of the Scourging. In the first, Pilate gives the instruction—'Frappez fort, frappez, ribaudaille / Homme ne se mecte en oubly' ('Strike hard, Strike hard. Let it never be forgotten'). His words are copied by three Torturers before he repeats them (ll. 22755-62). In the second, the four Torturers together then speak lines in turn about the rods they will use. Urged on by Pilate they deliver blows by numbers in four voices —'Empreuf. / Et deux. / Et trois. / Et quatre, / Et le cinquieme de surcrois.' ('One. And two. And three. And four, And the fifth one as well')—in an eleven-line rhyming sequence. This rhythmic and heightened speech suggests an increasingly frenetic tempo for the beating and it culminates in a stage direction: *Icy le batent une espace sans parler* ('Here they beat him for a while without speaking', l. 22818sd). Pilate then calls a halt and begins to show some pity. Other examples are found at the point where Pilate washes his hands and the Jews accept blood responsibility for Christ's death (ll. 23567-82); and in the refrains which accompany pulling Christ's limbs and raising the cross (ll. 24705-12; and ll. 24785-92). These episodes bring several voices into close interaction. Together with the 'Pauses' noticed above, which themselves may have had a musical component, these formally rhymed sequences play a valuable role in the cycle as a means of emphasis and variation. Neither convention appears in the English cycles.

The physical appearance of the characters, especially Christ, is much in evidence. At the preliminary beating before Caiaphas, his appearance is noted by a line in the accompanying refrain 'and his face completely deformed' (ll. 20882 and 20890). Later, when he refuses to answer, Herod has him dressed in the white robe of a fool (ll. 22349-80). The passage contains the action of putting the robe on his naked body. As he is again stripped for a beating after his condemnation, one Torturer comments: 'He has a beautiful body, well shaped' (l. 22707). During the beating his appearance changes: blood appears (ll. 22760 and 22851-2). The purple robe and crown of thorns are placed upon him (ll. 22901-4). These actions are made to lead up to an iconic moment in the stage presentation. It may well be that the conventions of the visual arts had an influence upon how Christ was actually made to appear in the *Passions*.[28] In the York and Chester Cycles there is a similar iconic dimension, and this is recalled in the spectacular flowing of Christ's blood during the Chester Judgement (24/421-8 and sd).

In a strikingly different context, Caiaphas requires that for the procession to Calvary, Christ be dressed in his familiar clothes so that the people will recognise him and understand what he has come to. The Torturers strip him, but the robes stick to his wounds 'like a skinned lamb' (l. 23853). They look upon him stripped, put on his old clothes and mock him. During the procession both the Torturers and those sympathetic to him draw attention to his dismal appearance. When the procession reaches Calvary, the Pharisees again intervene to make sure that he has the right appearance for them. Annas will not have him hanged in his 'chemise', but naked as a worm (l. 24566) without a scrap of cloth to hide him, just as he was born. Cruel though this is, the iconic significance running back to the Nativity cannot be missed. The Torturers mention the seamless garment he is wearing as they strip him (l. 24588sd). Mary is horrified, and she covers him with a cloth (l. 24626sd). These details may be paralleled by the special attention to the clothing of Christ in Memling's *Scenes from the Passion* noted in Chapter Two.

The *Passion d'Auvergne*, performed in 1452 and 1477, appeared at roughly the same time as Gréban's, but the three fragments surviving are independent of it. However in their use of staging conventions, and in a number of other features, including the use of discrete rhymed passages (*rondeaux*, *ballades*, and other patterns), they match the practices found in Gréban and Michel. The existence of this material at this time helps to increase the sense that the second half of the fifteenth century was significant for the development of the idea of cycle plays, and the enlargement of their scope. However the distribution of days for performance in Clermont Ferrand is somewhat different. The reconstruction proposed by Runnalls and Elliott for the 1477 performance involves playing on six successive Sundays, from April 13 until May 18 or 25, followed by the last day on May 26, Whitmonday (seven performances in all), in relatively short sequences of up to 2500 lines approximately.[29] For these, texts are extant for the first, third, and fifth days, respectively the Preaching of the Baptist to the Temptation of Christ; the imprisonment of the Baptist to the Healing of the Deaf and Dumb Man; and the Trial of Christ before Pilate to his Burial. The likelihood is that this cycle broadly follows the convention of Baptism to Pentecost common in many other Passions (but not Gréban's or *Semur*, as we have seen). The state of the surviving manuscripts is complicated because that relating to the first day has become separated from the other two, and because the three are each different in scope. They are all closest to the 1477 performance for which the first day is represented to us by a manuscript copied some time after the event;[30] the third day by a composite manuscript made up in part by an earlier version, perhaps from a previous performance in 1452 and supplemented by additions in 1477; and the fifth day by a manuscript copied completely in 1477.[31] This variety of status is entirely in line with the practices of development and adaptation we have noted in the texts of other contemporary cycles. If there were a performance in 1452, it is by no means certain that the texts would have been exactly those which have survived.

If this proposal is correct and the lost texts were similar to those surviving, the overall length might have been 7 x 2500, which is 17,500 lines, about half the length of Gréban's *Passion*. Judging from the survivals, the texts were compressed effectively: the dramatic style was crisp, and the texts were well packed with detail from the bible and other sources. But even so the texts are distinguished by many poetic episodes where the emphasis is upon highly complex patterns of verse, and many different choices of form are made. We shall return to this lyric element in the following discussion which addresses a series of structural features of the cycle. These are the role of Mary, the treatment of John the Baptist, and the use of the Devils in separate scenes as well as the interventions in the story. In all three there is a good deal of reliance on traditional sources.[32]

The management of the role of Mary is perhaps the most striking feature, pervading the texts for all three days. At the end of each day in the extant texts Mary is reunited with her Son, even though doing so requires remarkable liberties with traditional material and indeed with what might be considered probability—though probability usually gives way to the symbolic in the cycle plays. Towards the end of the first day as Christ triumphs over Satan's third temptation on the mountain and as the noises of strife in hell fade away, Mary asks God for some comfort. In this cycle, interventions by God the Father are a frequent resource, and here he sends three angels carrying bread to Christ ('even though he is the living bread', l. 871). First they call at Mary's 'ostel' where she is delighted to hear the news. She adds her 'supper' to the bread, and they proceed to the mountain. There Christ says he would eat some of his mother's supper, if only he had it (ll. 924-7). The angels offer what they have brought and Christ admits to human frailty. They all set off back to Mary's, while a song in her praise is sung. On his arrival, Christ is greeted by Mary and he accepts her offer to sleep there. Mary ends, saying 'We shall do no more today'.

When the dramatist brings Christ and his mother together at the end of the third day, he is content with a shorter passage. Having cured the boy possessed by a devil, Christ declares, after a Pause, that he must visit Mary, and, in a lyrical response arranged in quatrains, she welcomes him with praise and joy (ll. 1896-1911). For the fifth day, however, the treatment is more elaborate. Her role on this day during the crucifixion and burial is extensive, as we shall see in a moment, and the final ceremonial moments are impressive. She speaks two ballades of twenty-eight lines in the first of which she addresses God the father asking, in the refrain, that she might see her Son with Him. After the first, there is a stage direction indicating that she is to be lifted up, presumably into the scaffold of Heaven. God salutes her in language reminiscent of her own greeting to Christ at the end of Day 3: 'M'amour, Marie, mon doulx lis' ('My love, Mary, my sweet lily').[33] From this new location, in her second ballade, she looks down upon Christ in limbo where he has overcome the devils. Presumably at this point the attention of the audience is divided between Heaven and Limbo, perhaps some distance away across the acting area. As she celebrates the Trinity, she prays for all those who love her, that they might be admitted into Paradise. In the very last words of the day she includes especially the spectators who have watched the Passion, and prays that these people may always be beloved (ll. 4583-8).

Her presence throughout Day 5 follows a number of traditional interventions: the purpose is clearly to heighten the emotional impact, using a variety of dramatic methods. The Arrest of Christ sparks a remarkably tense dialogue as John reluctantly reports what has happened:

> *S. Jehan* Hee, dame!
> *Marie*   Quoy, Jehan?
> *S. Jehan*   En verité
> Mon bon maistre, voustre doulx filz,
> Est entre ...
> *Marie* Quoy, Jehan?
> *S. Jehan* ... est entre les mains ...
> *Marie* Las, de qui?
> *S. Jehan* Il est entre les mains des ...
> *Marie* Las, dy moy, amy!
> *S. Jehan* Il est entre les mains des Juifs!
> *Marie* Hee, Dieu, conment?
> *S. Jehan*   Dame, il fust pris
> La nuit passee fort laydement. (ll. 2359-70)

('Alas, Lady. What, John? In truth my good master, your sweet Son, is in ...What John? ... is in the hands ... Alas! Of whom? He is in the hands of the ... Alas! Tell me, beloved! He is in the hands of the Jews! Alas, O God, how? Lady, he was taken full wretchedly last night')

This is followed by a sequence in which she follows Christ as he carries the cross towards Calvary. As the Executioners jestingly call the blows they give him eggs, and coins to buy drink, she cannot find him. Looking into his face, she does not recognize him: 'ce n'est pas luy certainement' ('surely this is not he!', l. 2439). She begs two or three words of farewell from Christ, but he does not reply. As the Executioners proceed with the Crucifixion, she calls upon their hard hearts, begging them not to strike on the huge nails (l. 2592). She is given a complex stanzaic lament in which she calls upon God, addresses Christ in farewell and again condemns the Executioners and the Jews. Here her speech is in long, concatenated stanzas, and, even though this was spoken, it might have seemed more like an aria in performance.[34]

At this point the dramatic texture is rich and the tension high as events move to a climax. Whilst Mary suffers, the cross is brought to Calvary amid the jokes of the executioners; Christ speaks the Last Words; the two thieves are given strong wine to drink before their execution; God the Father himself says that he can longer endure the outrage upon his Son and he sends Michael to warn the Jews with the earthquake which shatters the Temple. We should bear in mind here that the pressure of events is made all the greater by the economy of language, and the dramatist's power of concision. Mary's part through this climax contains lamentations, but from time to time she also gives retrospects: as Christ's body is brought from the cross, she recalls that he must pay the dues for the deed of Adam and Eve (ll. 3541-4). It is at this point that she falls down twice as she says farewell, an incident we have found of interest in considering the visual cycles.[35]

In the *Passion d'Auvergne* the treatment of John the Baptist, the forerunner, is presented as a kind of structural parallel, and so an anticipation, of some aspects of the life of Christ. He preaches a sermon at Bethany, and he is provided with disciples whom he summons. At the beginning of Day 3 he makes a prophecy to them of his coming death, and they are obedient to him after it. After he has baptized Christ, he himself is baptized in return. This unusual reciprocation does not often appear in the drama, but it has some exegetical authority in Chrysostom.[36] At his death, which he accepts with the same dignity as Christ does, the extended lamentations of his disciples are placed alongside the regret of the executioner and also of the Le Duc, the unscriptural brother of Herod, who denounces the malice of those who have sought his death. Afterwards the angels defend his soul from the devils come to seize it, and he triumphantly enters Limbo where he is welcomed by Adam, Abraham, Isaac and Zachariah. All these items in some measure anticipate the story of Christ himself.[37]

The devils are in another way linking the cycle together. They have their own scaffold and action is conducted within it, and it is a base for intervention in worldly matters. There are hints of the longer view of the conflict with the divine in Lucifer's fear that Christ in the desert is showing greater penitence than anyone before him (Day 1, ll. 572-4) and with Satan's recognition at the Harrowing that Christ is 'homme Dieu' ('God-man', Day 5, l. 3264). Devils are closely associated with the death of the Baptist in Day 3. While the Daughter enchants Herod with her dancing, Lucifer sends Asmo to her, Beelzebub to Heriodas, and Satan to Herod. Their mission is supported by the appropriate documentation, which they celebrate in a *rondeau* (ll. 165-72). But the intervention of Gabriel forces them to accept only partial success (ll. 656-61). For Satan's mission to tempt the 'prophet' Christ there is another commission from Lucifer, written on the skins of whores and sealed with sulphur and pitch (Day 1, ll. 673-6). On this mission Satan is assisted by Asmo, and they rejoice in their past successes over Adam, Cain, David, Absalom and Joab. Asmo's boast that he can induce lechery, gluttony and avarice (ll. 648-58) is probably to be associated with exegetical interpretations of the sins of Adam, which were thought to be also involved in the temptation of Christ.

These details indicate the ingenuity of the dramatist. Satan's devices for beguiling Christ include appropriately disguising himself as a priest for the temptation on the pinnacle of the Temple, and as a king for that on the mountain. Afterwards he and Asmo are received as failures in Hell and they are beaten by Astorath and Beelzebub. This interest in the grotesque details of Hell's management is echoed in Asmo's earlier request for Lucifer's curse as a blessing for their mission. It reappears in Day 5, possibly, in the reception of Gestas, the false thief who curses Christ on the cross, and whom the devils prepare to eat with relish when he arrives in hell (ll. 3804-17). Such details may be conventional in iconography, but they add a lively realism, which is characteristic of the *Passion d'Auvergne*.

Though we have been concerned in this study with cycles dealing with the narrative of salvation, the interest in cyclic form was so great in France that we should take some account of some cycles which, in different ways, illustrate the adaptability of the form, and indeed are evidence of its popularity. The organization of *Le Mistère du Viel Testament* has been described as 'chaotic' and 'clumsy',[38] but this line of criticism does not prevent the collection from making a significant contribution to the history of cycles. Some of it was written in the fifteenth century, appearing in combinations with other plays as in the *Passion de Troyes*, but no comprehensive manuscript has survived. The cycle was printed in Paris in *c*. 1500, *c*. 1520 and 1542. The first edition claims that the cycle had already been played there, and the Confrérie de la Passion subsequently played it in 1542. The structure of the texts presents difficulties for interpretation because of its discontinuities, and we do not know whether these printed versions are the same as those in any performance: they may indeed be entirely the result of a compilation process after a number of episodes had come into existence. The enormous length, which is approaching 50,000 lines, may in itself raise questions about whether it could ever be done in full. Nevertheless many of the episodes in their stage directions support the assumption that performance was at least conceived.[39]

The text falls into two differing parts. The Old Testament narrative is more or less continuous, on a selective basis, from the Creation of Heaven and Earth to the encounter between Solomon and Sheba. During the latter, the text breaks off and becomes a series of episodes covering Job, Tobias, Daniel, Susanna, Judith, Hester and Octavian and the Sibyls. In the first sequence continuity is sustained by running the individual stories alongside the debate between the Daughters of God, who repeatedly appeal for his response to the enormity of human misdemeanours. This provides a framework especially as there is a development within these scenes showing how God becomes more and more concerned: at one point he regrets that he has made human kind. The story of the Oil of Mercy is gradually unfolded in the episodes dealing with the life of Adam, and after Abraham's saintly conduct with Melchisedek, God regrets that Mankind is still suffering from the sin of Adam.[40] Justice, consistently a severe advocate, complains that God is too full of kindness, but God nevertheless announces that mankind will be redeemed ('rachater', l. 8318). Much later, in the episode dealing with Hester, there is also an anticipation of the Passion (l. 47320). However, in these episodes there is no indication of the continuation of the *Procès de Paradis*, and the individual stories are somewhat arbitrarily added. There was a practice of printing episodes separately: Rothschild records a *Joseph* in c. 1538, and a *Susanna* in 1625.[41] In spite of this however it is apparent that this cycle was deliberately assembled in such a way as to give continuity to the narrative and also to prepare the way for the coming of Christ and to anticipate the Redemption.

The interest in representing a pre-Passion narrative was also met by *L'Incarnation et Nativité de Nostre Sauveur et Rédempteur Jésus-Christ*, which was played in 1474 at Rouen, and printed at about the same time, probably also at Rouen. The text is divided for two days, from the Prophets to the Annunciation and from Octavian's decree for the census to the celebration of the Shepherds after the Nativity. Some aspects match material in other cycles, including the *Procès de Paradis*. In this case the need for a good, dead man to pay for the sin of Adam is established, but Verity fails to find one in the world, the consequence being the Incarnation. There are other narrative devices such as Simeon's prayer for the completion of God's promises, and the persistence of the Roman framework through several scenes involving Octavian. However it is perhaps the Shepherds who make the strongest impact in this joyful cycle. They sing, adore, pay taxes, have a comic interlude, and, significantly for the cyclic structure, they praise the heroes of the past, including David. They also conclude the cycle with a song. There was apparently a strong local tradition for the performance of cycle plays in Rouen where there was a Confrérie de la Passion from 1374: Petit de

Julleville refers to performances in 1445, 1452, 1474, 1492, 1498, 1502, 1520, though the texts used are not known.[42]

Other surviving cycles in France continue and extend narratives well beyond the Passion itself. *Le Mystère de la Résurrection*, played in three days at Angers in May 1456, concentrates upon the narrative after the crucifixion, from the Harrowing to Pentecost. The sense of the past is enlarged by the recital of thanks rendered by the souls in limbo, kneeling before Christ (ll. 2855-3458), and by Satan's discussion about the possible divinity of Christ (ll. 1732-1919). The didactic intention of this cycle is emphasised by the preaching of Peter to the Jews at the end, in which he recited the Creed in Hebrew, Greek and Latin, and in the announcement that Christ will come to Judgement (ll. 18320-18340).[43]

Eustache Mercadé's *La Vengeance Jhesucrist* presents a narrative after the Resurrection and follows the fate of Pilate and the Jews, as Justice catches up on them for the killing of Christ. Wright has made it clear that this early fifteenth-century version was one of several in what became a popular mode.[44] He notes that there were a dozen full-scale productions in the years 1396-1541. There was also a vigorous interest in publishing the texts, there being seven editions between 1491 and 1539, making it comparable with the printing of Michel's *Passion*. For Mercadé there was a continuity between the *Passion* and the *Vengance* as the Preacher indicates at the beginning of the latter. Both plays were performed in the smaller market place at Metz in 1437, requiring four days for each. This was on a massive scale and gave much scope for the spectacularly terrible effects written into the destruction of Jerusalem. The sky showed omens; there was a shipwreck and a rain of fire. The anti-Jewish sentiment was strong and much cruelty was enacted.

The relatively early date of this cycle means that its development went alongside that of the *Passions*. The style of performance is an important link between the two, as is the sense of continuity and of cause and effect. However, most of this material is not biblical, and its appeal is more concerned with sensational events. The cycle has, in part, a sense of romance, allowing additions and developments which are but loosely connected to one another. It also permits the pursuit of themes like justice, and the anger of the Lord, and it gives scope to characterisation of monstrous tyrants like Pilate and Nero, who are pursued by devils. The critical question which arises is how far this tradition added to that of the *Passions*. The sharing of the mode of performance may have been one which was likely to increase the element of spectacle in the latter. But the difference between the story of salvation which could be carefully integrated and framed, and that of vengeance is remarkable. The latter allowed a much freer hand for invention, but it did not inherit the much more extensive interpretative corpus from exegetical literature which again and again influenced the management of the biblical cycles.

Such freedom of invention is also discernible in *Le Mystère des Actes des Apôtres*. This collection of episodes, numbering nearly 62,000 lines of 'authentic legends and saints' lives accepted by the Church', according to the title-page of the first edition, was written in the late fifteenth century, possibly by Simon Gréban, brother of Arnoul, but the surviving printed texts date from 1536 (Bourges) 1540 and 1541 (both Paris). They are associated with performances at these two cities: Bourges in 1536 at the Roman amphitheatre, lasting forty days, and Paris at the Hôtel de Flandres in 1541, by the Confrérie de la Passion, lasting thirty-five days. These very large dimensions seem to have been matched by many spectacular devices in performance.[45] However, the contents of the episodes are of most interest here because they show a vast range of incidents beginning after the Ascension with the election of St. Matthias. The stories of the apostles are sometimes scriptural, as with Peter and Paul, and there are other events such as the Burial and Assumption of the Virgin, which we have encountered in the salvation narrative. But the lives of the apostles are often presented in terms of their violent and spectacular deaths. Though these may echo one another, they do not have the same sense of purposeful chronology as in the *Passions*. There is an interest also in the lives of the emperors and kings, and because these present an evil contrast with the apostles, they have a structural function. The devils perform their conventional roles, but things become so unsatisfactory for them as Christianity spreads, that they decide to become mortals. This cycle, which seems to have the support of at least three monarchs, presents us with a kind of paradox. Because it deals with a series of only loosely related lives it seems unfocussed, but it can be seen as having a place as the third in a chronological panorama comprising the origins and the Old Testament, the life of Christ, and the spectacular and miraculous aftermath.[46]

Cycles in German

The review of German cycles in Chapter One has indicated the breadth of the surviving material, and has drawn attention to its fragmentary nature. From the records, which are still being assessed, there is now no doubt that a good deal has been lost, and that the biblical drama, some of it cyclic, was widespread. The texts available to us suggest that there was a strong vein of liturgical material in the German tradition and much music, an aspect which must have circumscribed the nature of some of the dramatic experience in particular ways to which we shall return later in this section. Studies of origins point both to the liturgical drama and also to the continuing influence of the liturgy itself.[47] They indicate that there was a development of Easter and Christmas plays, as well as of Passion plays, which had independent status. There were also considerable local variations in style, scope and influence. Methods of performance were varied. Perhaps the commonest location was the market place or other public square, but many plays were done in churches. In general, the texts of the cycles were not as long as those found in France, and although some cycles were performed over two or three days, the time required for the German examples was not generally as great as for some French plays. There is also a question of the influence and role of processions upon the performance. Not all the cyclic plays were associated with Corpus Christi, but where they were, they were likely to retain some reflection of the processions at the heart of the day's celebration. This means that the interpretation of the nature of individual cycles does not permit ready generalisation and that the particular nature of every individual text has to be considered on its own. The texts themselves should not be seen simply as copies of plays in a purely literary sense. As elsewhere, the manuscripts are rather reflections of the performance, or at least of plans for one. There are no early printed German cycles to compare with the examples in France already discussed in this chapter. Nevertheless there are a number of cycles showing careful overall planning, and which embody a broad scope of biblical narrative. Here we shall deal primarily with those from Alsfeld, Künzelsau and Lucerne, all of which begin the narrative with the Creation and continue to the Ascension, that from Künzelsau going on to the Last Judgement.

The development towards cyclic form appears quite early, as the surviving *Dirigierrole* from Frankfurt-am-Main from between 1315 and 1345 indicates. No doubt the spread of Corpus Christi processions in the fourteenth and fifteenth centuries was also an influence. This was the period which saw much interest in developing the Passion play as such. Of the three cycles to be discussed here, that from Alsfeld relates to performances in 1501, 1511 and 1517, the Künzelsau manuscript is dated 1479, and the complex and extensive Lucerne material (texts and records) attests to a Passion play performed from *c*. 1450 until the early seventeenth century. From about 1500 this extended to two days. The surviving texts relate in different ways to performances at Lucerne in 1545, 1571, 1583, 1597, and 1616.

There is little doubt that the *Alsfelder Passionsspiel* was intended for performance in the town's market place. The manuscript does contain a simple diagram giving some idea of the layout of the acting areas in the square, and it provides some important clues as to the method of performance. It also contains a detailed list of the order of a procession to take place at the start of the first day.[48] This list is no doubt a witness to the close link between procession and performance, and it hints that the cycle had a processional origin. It begins with standard bearers and Majestas (God) followed by Angels, Adam and Eve, and John the Baptist and Herod and his supporters. However, the change to New Testament figures does not follow the narrative order: Pilate comes first, with his Wife, Soldiers and Torturers, followed by Mary Magdalene and then the Jews, and Sinagoga, who embodies the Old Law. Annas and Caiaphas have their own standard and they are followed by the Maidservant and the Cock. After another standard bearer and the scholars (presumably choristers), come the Saviour, the disciples, Judas, the Virgin and the other Marys, the Daughters of Jerusalem and the Woman of Canaan followed by Lazarus, the Thieves, Barrabas, Longinus, the Blind Man and the Centurion. The departure from the conventional narrative sequence persists until the end of the procession with the figures of Joseph of Aramathia and Nicodemus, Ecclesia, Simon the Leper, and then Moses, Daniel, Isaiah and Simeon, followed by four Condemned Souls. The last figure of all is Death. The first direction in the play itself calls for the angels to sing 'Silete', a prompt for silence which like the 'Pauses' above may have had a musical element. This occurs once all the characters in order are settled in their own places. It is noteworthy that this list does not indicate the same character being performed by several actors, as we shall find below with the *Künzelsau Fronleichnamspiel*. The action which follows throughout the three days of performance is essentially dialogue based, though there are significant musical elements and a great deal of action, as is made clear by the *Dirigierrole*. We shall see that the action does entail a great deal of processing as the narrative of the Cycle is unfolded.

The division of *Alsfeld* into three days is an important structural factor, and indeed Nowé has interpreted it as emphases upon different areas of the acting space for each of the days. The first, which begins with an extensive devil scene, he connects with playing centred upon Hell at one end of the acting space. The third day deals with events based upon Heaven, including the Crucifixion itself, at the opposite end from Hell. In between, the second day is concerned with the events from the Last Supper to the Scourging, and here the action takes place in the middle of the acting area, which includes the scourging column, and in the locations set up for Annas, Caiaphas, Herod and Pilate. The identification of these latter in the diagram and the sequence of events within the narrative make this reading credible. If it is accepted, it implies a symbolic intention for each of the days.

Given this organisation, the devils have a significant impact at the beginning of the first day, and their influence also spreads through the other two, albeit on a lesser scale. The German tradition was indeed rich in the use of devil scenes, but it is clear here that the design of *Alsfeld* gives a strong sense of their influence on the development of events, even though they are circumscribed by divine authority. The preliminary addresses to the people by the Proclamator and others do not mention the devils, but concentrate rather upon the sufferings of Christ at the Passion, and the need for and benefit of paying close attention. But the action begins theatrically, with Luciper [*sic*] climbing on to a barrel and summoning his followers, who sing and dance around him (ll. 132sd and 138sd). Luciper recalls his lost glory, but is beaten by the other devils for being a preacher ('predigere', l. 164). He then whips up the animosity of his supporters against 'the sorcerer' ('zeuberer', l. 178), Christ. They in turn single out individuals whom they will each seek to suborn: Satan targets Judas, Milach, Annas and Caiaphas, and Rosenkrancz, Pilate:

> daruff wel ich dencken myt syn und wiczen
> das hie sal eyn falsch ortel uber Jhesum geben.   (ll. 255-6)

(For that I shall manage my wits and senses / So that he shall pass a false sentence upon Jesus)

The devils also indicate that they will corrupt the Jews, as well as setting out to encourage sinful behaviour related to the Deadly

Sins. Some of them introduce comedy: Hellekruyck intends to encourage idle chatter among women in a way reminiscent of Titivillus (ll. 432-41). Satan summarizes these evil intentions and Luciper rejoices. The long sequence ends as all the lesser devils run off to hell. Luciper comes down from the barrel and he and Satan go off singing (ll. 454-63 and stage directions). The Proclamator then restarts the play with the narrative of John the Baptist. The theatricality of this opening sequence cannot be doubted, and if we think of it in the context of other such performances it is clear that the intention is to provide a visually exciting beginning, but also to evoke emotional responses to the enemies of Christian virtue. This elaborate anticipation of some details of what is to come is a significant contribution to cyclic form here.

The narrative of this cycle continues through the events of the Baptist's death, and proceeds to the Temptation of Christ and the worldly life of Mary Magdalene, in each of which the devils play a role. For the first they join in the preparation for Herod's feast, though one stage direction suggests that the devils, or the Jews should dance (l. 897sd). Satan disguises himself as an old woman and instructs Herod's wife to persuade her daughter to ask for the head of the Baptist. When this is achieved, he leaves his disguise on the ground and runs to tell Luciper the good news. While Luciper roars (l. 1105), Satan and other devils drag off Herod's wife and her daughter to the fires of hell: 'mit swebel und bech woln mer uch trencken!' (We shall soak you in sulphur and pitch, l. 1109). Satan's disguise to tempt Christ is that of a Lollard (l. 1143sd), indicating that there is an underlying pro-Catholic programme for this cycle. A barrel is used again, this time to represent the pinnacle of the temple.

For the worldly life of Mary Magdalene, Luciper is apparently able to leave hell again, for he dances with her, and encourages her to resist the protests from Martha (ll. 1893-5). The devil Natyr acts as her servant and brings her a mirror so that she can admire her own beauty, and she dances with him as well (ll. 1834-45).[49] After her conversion, Luciper weeps and laments:

> O Maria Magdalene,
> wie werestu yn mynen augen sso schone!
> do werest myn fass der unreynnikeyt,
> das vol was aller bossheyt! (ll. 2892-5)

(O Mary Magdalene, / Why were you so beautiful in my eyes! / You were my cask of uncleanness, / Which was full of all evils.)

During the second day, though the devils do not take such a strong lead, they intervene in the episodes concerning Judas, and that of Pilate's wife's dream. Satan prompts Judas at a critical moment at the Last Supper, the point where Christ offers Judas the bread. The temptation is for a reward, but Satan urges him not to let his master live (l. 3137). Apparently there is no disguise here, and Judas must be aware of who is speaking to him. Later, when he is in despair, Judas specifically summons all the devils (l. 3666). They bring him a rope, the Chorus sings 'Alas' while he hangs himself, and the devils lead his soul to hell (l. 3669sd).

These events are quite conventional, but in the third day Satan appears at the Crucifixion in a striking episode, suggesting that he was given a special function by those who arranged this cycle. At the moment when Christ receives the vinegar, he mounts the left side of the cross, while an angel mounts on the right (l. 6267sd). As Christ dies the angel releases a white dove and Lucifer comes to the foot of the cross. He asks Satan what he is doing and finds that Satan is still seeking the soul of Christ, the man. As another angel drives them off with a sword, Lucifer explains that they have been deceived, and that this really is the Son of God (l. 6317). He is afraid that the devils will now lose the souls they have gathered over the past five thousand years. We shall return below to the highly theatrical presentation of subsequent events, in which there is a marked increase in the music, but the last significant sequence involving the devils takes its place in this imposing spectacle. After the burial the Saviour and the angels make a procession to hell singing (l. 7076sd). The tomb of the Saviour was probably at the same end of the acting space as Heaven and the crosses, and the movement is now through the whole length to the opposite end where Hell stands. The souls, waiting there in limbo, join in the singing and in the dialogue the panic of the devils grows. Remarkably the singing by the angels and the souls continues, but the devils' parts, in contrast, are only spoken. Even during the liturgical sequence, 'Lift up your heads, O ye gates, [that the King of Glory may come in]', the devils reply in words, 'Who is this king of glory?' (l. 7134sd). From these details it appears that the devils were very much part of the spectacle and they added a good deal to the dramatic versatility of this cycle. Being supernatural, not confined within the scriptural narrative, though sometimes contributing to it, they also played an interpretative function, even though much of what they said had to be understood with some scruple.

Apart from the devils, the Jews, including both the scriptural Annas and Caiaphas and also other figures drawn from different sources, such as the Counsellors and Sinagoga, function as the enemies of the Saviour. This is recognised by allowing them to perform from their own locations. Parallel with these are the locations for Herod and Pilate, which also are placed around the edge of the acting area, as the sketch in the manuscript indicates.

In turning to some of the staging arrangements embedded in this text, we find that the distribution of locations stimulates movement between them, and we have already noticed how the processional mode is embodied within the action of this cycle. The symbolic opposition of Heaven and Hell could be contrasted with detailed dramatisations of certain elements in the narrative, especially in the sufferings of Christ. It also seems that to visit the locations of individual characters in itself contains dramatic emphasis. We can trace this in the sequence of events on the second and third days from the Last Supper to the Arrival at Golgotha.[50] At the beginning of the second day, the Last Supper takes place in the house of the Pater Familias on the left side of the square, looking from the end for Heaven. After the meal and the prophecies of death, Christ and the disciples move to the Garden of Gethsemane situated at the lower end of the square. The Arrest takes place here, and Christ is then taken progressively to the houses of Annas and Caiaphas on the right side of the square, and then across it to Pilate's and on to Herod's and back to Pilate, these on the left side. Thus Christ will have been led right round the acting area, ending with the sentencing by Pilate. The third day begins with the Scourging, which takes place at the column in the centre of the square. If the processional mode were continued, the way to Golgotha would now involve Christ and Simon carrying the cross around the square and back to Golgotha at the upper end.[51] Such a method of presentation could emphatically reveal his suffering to the whole audience, especially as there is a good deal of realistic, even sadistic detail in the text. But the dramatic effect is complex because such an extended movement was embellished by music along the way.

To give a more accurate impression of the *Alsfeld* performance we need to focus upon the richness of the musical aspects. Dreimüller counts sixty-seven German songs with notation, in different metres and tunes, only some of which are in traditional style. Indeed, he finds a wide variety of styles, with the liturgy as the most important.[52] There were substantially three modes of performing the music. A main Chorus, which does not have a role as characters, provides many narrative links. Several groups of characters such as angels, Jews, and apostles take an active role in the dramatisation in the form of choric singing. The disciples, for example, sing when Mary Magdalene is forgiven (l. 2826sd). Thirdly some individual roles such as Christ, the Virgin and Mary Magdalene also require extensive singing. For example Christ, whose role contains more than eighty songs, sings frequently when on the cross, giving versions of the scriptural words, no doubt making use of liturgical settings. It is striking that on several occasions he sings the liturgical setting first and then gives a paraphrase in German, as for 'Father, forgive them, for they know not what they do' (ll. 5756-9 and sds). This must have given a special effect to the dramatisation. One could interpret the technique as simply didactic, but equally it might be essentially a religious ritual which allows the words, in Latin and German, to be appreciated for what they mean, and for their emotional association. Such an effect may accord with Dreimüller's suggestion that the exchanges between Christ and his mother are virtually operatic in style.[53] Of the liturgical music there is an especially intensive use of recitative, mostly drawn from the Gospels. Some of the music is sung from stationary positions, but it is also sung on the move, using processional antiphons. There is an abundance of special effects, and it is not an exaggeration to say that the text has its own musical vocabulary. The Jews dance and sing around the Cross at the Crucifixion (l. 5793sd). On the other hand Christ sings at the moment when he lies down upon the cross, but the leader of the Scourgers says: 'Herre Jhesus, loiss dyn singen!' (Sir Jesus, stop your singing! l. 5566) There is no further singing by any of the characters or the Chorus until the dispute about his garments, for over a hundred lines of dialogue, during which he is stretched and nailed to the cross and the cross is raised.

From the manuscript it is evident that some of the singers came from the Augustine monastery. But even the presence of such highly trained specialist singers does not alter the high probability that on the days of performance such a complex musical programme could only be performed once, or, at most, for only a very small number of times. This is consistent with the scheme of performance proposed above. We shall see below that there is a comparable use of music in *Künzelsau*, suggesting that it had much to contribute to cyclic form, but we shall also note that the forms of musical expression could be much varied according to the needs of local ideas and circumstances. In both cases the cycles were constructed for public, secular performance, which gives a special context for the use of so much music derived from the liturgy.

The actions presented in *Alsfeld* are framed by the speeches of the Proclamator at the beginning and end of each day. Unfortunately, though his 'verses' are mentioned at the end of Day 2 and the start of Day 3, they are not actually recorded in the manuscript. Otherwise the existing passages are addressed to the audience and express concern about their attitudes to the play. There is a distinct preoccupation with the narrative outline. At the start of Day 2, before the enactment of the Last Supper, the Proclamator turns to the wonders of Creation, and he links this with story of Adam and Eve and the divine compassion of the Incarnation. He looks forward into the events of the Ministry and Passion, which are to come, and the hope of Salvation (ll. 2930-3013). The appeal to emotions is direct:

> uwer hercz sollet er uffslysssen
> und umb Jhesus lyden trene gyssen!   (ll. 2996-7)

(You should open up your hearts / And pour out tears for the sufferings of Jesus!)

There is also a warning to take heed of how the evil Jews hated Christ (using 'bösen', the same word as for the evil of the devils). At the beginning of the cycle, the people are urged to watch devoutly ('mit andacht') and, with wisdom, to help Jesus to carry his cross ('tragen', l. 54, also implies endure, and suffer). A few minutes later, however, the Proclamator turns to more practical things, asking for the mayor to proclaim a circle as an acting area and threatening anyone not belonging to the play who enters it with devilish punishment (ll. 109-16). He also speaks to the people after the long introductory scene by the devils (ll. 463sd), as we have noticed, but his words are not recorded. This intervention, however, is significant in setting off the devils scene from the rest of the play. In his concluding speech, the Proclamator recalls the sorrow the people should feel for Christ's suffering in almost the same words as he had done on the previous day:

> uwer augen sollet ir giesssen
> umb das liden unssers herren!   (ll. 8071-2)

(Your eyes should pour out tears / On account of the sufferings of Our Lord!)

But soon this is changed to joy, as he urges his listeners to go home, eat and drink and go to church.

Finally the *Alsfeld* text leaves us with some paradoxes, but these help to illuminate this particular way of adapting the cyclic form. It accommodates an overall design, carefully framed by the Proclamator, but also sustained by structural devices, including the devils. Dramatically it gives us a challenge concerning its mode of performance, which exploits the market place setting skillfully, both in terms of procession and of static playing, and puts together a rich and complex musical experience with one based upon vigorous and realistic dialogue. The dramatisation also allows scope for symbolic presentation alongside the latter.

The text of the Künzelsau cycle is headed *Registrum processionis corporis Cristi Sic ordinatur* ('The Register of the Procession of Corpus Christi is thus ordered') and the relationship between procession and performance pervades the manuscript and needs to be considered carefully.[54] It is much more complex than the arrangement in the Alsfeld manuscripts. There are many episodes, and nearly every one is introduced by a speech from the *Rector Processionis* (also called *Rector Ludi* at some places in the manuscript). The scope of the episodes varies considerably. Some like Noah, which comprises seventy-one lines, contain only two or three speeches following the Rector's introduction, whilst some develop considerable complexity of dialogue. The action of the Noah play, for example, is very limited. The episode begins with a typical but revealing stage direction: *Noe accedat cum archa* (Noah comes with the ark, l. 548sd). In this we can remark upon two things. Firstly Noah is presumably carrying a replica of the ark, or he comes in accompanied by a larger representation of it. In either case the symbolic nature of his arrival is clear. The second point is that *accedat* is the normal word in this text for marking entry at the beginning of each episode, and it implies coming or arriving: as such it is appropriate to the successive items in a procession. In his introduction the Rector makes the traditional figural link between the ark as preserver of mankind and Mary, who nurtured Christ in her womb (ll. 557-60). When the action itself begins, Salvator tells Noah to make the ark, taking aboard his children and the animals, which Noah agrees to do. Similarly the Offering of Isaac, lasting only forty-four lines, has a very simple plot, with two angels, Abraham and Isaac each in turn speaking only once. The Rector draws attention to the theme of Obedience (l. 622). Action is required, however, as a stage direction tells how Abraham seizes the sword to kill Isaac, and the angel in turn seizes it from him (l. 652sd). It must be conceded that there are some longer episodes with more complex dialogue and action, such as the opening sequence comprising the Creation and Fall of Man, accompanied by much laughter from Lucifer and Satan (ll. 211-424); the sequences dealing with the Kings and their encounter with Herod and at the crib (ll. 1664-1997); and the episode concerning the Baptist, from his criticism of Herod to when the devils carry Herodias and Salome off to hell (ll. 2140-2406). But the frequency of the shorter episodes needs to be accounted for. Such limited verbal and physical activity may well be clues to the nature of the performance. If we look at some of the stage directions—all of which are in Latin—we find a number of details which must help to determine how the play was done. It seems that the text encompasses several dramatic styles.

Apart from the initial heading already noted, the cycle begins: *Primo Duo Angeli cantant:* Silete, Silete, Silencium habete! (To begin two angels sing: 'Silence, Silence. Have Silence!') After they call for silence in German, the following direction appears: *Rector Processionis vertat se ad sacramentum et dicat* (The Ruler of the Procession turns himself towards the sacrament and says). This indicates that the sacrament must have been present as part of the Corpus Christi procession.[55] His next speech is a prayer, at the end of which another direction tells him to turn towards the people and speak to them (l. 26sd). There are no instructions for movement, but two later directions imply that movement has taken place:

> *In Secunda Staccione Angeli cantant*: Silete, *ut supra* (l. 685sd)
> (In the second station the Angels sing: Silence, as above.)
>
> *In tercia staccione Angeli cantant*: Silete, *ut supra* (l. 2139sd)
> (In the third station the Angels sing: Silence, as above.)

These are the only directions referring to stations; the first station is not so designated. However, the presence of the Angels' Silete, which is probably a fanfare or some other musical device demanding that the audience pay special attention, and the use of '*ut supra*' connect these three directions. Though there remains some uncertainty, and a good deal of academic debate, the most likely explanation, or way of fitting together these clues, is that the procession begins with the Rector as described but that the plays themselves were not spoken until the procession was completed, perhaps in the market place. On the way it passed through two important stations where limited activity surrounding the two prompts for Silete took place, making a pause there. At the second station the episode which follows in the manuscript is the Ten Commandments, and at the point where the third station is mentioned there begins the play of John the Baptist. The possibility remains open that some part of these was given at these two stations. At the final stopping place, probably the market square, the Rector would be in a position to carry out his role of introducing most episodes as they were performed one by one. In these speeches he usually anticipates or summarizes the story and adds to the devotion of the people by his injunctions.

The suggestion made here does still leave some details unexplained, but at least it shows that a processional mode must have contributed something to the process of appreciation of the cycle, as we have found that it did at York, even though the actual details of the form of the dramatic procession were different in radical ways. It is apparent that many plays were done in Germany in connection with procession, as N. C. Brooks has made clear.[56] His discussion is all the more intriguing because he finds eight ways in which procession and dramatic performance might interlock. If the proposal here is correct, it implies that it would be possible for members of the audience to go along with the procession through all its stages, but conclusive evidence for this is wanting.

We need to consider also that the stage directions sometimes give a very compressed account of the action. Following the kiss, at the scene of the Arrest, we find: *Tunc accedunt Judei et capiunt, ligent et percucient Jhesum cum magno strepitu. Et omnes apostoli fugiunt* (Then the Jews come and they seize, bind and beat Jesus with a great noise. And all the apostles run away, l. 3271sd). It is difficult to see how this could be done in a procession: it seems rather to demand a fixed place for performance.

The text presents the climax of the Crucifixion quite differently. The actions are not as realistic as in the last example, but work symbolically. The few spoken words in the texts, amounting to only forty-six lines (ll. 3670-3715), are addressed primarily to the audience: indeed they are not really dialogue at all. There is a strong musical element. Three stage directions in Latin, as is usual for this text, occur within nineteen lines, and make it clear that at this point there were three actors playing Christ (*Salvator*): one with a crown (of thorns, presumably) accompanied by two soldiers (l. 3671sd); one with a column (*statua*) and two soldiers (l. 3679sd); and one with the Cross, also accompanied by two soldiers (l. 3689sd). After each of these the Rector addresses the people briefly. The last of these is followed only eight lines later by another direction, which I translate as follows:

> Then comes a Chief Priest, and a lay person with him, carrying the sign of the cross. Then the same Priest, holding a cross in his hand, sings: *Ecce lignum cruces* ...[Behold the wood of the cross ...]
> The Chorus responds: *Beati in maculati in via* ...[Blessed are those ...]
> Then the same Priest speaks to the people.   (l. 3697sd)

The sequence of the three Christs, followed by the Priest, is clearly a ceremonial climax to the performance, enhanced by liturgical music, and it seems that this is largely determined by the processional concept which is at the basis of this cycle.

But the nature of the performance must also have been affected by playing on a fixed site, in accordance with what is here suggested. There are a good number of stage directions indicating that individual characters had a fixed base, a *locus*. For example in the Visit to Elizabeth, Mary's first move is: 'Then Mary rises from her place (*de loco suo*), coming to the place (*ad locum*) where Elizabeth is seated'. (l. 1479sd) When they have greeted one another Mary is directed to go to her own place (l. 1487sd) where she sings the *Magnificat* with the Chorus (in Latin). At the end of this she embraces Elizabeth and returns to her own place (l. 1491sd). It also seems that some of the fixed places had special significance as in the Four Daughters episode where the Saviour, as Creator, sits in the place of the Father, and the Saviour, as Resurrected, sits in the place of the Son (l. 1098sd). It will be seen from all this material that the manuscript needs careful interpretation and the actual theatrical events which it embodied are not easy to define. Nevertheless there are sufficient indications in line with the mode of presentation suggested here, and it seems that those responsible for the cycle might have been aware of the advantages of processional aspects of the presentation even though the culmination took place on one site.[57]

The sense of a spectacular event implied in these aspects of the *Künzelsau* performance may be considered along with the selection of events in the cycle. If we take two hundred lines as a benchmark, only one play from the Old Testament, the Four Daughters, exceeds it, and only the Fall of Man, and the Ten Commandments come near to it. In the New Testament there are three long sequences of interrelating events, the plays dealing with John the Baptist, the Three Kings and the Passion. Apart from these, the episodes exceeding two hundred lines are The Twelve Articles of Belief, the Debate between Ecclesia and Sinagoga, the Ten Virgins, The Antichrist, and the Last Judgement. This list of the longer plays seems to betray two preoccupations:

the need to clarify abstract considerations of design and faith, and the need to respect a number of traditional narrative sequences which are scriptural or legendary, and may well have had liturgical precedents. In the first, more abstract group, in such plays as the Four Daughters, and the Debate between Ecclesia and Sinagoga, some of the material comes from theological discourse, and yet there is also a tendency to reflect upon and use fragmentary narrative references which recall and sustain the overarching narrative, as with the reference to Adam and the apple (ll. 1129-30). This is especially true in the sequences which follow the Ascension, where we have noted in cycles in other countries that there is some difficulty in providing a continuous narrative. In the Procession of Saints, Juliana the Virgin beats the devil Beal who recalls prompting Cain to kill Abel (ll. 4391-2).

The episode of the Kings (ll. 1664-1997) is rich in dialogue and action. It cannot be seen as anything but a word-based play, even if there are considerable scriptural echoes in places. In spite of the musical tradition, it is striking that there are few such items here. The Rector intervenes on several occasions to indicate what is about to happen, and this function of doubling the action, so to speak, cannot but serve the same function of repetition we have noticed in other cycles. The Kings speak of their intention, impressed by the star (ll. 1702-5), and they set forth to make their offerings. When he is told about the birth of Jesus, Herod sends his soldiers to intercept them. Herod at once has Singoga check the Scripture, and when the birth is confirmed there, the Kings depart, still praising the star. Eventually they reach Bethlehem where they offer the scriptural gifts. The effect of this quasi-realistic dialogue, with its interchange of personalities and its underlying motives, good or bad, is in strong contrast with much else in the *Künzelsau* play. For this sequence at least the medium is primarily a verbal drama, supported, but probably not exceeded by other semiotic material. The action itself also moves through three or four different places. Such liveliness in the dramatic texture may also be discerned in some other episodes even though they are not particularly long. One example is the way Singoga, representing the High Priests, counts out the money into the hands of Judas (ll. 3038-51). Another in the episode of the Woman taken in Adultery, is even more graphic. Sinagoga brings the woman to Christ and when he has spoken a version of the scriptural response about the innocent throwing the first stone, a stage direction embodies the action: 'The Lord again leans over the earth and writes. Sinagoga and the other Jews inspect the writings. One after another leaves. The woman remains alone.' (ll. 2729sd) From this discussion of the variety of dramatic styles, it is apparent that the text as preserved is really the embodiment of changes, and it is not always possible to be certain what these actually were.

The *Lucerne Passion Play* gives further valuable detail about the ways in which the cyclic form could be developed. Because this cycle was performed on the Wednesday and Thursday of Easter week, it is usually called an Easter Play ('Osterspiel'), but it is more strictly a Passion since it includes some Old Testament episodes as well as the life of Christ.[58] The cycle has a long history, from 1450 onwards, and in 1495 the Brotherhood of the Crown of Thorns, the religious guild responsible for the play at the time, decided that performances were to take place every five years in memory of the five wounds of Christ, though this was by no means always achieved. The first known reference to a two-day presentation occurs shortly after this, but the earliest indication of the incorporation of the Old Testament material is 1538. In spite of the uncertainty in this chronology, the impulse to develop a more comprehensive cyclic form cannot be doubted.[59]

There are eight extant play manuscripts, all of them incomplete. They relate to one or other of the five performances in 1545, 1571, 1583, 1597 and 1616, and between them they cover all the incidents from the sequence of Adam to the Blind Man on the First Day, and that of Lazarus to the Ascension on the Second Day. Though they show considerable similarities, there is no doubt that each manuscript was specific to a performance and each thus evidences a different text. It is apparent from annotations made by Renward Cysart, who was Director for the performances of 1583 and 1597, having also done much of the work in 1571, that the demands of performance, and indeed of innovation continuously contributed to change. The phenomenon is similar to that we have observed in the development and adaptation of the Gréban *Passion* in France, and it effectively means that there is not really one text but several. For example, episodes about Hester and Judith were added in 1597 and deleted in 1616. This positive evidence about the multiplicity of texts prompts reflection upon the context of the extant English cycle manuscripts to be discussed in Chapter Five. In the case of York we have only the one witness from nearly two centuries; and for Chester the surviving complete manuscripts are so late that we may assume much earlier material, perhaps with many variations, has been lost.

Cysart also worked on the archives for the Passion and thus he is an important source for earlier material; but his major contribution is his extraordinarily detailed notes for the 1583 performance. These cover a large range of topics and give valuable information about performance, including general arrangements for rehearsal and organisation, staging and arranging the sets, music, costume, casting, and movement about the stage. This material is amplified by the stage plans for the two days of the performance in 1583.[60] There is no doubt that there was very considerable municipal commitment to the undertaking of the performance of this cycle, Cysart being the City Clerk from 1575 to 1614.

The broad principles of performance were not dissimilar to those we have noted for *Alsfeld*. The Weinmarkt, then called the Fischmarkt, was fitted with Heaven at the east end, with Hell opposing it, and there were a number of identified locations on each side of the square which could be assigned differently on the two days. As with *Alsfeld*, and many other cycles, the continuous organisation over two days meant that the same actor played the same role throughout. But those items of the staging plan which also remained constant must have been another of the features which tended to make for the coherence of the whole cycle. Thus Heaven and Hell remained in the same place, and the stalls of Herod, Annas and Caiaphas were also constant. As Tailby has pointed out, the stall for Pilate at the west end of the square is designated for him and his supporters on both days, even though he does not contribute anything to the action of Day One.[61] The effect of the continuing identity of these places must have been to give cross reference from one day to another. Moreover the stall for Pilate is adjacent to Hell, and as in other German cycles, there is plenty of direct intervention by devils. Another highly significant fixture was the Temple on the south side. This was used on both days for many of the activities of the Jews who in this cycle are persistent opponents of the righteous. The use of space and fixed locations seems a particularly strong feature of the Lucerne Play and this may well be reflected in the meticulous attention to the physical orientation implicit in Cysart's stage drawings. One should not, however, lose sight of the relativity between time and space which is characteristic of this and many other cycles. Because of the scope of cyclic form and the extended time which cycles took to perform, an opportunity was created to make the most of interplay between physical locations, and one of the key features of this is undoubtedly movement between places, often having symbolic importance. We shall now look at this, with special reference to processions in this text.

Each of the two days began and ended with a procession, a procedure established at least as early as 1538. There was an assembly point at the St. Peter's Chapel, and the order of processing was carefully documented by Cysart in 1583.[62] For both days it began with the Proclamator, followed by musicians, schoolmasters and learned authorities of the Church (in 1570, Isaiah, Jeremiah, Gregory, Jerome, Ambrose and Augustine) who later introduced individual episodes, and then Pater Eternus accompanied by angels. For each day, in broad terms, the subsequent order referred to the action to follow. Thus on Day One the procession continued with Adam, Eve and the Serpent, followed by Cain and Abel, Abraham, Isaac and Jacob. The principal Old Testament figures had many attendants. Towards the end of this procession appeared the Salvator and the disciples. Pilate was the last principal figure on this day even though he had no part in the action. It appears, however, that some elements which appeared in the action did not appear in the procession, notably the mounted entry of the three Kings, Balthasar on a camel, Caspar on an elephant and Melchior on a dromedary. These exotic beasts were horses in disguise,[63] and they may have been a prized feature held back for a special moment in the performance. On the following day, after the same figures at the beginning, the procession was continued by the Salvator and the disciples, followed by the chief actors in the Passion itself, Caiaphas, Pilate, Herod and Annas. No doubt because the Harrowing came late on the Second Day, Adam, Eve and the Fathers came towards the end, in respect of their position in limbo. This formulation reminds us of the preoccupation within cyclic form to set up echoes, and retrospects. The devils were originally last, but Evans shows that they were moved to almost the head of the procession by 1583.[64]

Within the action of each day there were a number of significant movements about the central acting space. A good deal is made of the intended battle between the armies of Saul and Goliath (in Actus 7). In the text of the play participants of Saul's are listed (l. 2186sd). The principal figures wearing armour, and carrying weapons, or with them carried for them, are listed in order. There are again many attendants, standard bearers, as well as musicians (trumpeters, drummers, pipers) and even a barber-surgeon. Saul's army makes a circuit and returns to his stall.[65]

In discussing the Gréban *Passion*, we noted the importance of the order of procession after Christ's arrest, and such items, as we have seen in Memling's work discussed in Chapter Two have a role in the iconographical tradition. Here we find that the order of the Procession of the Cross is specified, this time in the stage direction (l. 8773). It comprises Pilate and Herod with the Murderers in front, Annas and Caiaphas, with other Jews, then the Salvator with the cross, followed by Mary and John and then Mary Magdalene, Martha, Veronica and the three Marys (l. 8773 sd). If the procession starts at the court of Pilate at the west end of the square, it must have crossed the full length of the square to reach Golgotha which was located at the east end, below Heaven.

Turning to the nature of the dialogue, we find that it accords closely with highly detailed and realistic mode we have found in movement and action. The large quantity of information about the staging and organisation of the cycle, as evidenced by the invaluable surviving material coming though the work of Cysart, should not detract from the quality of the dialogue and its capacity to embody a large variety of dramatic effects. There is no doubt that the cyclic form gave rich opportunity for this, and that the attention to the texts themselves reveals that this was of importance to contemporaries. Some of the features noted in other cycles appear here. Mary begs Christ to seek the redemption of Man in another way than by death on the cross (ll. 6785-8), but Christ follows his Father's will: 'am holtz des Crüzes muss ich sterben' (on the wood of the cross I must die, l. 6804). The blind Longinus aims to kill Christ and aims for the heart (l. 9410). Pilate before giving sentence emphatically distances himself: 'Ich bin unschuldig an disem blut!' (I am innocent of this blood, l. 8661). As to characterisation, there are many who cause Christ to suffer. The role of Malchus is elaborated into one of his tormentors, and there is much attention to Judas's states of mind as he twists and turns at the time of the Arrest and afterwards. On his death the devils take him to Hell where Lucifer receives him (ll. 7854-8054 and sd). The tormenting of Christ is much emphasized, and the slowly-conducted move from Annas to Caiaphas is accompanied by jeering, blows, pushing, and bullying (7759sd in 1559 copy). There are also significant iconic moments, perhaps the most striking being the stage direction for the Resurrection: 'Dann stost der Salvator das grab uff unnd stygt mit eim Füss us dem grab' (Then the

Salvator comes from the grave and steps with one foot out of the grave, l. 9825sd). At the Harrowing he leads Adam by the hand out of Hell (l. 9871sd), and he binds Lucifer (l. 9853sd). The dramatic texture is also much enhanced by the interventions of the doctrinal figures who are used to introduce and comment upon episodes. At different times Jerome, Augustine, Ambrose, Chrysostom and Gregory are used in this way, and their interventions, such as Gregory's recall of the false kiss when speaking directly to the audience (ll. 9572-8), suggests that there is an persistent concern for the interrelationship between episodes. Ambrose has a narrative role at lines 7139-7250.

There is no doubt, from these details, that the occasions of the performances were conceived on a grand scale and that they embodied rich and complex dramatic effects. Among these was the music, but we shall find that it was not used in quite the same way as the other two cycles in German we have discussed. For example, we noted that the parts of Mary and Christ in *Alsfeld* were virtually operatic in style, whereas here there is no interest in conveying the dramatic experience by such a means. Indeed Cysart, who took a very active interest in the incorporation of some of the music and who may well have been responsible for putting it together, specifically warns about the danger of distraction by music: 'Nota, der wylen man im spil ettwas agiert, sol man kein Music gan lassen, damitt man uffsehe' (Note that while something is being enacted, no music should be allowed whereby attention might be attracted).[66] As we have seen, Cysart's contribution came late in the life of the Lucerne Play and before his time no doubt many practices had been developed, some from the liturgy, and some from more secular customs. For example it is recorded that a crowd of some 156 musicians came from all over Switzerland to participate in the performance of 1571, but Cysart, fully in charge by 1583, cut this drastically. Nevertheless, for the surviving texts there was much music, which must have given a variety of effects. Some of the characters sang during the action: Mary, for example, at the tomb, where the angels sang the *Quem*

Quaeritis giving scope for liturgical performance. Michael sang in consolation to Christ at the Mount of Olives, and the Fathers sang while in Limbo. At other times the *Sanctus*, the *Benedictus* and the *Agnus Dei* also were performed. In 1583 there were three trained choruses: the angels, consisting of eight voices; the Cantory, consisting of twelve and situated at the east end of the performing area, below Heaven, as the plan shows; and the *Synagogschuoler,* twenty or twenty-four singers placed in the Temple on both days. Cysart was the composer of the music for this last group, and it has survived in the form of decorated books showing words and musical notation. As they contain some nonsense from children's rhymes, scraps from different languages, and bits of magical incantation, it appears that the performance of this music was part of the process of belittling the Jews evident elsewhere. In contrast the Angels sing in the action, and there are four song cues for them at the Nativity (ll. 2785sd-3136sd), and six at the Crucifixion (ll. 9547sd-10019sd).

Instrumental music was provided by drum, trumpets, organs, lutes, zithers, viols and krummhorns.[67] There was a strong contribution from most of these at some of the processional episodes discussed above, and this must have been a salient effect. Mary Magdalene's worldly party was enhanced by a lutanist. Together with the vocal music discussed above these aspects suggest that the Lucerne Play was rich in musical effects, and that by the time we reach the elaborate written texts it was deeply embedded in the dramatic experience, and required careful management at the performances. But in this cycle at least music had to take its part along with a wealth of other dramatic systems, including language, and movement on the acting areas.

Notes

1. Anne J. A. Perry [ed.], *La passion des jongleurs: Texte établi d'après la bible des sept estaz du monde de Geufroi de Paris*, Paris, 1981 [*Textes, dossiers, documents*, 4].
2. Graham A.Runnalls, 'Un mystère de la passion inconnu? Les fragments

du MS BN, N. A. F. 10660', *Romania* 111 (1990), pp. 514-41.
3. Graham A.Runnalls [ed.], *Le mystère de la passion Nostre Seigneur: du manuscrit 1131 de la Bibliothèque Sainte-Geneviève*, Genève, 1974, p. 33.
4. *Ibidem*, p. 30.
5. Jean-Pierre Bordier, *Le jeu de la passion: Le message chrétien et le théâtre français (XIIIe–XVIe s.)*, Paris, 1998, p. 713. For text see Jules-Marie Richard [ed.], *Le mystère de la passion: Texte du manuscrit 697 de la Bibliothèque d'Arras*, Arras, 1891 [rpt. Genève, 1976].
6. Literally, 'Why was God made Man?'; see Charles Mazouer, *Le théâtre français du moyen âge*, Paris, 1998, p. 194. The configuration of the Four Daughters is thought to have been derived from Psalm 84:11 (Vulgate) by St. Bernard; see Lynette R. Muir, *The Biblical Drama of Medieval Europe*, Cambridge, 1995, p. 182.
7. Mazouer, *Théâtre français du moyen âge*, pp. 176-7.
8. Omer Jodogne has a review of ten manuscripts, some of which are incomplete, in the Introduction to his edition of Arnoul Gréban's *Le mystère de la passion*, 2 vols., Bruxelles, 1965-83. References are to this edition, except where stated. For a sixteenth-century printing of part of Gréban's *Passion* see note 18 below.
9. Bordier, *Jeu de la passion*, p. 721.
10. 'Pour monstrer la differance du peché du deable et de l'homme et pour quoy le peché de l'omme ha esté reparé et non plus celluy du deable.' (Gaston Paris & Gaston Raynaud [eds.], *Le mystère de la passion d'Arnoul Greban*, Paris, 1878, p. 2.)
11. Dominique Gangler-Mundwiler, 'Les diableries nécessaires. Le role des scènes diaboliques dans l'action des mystères de la passion', in: Marie-Jeanne Drury [ed.], *Mélanges de littérature: Du moyen âge au XXe siècle, offerts à Mademoiselle Jeanne Lods*, 2 vols., Paris, 1978, vol. I, p. 266.
12. Mazouer, *Théâtre français du moyen âge*, p. 195.
13. Maurice Accarie, *Le théâtre sacré de la fin du moyen âge: Etude sur le sens moral de la 'Passion' de Jean Michel*, Genève, 1979, pp. 133-5 and 431-4.
14. Omer Jodogne [ed.], *Le 'Mystère de la passion' (Angers 1486)* [de] *Jean Michel*, Gembloux, 1959, p. 109.
15. For bibliographical details of editions see Graham A. Runnalls, *Les mystères français imprimés: Une étude sur les rapports entre le théâtre religieux et l'imprimerie à la fin du moyen âge français, suivi d'un répertoire complet des mystères français imprimés (ouvrages, éditions, exemplaires), 1484–1630*, Paris, 1999, pp. 140-8. Overarching

themes in Michel are discussed by Accarie, *Théâtre sacré de la fin du moyen âge*; and for Fortune and earthly and heavenly kingship, see Sandra Billington, 'Social Disorder, Festive Celebration, and Jean Michel's *Le Mistere da la Passion JesusCrist*', *CD* 29 (1995), pp. 216-74.

16. Graham A. Runnalls, *Les mystères dans les provinces françaises: En Savoie et en Poitou, à Amiens et à Reims*, Paris, 2003, pp. 244-5.
17. See the account of a document written by Jacques Le Gros, the father of a ten-year-old boy who played three roles including the soul of Christ in the 1539 performance, Graham A. Runnalls, '*Le Livre de Raison* de Jacques Le Gros et *Le Mystère de la Passion* joué à Paris en 1539', *Romania* 118 (2000), pp. 138-93. The boy's speeches are identified with passages in the 1507 *Passion Cyclique*.
18. BL shelf mark C34.g.27. Jodogne's edition of Gréban takes account of five versions of his Day 4, which were printed to accompany the printed versions of Michel's *Passion*; see Jodogne [ed.], *Mystère de la passion* [de] *Gréban*, vol. II, pp. 13-4, Runnalls, *Mystères français imprimés*, p. 152, *Résurrection* (i) (1541).
19. Perry [ed.], *Passion des jongleurs*, pp. 89-90.
20. Grace Frank [ed.], *La passion d'Autun*, Paris, 1934 [*SATF*], pp. 7-8. The Sion fragment is reprinted on pp. 160-5; see also Jean Bédier, 'Fragment d'un ancien mystère', *Romania* 24 (1895), pp. 86-94.
21. Graham A. Runnalls, 'The Evolution of a Passion Play: *La Passion de Semur*', *Le Moyen Français* 19 (1986), pp. 163-202. Bordier, *Jeu de la passion*, pp. 36-8, lists thirteen short passages with marked verbal similarities.
22. See Marcel Couturier & Graham A. Runnalls, *Compte du mystère de la passion: Châteaudun 1510*, Chartres, 1991; and Graham A. Runnalls, 'Were They Listening or Watching? Text and Spectacle at the 1510 Châteaudun *Passion Play*', *METh* 16 (1994), pp. 25-36.
23. Runnalls, 'Un mystère de la passion inconnu?', p. 519, and ll. 216-50 on p. 524. For details of *Mystères* in and around Poitou, see Runnalls, *Mystères dans les provinces françaises*, pp. 191-225.
24. Aileen Ann Macdonald [ed.], *Passion catalane-occitane*, Genève, 1999, p. 16.
25. Compare ll. 1979-93 with ll. 2962-76, Macdonald [ed.], *Passion catalane-occitane*, pp. 218 and 322.
26. Jacques Chocheyras, *Le théâtre religieux en Savoie au XVIe siècle: Avec des fragments inédits*, Genève, 1971, pp. 43-5. See also his *Le théâtre religieux en Dauphiné du moyen âge au XVIIIe siècle (domaine français et provençal)*, Genève, 1975. The infuence of Jean Michel has been further examined by Runnalls, who shows that in the sixteenth century the text was subject to considerable modification: see his *Mystères*

dans les provinces françaises, pp. 33-126.
27. Nadine Henrard, *Le théâtre religieux médiéval en langue d'oc*, Genève, 1998, pp. 210-3.
28. Véronique Plesch, '*Etalage complaisant?* The Torments of Christ in the French Passion Plays', *CD* 28 (1994-95), pp. 458-85, relates the increasing violence shown towards Christ in the *Passions* to a desire to present the story in a more concrete and tangible way.
29. See Graham A. Runnalls [ed.], *La passion d'Auvergne*, Genève, 1982, p. 41; there is a possibility that there were more than seven days of performance, but the scheme outlined here is distinctly credible.
30. John R. Elliott jr. & Graham A. Runnalls [eds.], *The Baptism and Temptation of Christ: The First Day of a Medieval French Passion Play*, New Haven, 1978, pp. 23-7.
31. Graham A. Runnalls, 'Les mystères de la passion en langue française: Tentative de classement', *Romania* 114 (1996), pp. 507-11.
32. Elliot & Runnalls [eds.], *Baptism and Temptation*, pp. 24-35.
33. Line 4553, cf. l. 1898.
34. At ll. 2628-56 the rhyme pattern is 'aabaabbbcbbd defedfffgffg gghh'. Such prosodic complexity may well parallel that of York and Towneley.
35. In Gréban and Michel she faints at the crucifixion with the cry: 'O mon filz', ll. 24245 and 26832.
36. Elliott & Runnalls [eds.], *Baptism and Temptation*, p. 146, note 340.
37. Compare the iconographic interrelationship in the Baptistery of San Marco discussed above, p. 71.
38. Mazouer, *Théâtre français du moyen âge*, p. 209; [Louis] Petit de Julleville, *Les Mystères*, 2 vols., Paris, 1880, vol. I, p. 208.
39. James de Rothschild [ed.], *Le mistere du vieil testament*, 6 vols., Paris [*SATF*], 1878-91, vol. I, pp. xxi-xxviii.
40. For the Oil of Mercy, see Muir, *Biblical Drama*, pp. 71-3.
41. De Rothschild [ed.], *Vieil testament*, vol. I, pp. xxxiii-xxxiv.
42. Petit de Julleville, *Mystères*, vol. II, pp. 184-5. The text is in Pierre le Verdier [ed.], *Mystère de l'incarnation et nativité de Notre Sauveur et Rédempteur Jésus-Christ répresenté à Rouen en 1474*, 3 vols., Rouen, 1884-6.
43. Text in P. Servet [ed.], *Le mystère de la résurrection. Angers (1456)*, 2 vols., Genève, 1993. The dating for this performance anticipates that of Michel's *Passion* by a generation.
44. Stephen K. Wright, *The Vengeance of Our Lord: Medieval Dramatizations of the Destruction of Jerusalem*, Toronto, 1989, p. 97. See also, by the same author, '*The Destruction of Jerusalem*: An Annotated Checklist of Plays and Performances, *c*. 1350-1620', *RORD* 41 (2002),

131-56.
45. Petit de Julleville, *Mystères*, vol. II, pp. 130-3, and Grace Frank, *The Medieval French Drama*, Oxford, 1954, pp. 192-3. There is no modern text of the *Actes*: for general information and performance details, see Raymond Lebègue, *Le mystère des Actes des apôtres: Contribution à l'étude de l'humanisme et du protestantisme français au XVIe siècle*, Paris, 1929.
46. For a later modification of the text showing the selective principles of a possible director, see Jelle Koopmans [ed.], *Le mystère de Saint Remi*, Genève, 1997, pp. 33-40.
47. Johan Nowé, *Von Gottesdienst zum Menschenspiel: Eine Einführung zum biblischen Dramas des deutschen Mittelalters*, Leuven-Amersfoort, 1987, p. 90.
48. Richard Froning [ed], *Das Drama des Mittelalters: Die lateinischen Osterfeiern und ihre Entwickelung in Deutschland*, Darmstadt, 1964 [rpt.], pp. 858-60; and Nowé, *Von Gottesdienst zum Menschenspiel*, pp. 108-19, for an interpretation.
49. In some pictures of this story, Mary looks at herself in the mirror, but sees only a devil.
50. The following description is indebted to Nowé's reconstruction. He gives diagrams, *Von Gottesdienst zum Menschenspiel*, pp. 118-9.
51. This measured exploitation of procession within the acting place recalls that for the passion sequence in N-Town, 31/01: see below, pp. 289-91.
52. Karl Dreimüller, 'Die Musik im geistlichen Spiel des späten deutschen Mittelaters: Dargestellt am Alsfelder Passionsspiel', *Kirchenmusikalisches Jahrbuch* 34 (1950), p. 28.
53. *Ibidem*, p. 29; Larry E. West [ed. and trans.], *The Alsfeld Passion Play*, Lampeter, 1997, p. xxviii.
54. Details of the three interrelated manuscripts are in Peter K. Liebenow [ed.], *Das Künzelsauer Fronleichnamspiel*, Berlin, 1969, p. 224. For some episodes he prints parallel texts, especially for the Three Kings, pp. 62-90.
55. This was the case for the Innsbruck play, see William Tydeman [ed.], *The Medieval European Stage, 500–1550*, Cambridge, 2001, p. 191.
56. N. C. Brooks, 'Processional Drama and Dramatic Procession in Germany in the Late Middle Ages', *JEGP* 32 (1993), pp. 141-71.
57. We have noted above (p. 56) that the *Bliscapen* were presented in Brussels as a procession in the morning followed by a dramatic performance in the afternoon. Similarly the plays at Lille were managed in the form of a procession during which the episodes were mimed *en route*, and then performed in full in the Market Square: see Alan E. Knight [ed.], *Les mystères de la procession de Lille*, vol. I: *Le pentateuque*,

Genève, 2001, p. 55. There are, however, some problems in assuming that this collection of plays was cyclic. Professor Knight makes it clear that although forty-nine biblical items in the manuscript are arranged in a roughly chronological order, Old Testament followed by New Testament, the plays were not performed in this order (pp. 26-7). Thus we may have here a manuscript which had some limited cyclic pretensions even though they were not fully carried out, but a performance which did not. It is also apparent that the aldermen of Lille took control of Passion material in the 1520s as a response to Lutheran activity. They introduced a system of linking scenes by pre-figuration in the traditional Catholic manner: see Alan E. Knight, 'Processional theatre and the rituals of social unity in Lille', in: Alan Hindley [ed.], *Drama and Community: People and Plays in Medieval Europe*, Turnhout, 1999 [*Medieval Texts and Cultures of Northern Europe*, 1], pp. 106-8.
58. John E. Tailby, 'Lucerne Revisited: Facts and Questions', *LSE* n.s. 39 (1998), p. 358. For the text see: Heinz Wyss [ed.], *Das Luzerner Osterspiel*, Berne, 1967, 3 vols.
59. An earlier form of the *Luzerner Osterspiel* is thought to have been preserved in the *Donaueschinger Passionsspiel* which dates from about 1480. See the diagram in Antonius H. Touber [ed.], *Das Donaueschinger Passionsspiel*, Stuttgart, 1985, p. 14. The first episodes of this cycle are the Worldliness of Mary Magdalene and the Temptation of Christ.
60. The most accessible version of these is the endpaper foldout section in Peter Meredith & John E. Tailby, *The Staging of Religious Drama in Europe in the Later Middle Ages: Texts and Documents in English Translation*, Kalamazoo, 1983 [*Early Drama, Art and Music Monograph Series*, 4].
61. Tailby, 'Lucerne Revisited', p. 354. The practice recalls that used for the Cornish *Ordinalia* (see p. 282).
62. Bernd Neumann, *Geistliches Schauspiel im Zeugnis der Zeit*, München-Zürich, 1987, pp. 449-59, presents the document containing the actors' names.
63. Marshall Blakemore Evans, *The Passion Play of Lucerne: An Historical and Critical Introduction*, New York, 1943, p. 201.
64. *Ibidem*, p. 217 and note 4.
65. Meredith & Tailby, *Staging of Religious Drama*, p. 168.
66. Evans, *Passion Play of Lucerne*, p. 62. I should like to acknowledge a considerable debt here to his account of the music, pp. 61-76.
67. Meredith & Tailby, *Staging of Religious Drama*, pp. 158-9.

Chapter Four
Continental Analogues: A Review of Allied Forms – Italy, The Netherlands and Spain

Though cyclic plays are less plentiful in the languages discussed in this chapter the extant texts as well as records about performances and their preparation all give us something to consider. Cultural and social differences have played their part in leading us to perceive that cyclic drama was more limited in all three.

Italy

There is some controversy about the extent of dramatisation of cycle material in Italy. Of the three examples from Bologna, Rome and Revello to be discussed here, that from Bologna is perhaps the least convincing as a continuous play, though there is undoubtedly dramatic dialogue by living actors in some parts. The episodes, which De Bartholomaeis entitles a *Rappresentazione Ciclica*, form part of a spectacle on carts or waggons, each making a moving stage (*palcoscenico ambulante*). He thought the whole event was organised with a unified concept, thus making a dramatic cycle.[1] There is certainly an extensive chronological scope from the Creation through and beyond the life of Christ up to some fairly recent saints. The episodes with the most sustained dialogue are those of the Creation and the Annunciation. In both these there are vigorous exchanges between characters, in the eight-line stanzas standard for the whole work, and in these the narrative has a distinct development. The Annunciation is closely modelled on the scriptural account, and the Creation shows some invention as to events and interchanges. There were other dramatisations of the latter episode at this period, but this one is distinct. The devil has an extensive role and he exploits the relationship between Adam and Eve.[2]

After the Creation, the narrative contains Prophets, Sibyls and the Plea of the Virtues, a version of the Debate of the Four Daughters, in which each of the four speaks in turn. As a result, God the Father orders a search for a pious person ready to die for the sins of the first parents (ll. 821-4). The Annunciation follows as a consequence, with dialogue, actions and gestures noted in the text, undoubtedly in the form of a play. Here the purpose of redemption is recalled, linking it with the Creation and the Plea, and the episode ends with rejoicing in heaven (l. 944sd).

However, there is something of a turning point in the dramatic style of the text after this. An elaborate stage direction following line 944 calls for another structure (*edifizio*) showing the Nativity, with Our Lady holding the Child in her arms. Angels sing and the ox and ass are part of the setting. Accompanied by their followers, the Magi come to make their offerings. But there is no dialogue, and any action is implied rather than stated. The next item appears to be purely static, showing St. Michael with scales (to weigh souls): 'the infernal enemy' is with him. Then come seven angels, each carrying one of the signs of the Passion: each speaks one stanza (ll. 945-1000). The Crucifixion follows, though the manuscript is incomplete here. There are no directions as Christ speaks generally, perhaps directly to the audience, and he is followed by the Good Thief and Our Lady, who says that Christ has opened heaven with his blood (l. 1027), and she recalls the first sin and the apple. After this, the narrative virtually disappears and the show consists of a sequence of single speeches in eight-line stanzas, usually one for each participant, by groups of apostles, martyrs, confessors, popes, doctors of the Church, abbots, saints, virgin martyrs, widows, the Seven Virtues, Constantine, the Mother Church, and finally the four evangelists (ll. 1033-1760). De Bartholomaeis, with some justification, calls this part 'interminable'. However, there remains the possibility that this manuscript is a compilation deriving from different elements, and this may explain the variety of dramatic texture. If it does represent an original performance or performances, the concept of a cycle is clearly present, however disjointed. If it does not, the cyclic idea may be attributed to the work of the compiler.

The *Passione* presented in the Colosseum in Rome gives us some problems of interpretation, but it does show that there was here a significant attempt, for a considerable period of time, to achieve cyclic continuity, and also to grapple with related performance issues in a number of ways. It is comparatively short, comprising a narrative from Peter's Denial to the Deposition, 676 lines in all, and it is known to have been performed on Good Friday from the second half of the fifteenth century until 1539. It is not clear what had gone on before this period, but the Confraternità del Gonfalone, who were responsible for mounting shows in Rome, had a varied history of devotional activities going back to religious groups of the thirteenth century. These included processional shows outside the churches of St. John Lateran and St. Peter's. Surviving registers of expenses for performances begin in 1486.[3] It was on those sites that they also presented the *Resurrezione*, for which a text survives, though details about the time and nature of performances are less apparent. This fragment has 337 lines, starting with Setting the Watch and breaking off at the Appearance to Luke and Cleophas. There is a distinct possibility that in some years the *Resurrezione* was performed after the *Passione*, perhaps on the following day.[4] We are able to reconstruct a number of significant aspects of performance of the *Passione*. The text itself, which has lacunae and is incomplete at the end, allows us to perceive that this was distinctively a dramatisation which depended upon the nature and quality of its dialogue, as well as having a number of associated effects comprising a rich texture of performance. The text of the *Passione* was printed in 1496 and reprinted up to twenty-one times before 1601.

The choice of the Colosseum must have had a variety of implications, not least the grim antecedent of early Christian martyrdom in this very building. Any dramatic presentation must take account of its enormous size: both its advantages for large-scale spectacle, and the difficulty of projecting over a huge area as well as of concentrating the numerous audience's attention upon specific dramatic moments. However, the presentation of the cycle over many years suggests that the advantages probably outweighed the difficulties. By comparison the town square at Alsfeld and the streets of York must seem intimate.

The mode of performance was similar to the place and scaffold types we have encountered in both France and Germany. The acting area was covered by a black tent, which may have helped acoustics as well as providing some protection from the weather. There were various *edifizi* (structures) including the Mount of Olives and a hill for Calvary. The Temple, Hell and Paradise were separately located, the last with painted clouds and provided with a turning wheel with lights. The Palace of Pilate was elaborated with four columns in front, perhaps related to the importance of his dramatic role, which is discussed below. That for Herod was on a somewhat smaller scale. The use of this acting area involved action at these different places, intercutting of episodes, together with movement between locations, as in other similar layouts. Here there is a distinctive use of music to cover some of these transitions. When Pilate, who plays a dominating role here, sends Christ to Herod, there is a stage direction: *Mentre li Farisei conducono Cristo dinanzi a Erode, li Cori cantano* (While the Pharisees lead Christ in front towards Herod, the Choruses sing; l. 128sd). One of the Choruses was of Shepherds, who here sing of the envy and fear of the Pharisees: the other consisted of Kings, whose song is about the plague, hunger and burning war to come upon this guilty people (ll. 129-44). This topic anticipates the vengeance of the Lord and it notably extends the historical reference. It is striking that Shepherds and Kings are normally part of the Nativity rather than the Passion. Their appearance here cannot but interconnect these two events. Apart from their usefulness in relation to movement, these Choruses manifestly take a significant dramatic role and indeed they may recall the function of the Chorus in classical tragedy. While Christ is being nailed to the cross, they widen the emotional range of the action. The Shepherds sing of the pride and envy of the Jews; and the Kings of the cruelty of Christ's death to come and the poison, hatred and fury of the Jews (ll. 385-99). The end of the play is also presented by means of music. After the Virgin Mary and Mary Magdalene have lamented the cruelty of Christ's death as he is placed in the tomb, 'All the Marys' (presumably Mary Magdalene, Mary Cleophas, and Mary Salome) 'in musica' introduce a note of hope:

> Tollera, Madre, questa Passione
> Con fede della sua Resurrezione.

(Endure, Mother, this passion With faith in his resurrection, ll. 659-60)

This does not make it clear that they actually sang: it might just mean an accompaniment, as there were musical instruments available. The two Choruses then end the play. The Shepherds sing of Jesus as example and standard for the Jews, and the Kings of the new form of His precious body which, triumphant and glorious, will open the way to Heaven (ll. 661-76).

The dialogue of the *Passione* makes Pilate a driving force in the action. The main thrust is to emphasize his reluctance, a move in line with the heavy condemnation of the Jews in this text. This is presented in what he actually says, but it is also reinforced by a series of stage directions making plain that the demands of the Pharisees are repugnant to him. The sequence begins when Christ is brought back from Herod, now wearing the fool's white robe (ll. 160-2 and sd). The interview with Herod lasts only seventeen lines. The stage direction indicates that Pilate responds *turbato* (disturbed, l. 165). The next has *Pilato, credendo di liberar Cristo, dice...* (Pilate, thinking to free Christ, says ...) and he offers to release Christ or Barabas. When the Jews choose the latter, the direction reads:

> *Pilato cerca di liberar Cristo per altra via e comanda al Cavaliero che Cristo sia flagellato, e dice questo con intenzione poi di lasciarlo.*
> Giesù a me non par degno di morte,

> Ma poiché piace a voi che cosi sia,
> Coreggerollo amaramente e forte,
> E flagellato manderollo via.

(*Pilate seeks to free Christ by another way and orders the Knight to have him flogged, and says this with the intention of then letting him go:* In my view Jesus does not deserve death, but seeing that it may please you thus, I will correct him bitterly and hard, and I will order him a flogging, ll. 193-6.)

Afterwards another direction indicates that he speaks *thinking to have satisfied the Pharisees* (l. 234sd). When they continue to press for Christ's death, he, *shy, takes Christ by the hand* (l. 246sd). He then moves on to yet another device, suggesting that they should not kill their 'King'. Some of this material is adapted from scripture, but the dramatisation is pointed to emphasize Pilate's dilemma, especially when the Jews threaten him with the power of Augustus (l. 270). Although it is not directly related to the *Passione*, the *Resurrezione* picks up on this troubled Pilate who hopes that, now Christ is dead, he will be able to escape from 'these treacherous, cruel and proud people' (l. 742), and he speaks of their 'insatiable appetite' (l. 758).

The exploitation of the possibilities of dialogue is found in a number of places in both plays. In the *Passione* Christ asks the people why he has been beaten (ll. 211-6); he accepts the weight of the cross willingly (ll. 343-8); and he prays to God twice from the cross (ll. 373-8, 524-9). In the *Resurrezione*, Mary is articulate about the loss of her Son (ll. 859-64, 951-57). In this section of the cycle there is also a good deal of music, sung and instrumental. De Bartholomaeis notes that the *Resurrezione* was a spoken performance, but that the dialogue was interrupted by musical *intermezzi*.[5] There were also Choruses who sang, but their words are lost.

The *Passione di Revello* comes from near Saluzzi in Piedmont. In broad terms it is untypical of Italian practice, even though we have found there are some cycles originating in Italy.

Revello is close to the modern French border, and it may well have been influenced by *Passions* written and performed in the south east of France, or Provence, where there was a demonstrable tradition, as for example at Draguignan in 1439. Passions were shown at Grenoble in 1398 and Vienne in 1400. There is a possibility that this French influence was of some political importance locally. It may well have been encouraged because of a need to preserve some independence from the powerful political forces of central Italy.[6] The *Revello* follows many French analogues in starting with the Nativity, though this is different from the influential Gréban model. However, we shall see that although there are number of links with French practice, it is intriguing to note that the dialect has been identified as Tuscan.[7]

This cycle is divided for performance into three days. Because the first, with 7717 lines, is about twice as long as the other two (2412 and 2385 lines respectively) it has been suggested that it ought really to have been divided into two. But the limited data about actual performances makes this difficult to confirm. The first day starts with sermons looking forward to Christ's death and the Redemption, and recalling the sin of Adam (Day 1, ll. 7-42, 75-80) and there is a distinctive didactic element which is thought to be Dominican. Demons begin the action as Belial tells of 'a great prophet called Christ' (l. 1079). Broncano suggests sending Satan to tempt Joseph to reject Mary on the grounds of adultery, which would make her worthy of stoning (ll. 1179-84). The narrative on this day continues through the Nativity, with Shepherds and Magi, to the Flight into Egypt. After the Baptism and Temptation of Christ, the Demons intervene again, possibly at the point where a division might have been made. There follow the episodes of the Ministry and Mary Magdalene and Lazarus; and the day ends with the arrival of Judas at the palace of Cayphas. The second day, after an initial sermon, runs from the Feast at the Passover to the gathering of the Jews at the palace of Pilate for the trial. The third day also begins with a sermon and carries the narrative from the Condemnation through the Crucifixion to the Burial, the Resurrection and the Appearances to the Virgin and Mary Magdalene.

At this end point the manuscript is dated 15 July 1490 (after Day 3, l. 2385). There is some evidence that there was a performance at Easter on the "piazza" in front of the church of Mary Magdalene in 1481.[8] Internal information places a good deal of importance upon a scaffold (*zafaldo*) for the performance. This seems to have been quite large. When the Centurion orders the trumpeter to sound before the Crucifixion, in itself a parallel with some French practice, the stage direction says he is to go to three or four places on the scaffold, and make a noise with his trumpet 'in each place on the scaffold' (Day 3, l. 245sd). The word *zafaldo* is always used in the singular, suggesting that it was a comprehensive structure, but it is apparent that on it there were a number of designated locations. In the third day there are references to the scaffold of Caiaphas (l. 66), and movements to and from Pilate are recorded (ll. 287, 1273). There is some detail in records about material required for building scaffolds, and for payment for the work done.[9] Some of the locations were doubtless adapted for different episodes. Thus there is a hill or mountain used for the Magi to see the star (an episode with iconographic parallel with Giotto), for the Transfiguration of Christ on Mount Tabor, and for the hill of Calvary. Similarly a 'river' is used for the Baptism, for the Magi to take a boat, and for Lake Tiberias. Some of these scenic links may well have carried symbolic interrelationship between episodes. In total the number of such places is about twenty and there may well be others not specified, which means that the organisation of the spectacle must have been complex, but the opportunities for effects would have been rich and varied.

There are a number of crowd scenes where management would be critical. The shortage of evidence for specific performances is somewhat outweighed by the generously provided stage directions which frequently give details of movements, and also advise how the actors are to say their lines. Sometimes the gestures or movements are meant to point up meaning in a dramatic

203

way. When the darkness falls at the death of Christ, the Centurione, who in this cycle is not particularly sympathetic, 'begins to beat his breast' (l. 1268sd) as he acknowledges the outrage of the Crucifixion. One direction gives details for the role of Christ. There were a number of children in the performance, including such roles as little devils, and at a critical moment *Jhesu picolo* is instructed to give way to allow *Jhesu grando chi debi esse cruciado* ('big Jesus who must be crucified') to take over (Day 1, l. 3458sd).

Like some other cycles, *Revello* uses devils structurally. Always effective as a means of riveting attention, they are inserted here at frequent intervals, often to stimulate further actions, or to remark upon what has just occurred. It is apparent that there was a Hell: one stage direction says 'When they have placed Jesus in the tomb, Jesus departs from the tomb very secretly and goes to Hell' (Day 3, l. 1935sd). Allegri notes that unlike other Italian plays, *Revello* has a Hell in the form of a monstrous throat. The Council of Hell takes place in front of this, with Lucifer in a high seat.[10] Apart from the appearances noted above as marking significant episodes, there are a number of other places where devils make an impact. One is the council of devils after Christ's Descent into Hell to free the patriarchs, a challenging moment for the infernal aspirations. Earlier a devil called Legio appears to Pilate's wife in order to try to prevent the Crucifixion. He tells her that Christ is a just man, and he claims that he himself has been sent from God to warn her (Day 2, ll. 1397-1401). Belzebub takes a vigorous part in the death of Judas. Once Judas has climbed a ladder and attached the rope from his neck to the tree, Belzebub removes the ladder, leaving Judas hanging by the throat (Day 3, l. 464sd). He then takes the soul of Judas to Hell, but as he arrives he meets Mamona, another devil, who claims that he has the right to it on the grounds of avarice. Belzebub bases his claim on despair and a fight ensues, which he wins, and so he sings as he takes the soul inside (Day 3, ll. 466-540).

The dramatic qualities of the cycle are considerable and there is a good deal of inventiveness in dialogue and action. The trial before Pilate is particularly lively. Some of the material is traditional but the management of the dialogue is effective. Accusations are made to show that Christ is worthy of death because he claimed he could rebuild the Temple in three days, because he denied tribute to Caesar and because he claimed to be King of the Jews. But here there is also a defender in Samuello who claims that the witnesses against Christ are disreputable (Day 3, ll. 109-18). Pilate cannot free Christ, and he pronounces the sentence 'piteously'. Mary is articulate and moving. When she encounters Christ on the way to Pilate's she laments the prophecy which had been made:

> O Signor Dio, el quale ày voluto
> abia el tuo figlio carne recevuto
> nel myo ventre, et poy qu'el regnasse
> in casa di Jacob, et may non finasse
> el suo regname unqua in sempiterno,
> questa promessa è ben stata inderno.
> Ove è el regno che ora gly ày dato?

(O Lord God, who wished me to receive your Son in the flesh in my womb, and so that he would reign in the house of Jacob and that his kingdom would never end for eternity, this promise has remained secure within me. Where is the kingdom which once you gave him? Day 2, ll. 1221-7)

At another point often made the subject of her pathos, she observes that Christ has been denuded by his torturers and she cannot get to him because of the crowd surrounding him. She gives a handkerchief to the Centurion that he may be covered (Day 3, ll. 1000-8 and stage directions).

Though *Revello* is only about one third of the length of Gréban's *Passion* it is significant because of its presumed date, its scope and its method of presentation. These all suggest that it followed the French initiative, but it is apparent from closer comparison that it was an independent creation in which its own dynamics are present.

The Low Countries

The two surviving parts of the *Bliscapen* present us with a number of different aspects of cyclic form, and their significance for this study is partly that they take a stance which is somewhat different in scope and intention from many other examples we have under consideration. The manuscripts date from about 1455, but we have already noticed that the pattern of performance, established by 1448, continued at least until 1566. Although this is a long enough period for changes to creep in, the manuscripts do seem to have been close to the early performances, to have been updated, and to have been still in use in the mid-sixteenth century. This has been established by manuscript studies, showing that the original language is characteristic of mid fifteenth-century South Brabant, and that the hand of François van Ballaer, the factor, or poet of one of the guilds involved in the 1559 production of the *Sevenste Bliscap* (Seventh Joy), is found in the manuscript.[11] Within this general chronology it seems that the cycle was established by means of the concept of presenting seven different Joys of Mary, one each over a seven-year period. Each year the plays were performed in the "Grote Markt" at Brussels, in the afternoon of the Sunday before Pentecost, there having been a procession also in honour of Mary in the morning. This setting would have given the opportunity to present the play in manner similar to that used in France and Germany, based upon the construction of a number of fixed stages and using them and the space between them for the action. We also find that in some way the dramatic presentation was linked with a procession, a phenomenon already noted in Germany, and one which must have enhanced the sense of occasion in a number of ways. However, we shall see that it is difficult to be sure how closely variations in the processions may have been linked to the dramatic performance on the same day. It is not clear whether the document referring to the arrangements in 1448 represents an innovation or just a codification of existing arrangements, but it is perhaps significant that the date is close to the middle of the century when so many other cyclic arrangements seem to have been established or confirmed in other countries.

There is some speculation that the *Bliscapen* owe something to contemporary French influence.[12]

Our sense of the overall concept of the cycle is enhanced by information which can be gleaned from Prologues and Epilogues. Thus the Prologue to the *Eerste Bliscap* (First Joy) shows that there is a deliberate selection in making clear that it is not proposed to show the Fall of Lucifer (though the Fall of Adam is presented), but that the play would concentrate upon the first Joy, that of the Annunciation (ll. 36-40, 49-50). The expectation of a further six plays, at the behest of the city is confirmed (ll. 43-4). This is echoed in the Epilogue, which again refers to seven plays and looks forward to next year, though it does not specify exactly what the subject would be (ll. 2062-6). In the *Sevenste Bliscap* the Prologue refers to the sixth play last year, again without specifying its subject matter (ll. 15-8). The Epilogue, however, does list the seven joys which have been shown over the past years: the Annunciation, the Nativity, Epiphany, Christ in the Temple, the Resurrection, Pentecost, and the Assumption (ll. 1701-22). The actual content of the two surviving plays corresponds, but the dramatisation is extensive and contains a good deal of material not closely related to the Joy at the focus of each. These references keep the overall structure of the cycle before our attention, even though it was decided to extend it over such a long period.

On the other hand, the evidence of Juan Christoval Calvete de Estrella's account of the procession on the morning of June 2, 1549, the day of the presentation of the *Vierde Bliscap* (Fourth Joy), provides us with another way of seeing the comprehensiveness of the idea of the Joys. The play itself has not survived, but the scheme from the *Sevenste Bliscap* noted above indicates that the subject of the play would have been Christ in the Temple. However, De Estrella's account indicates that there were thirteen waggons in the procession, each devoted to an episode in Mary's life, and it appears that these did not include Christ in the Temple.[13] Although he does not remark upon this, it may perhaps be that this is not a casual omission, but one determined by the topic of the play to follow in the afternoon. Unfortunately such a suggestion cannot be confirmed by evidence from other sources, but it remains plausible. As we have seen in the work of Hans Memling in Chapter Two, the number and subjects of the Joys was not necessarily stable. Some works identified only five, the Annunciation, the Nativity, the Resurrection, the Ascension and the Assumption, designating them as earthly Joys. Memling's painting in Munich which deals with Mary's life is no longer called the 'Seven Joys', chiefly because it covers a much larger number of incidents.[14] Besides these indications of overall completeness in the *Bliscapen* we should also consider some aspects of the dramatisation and staging. The two plays are really quite different in their dramatic structures even though there are aspects of the staging which suggest that as far as details of performance were concerned they conform to a norm. Such divergence, however, is not unknown in cyclic form elsewhere. These plays are manifestly not Passions, and yet the idea of Christ's life and suffering is constantly present, and there is frequent reference to it. For example, in the Debate Christ says he is willing to undergo death (*Eerste Bliscap*, ll. 1337-8); and Michael recalls Christ's expiation with his blood of the sin of Adam (*Sevenste Bliscap*, ll. 1124-5). It remains a basis to which the cyclic elements in the Joys are related. This shows itself in the construction of the *Eerste Bliscap* where there is a marked effort to produce a narrative leading up to the Annunciation. Thus after his fall, which is enacted, Adam lives a long life, and, becoming burdened with age and illness, sends Seth to find a cure. This leads Seth to Paradise from which he returns with a branch of the Tree to be placed under Adam's head. Embodying Adam's suffering, Bitter Misery sends Fervent Prayer to ask for help from Heaven, and the latter's petition leads her to Mercy, one of the Four Daughters. Hence there is set in motion the debate of the Four Daughters, which in turn reaches to the Trinity and the decision to bring about the Incarnation. This is ensured by bringing about the Birth of Mary, followed by her upbringing and marriage to Joseph. The last episode of the play culminates in the visit of Gabriel to Nazareth to announce the birth of Christ to Mary, and the play ends with rejoicing. Although many of these episodes are not directly concerned with Mary, they are structured to point directly to the Joy of the Annunciation, and there is a marked causal element in the narrative, as well as a distinctly selective approach to narrative detail.

The Debate comes at roughly the mid-point of the *Eerste Bliscap*, occupying as much as ll. 961-1400, with the kiss of Truth and Justice at l. 1345sd. (The whole play has 2081 lines.) We have seen elsewhere in cyclic drama how this episode can be fundamental to the organisation of the quasi-historical structure of such plays, and the procedure here is no exception. In dramatic terms it receives marked emphasis.[15] There is also a spectacular effect in that the episode begins with the revelation of God the Father sitting upon his throne (l. 960sd), the whole scene taking place in some part of Heaven, which, it seems, was a specially-built raised platform in the "Grote Markt". This particular edifice may have been a traditional one: it appears again in the *Sevenste Bliscap*, along with Hell.

To return to the narrative structure, the plenitude in the *Eerste Bliscap* is contrasted with a much simpler development in the *Sevenste Bliscap*, where the play is centred upon the death of Mary and the Assumption. The story of Mary's tender relationship with the Disciples, her death and the greeting she receives when she comes into Heaven, without having died in a physical sense, is interwoven with a series of conspiracies by the Jews and by Lucifer and other devils against her.[16] This is no doubt a manifestation of the particular antipathy between her and evil forces which is traditional. In the end the Jews are blinded, and the devils can do nothing to affect her goodness and dignity.

These indications of the narratives of the two plays can be supplemented by a consideration of their dramatic texture. There is quite a range. Apart from the Debate, there are death scenes for Adam and Mary which embody their self-regard as well as revealing the attitude of their followers and supporters. It looks as though these scenes involved a separate location which would be the chamber of each of these characters. They are an occasion for praise and thanksgiving as well as an opportunity to prompt divine intercession. Underlying them both there is the iconography of dying, as well as the necessity to make preparation for death, a theme which is common in the Rhetoricians' plays, including *Elckerlijc* (translated into English as *Everyman*). In both plays the human characters are made to interrelate with supernatural ones repeatedly. Besides the divine figures, this includes angels and devils. Thus human circumstances are enveloped in broader implications of spiritual history and the sense of a cyclic mode is reinforced.

The sequences of praise and celebration, which are endemic to the Joys, show many variations, but rondeaux are common here: as for example one by the two Priests when the Angel has given Mary her name (*Eerste Bliscap*, ll. 1644-51); and Mary expresses her joy in a rondeau when the Angel foretells her high position in Heaven (*Sevenste Bliscap*, ll. 491-501).[17] It remains uncertain whether these items were sung, or whether they might perhaps have had some musical background or accompaniment. Perhaps linked with them are other musical elements in the performance. There are a number of *pausae* or *seletes* designated in the text, which were probably musical punctuation marks, underlining emotional moments, or perhaps marking a change of mood at the end of an episode.[18] The *Eerste Bliscap* has several specifically musical cues giving the choice of instrumental or vocal performance, or indeed of using both. Beuken lists seven of these, of which one follows the successful completion of Seth's mission (l. 738sd), and one is a prelude to God's despatch of the Angel to tell Anne of Mary's impending birth (l. 1460sd). In the latter, the effect was no doubt spectacular; *Hier singen ende spelen in den trone* (Here sing and play in the throne). As the previous action had been the quarrel, in which Joachim had been ejected from the Temple by the priests on the grounds of his unworthiness, the switch to God's commanding presence must have been dramatic. We should also note that this is a shift of location as attention moves across the acting area from the Temple to Heaven. A similar spectacular shift in location, which may well have been used for its implications as a miracle, is Saint John's translation from Ephesus to Mary's bedside: *Hier selen comen twee ingle met enen cleede ende omslaen Sint Janne ende tcleet sal scinen als een wolke. Ende soe bedect selen sine voeren vor Marien dore, oft anderssins, soet best es* (Here shall come two angels with a cloak and enfold St. John, and the cloak shall glitter as a cloud. And so wrapped they transport him to Mary's door, or otherwise, as seems fit, *Sevenste Bliscap*, l. 571sd).

The skillful manipulation of dramatic space and time is seen in the sequence in the *Sevenste Bliscap* when the Jews attack the Disciples who are carrying Mary's bier to burial (ll. 1356-1516, although here a lacuna prevents our knowing the end of the conflict). After Mary's death (l. 1250sd), God intervenes to instruct them to take her body to the Vale of Jehosophat. Praising the Lord, the Disciples take up the bier and, singing the anthem *Exit de Egypto*, they set off, presumably using the central acting space for their procession. The effect is enlarged by the instruction that the angels in heaven should also sing and play organs (l. 1397sd). The Jews are disturbed by the sound, and, determined to turn the singing to misery, they report their concern to their leader (*Potestaet*) while the Disciples continue their movement. He decides to surround the procession, in battle array (l. 1451). Though violence is threatened, there is a verbal battle as the Jews attempt to throw the corpse into the mud (l. 1496). But suddenly, and miraculously, a panic breaks out. The Jews cannot see, and their leader calls for water for his burning hand. Another's is as dry as the bark of a tree (ll. 1500-13). This sequence is rich with dramatic inventiveness and shows the dramatist making effective use of the staging resources at his disposal. It implies that, although there might have been some influence from the dynamics of procession, there was a deliberate intent to use dramatic devices, especially in the managing of the complex acting area, and the close interplay of words and action. This theatrical strain is in sharp contrast to the *Maastricht Passion* where most of the action depends very closely upon the scriptural narrative, and many speeches are also much more limited in dramatic range.

However, the *Maastricht Passion* does provide some useful information about the development and nature of cyclic form. Julius Zacher, the nineteenth-century editor, thought it was written out in the late fourteenth century, but that the composition was probably fifty years earlier.[19] The manuscript is rather fragmentary and the dialect somewhat inconsistent. Although there are some extensive continuous passages showing the style and scope of the dramatisation, there are a number of lacunae, and the play breaks off just as Judas and the Jews are about to arrest Christ (1500 lines in all). Thus we do not know how this cycle ended, but the beginning is sufficiently clear with a kind of stage direction saying that the Lord made the world and said 'Alpha and omega'. Because of the relatively early date proposed, the decision to start with the Creation is remarkable. However, the pace of the dramatisation is variable. Sometimes it is very rapid. By line 22 Lucifer has spoken, received support from Satan and been sent off to Hell; at line 40 the Lord, having created the world, addresses Adam, who is already feeling guilty and aware that he is naked. There follows a brief retrospect in which Adam blames Eve, and Eve the serpent; and the Expulsion is soon completed by a stage direction at line 90: *Hie driuet Cherubin, der engele, Adame ende Yuen usser dem paradyse mit einen swerde* (Here Cherubim, the angel, drives Adam and Eve out of Paradise with a sword). Such brevity may imply that here at least the presentation was more like a tableau with a few words added. A similar conclusion suggests itself with the 'Debate' of the Daughters which follows immediately upon the Expulsion. Only Truth and Mercy speak, and Truth soon prophesies the maid who will bear a child (l. 147).

With the Annunciation the dialogue becomes more expansive and it comprises more complex exchanges between the characters. This is especially so with the episode of the Kings with Herod and at the Epiphany. But the most extensive dramatic sequence with ample dialogue is that which runs from the worldliness of Mary Magdalene to the raising of Lazarus (ll. 776-1211). We should note here that the language of this Passion has some links with German, and it is quite probable that both the Kings and the Magdalene episodes were much influenced by the German tradition we have noted elsewhere. In the latter the action requires movement between at least two locations.

German influence is also suggested by the approach to music. There are a number of places where characters are instructed to sing. For Mary Magdalene in her phase of worldliness a lyric is provided in the text (ll. 796-807). This being so, it seems likely that there was also singing at the places in the text where speeches begin with a Latin scriptural phrase, usually ending with '&c'. This occurs when Gabriel addresses Mary and she replies (ll. 253, 257, 261, 265), and in the sequence when the Kings meet Herod. For the latter moment the text actually reads: *Hie kument die dri kunincge vor Herodes ende sengent* Vive rex in eternum (Here the three Kings come before Herod and they sing 'O king, live for ever', l. 403sd). Though the manuscript is a little inconsistent, it seems that these entries are music cues, and they may indicate the insertion of liturgical music in the German manner.

The presence of the figure called Ecclesia, who acts as a link or introduces in some episodes, suggests that the cycle was conceived as a whole, and that the author felt the need to shape his material in order to meet the didactic requirements of salvation history. Here Ecclesia introduces the prophets (ll. 200-34), and also speaks to Mary, praising her as a rose amongst women, and foreseeing her coronation in heaven (ll. 270-85). Thus the performance characteristics of this cycle fit in with other examples, and it is important not only for its intriguing link between Dutch and German, and also, because of its early date, for its significance in the wider context of European plays.

Spanish Cycles
We have noticed that the development of cyclic drama was relatively late in Spain, but there now seems little doubt that there were cycles in Catalonia in the fifteenth century, and that for the rest of Spain there are details which suggest that dramatic cycles were not unknown.[20] The deep and early interest in Corpus Christi may have been both an inhibiting factor, but also one which eventually facilitated the development of cyclic drama. From its inception there was a general interest in the processional aspects and this led to highly complex and sophisticated processions, with many different mimetic elements including costume, models of supernatural and human beings, scenic effects, stage machinery, sound and music, as well as *tableaux vivants*. This conscious use of processions and the development of skills associated with it may well have been a strong factor in the eventual emergence of cyclic form in Spain, but initially its emphasis upon spectacle rather than the spoken word may have delayed the development of cycle plays as such. The Corpus Christi processions certainly had significant social status, and, as in some other cultures, guilds, whether deriving from crafts or religious brotherhoods, were much involved in preparation, financing and presentation of the processions. In Catalonia, however, there is every chance that French influence would have been strong as the large-scale production of cycles gathered pace in the second half of the fifteenth century. It is there that the idea of cycle form is unmistakable.

The evidence for its development in Spain as a whole comes from the content of Corpus Christi processions, the methods of dramatic presentation, and the survival of some texts which show that the arrangement of material has deliberate design. The details come from Barcelona, Cervera, Gerona and Valencia in the east, together with the *Passion Catalane-Occitane*; and from Burgos, Seville, Toledo, and probably Madrid in the rest of Spain.[21]

The content of the processions sometimes contains a sequence of biblical episodes in such a way that the notion of sacred history is employed. At Seville there is an early record of Corpus Christi celebrations in 1282 (before the confirming Papal Bull *Transiturus*), and by 1532 the Chapter of the Cathedral set down that there would be representations on *castillos* (floats) of six episodes from Adam and Eve to the Judgement. Usually these were carried by about twelve men. It must also be noted that the subjects were not usually confined to biblical history.[22]

In Toledo, where again there was a very early Corpus Christi celebration in 1280, there is evidence for the years 1493 to 1510 of the recurring choice of particular biblical incidents on *carros*. Out of a total of thirty-three subjects on floats known for these years, twenty-one can be identified as showing episodes in the biblical cycle. Usually up to nine subjects were selected, and several were chosen quite often: Adam's Sin appeared in fourteen years; the Holy Fathers in twelve, and the Judgement in eight; while the Decolation of John the Baptist, the Resurrection and the *Pieta* each appeared on six occasions.[23] This observation accords with arrangements of cyclic material over a longer period than one coherent and complete performance, as we find in the *Passion d'Auvergne*, and the Dutch *Bliscapen*. Floats were being drawn through the streets in Valencia by 1373. For the years 1571-83 seventeen subjects are known, of which nine come from salvation history including the Sale of Joseph, Herod and the Three Kings, the Flight into Egypt, Emaus and Judgement.[24] The concept of the cycle in the *Passion Catalane-Occitane*, and the *Pasión* from Cervera, by contrast, was not manifested in the form of Corpus Christi processions as we shall see.

The details of processional presentation show a range of possibilities even in the limited number of medieval references which are available to us. The persistence of processional street drama into modern Spain gives us indications of the overwhelming strength, flexibility and popularity of this tradition. Whilst it is not at all demonstrable that the modern examples all have specific medieval predecessors, a few like the *Festa d'Elche* can be shown to be 'descendants', and the procession at Valencia, which today includes biblical figures, still makes use of some sixteenth-century waggons.[25] The methods of dramatic presentation in earlier times show that on the floats there was dialogue and movement on the *carros* at Toledo in 1425. At Seville in 1557, by which time a professional element had come into the performance, two waggons were used in conjunction for the Last Judgement, one for Paradise and one for Hell.[26] For the Samson episode in the *Codice de los autos viejos* two waggons were also used, with a stage linking them. The action, which accompanies a written text in this case, includes the pulling down of the columns of the temple, as in scripture, as the last moment of the play.[27]

On the eastern side of Spain, French practice seems to have been influential. In Valencia, however, there was a processional tradition. By 1425 there were stopping places where some sort of performance or perhaps demonstration was given. It is not thought that these stops were for more than a few minutes, but it seems likely that the settings were complex enough for some episodes that a multi-centred performing area was developed and that the practice of *decor simultané* was incorporated. Details available show that the staging was indeed ambitious, and included doves and fireworks as well stage hands to help with the ladder for the Deposition and with the Opening of the Tomb. Although some dialogue was introduced, many floats retained *tableaux vivants* for many years. The staging appears to have become so complex that the number of representations was reduced by the seventeenth century.[28]

The two Catalan Passions made use of several static scaffolds in the acting area. At Cervera, in 1534-45, the performance was mostly in the Church of Santa Maria, and was spread from Palm Sunday to Good Friday. For the Citació (Trial) there were five different locations with movement between. At the beginning of two days there is a procession of characters to take their place on their locations. The performance contained sung liturgical extracts, including passages to be sung by Christ as well as by his accusers. This may well have been reinforced by the ritual element in the sequence involving Mary Magdalene in which she holds up the crown of thorns and the nails to the audience. Nevertheless the dialogue at various passages in this cycle is highly complex and involves sustained argument and the portrayal of conflicting emotional states. Even though the fourteenth-century *Passion Catalane-Occitane* may be substantially Catalan, the French elements in the text are supported by the use of *maisons* for different characters, and these may have been given different designations at different points in the performance. The actual number of locations which might require a scaffold is formidable, and it reflects the characteristic requirements of many French Passions. These include the conventional places like Jerusalem, the temple, the house of Simon, a scaffold for the Jews, Pilate's palace, Calvary, hell and heaven, the tomb and Galilee. There is also a great deal of movement between them and for much of the text the dramaturgy appears to depend upon the facility afforded by having so many places.

When we consider the survivals of actual texts we find that those from the eastern side of Spain show the strongest signs of being composed and arranged to conform with cyclic design. The *Passion Catalane-Occitane* is a text consisting of a series of fragments, and it is quite possible, as the most recent editor suggests, that these were assembled from different provenances to make up the present form. Possibly the section dealing with the Resurrection (ll. 1531-2370) was added to that dealing with the narrative from the miracle of the blind man to the crucifixion (ll. 1-1494) after the injection of the lament of the Virgin (ll. 1495-1530).[29] Various aspects of the text suggest that it derives from a distinctly literary tradition, one closely related to the French analogues, with extensive passages of dialogue sustaining the stage effects. There are also a number of lyrical or narrative soliloquies with a high emotional level, in the account by Judas of his life before the Passion (ll. 433-594), the lament of the Virgin and that of Mary Magdalene (ll. 1977-2050).

As the surviving text from Cervera amounts to only 1979 lines, of which the *Passió* has 1012, the scope for cyclic development is somewhat limited. But the texts as assembled in the modern edition do cover events from Palm Sunday to the Deposition. There is distinctive characterisation for Judas and the Porter, and the part of Pilate is prominent. At Valencia where we have noted that the culture is more emphatically processional three texts have survived dealing with Adam (278 lines), Herod (593 lines) and the Assumption (816 lines). The text of the *Misteri del Rey Herodes* covers a considerable span of the biblical events surrounding the Nativity. The three Kings visit Herod, and worship Christ; Joseph is warned by the angel and he leaves with Mary and the Child; Herod orders the Slaughter of the Innocents, and the Mothers lament.

Finally, having mentioned some performance aspects above, we should also consider the collection known as *Codice de los autos viejos*. The purpose of the manuscript is obscure and one must regard its ninety-six plays (amounting to over 50,000 lines) as largely independent from one another.[30] There are a substantial number of biblical plays on Old and New Testament subjects, many in the range 400 to 500 lines. There is no doubt that these are dramatic texts, and three of them are attributed to specific authors. Some of the plays, known as *farsas*, are allegorical in concept: one (no. 9) deals with the Impeachment of Man and includes the World, the Flesh and the Devil, together with Conscience, Justice, and Mercy. Though there is some distinctive action in some of the plays, several of them, including no. 9, seem to put emphasis upon recitation rather than a fully evolved dramatic performance. Several prologues draw attention to this, but their very presence suggests that the effect upon an audience was a distinct consideration. But it must be that the existence of such a large collection of plays, probably emanating from Madrid, is evidence of a vigorous dramatic tradition however kaleidoscopic.

Notes

1. Vincenzo de Bartholomaeis [ed.], *Laude drammatiche e rappresentazioni sacre*, 3 vols., Firenze, 1942 [rpt. 1967], vol. III, p. 190.
2. For a contrasting text from Florence, see Nerida Newbigin, *Nuovo corpus di sacre rappresentazioni fiorentine del quattrocento, edite e inedite tratte da manoscritti coevi o ricontrollate su di essi*, Bologna, 1983, pp. 3-28.
3. Vincenzo de Bartholomaeis, *Origini della poesia drammatica italiana*, Torino, 1952 [2nd ed.], vol. III, p. 365, and Luigi Allegri, *Teatro e spettacolo nel Medioevo*, Bari, 1988, p. 245. See also William Tydeman [ed.], *The Medieval European Stage, 500–1550*, Cambridge, 2001, pp. 439-41.
4. Fabrizio Cruciani, *Teatro nel rinascimento: Roma 1450–1550*, Roma, 1983, pp. 263-5. The *Passione* was seen by Harnold von Harff on Holy Thursday in 1496. He seems to distinguish particularly the performance he saw, or parts of it, from models or images because he says: 'Uomini viventi figurano le flaggelazione ...' (living men represented the flagellation ...), p. 266.
5. De Bartholomaeis, *Origini*, p. 370.
6. Anna Cornagliotti, *La passione di Revello: Sacra rappresentazione quattrocentesca*, Torino, 1976, p. xiv. Marco Piccat, *Rappresentazioni popolari e feste in Revello nella metà del XV secolo*, Torino, 1986, p. 89, suggests that one important political concern was to sustain the Marquisate of Saluzzo.
7. Cornagliotti, *La passione di Revello*, p. xxx.
8. Allegri, *Teatro e spettacolo*, p. 248 and note 46.
9. Piccat, *Rappresentazioni*, pp. 66-7.
10. Allegri, *Teatro e spettacolo*, p. 245; Piccat, *Rappresentazioni*, p. 66. Cornagliotti, *La passione di Revello*, pp. 205-6, indicates separateness from the Italian tradition for this detail.
11. Some of the evidence also comprises changes in spelling: see W. H. Beuken [ed.], *Die Eerste Bliscap van Maria en Die Sevenste Bliscap van Onser Vrouwen*, Culemborg, 1973, pp. 14, 21-2, 40-1.
12. Beuken [ed.], *Eerste en Sevenste Bliscap*, pp. 46, 49.
13. P. Leendertz [ed.], *Middelnederlandsche dramatische poëzie*, Leiden, 1907, pp. 493-4. B. A. M. Ramakers, *Spelen en figuren: Toneelkunst en processiecultuur in Oudenaarde tussen Middeleeuwen en Moderne Tijd*, Amsterdam, 1996, p. 415, notes this absence.
14. Dirk De Vos, *Hans Memling: The Complete Works*, London, 1994, pp. 173-9. From before the fourteenth century there survive English rimes or jingles about the Five, as in 'I pray thee for thi ioyes fyue / Me to amende here in this liue' (see Carleton Fairchild Brown, *A Register of*

Middle English Religious and Didactic Verse, 2 vols., Oxford, 1916-20, vol. II, p. 162). The *York Plays* also have five: Incarnation, Nativity, Resurrection, Ascension, Assumption, Play 42, ll. 113-28.

15. For a detailed comparison of the use of this device between the *Eerste Bliscap* and English cycle plays, see Peter Meredith and Lynette R. Muir, 'The Trial in Heaven in the *Eerste Bliscap* and Other European Plays', *Dutch Crossing* (1984), n° 22, pp. 84-92.
16. These are in the *Sevenste Bliscap* at ll. 166-305, 991-1137, 1398-1516: 406 lines out of a total of 1733.
17. Beuken [ed.], *Eerste en Sevenste Bliscap*, pp. 47-8, lists sixteen rondeaux and comments on their functions.
18. See W. M. H. Hummelen, '"Pause" en "selete" in de *Bliscapen*', in: Hans van Dijk, Bart Ramakers *et al.*, *Spel en spektakel: Middeleeuws toneel in de Lage Landen*, Amsterdam, 2001, pp. 133-53 and 339-44.
19. Julius Zacher, 'Mittelniederländisches Osterspiel', *Zeitschrift für Deutsches Alterthum* 2 (1842), p. 302.
20. For a chronology showing the extent of dramatic activities, see Charlotte Stern, *The Medieval Theater in Castile*, Binghamton, 1996, pp. 246-55.
21. For documentation see Tydeman [ed.], *The Medieval European Stage*, pp. 569-77.
22. Jean Sentaurens, *Séville et le théâtre de la fin du moyen âge à la fin du XVIIe siècle*, Talence-Lille, 1984, pp. 190-3.
23. Carmen Torrojá Menéndez & Mariá Rivas Palá [eds.], *Teatro en Toledo en el siglo XV: 'Auto de la pasión' de Alonso del Campo*, Madrid, 1977, pp. 44-7; Stern, *Medieval Theater in Castille*, pp. 119-20.
24. Hermenegildo Corbató, *Los misterios del corpus de Valencia*, Berkeley, 1932, pp. 82-3.
25. Pamela M. King, 'Corpus Christi, Valencia', *METh* 15 (1993), pp. 103-10, and *Idem*, 'The *Festa d'Elx*: Civic Devotion, Display and Identity', in: Meg Twycross [ed.], *Festive Drama*, Cambridge, 1996, pp. 95-109. For performance parallels between medieval and modern see Rafael Portillo & Manuel J. Gomez Lara, 'Holy Week Performances of the Passion in Spain: Connections with Medieval European Drama', in: Twycross [ed.], *Festive Drama*, pp. 88-94.
26. Sentaurens, *Séville*, p. 190.
27. Léo Rouanet [ed.], *Collección de autos, farsas y coloquios del siglo XVI*, 4 vols., Madrid, 1901, l. 13.429sd.
28. Corbató, *Valencia*, pp. 82-4.
29. Aileen Ann Macdonald [ed.], *Passion catalane-occitane*, Genève, 1999, pp. 14, 263-5. The text contains the work of several scribes.

30. N. D. Shergold, *A History of the Spanish Stage: From Medieval Times until the End of the Seventeenth Century*, Oxford, 1967, pp. 89-92, 111.

Chapter Five
English Practice

Having looked at some characteristics of cycle drama and at ways in which it was projected on the continent against a background of long-term iconographic conventions, we can now return to the dynamics of the five English cycles to consider how each one of them, in its different ways, makes use of this concept. It will appear from most of them—and also from some cycles which are lost but about whom information concerning their design still survives—that the outline of a narrative from Creation to Doomsday was usually adopted in England, and often the choice of episodes was remarkably similar within this overall structure. However, the tactics of how this narrative was handled remain variable. In some, the sense of progression from one event to another is plain enough, but the facility of analepsis and prolepsis, and the technique of simultaneity are widely used, especially as the dramatic texture of each of the cycles, distinctive in itself, tends to vary within each. We also need to bear in mind that the content and the presentation of the cycles were constantly changing, and that these changes themselves bear witness to the strength of the genre. At the end of this chapter I shall also consider the work of John Bale whose three surviving plays show how the idea of a cycle could be modified polemically.

Each cycle comes to us now with an accompanying cluster of critical material, and this varies in relation to the preoccupations of the historical processes of scholarship by which each cycle has been transmitted. Thus the work on York has been much affected by the existence of a substantial amount of archive material which has raised interest and controversy about the practicalities of guild performance on pageant carts on the feast of Corpus Christi. It is of course easy to oversimplify such considerations, but at the same time it is clear that at Chester, where there survives a comparable amount of non-dramatic archive material, critical endeavour has been largely controlled by the circumstance that the extant texts are later than the period of performance, and by the political circumstances of performance and of the creation of the extant manuscripts. At Wakefield the question of the individuality of the Towneley Cycle has been much debated in the light of the extensive borrowings from York and of the extensive contribution of the Wakefield Master. For N-Town there has been much activity over its provenance and the nature and purpose of its manuscript in the absence of an established place of origin or clearly identifiable circumstances of performance. The Cornish cycle has its own critical issues in its different scope and style of performance. Quite often it is seen as an "other" to the English language cycles, definable largely by its differences from them. The effect of these dominating approaches has been to make it more difficult to compare like with like, and to see that as plays they have a great deal in common which, it is suggested here, is largely dependent upon the concept of the cyclic drama. In short I am concerned here with the English cycles from a consistent point of view in the light of their continental and iconographic analogues. At the same time it must be admitted that it is very difficult to ignore the fruits of investigation achieved by these means which have substantially increased our knowledge of these plays and their contexts.

The York Cycle

The extensive archival detail surviving from York has given us a rich picture of the possibilities of performance for this cycle. It is widely accepted that, in spite of the apparently inherent logistical difficulties, the cycle was performed on an annual basis at Corpus Christi for more than a century and a half. In the records it is striking that, even though it was not always achieved, there is a general assumption that the plays would be done annually, as for example *annuatim* and 'yerelie'.[1] This assumption survives in spite of the immensely complex operation of managing about fifty pageant carts and perhaps three hundred actors (allowing an average of six for each play) through narrow streets and twelve or more stations, for performances on a summer day from 4.30 a.m. until half an hour after midnight.[2] In spite of what looks like an immensely demanding schedule for performers and their supporters—imagine being 'crucified' twelve times in about seven hours—it is apparent from the text (usually known as the 'Register', and so henceforward) that a huge variety of dramatic styles was possible, and that there are many features which could be brought into play within the scope of the cycle.

The variety of dramatic styles indicates that the Register is not the work of one author. It was probably compiled for official purposes in the years 1463–77, though how this series of plays was dovetailed into one another (with a few rough edges) still presents us with some puzzles. If we take two contrasting sequences we find remarkable differences. The first six plays, comprising The Fall of the Angels, The Creation, The Creation of Adam and Eve, Adam and Eve in Eden, The Fall of Man, and The Expulsion, all have less than 200 lines each, and that in itself limits the complexity of the action. Material which might have been used for one long play has been deliberately presented in brief episodes, and in each there is a good deal of exposition of symbols, especially by Deus, who has a number of soliloquies. Some of what he says at the beginning touches upon overriding theological or metaphysical themes:

> I am gracyus and grete, God withoutyn begynnyng,
>   I am maker vnmade, all mighte es in me...   (1/1-2)
>
> Sen I am maker vnmade and most es of mighte,
>   And ay sall be endeles and noghte es but I...   (1/9-10)
>
> But onely the worthely warke of my wyll
>   In my sprete sall enspyre the mighte of me.   (1/17-18)[3]

In this first play the fall of Lucifer is shown. He begins with a kind of parody of the self-revelation by Deus:

> All the myrth that es made es markide in me!
> The bemes of my brighthode ar byrnande so bryghte,
> And I so semely in syghte myselfe now I se... (1/49-51)

But his actual fall could be described as dramatic, even sensational, in its suddenness. Though there is a hint of pride going before a fall, the psychological preparation is brief:

> I sall be lyke vnto hym that es hyeste on heghte.
> Owe, what I am derworth and defte - Owe! Dewes! All goes downe!
> My mighte and my mayne es all marrande -
> Helpe, felawes! In faythe I am fallande. (1/91-4)

This event could hardly have been more well known to the audience, and it must have been expected, even eagerly awaited. No doubt Lucifer's appearance would have been striking enough—there is plenty of archival evidence about his grotesque costume—and some kind of physical change as well an actual falling down could have been engineered on or from the pageant waggon. In short the dramatist here is relying upon expectation and the physical circumstances rather than upon complex linguistic effects. On the other hand the acts of creation are much simpler physically: the whole of the Creation (Play 2) is a speech by Deus as he brings forth the various elements in the world. Notably he begins with the repetition of the theme of his sublimity, this time with some Latin:

> *In altissimis habito,*
> In the heghest heuyn my hame haue I;
> *Eterne mentis et ego,*
> Withoutyn ende ay-lastandly. (2/1-4)

There is an emphasis upon the created world being in order and responding to his command (2/41-2, 65-6); as well as upon natural fertility (2/167).

With the introduction of human characters in Eden, and the Fall of Man, the stanzaic verse is developed for dialogue. Satan offers God's knowledge to Eve, and, in spite of her suspicions, she is persuaded on the grounds of being 'wirshipped' (5/55-6). Besides the intricacies of temptation and persuasion, the language is also enlarged emotionally to encompass the lament for a lost paradise:

> Gone ar my games withowten glee;
> Allas, in blisse kouthe we noght bee. (6/87-8)

But the narrative line in these initial plays remains simple and there are no problems about how to use the waggons to present the action: it usually has only one centre.

By contrast, in the sequence of the Passion (from 26 The Conspiracy to 38 The Resurrection) the plays are rather longer: up to 548 lines for Pilate's Wife's Dream, and most of them well over 300. The number of speaking parts also tends to be much larger, often more than ten, and the action of these plays frequently requires more than one location. We have to be aware that the individual waggon might have to be adapted in some way, or the movements on and off it might have to be carefully arranged to allow for changes in location. There are also developments in the poetic style and in the management of complex stanzaic forms to accommodate extremes of feeling, and to portray interactive dialogue between several speakers. It is of course possible that this more ambitious dramatic style is the result of the work of a different dramatic poet from the composer or composers of the initial plays in the cycle: but without venturing to decide on that, we can still see that the cyclic form embraces such a variety.

Let us now look more closely at Play 30, The Dream of Pilate's Wife, Play 32, The Remorse of Judas, and Play 37, The Harrowing of Hell. The first, a colourful play rich in incidents, was inserted into the cycle at some time between 1415, when Roger Burton, the Common Clerk, compiled a list of the plays, and the writing of the Register after 1463. His note, including a brief summary, gives no hint of much of the action: it says only that Annas and Cayphas, Pilate and Christ were present, and that four Jews accused Christ.[4] The expansion to the extant form of the text is interesting in itself since it sheds light on the dynamics of performance and the process by which a segment of the Passion story, some of it scriptural and some not, was translated into a performance script and played for a number of years. The later Common Clerk, John Clerke, who sat at the first station at Holy Trinity church on the day of performance for many years in the sixteenth century, has not indicated on the manuscript that the players he witnessed departed substantially from the fifteenth-century text of this particular play.[5]

This text now comprises the following incidents. Pilate boasts of his descent and family, and is encouraged by his wife Percula over his impressive 'genologie'. They kiss, and after the Beadle hints that the day is in decline, she leaves, having convivially drunk wine with Pilate. Pilate lies down to sleep (30/1-148). This first sequence, which has rich comic possibilities in its overripe style, seems to be largely the invention of the York dramatist. In a separate location the wife herself goes to bed, where she is visited by the Devil in a dream. He reveals to the audience his increasing doubts that Christ is God's Son, as expressed earlier in The Temptation (22/49-52), and he is now fearful that to engineer Christ's death would be disastrous for his own interests. He frightens Percula into sending her son to warn Pilate against killing Christ.[6] The son, however, says he will wait till morning (30/149-96). Starting from a third location Annas and Cayphas have Christ bound and, accompanied by soldiers, they take him to Pilate's palace (30/196-232). Pilate is awakened and sets up his court to hear the charges against Christ. His son intervenes bringing his wife's warning, but this is disregarded as being allegedly the result of Christ's witchcraft. Annas and Cayphas (not the four Jews of Burton's list) make their accusations. Pilate speaks to Christ, asking him about his reported aspiration to a kingdom, and Christ's four-line reply, his only speech in the play, is an echo of the brevity of his scriptural reply at which Pilate is said to have marvelled (Matthew 27:11-14). As further accusations indicate that Christ comes from Galilee, Pilate, again following the scriptural account, shifts responsibility and sends him to Herod. Pilate, at the end of the play looks for vengeance (30/233-548).

The presence of these three locations in the text means that either the dramatist must have envisaged some movement on and off the waggon and some playing away from it, or, if the play was strictly confined to the waggon, the players would have had to accept very cramped playing spaces. One must suppose that here, as well as in a considerable number of other plays such as The Entry to Jerusalem (Play 25), that there was movement around three centres and that this would have been part of the spectacle. In fact here, and elsewhere, the action comprises interlocking times and locations, for when the son says he will sleep before delivering his mother's message, he brings to an end one sequence of time in order to allow the next, the conference between Annas and Cayphas, to develop.[7]

The process we are describing has thus both physical and temporal aspects, but it also has implications for the presentation of narrative which are inherent in cyclic form. In the York Cycle, with its many separated individual plays, there is plenty of scope for narrative elements to be started anew, or to be repeated, or to be recalled in some way. It has been pointed out that the York Cycle is rather special in its use of short scenes. This may well have been an effect of the intense rivalry between the trade guilds responsible for each episode. The interrelationship between plays and guilds is a matter of current debate. Though the plays were important to the status of the guilds, it has been argued effectively that the establishment of the plays also contributed to guild development.[8] Like many other episodes in the Passion sequence, Play 30 gives examples of the multivalent narrative, enabling a series of approaches to be made to it. The effect is not that there is one narrative, but a series of versions of it which are appropriate to the circumstances of various individual episodes. Even though the York Cycle is arranged in the separate episodes we are considering, it is also apparent that similar processes of narration are discernible in N-Town, a cycle using a different form of presentation for individual plays, especially in the Passion sequence. And further, the continental cycles which are not usually divided into separate segments like York, show parallel techniques in the manipulation of narrative.

The recall of past events comes in two contrasted ways in Play 30. The Beadle, a rather efficient, but slightly officious character, introduces a reminiscence of Christ's entry into Jerusalem on Palm Sunday. It had been elaborately presented an hour or so before in Play 25. His recall is now worked neatly into the action. When he is sent by Pilate to fetch Christ into court, he recalls the crowd singing 'Osanna', and he himself does reverence to Christ now (30/312-5). One of the soldiers reports him for this, and under Pilate's enquiry he describes how the crowd had sung, calling Christ the son of David. He explains to Pilate that 'Osanna' means 'oure sauiour and soverayne thou saue vs we praye' (30/350). This exegesis is grudgingly confirmed by Cayphas who nevertheless warns that the Beadle is subversive.

The second cluster of references comes a few seconds later when Cayphas and Annas make allegations against Christ at the bar of Pilate's court. Their two voices press hard upon one another. Annas complains of Christ's abuse of the Sabbath (30/418), and of his raising of Lazarus (30/447-9), while Cayphas seeks to add outrage by references to healing the lame, deaf and dumb (30/441-2) and Christ's claim that he will save the people (30/464).The dramatic irony here invites the audience both to recall the earlier events, and also to interpret them quite differently from the way intended by the two prelates. Both of them come to a climax with a politically sensitive recapitulation: Annas distorts Christ's advice about the tribute to Caesar (30/462), and Cayphas reports that Christ aspires to his own kingdom (30/466). In these two sequences it is apparent that the references to past events are used to guide audience response to the current circumstances: they are working upon previously established information. These lead to Pilate's bafflement about what to do about the case against Christ—like the audience, he does not trust the prelates—and his decision to pass the buck to Herod.

Besides the interlinking of narrative between plays, there are also arise a number of themes to which reference is constantly made. One of these is treachery. Indeed it is more than a theme since it becomes a main spring of the action in the betrayal of Christ by Judas. Because there are also a number of tyrants, or at least morally dubious characters, who make boastful speeches to bolster up their rather shaky worldly authority, we find plenty of references in their words to their anticipation of treachery as they try to impose their authority. This is not confined to the York Cycle, nor indeed to English practice. Characters like Herod, Pilate and Caesar are generally overbearing and scenes in which they appear frequently begin with their boast. This is a particularly good device for gaining attention in the open air when the pageant cart has arrived and the play must now make its mark. In Play 30 Pilate makes a threat against treachery at the end of the first stanza of his first speech, and it is apparent that, later in the play, the prelates use the alleged treachery of Christ to the civil authorities as one of the means of causing anxiety to Pilate.

In turning to the text of Play 32, The Remorse of Judas, we find that it appears to have undergone some revision, and difficulties of lineation together with the marginal annotations of John Clerke indicate that it was perhaps not as stable as some of the others.[9] The two main episodes show Annas and Cayphas continuing to malign Christ to Pilate, and the attempt by Judas to escape from his sense of guilt over the betrayal of Christ. It concludes with a brief exchange between Pilate and a Knight, to which we shall return. From the point of view of staging, this is a much simpler play. Judas does speak apart before approaching Pilate and the prelates, but this could be easily managed on or off the waggon. Much of the material here is not scriptural and shows how the dramatist(s) sought to evolve a coherent episode from what could be found. It was felt to be important, no doubt, to show the despair of Judas which is scriptural (Matthew 27:3-8), but the development, particularly of the idea of treachery goes well beyond what was inherent in scripture. To some extent the first part of the play is a repeat of part of Play 30. Again we have a boast from Pilate who warns his listeners against unruly behaviour; this time it is embellished with claims about his outstanding physical beauty, a feature which makes one wonder whether the performers made a point of making him hideous to behold. Again the prelates, this time with corroboration from the Soldiers, raise the accusations against Christ concerning miracles, the misuse of the sabbath, his claim to be God's Son, to be able to re-build the Temple in three days, and his aspiration to be King of the Jews. The truth is that this part of the play adds nothing to the narrative: Christ is absent, and a brief reference is made to the examination by Herod which is currently going on. Possibly the play about Judas had to be enlarged to reach some minimum size necessary at this point in the cycle, and the option chosen was to exploit the value of repetition and recapitulation of known details we have been considering. However, treachery again becomes a main concern here: both Annas and Cayphas refer to Christ as a traitor (32/42, 112, and 64). At the point when these details reach a climax the attention is shifted to the troubled Judas who admits that he 'betrayed hym traytourly / With a false trayne' (32/138-9). As he admits his treachery to Pilate and the prelates, they merely endorse it and Pilate mocks his change of heart. Judas even promises to be faithful to Pilate himself if he will release Christ, but this excites a bitter rebuke from Pilate:

> Fynde the faithfull? A, foule mot the falle
>   Or thou come in oure companye,
> For by Mahoundes bloode thou wolde selle vs all.   (32/224-6)

Cayphas twists the knife by saying that Judas had claimed Christ was a traitor and that they had all agreed it was so, and he adds grimly that the bargain had a purpose: 'We bought hym for he schulde be spilte' (32/247). Unlike Pilate, Cayphas pursues an unyielding hostility to Christ and is uncompromising towards Judas. When the latter curses them, Cayphas again charges Judas with treachery, but by now the concept has been worked up to have ironic meaning, and the audience would have understood his accusation differently:

> Whe, fye on the, traytoure attaynte, at this tyde,
> Of treasoune thou tyxste hym that triste the for trewe. (32/288-9)

Judas calls for vengeance, but such is his despair that he leaves with the intention of killing himself (32/316-7). From a second list, also recorded by Burton in 1415, it is apparent that at one time there followed a separate episode of The Hanging of Judas, but probably because of difficulties between the guilds, this had disappeared by the time of the Register.[10]

This brings us to the brief episode at the end of Play 32 concerning the Knight (*Armiger*): it is itself an act of treachery, and so a fitting conclusion. When Judas has left in despair, Pilate decides that the thirty pieces are the price of blood and that they shall be used to buy a plot of land to be used for the burial of pilgrims, and 'othere false felons'. He is immediately approached by the Knight who wants to raise a mortgage of thirty pieces on his own field. Pilate apparently agrees, implicitly the money of Judas might be used, and he asks to see the deeds. When the Knight hands them over, Pilate takes possession of them and drives him away empty handed (32/338-67). Thus the dramatist exploits two aspects of Pilate's character: his uncertainty about accepting the prelates' accusations against Christ, and his selfish assertion of his own authority, especially when he thinks it is being threatened. The York author's differentiation between Pilate and the prelates is one of the ways in which the Passion sequence is made dramatically interesting.[11]

The Harrowing of Hell (Play 37) is one of the six plays which were borrowed wholly or in part by the compilers of the Towneley Cycle. The York Register shows that it was still being performed in much the same form in the mid-sixteenth century as John Clerke's annotations are rather limited in scope.[12] The subject of Christ's descent into hell between his burial and the Resurrection, is not scriptural, but it appears in the Apostles' Creed, which makes it an article of faith; and indeed it was much elaborated in exegetical works, especially by Aquinas, as well in works more concerned with narrative such as the *Gospel of Nicodemus,* and the poetic Passions such as *Cursor Mundi.*[13] In the cyclic structure it takes its place as part of the continuous strife between God and the Devil, as well as being presented here as reflecting the overall promise of God for the Redemption of man. In his initial speech Christ sets up this and other thematic links, as well as recalling earlier episodes in the cycle: creation, the sufferings of Christ, the trickery of the Devil, and the apple are all adumbrated. Indeed the first stanza is remarkably compressed:

> Manne on molde, be meke to me,
>   And haue thy maker in thi mynde,
> And thynke howe I haue tholid for the
>   With pereles paynes for to be pyned.
> The forward of my fadir free
>   Haue I fulfillid, as folke may fynde,
> Therfore aboute nowe woll I bee
>   That I haue bought for to vnbynde.
>   The feende thame wanne with trayne
>   Thurgh frewte of erthely foode;
>   I haue thame getyn agayne
>   Thurgh bying with my bloode.   (37/1-12)

In the following stanza he makes the further point that while the fall of Lucifer cannot be reversed, mankind shall be restored to everlasting bliss (37/13-16). In his third stanza he explains that prophecies will be fulfilled, and he foresees his Resurrection and his coming at the Last Judgement: 'Thus is my fadris will' (37/36). From a dramatic point of view, this play brings to an end the long earthly narrative of the Passion, and, by stepping aside, physically out of this world, and intellectually into the transcendental structure of Christian history, it opens up a separate range of feelings.

One of the most significant aspects of this episode cyclically considered is that its supernatural setting facilitates the figurative linking with other elements in the cycle. Christ here, as the second Adam, releases the souls of the virtuous from limbo. It is Adam who first sees the 'glorious gleme' which heralds Christ's approach to hell (37/42), and he twice draws attention to the four thousand and six hundred years he has spent awaiting this moment (37/39, 354). When Christ has triumphed over Satan, he speaks to Adam and the others, and instructs Michael to lead them into Paradise. It is Adam who brings in the final song in the play: *Laus tibi cum gloria*.

The main action of the play, however, is the confrontation between Satan and Christ. It has been pointed out by Kolve that this contest of power is found in most versions of the Harrowing, and he notes that the battle metaphor is extended in the York version.[14] This may not be denied, but there is also a sharp verbal battle between them here. Even the subordinate First Devil notices that the attack is being made by the Jew that Judas sold (37/147). When Satan appears in response to the urgent summons of his followers, he is quick to call Christ a traitor, and he also recalls Judas, as well as the devils' failure to keep Lazarus in hell once they had got him there (37/161-2). Thus the familiar technique of recapitulation is brought into the argument. During the subsequent exchange in which Satan tries to belittle Christ by showing that he lived like a simple knave, a number of subjects from elsewhere in the cyclic history are evoked by Satan. He argues legalistically by claiming that Christ cannot release the souls because Solomon had argued that no one could come out of hell, and Job had supported this. Satan comforts himself by saying that he will always have some inmates. Christ agrees that these include Cain, Judas, Achitophel, Datan and Abiron, 'tyrantis euerilkone' (37/305-12), but he claims, anticipating the future, that after his Resurrection, he will come to judge them. Although Satan thinks that the judgement will give him more opportunity of extending his power, Christ counters by showing that Satan will be held fast, and that he will not be allowed to wander about the world. Satan then falls quickly into hell pit in a way reminiscent of Lucifer's fall in Play 1, as noted above. Thus this particular play contributes much to the sense of the cyclic form by its place in the battle between God and the Devil, and it brings into focus a number of events scattered through the history of salvation which can here be made to function in the destruction of Satan and the apocalyptic release of the good souls in limbo into Paradise. In the York Cycle at least the devils are never the same again: it is notable, for example, that in the Judgement Play they have a minor role comprising only twelve lines of text.[15]

These discussions of three plays in the Passion sequence, which have some similarities, but which are not necessarily the work of the same author, give an indication of the way the devices of retrospect and anticipation (often in the form of traditional biblical prophecies) were integrated into the texture of individual plays. A broader look at the cycle indicates a high incidence of them, especially retrospect. The function of such items is to make constant reference to parts of the narrative which are essential to belief and doctrine, but dramatically they offer further advantages, especially within groups of plays in similar mode. Such items are not new information: they are mostly well known incidents. They help to identify the role of individual characters, good and bad, and they assist in the management of the plot of individual plays and also more comprehensively. Thus in The Expulsion, Cain and Abel and The Building of the Ark there is recall of the Tree of Knowledge, Lucifer's Fall and Adam and Eve (6/9, 7/18-22, 8/6-16). We have noted how they frequently overlap in the Passion sequence. After it the audience are reminded of the crucifixion by the Centurion in the Resurrection (38/37-42) and Mary Magdalene in The Appearance (39/11-2), a play which also shows a visual recall by Christ's display of his wounds. In the next play the Pilgrims give a graphic and extended account of Christ's suffering and the surrounding events. The passage (40/17-66) is introduced in such a way that the retrospect is made self-conscious: 'But take vs tome [leisure] at this tyme to talke of sume tales' (l. 17). The richly alliterative verse summons a mood of affective piety:

> For all the swette that he swete with swyngis thei hym swang,
>   And raffe hym full rewfully with rapes on a rode.
> Than heuyd thei hym highly on hight for to hang,
>   Withouten misse of this man, thus mensked thai his mode

> That euere has bene trewest in trastyng. (40/41-5)

This poetic mode is extended further into the group of plays associated with the Virgin which form an extended sequence before the Judgement (Plays 44-6).[16] In The Assumption Thomas begins by 'waylyng and weping' (40/1) and he gives a comprehensive account of the cruelty shown to Christ, and of the contrast between the true teaching and the treachery surrounding it: 'Thai toke hym with treasoune, that turtill of treuthe' (45/32).

As for anticipation of coming events, Abraham reveals God's instructions over his family (10/12-24), and at the Last Supper Christ marks the establishment of the New Law, and warns Peter and others of the dangers to come from the Devil (27/116-9). In the following play in the Garden of Gethsemane Peter anticipates the Crucifixion (28/25-6), and in the Harrowing Christ speaks of his Resurrection to come, according to the prophecies (37/25-32).

Prophecies for the Nativity which are perhaps more conventional and more widespread in the cycles come through the Doctour as an extended prologue to The Annunciation and Visitation (12/1-132). After Christ's birth Mary refers to the prophecy of Balaam concerning the star and a maiden (14/99-105). The Kings in the presence of Herod and on their way to Bethlehem pick up the same theme and add several more witnesses (16/209-34). Traditionally John the Baptist came at the end of the line of prophets, but in Play 21 he specifically denies being one and claims that his role is that of a forerunner, and a voice crying in the wilderness (21/15-28). His function is to persuade the people to make themselves ready for the Lord to come to them. Christ marks his Baptism by John as a turning point in the destruction of the dragon's power, and the salvation of mankind (21/157-61).

These techniques of reduplication, forward and backward, are especially appropriate and necessary in a cycle performed in short episodes, where the dynamics of the performance depend upon the arrival and departure of the waggons at the designated stations. Rosemary Woolf's comment that the English cycles do not have essentially one plot is thus borne out by the abiding sense that approaches are made to the central material again and again from different viewpoints and with different objectives on the part of author and performers.[17] Nevertheless the central material, together with many of the subordinate interpretations of it, are the same substantially and this process of touching upon it in a variety of ways is in fact a way of enhancing it, however diversely.

Recent work on the cycle adds two further considerations which evidence the concept of cyclicity by pointing to significant unifying factors. We have already noted that all four English cycles have distinct and particularly local linguistic characteristics. In the case of Towneley, for instance, it is demonstrable that the episodes borrowed from York show systematic differences from the original York versions. But beyond this, there is in York the selection of words, the register, which is used consistently from play to play. It appears that within the York Cycle itself there is a remarkable homogeneity of language, showing itself in the use of the same vocabulary and restricted choice of words even though the plays were written over a long period and by different authors. Beadle describes this as 'the repetition from one play to the next of a significant proportion of the total vocabulary' and he argues that the authors shared a 'tacit assumption of stylistic restraint'.[18] I take this to mean that those who added to and revised existing material were conscious that they must fit in with what already existed.

Alexandra Johnston's discussion of language points similarly towards unity. Her interpretation of the dramatic realisation foregrounds language.[19] This is in part a theological approach depending upon the concept of the Word. Her discussion of Christ's presence as a speaker and preacher of truth in the Ministry in contrast with his silence in most of the Passion sequences implies much of the spirituality we have noticed in Chapter One. She pointedly suggests that his role as the Image of Pity is replaced by that of Christ the Victor.

The concern for overall design also manifests itself in a number of scenes which are mainly representations of events on a supernatural plane rather than being a reflection of earthly history. Such a distinction is admittedly a rather modern one, but it may be perceived that although some of these do have biblical authority, the deployment is the result of thinking about the unfolding of events in a different way. It takes into account the supernatural forces which were believed to overshadow all human affairs. The plays which most reflect this are The Fall of the Angels (Play 1), The Transfiguration (Play 23), The Last Supper (Play 27), The Harrowing of Hell (Play 37), Christ's Appearance to Mary Magdalene (Play 39), The Ascension (Play 42), Pentecost (Play 43), The Assumption of the Virgin (Play 45), and The Last Judgement (Play 47). It is largely in these scenes that the eschatological issues are made explicit in terms of the conflict with the Devil, the divinity of God and of Christ, the special role of the Virgin and of Mary Magdalene, and the vision of heaven to which the Christian must aspire. Some of these are well supported in scripture, and the playwright's task is to bring out the larger issues, as in the Last Supper and the Appearance to Mary Magdalene, but The Transfiguration and the Assumption are especially interesting because they show an exchange between people on earth and those beyond. In the former, three disciples are allowed a vision of Christ in the presence of Elijah and Moses. The stage effects are spectacular. Christ appears in white clothing with his face shining like the sun (23/97-8), and clouds come down as God speaks from within (23/168sd).[20] In the Assumption, which we have noted contains Thomas's substantial recall of Christ's suffering, he is granted a vision of the Virgin who tells him that she is now on her way to join her Son in heaven. By tradition, her sinless state meant that she could not die like others, but she was carried into heaven at the end of her physical life. She gives Thomas her girdle and instructs him to recount the truth of what he has seen to the other disciples. Again the play is spectacular, not only in the management of this miraculous event, but also in the inclusion of music (unusually the Register actually gives the musical notation for this play). The poetic language is ambitious: several stanzas are concatenated, and there are several passages of anaphora extending over many lines (45/105-13, 114-7, 132-43, 170-8, 196-9, 200-8) as the exultation rises. The effect must have been very striking and it seems likely that this kind of presentation was particularly aimed at the stimulation of devotion.

For the Last Judgement there survives among the Mercers' pageant documents an indenture of 1433 giving details of costumes and properties and some particulars of the physical construction of the waggon. The latter makes it clear that there was lifting gear for God (Christ) when he was to be raised up to heaven, and painted clouds and beams of light.[21] It might appear that physical action is limited, but there is both spectacle and the recall of events at this climatic moment. Most of the performances of this last episode must have been in twilight or darkness, necessitating the use of artificial light. Deus (= Father) initially summarizes Creation, the disobedience of Man, the Fall, the Incarnation, the Crucifixion and the Harrowing of Hell (47/9-40). He repeats his regret over the sinful ways of Man, echoing his initial speech at the Building of the Ark (47/6-8 and 8/13-16). After the trumpets are blown by the angels, the Good and Bad Souls describe their lives. God (= Christ) descends to sit in judgement (no doubt by means of the lifting gear). In delivering sentence he finds the Bad Souls guilty of his own suffering at the Crucifixion, which he details (47/245-76). At this point we may be aware that the two aspects of the dramatization of Deus, God the Father and God the Son, bring out and recall differing recollections of the past. The main purpose of his teaching is to encourage the Works of Mercy. The Bad Souls are sent to sit by Satan. In the final stanza he brings the world to an end, relating it to his own anticipation:

> Nowe is fulfillid all my forthoght,
> For endid is all erthely thyng. (47/373-4)

His last movement is to return to heaven accompanied by the music of the angels (47/380sd).

The Chester Cycle

The Chester Cycle may now follow York in that it covers the narrative from Creation to Doomsday, but there are many significant differences which in themselves help to reveal the ways in which the idea of a cycle of plays could be developed and used in England. Many of the incidents are ostensibly the same in the two cycles, but the structure of Chester shows some quite different objectives. There are only twenty-four plays, and in general the plays tend to be rather longer than most of those at York. Often episodes are combined because there is a thematic link between them. It does not appear that the cycle was performed annually and many decisions had presumably to be made when each performance was proposed. From evidence of varying degrees of certainty, it appears that there may have been performances in 1532, 1540, 1546, 1550, 1554, 1561, 1567, 1568, 1572, and 1575.[22]

First though, we need to recollect that the surviving texts of the full cycle are all later than 1591, and that they have differences between them which are of importance in showing how the cycle was conceived and used. In spite of a tradition to the contrary, it now seems that the common ancestor of these late manuscripts, usually known as the 'Regynall', was actually evolved at some point after 1521. There is little doubt that some form of the cycle goes back as least as far as 1422, but in the absence of convincing textual evidence, its nature remains very shadowy and we can only be sure from records of the existence of a few individual episodes in the fifteenth century. These indicate that the earlier performances were on Corpus Christi, but it seems likely that this earlier form of the cycle was given only once on that day at a location by St. John's Church.[23] This means that, though there may have been a procession, the performance itself at one time was not truly processional.

The changes which came about in the early sixteenth century certainly indicate that the idea of the cycle was held very firmly in mind. It seems that a major re-writing was undertaken and that the author or authors were able to incorporate many aspects which were consistently sustained throughout the cycle. Indeed, instead of a sense that the cycle was just an accumulation of episodes there are many devices and themes which suggest that specific programmes were being pursued. This persistence with objectives may also account for the two most striking innovations: the shift of the occasion of performance to Whitsun and the division of the performance into three days. It has been suggested that a practical reason for the division was that the pageant carts—called 'carriages' at Chester—could be re-used on each of the three days, and indeed that is what certainly happened to the pageant shared by the Innkeepers in 1531.[24] But we should look further into the wider issues which this change embodied, and these lie in the religious objectives which the reviser-author set himself. Reference will be made to such a person in the singular in what follows, but it has to be admitted that we are dealing only with the probability that the changes were made by one writer. This probability is enhanced, however, by the fact that Chester of all the English cycles shows by far the greatest homogeneity in its versification.[25] There is also the fact that the *Stanzaic Life of Christ*, a text of local provenance was used as a source in many places in the cycle.[26]

Though there is something to be said about the earlier, now submerged version of the cycle and how it might have contributed to the revised form, the relatively late date of the latter means that there is a possibility that its author could also have drawn on other models from elsewhere. This would include the French *Passions* which were generated in quantity from about 1450, as well as the by now well-established and famous cycles at Coventry and York. There are a few specific similarities to other texts, as in the Doctors play, which is similar to the York, Coventry and Towneley versions,[27] but the essence of the situation is that the author seems to have been master in his own house. His major debt, it would seem, was to the circumstance that, by the time he came to effect his revision, the idea of a cycle was familiar and accessible. He could have been influenced by the previous Chester Cycle, by the successful English models, and by material from the Continent. Indeed, the ways in which he sets about concentrating and unifying his work seems to bear this out strongly. It is as though the text he created embodied a sense of what a cycle should or could be like, and how it could be put to use.

The unity of the Chester Cycle, however, is a matter for delicate critical judgement. Even though it has been described as 'self-consciously unified',[28] it would be incautious to attribute to the whole text one single objective which dominated every aspect of it. This would seem indeed to contradict the very flexibility which lies at the heart of the cyclic form. Some of the evidence which may be derived from the manuscripts puts it beyond doubt that there was more than one version of several episodes, and though the surviving full-text manuscripts are undoubtedly copied from the same precursor, the individual scribes made choices among alternatives in a number of places. The most striking is perhaps the conflation of the Passion into the play called 'The Trial and Flagellation' in one manuscript, whereas the others treat this as two separate plays (Plays 16 and 16A). Similarly in Noah (Play 3) an episode of forty-seven lines containing the sending out of the raven and dove occurs in only one manuscript.[29] The existence of such alternatives in the lost exemplar gives us a clue to its nature. It seems likely that it was a collection from which, in a year when it was decided that there was to be a performance, a selection would be made. This implies that the cycle had no single state, but that it was always a notional entity, constantly changing and constantly changeable. In the light of this we should rather be prepared to tolerate a series of unifying forces which interact intermittently. This occurs partly because of the long, complex and phased narrative which provides a linear structure to the cycles. It shows itself most strongly in the different considerations which frequently underlie Old Testament episodes as distinct from those dealing with Christ's Ministry, and then his Passion. The sequence after the Passion leading to Judgement forms another sequence which tends to generate its own dynamic, and we shall see that this is particularly marked in the Chester example. It is especially interesting that the Continental cycles embody markedly different approaches to this last sector.

The shift from Corpus Christi to Whitsun is only a matter of a few days, but it may have had pressing religious reasons, and there is also the interesting fact that the Continental cycles were not always tied to Corpus Christi, especially in France. There has indeed been a persistent thread in studies of the cycle suggesting direct French influence, but this has proved difficult to substantiate beyond the fact that Chester has a number of episodes not found in other English cycles, but traceable in various French examples.[30] The feast of Corpus Christi, as we have noted, placed its major emphasis upon celebrating the Eucharist. Whitsun, by contrast, was designed to mark the coming of the Holy Ghost, and it was also closely related to Trinity Sunday. It is apparent that the surviving Chester texts bear witness to these as major preoccupations, and the conclusion must be that this goes back, through the lost exemplar, to concerns at the time of the revising author at the beginning of the sixteenth century.

We can also notice that the division into three days may have had a meaningful purpose which relates both to doctrine and to the success of performance. The days would certainly be less crammed than Corpus Christi at York. The act of dividing is itself part of the semiotics of the play. It enables a new start to be made, as well as including emphatic endings. These are deliberate doctrinal and aesthetic choices. Anyone who has produced a five-act play will have asked themselves when to break for the interval: it is not just a matter of when the kettle boils. At Chester the breaks were made after the Magi's Gifts (Play 9), and after the Harrowing of Hell (Play 17). The narrative points here are thus at the point where the Old Testament preparation has reached the moment when Christ has become human, the prophecies being fulfilled and the Child manifest; and after the Harrowing of Hell when Christ has triumphed over Satan and released those in Limbo. Aesthetically these breaks are pleasing because of the honouring of the Child (9/191-9), and the completion of Christ's mission, celebrated 'with great solempnite' by singing *Te Deum Laudamus* in a processional exit (17/276sd).[31] The decision to break at these points may also have been related, as Mills suggests, to the Trinity in that the first day shows largely the work of God the Father; the second presents the mission of the Son; and the third shows the work of the Holy Ghost.[32] However the exploration of themes below indicates that we should not see such a categorisation too rigidly, and it is not made explicit in the doctrinal exposition within the cycle.

The intermittency noted above can indeed be traced in the ways the topics of the Trinity, the coming of the Holy Ghost and Christ's divinity are managed through the cycle. There is always the dimension of tactics as well as of strategy. References to the Trinity and to Christ's divinity are thus found throughout the cycle whereas those to the coming of the Holy Ghost are notable more from The Last Supper (Play 15) onwards. The initial speech by Deus quickly introduces his tripartite nature, drawing attention to the essential, doctrinal indivisibility:

> I ame the tryall of the Trenitye
> which never shalbe twyninge.   (1/9-10)

The theme is repeated later in the same play (1/28-31, 66-7), before Lucifer makes his challenge. When Deus returns to the scene to punish him, there is a musical cue for the anthem *Gloria tibi Trinitas*. In the Play of Abraham the Trinity is evoked by the Preco who introduces it 'in wirshippe of the Trynitie', and at the climactic moment when Abraham is about to strike Isaac he calls for the blessing of the Trinity upon his son, thus pointing up the theme of obedience to which we shall return later (4/10 and 335-6).

The Trinity is acknowledged in both the Shepherds Play and the Magi's Gifts (7/337, 9/117), and its occurrences there particularly point up the interplay of eternal time and human time in the cycle. In both cases, historically speaking, the knowledge of the

Son is still a kind of anachronism, and yet the references to the Trinity take their place alongside other preternatural aspects. These are perhaps more in evidence in the concluding plays of the cycle which embody the shift from human history to the supernatural world and the world to come. There is reference to the Trinity in Pentecost (Play 21), but in that play the role of the Holy Ghost is naturally more prominent. The Play of Antichrist, however, shows the last assault of the forces of evil, and the concept of the Trinity is dramatically and doctrinally of key significance. The play is built on the device of making Antichrist ape many of the actions and attributes of the true Messiah, including death on behalf of his followers and a resurrection. By his pretence of true religion he gains control of human faith. When this is challenged by Enoch and Elias they find him ignorant of the Trinity:

Antichristus	What ys the Trinitye for to saye?	
Helias	Three persons, as thou leeve may,	
	in on godhead in feere.	(23/491-3)

But the concept is beyond the understanding of Antichrist:

Owt on you, theeves! What sayen yee?
Wyll you have on God and three?   (23/498-9)

The craftiness of Antichrist is ultimately exposed by Enoch and Elias by means of the holy bread (of the Eucharist?) which is made potent by the invocation of the Trinity (23/569-76): it is this which shows up the devilish nature of the followers of Antichrist. This play shows a remarkable interweaving of historical characters and preternatural ones. Such devices do happen elsewhere in the cycles, notably in the York Transfiguration (Play 23).

The emphasis upon the Trinity is interwoven with the interest in the role of the Holy Ghost in later parts of the cycle, notably in the promise of his coming given by Christ at the Last Supper ('to abyde with you evermore' 15/245), in the Ascension (20/65-8), and at Pentecost itself where there is a spectacular stage direction in Latin showing that Deus sends the Holy Ghost in the form of fire upon the Apostles while the attendant angels sing the antiphon

Accipite Spiritum Sanctum (21/238). Besides his role as a comforter, the Holy Ghost is presented as a means by which the faith may be increased throughout the world. The Angel says:

> But look yee goe anon in hye
> into all the world by and by,
> and also preach the fayth meekelye
> and his workes so deare. (21/243-6)

This emphasizes a persistent thread in the cycle in the concern with preaching and the dissemination of the faith. It is striking, for example, that at the end of Play 7, the Shepherds give up their sheep and turn to holy work, Tertius Pastor specifically 'to preach this thinge in every place' (7/659). The role of the Expositor is perhaps another aspect of this, as we shall see. It is also in line that the cycle ends with speeches from each of the Evangelists in the final moments of the Judgement play.

Alongside the didactic emphasis upon the Trinity and the Holy Ghost, there is also a persistent strategy to emphasise that Christ really is the Son of God. In other English cycles this theme is often raised by means of the ignorance of Satan, especially in the Temptation of Christ which in N-Town is made a critical test. In Chester, Satan mentions the issue several times, and though the audience must be in no doubt who Christ is, Satan will not admit Christ's divinity in so many words. Nevertheless after Christ has overcome the temptations Satan eloquently laments the strength of his opponent:

> Owt, alas! That me is woe
> For found I never so great a foe. (12/141-2)

As the cycle develops the question of Christ as Son of God is dramatised in a number of ways. On the one hand the Ministry, through miracles such as the blind man and the raising of Lazarus (13/229 and 13/477), brings out the beneficent power of his divinity: indeed the collocation of these two scriptural episodes in the same play is a characteristic structural device. But the true identity of the Son of God is used more ironically in a number of episodes in the Passion sequence. While the Janitor, who gives the ass and foal to the disciples before the entry to Jerusalem, is generally sympathetic to Christ and the miracles (14/173-6), Annas and Cayphas use the idea as a means of tormenting him, as in scripture (16/298). However, when the evil First Thief on the cross uses the title ironically, he is reproved by the good Second (16A/305-12). After the miracle of the healing of the sight of Longeus, both Joseph (of Aramathea) and Nicodemus repeatedly assert that Christ is God's Son (16A/412, 417, 461, 470). In the Harrowing Christ himself refers to it at the moment when the gates of hell are forced open (17/155), and the Thief acknowledges that in retrospect he had seen this at the Crucifixion (17/262). After the Resurrection, which immediately follows the Harrowing, the Soldiers guarding the tomb are overcome by Christ's rising, and they regret what has been done to him. Tertius Miles admits that 'this ys Goddes Sonne verey' (18/227) and sets off to inform Cayphas. The principal theme of the Play of Antichrist is that he is a false version of Christ who seeks to impose himself by false signs of his supposed divinity. It is no surprise therefore that in the face of the challenge by Enoch and Elias, he makes the palpably false claim that 'Goddes Sonne I am, from him sent' (23/514). By the Judgement, however, the reassertion is no longer needed. Deus initially appears in the form of the Trinity, the scriptural quotation which appears in one manuscript recalling alpha and omega the first line of the first pageant. Later in the play, as required by a stage direction, Jesus descends as though in a cloud to carry out Judgement as the Son of God (24/356sd).

The function of these emphases may be largely didactic as the cycle seems concerned to strengthen faith by its presentation of the nature of the divinity. If the date of the remodelling of the cycle was indeed some time after 1521, this would have happened when the appearance of Protestant views and questioning made the reassertion of traditional beliefs all the more important. Remodelling, perhaps in defence of traditional belief also occurred in the 1530s at Coventry and Norwich. There is also a concern for moral values in the treatment of the sinful ways of mankind, and this is supplemented especially in the Old Testament episodes by repeated reference to the necessity of obedience. This is a primary theme for the plays about Noah, Abraham and Moses. In the Noah play especially the sinfulness of man is contrasted with Noah's willing compliance with God's wishes. It is perhaps expressed most strongly by the Expositor (Doctor in some texts):

> Such obedyence grante us, O lord,
> ever to thy moste holye worde;
> that in the same wee may accorde
> as this Abraham was beyne. (4/476-9)

The episode of Balaam and Balack which forms part of the Moses Play (Play 5) deals obliquely with obedience. Here again the collocation of two episodes, one concerning Moses and one Balaam, seems pointed. Balaam, the prophet is ordered by the tyrannical King Balack to curse the people, but prompted by Deus, and by the innocent obedience of his talking ass, he refuses to do so. In one version of the play this leads to a Prophets' sequence which foretells the Incarnation and the Passion.[33]

The presence of the Expositor, or sometimes the Doctor, in a number of plays further supports the sense that the author of the cycle felt there was something to be taught. Besides helping to explain the move from Corpus Christi to Whitsun, this in itself opens up for the modern reader or watcher the whole question of the relationship between didacticism and entertainment. They were not as polarized in the cycles as we might suppose today, and in many cases they were tempered by a sense of worship. This last element is somewhat muted in the Chester Cycle, though it must be admitted that the presence of a good deal of liturgical music, as we have noticed above, must have pushed the consciousness of the audience towards a participation in the customary modes of worship. Nevertheless the Expositor does present important issues in certain plays. He appears in Plays 4, 5, 6, 12, and 22, and he is made to interrupt the action at times as well as to point up significances at the beginning and end of the play or episode.

At the end of Play 12, for example, he puts a moral gloss on the story of the woman taken in adultery, indicating that Christ was intent on showing how the accusers were themselves guilty (12/297-312). He may be used to point up thematic unity as he does in Play 4 where he is used to link the Eucharist, Baptism and the Passion of Christ.[34] In this he enunciates the important theme of the replacement of the Old Law, as shown in the Old Testament, by the New Law depending upon Christ's sacrament. At the end of one version of Play 5 he is used to mark the end of the day's performance, but this may be specific to the last performance in 1575 only, when the cycle was shown over four days.

The cyclic devices of recapitulation and anticipation noted at York are rather more strictly employed in the Chester Cycle, suggesting that an overall design was intended, though once again this cannot be said to be comprehensive. Nevertheless it looks as though the episode of Adam's dream in Play 2 is a sophisticated dramatic device. This play is remarkable for the sequence of episodes which it combines. We see the completion of the Creation, including that of Adam and Eve, the Temptation and Fall, and, after time moves on, Cain's murder of Abel. At the point when God creates Eve during Adam's sleep (2/138-40), Adam is granted a vision which he recounts later, after the Fall and before Abel's murder. Framed in this skillful manipulation of the time sequence, Adam is made to give an account of how his spirit was transported to heaven. There he learned that God would come from heaven to slay the Devil, and that he would redeem Adam's blood, lost through his sin, and establish a new law. Destruction by water and fire would come because of man's sins, and God would come in the flesh to judge the good and bad (2/439-72). He tells this explicitly as a warning to his children, Cain and Abel, who apparently are listening, but it was no doubt also intended for the audience. This vision, by its nature, could not be in the bible, but Lumiansky and Mills note that the basis for it can be found in Augustine and Peter Comestor.[35] The fact that it is not original does not prevent its being an important structural device for the cycle.

There is much anticipation throughout the cycle of the principal events of the narrative including the Nativity, the Crucifixion and the Redemption, the Resurrection, and the Judgement: more than is convenient to detail here. We may however note that the defeat of Satan anticipated by Adam is also foreshadowed by Mary at the Nativity (6/519). Play 9, The Magi's Gifts, is especially rich in recapitulation and prophecy, perhaps because this was the play which ended the first day of performance. The moment when the Magi worship the Child with their gifts concentrates upon his attributes and it is here that Tertius Rex twice links the coming Passion with the defeat of Satan (9/168-83). At the moment of the Ascension, Christ appears red with the blood of the crucifixion, in what must have been a spectacular scene, with musical accompaniment for the physical ascent. In response to a question about his body and clothing he shows how the blood is a sign of his triumph in a speech which begins with his conquest of the Devil:

> For the devill and his powere
> that mankynd brought in great dangere.
> Through death one crosse and blood so clere
> I have made them all myne.   (20/125-8)

In discussing the Antichrist play (Play 23) we have noted how it is strategically placed before the Judgement. There it partly anticipates the doom which is to come, and thematically it also recalls the Fall of Lucifer, and the Resurrection and the Ascension.[36] The key figures opposing the Antichrist are Enoch and Elias. Their role is anticipated in the Harrowing of Hell where they are the last prophets to speak. Neither of them had suffered a normal death, as they recall, and Elias prophesies that it is ordained that they will fight against the Antichrist and, after they are slain by him, they will rise again in three days (17/229-52). As a means of explaining and anticipating their later role they are also built into Play 22, Antichrist's Prophets. John the Evangelist recounts how he saw a vision as he lay 'upon my maisters brest sleepinge'. In heaven he saw God commend two witnesses who would combat false faiths and confront the beast; they would be slain and rise again (22/173-212). John's account is in general terms and does not name the witnesses, but it is followed by the Expositor who makes the identification of Enoch and Elias, and also of the beast as the Antichrist, who will have the Devil's power (22/221-60). Thus the Expositor, having a special function for the revising author is to point up essential structural devices which both enrich the doctrinal content, and also to make more effective the dramatic management of the subject matter of the cycle. There seems little doubt that the author was constructing over a long span, and that this grasp of teleological aspects of his material is fundamental to the way in which he thinks about the cycle.[37]

But alongside these structural considerations we ought to take particular note of some of the ways in which the dramatist develops individual episodes, irrespective of the interlocking global significances we have been discussing. To some extent the dramatic quality of the cycle has been underestimated, and its style has been seen as plain, or even primitive. But in fact, given the kinds of strategy suggested here, it seems apparent that the author was acutely aware of his objectives and wrote skillfully so as to approach them. To illustrate the flexibility and variety of the dramatic techniques we shall look at Noah (Play 3), The Shepherds (Play 7) and Judgement (Play 24).

The Play of Noah derives from a strong biblical story and follows it closely. Though the whole play is written in one or other of the two main Chester stanza forms, the versification accommodates several changes of pace.[38] Initially God's stanzas have long lines and proceed at an emphatic pace which involves a sense of threat (3/1-40). When Noah and his sons begin their construction of the Ark the pace quickens:

Sem	Father, I am allreadye bowne:
	an axe I have, by my crowne,
	as sharpe as any in all thys towne
	for to goe therto. (3/53-6)

The list of animals in the ark runs excitedly, with interwoven alliteration:

> Here are cockes, kytes, crowes,
> rookes, ravens, many rowes,
> duckes, curlewes, whoever knowes,
> eychone in his kynde.   (3/185-8)

The dialogue sets up sharp opposition between Noe and his Wife: one stanza runs as follows:

Noe	Wife, in this vessell we shalbe kepte;
	my children and thou, I would in yee lepte.
Wife	In fayth, Noe, I had as leeve thou slepte.
	For all thy Frenyshe fare,
	I will not doe after thy reade.
Noe	Good wiffe, do nowe as I thee bydd.
Wife	By Christe, not or I see more neede,
	though thou stand all daye and stare. (3/97-104)

Finally God's promise is presented with graceful simplicity characteristic of much in the cycle:

> Where clowdes in the welkyn bynne,
> that ylke bowe shalbe seene,
> in tokeninge that my wrath and teene
> shall never thus wroken bee.(3/317-20)

This play also provides some ambitious staging. The Ark is built in front of the audience, with mast, yard, topcastle and bowsprit. The flood overwhelms the Gossips, as Noe and his family watch from within the ark. The stowing of the animals within the ark requires a special device (explained at 3/160sd): Noe and his family go into the ark and from within they point to pictures of the animals which are painted on boards around the ark, and name them, making sure that the names correspond with the pictures. This stage direction is in all the manuscripts, in Latin in one case. At the end, after the flood has receded, a rainbow appears. In the one text which has Noe send out the raven and dove, there is to be a second dove with an olive branch in its mouth which comes by means of rope from the mast into Noe's hands.[39] Apparently the difficulties of managing these technical devices on a pageant waggon were overcome.

The Chester Shepherds Play offers us valuable material for comparison with its treatment in the other English cycles. It shares many things with them including the portrayal of hardship in contemporary life, comic tone, feasting, the interpretation of the Angels' song, the visit to the Christ-Child to whom simple gifts are presented.[40] Whilst not all these characteristics are present in the other four versions, it is apparent that dramatic conventions had been built up, and no doubt if there was revision at Chester these would have been available to the author. There does seem to be an absence of exegetical material such as was used in many other parts of the cycles, a circumstance which might make it more likely that the dramatist would draw upon specifically dramatic conventions.

The Chester play presents us with Primus Pastor who is proud of his skills in healing his flock. When he is joined by the other two Shepherds (three were conventional in the plays, perhaps analogous to the three Magi) they set about a feast of enormous proportions. The staging is somewhat difficult to particularize, but the list of comestibles is so long that it must have been comic to have the shepherds produce so many items from pockets and bags. If however the items were mimed, there still seems to be plenty of scope for this comic presentation of gluttony and extravagance. When their bellies are full, they summon Trowle, their boy who is minding the sheep, with his 'good dog Dottynolle'. He turns out to be a very tough character, and one with a grudge. When they offer him food, he complains that 'the grubbes theron do creepe'. He challenges his masters to wrestle—'But warre lest your golyons glent' [testicles disappear]—and in the ensuing bouts throws all three. However, when the Angel delivers his message, it is Trowle who takes the lead in interpreting it, and in leading his masters:

> To Bethlem take wee the waye,
> for with you I thinke to wende

> that prince of peace for to praye
> heaven to have at our ende. (7/472-5)

His gift to the Christ-Child is 'a payre of my wyves ould hose' and it seems that his tangy subversiveness is part of his strength. He decides to retire to a hermitage to pray, and he is given the last words in the play, a farewell addressed to the audience. There have been attempts to allegorize this play, the feast being seen as a midwinter ceremony, and the healing skills an anticipation of Christ's miracles, but these are less convincing than the view that the conventions associated with Shepherds imaged fallen mankind who was transformed by the joy of the Nativity.

The Judgement reveals a large number of individual decisions by the playwright even though many of them may be traced to biblical or patristic sources. He seems to be working towards the completion of a design which is embedded in many different ways throughout the cycle. Thus the initial reference to *alpha et omega* recalls the first play and reminds the audience of the beginning and the end. Judgement of individual sinners has already taken place and the revival for judgement day is to confirm this. It is used by the dramatist to point up two important didactic points. Dramatically the two groups of saved and damned souls recall the dance of death—unusual in the English plays, but found on the Continent—by the way in which their sins and their virtues are related to their particular rank in society. But the structure of the sins confessed by both groups is concentrated on several of the Deadly Sins, notably Avarice, Gluttony, Pride and Lechery, and upon the Works of Mercy which require that the plight of others be remedied.

The traditional spectacle of the scene is exploited here in several ways. Initially Deus stresses the Trinity and perhaps he represents it visually, but when it comes to the judgement there is a spectacular descent by Christ to perform it. This is partly anticipated by the angels who from the beginning of the play exhibit the instruments of the Passion. After the trumpets, the rising of the dead and the laments of the damned, the instruments are again mentioned in the stage direction which requires that Christ descends as though in a cloud (24/356sd). Christ recalls the creation and the sinfulness of man and in doing so repeatedly refers to the shedding of his blood. The climax comes when he shows that the blood is still flowing:

> Behould nowe, all men! Looke on mee
> and see my blood freshe owt flee
> that I bleede on roode-tree
> for your salvatyon. (24/425-9)

The spectacle was no doubt heightened by the presence of two devils who put the case against the damned. They describe the torments to come, and Demon Secundus has a sack, presumably of misdeeds, which he can hardly carry. As the devils lead off the damned, the Evangelists remind the audience that each of them had given timely warnings about salvation and now the cycle ends with a grim sense that the time has passed. Thus the didactic intention which we have identified in many places in the cycle is fulfilled in a way which is pointedly disturbing, and remarkably different from the triumph in the last moments of the York Cycle.[41]

The Towneley Cycle

Though the Towneley Cycle contains in the Second Shepherds Play, the most famous and possibly the most frequently performed of all the individual English mystery-play episodes, it is the most fragmented of the five English cycles, and it now presents to us significant problems about its location, its date and its mode of performance. Moreover the manuscript, which has recently been dated as late as the reign of Queen Mary,[42] has been damaged in a number of ways, even though it was copied almost entirely by one scribe and prepared in such a way as to suggest that it was meant to be read rather than performed. Nevertheless this codex serves to enlarge considerably our perception of the potentialities of cyclic form, and in spite of the many inherent uncertainties, it is a manifestation of the sense that cyclic drama was a desirable model for a number of different reasons.

To follow up some of the points already made about English practice, we find that this cycle uses extensively the techniques of recapitulation and prophecy, having regard to its own specific emphasis, and there is again a persistent concern with the nature of the divinity, including the concept of the Trinity. It shows an abiding interest in the nature of the law, especially in a critique of lawyers, who are seen, in several plays, as oppressive exploiters. In some contrast to the other cycles, however, it places particular and sustained emphasis upon evil characters, human and supernatural, to the extent that for some sequences, including the Passion, the study of evil becomes a structural principle. Unlike some other cycles, Towneley contains no Expositor figure to act either as a link between episodes, or as a means of introducing doctrine. Instead there is more frequently a reliance upon soliloquy in character addressed directly to the audience.

In broad terms the cycle follows the English practice of a narrative from Creation to Judgement, but there are some unusual episodes, notably those dealing with Jacob and Isaac (Plays 5 and 6). There are also some striking omissions in that there is no Nativity play, and the episodes showing Christ's Ministry are not present except for the atypical Lazarus play (Play 31) which, as it happens, was added to the codex by the main scribe anomalously, after the Judgement. The layout of the manuscript is continuous, there being no spaces usually between the end of one play and the beginning of the next: thus the scribe did not have the recourse of inserting this episode in its normal place, and instead he added it as though it were an afterthought or it came late to him. It is a feature of the continuous layout that textual discontinuities or omissions have become all the more apparent.

Critical evaluation of the cycle has to take account of the highly individualised, and somewhat idiosyncratic contribution of the dramatic poet who was first called the Wakefield Master by C. M. Gayley in 1907, a nomination which has stuck and which has subsequently become inescapable for considering the nature of this cycle.[43] The extent of his contribution is controversial. On the one hand a rough guide may be found in the presence in several plays of his characteristic thirteen-line stanza whose rime scheme is *ababababcdddc*.[44] The accompanying table gives an indication of the distribution. It indicates that he wrote five whole plays (Plays 3, 12, 13, 16 and 21) and made extensive interpolations into two others (Plays 22 and 30). He contributed on a smaller scale to Plays 20, 24 and 31; and a further four (Plays 2, 23, 27 and 29) show signs of minor insertions. But his characteristic forms of expression, especially in the presence of demotic speech, and in his strong sense of the power of language have led most critics to widen the attribution beyond the occurrence of the stanza. This is strongly supported by the presence of his work alongside that of others in a number of plays, suggesting that at times he went carefully to work to expand or combine, rather than undertaking a wholesale rewrite.

But because the cycle as a whole does not show uniformly these signs of his work, we can look through the existing text for indications of a version or an original which is now lost but which may have been current before the present codex was assembled. Unfortunately there is no external documentary evidence for the existence of a cycle at Wakefield before a hint in 1556, and even at that late date it is difficult to be sure what was actually done in the streets, if indeed the play was actually performed continuously in the form that we find in the manuscript. The best support for an earlier cycle comes from the fact that some five plays bear a very close relationship to their counterparts in the York Cycle to the extent that they follow the wording verbatim for considerable stretches. These are Play 8: Pharaoh (York 11), Play 18: Doctors (York 20), Play 25: The Harrowing of Hell (York 37), Play 26: Resurrection (York 38), and Play 30: Judgement (York 48). We have seen that the York manuscript was created at some point in the years 1463-77, and these Towneley borrowings contain some indications that the York texts from which they were taken pre-dates the York Register, drawing presumably on originals which must have been modified before the Register itself was copied.⁴⁵

From the information already noted it is clear that the peculiar emphases in this text give some rise to difficulties about a coherent interpretation of the cycle as a whole, but evidence from other cycles suggests that the latter may rarely be found in any case. In fact Chester is rather special in having such a strong sense of re-creation at the beginning of the sixteenth century. Here at Wakefield the process of revision is more difficult to rationalize, even though the result of the Wakefield Master's innovations in particular is to create some piquant drama and to give us a sense that his plays are the work of an experienced, perceptive and indeed learned dramatist. We should notice that on linguistic grounds the proposed date for his intervention is presumed to be no earlier than the last quarter of the fifteenth century, and perhaps a bit later. Thus if he was revising an earlier original or a collection of plays, he would have had other pre-existing models from places other than Wakefield to guide him, or to excite his challenge. In this connection it is perhaps significant that some of his contributions are in plays which have been borrowed from York, indicating that he must have been familiar with the cyclic form there. But at the same time some of his plays are substituted for existing episodes, whilst others show a departure from the norm, especially the innovations in the two Shepherds plays (Plays 13 and 14), as we shall see.

Reference to the table gives an idea of the plays which do not suggest any apparent intervention by the Wakefield Master, and it is most probably here that we shall find some clues about the nature of the cycle before his re-working. Avoiding the borrowings from York for a moment, we can see a number of different dramatic strategies at work. The Creation and the Annunciation both begin with an Introduction by Deus, and these set up a teleological presentation of his concern for the world. In the former he begins with his eternal nature and he introduces the concept of the

Table
Towneley Cycle: York Plays; Wakefield Master by stanzas

#	Play	3	4	5	6	7	8
1	Creation						
2	Abel					W2?	
3	Noe		WM				
4	Abraham						
5	Isaac						
6	Jacob						
7	Prophets						
8	Pharaoh	Y11					
9	Caesar						
10	Annunciation						
11	Elizabeth						
12	1 Pastorum		WM				
13	2 Pastorum		WM				
14	Magi						
15	Flight						
16	Herod		WM				Herod, Soldiers
17	Purification						
18	Doctors	Y20					
19	Baptist						
20	Conspiracy				W6 + 4?		Pilate, Soldiers
21	Coliphizacio		WM				Cay, Ann ,Torts
22	Flagellacio	Y34 part +		W27			Pilate, Torturers
23	Crucifixion					W1?	
24	Talentorum	? (from lost Y?)			W9		Pilate, Torturers
25	Harrowing	Y37					
26	Resurrection	Y38					
27	Peregrini					W1	
28	Thomas						
29	Ascension					W2?	
30	Judicium	Y48 +		W40			Devils, Tutivillus
31	Lazarus				W7?		[Lazarus' solil.]
32	Judas						
		4 + 2 [+ 1]	5	2	+	3 +	4

Column 3:   Plays completely or partially borrowed from *York*.
Column 4:   Plays entirely in the WM stanzas
Columns 5-7:   Count of interpolated WM stanzas
Column 8:   Characters speaking WM stanzas (selected)

[Principal Source: Stevens and Cawley.]

Trinity (1/1-6). The Annunciation, which marks the most positive divine intervention in human history, begins with his retrospect to Adam's fall from Paradise and his promise of the 'oil of mercy' which had been previously mentioned by Noah (3/66), and Jacob (6/44). He refers to the release of souls from hell, and foretells the Incarnation, Passion and Resurrection. In a haunting quatrain he brings together Adam and Christ, Eve and Mary, and the Tree of Knowledge and the Cross:

> For reson wyll that ther be thre -
> A man, a madyn, and a tre.
> Man for man, tre for tre,
> Madyn for madyn; thus shal it be.   (10/31-4)

It is a striking decision to use Deus as an expositor rather than the human teachers of some other cycles.

There is always a temptation to identify verse forms as signatures of authorship, but these have proved to be somewhat unreliable. Nevertheless the reliance upon couplets in these two plays, taken with the overall management of the narrative, is suggestive of an underlying continuity. We have already noted that the Isaac and Jacob episodes are unique to Towneley, and we can extend this further to the treatment of Abraham (Play 4). There is some interconnection between versions of this episode in the other English cycles, but the Towneley stands very much on its own. It eschews typological links between Isaac and Christ found in other versions such as the Buffeting (the blindfold for Isaac) and the Crucifixion (Isaac bound to the altar), and Isaac as a lamb.[46] Instead the play begins with another historical retrospect referring to Adam, Cain, Noah and Lot, and presents an emotional sequence between Abraham and Isaac:

> Isaac   What have I done?
> Abraham   Truly, none ill.
> Isaac   And shall be slayn?
> Abraham   So have I het.
> Isaac   Syr, what may help?
> Abraham   Certys, no skill.

Isaac	I ask mercy.
Abraham	That may not let.
Isaac	When I am dede and closed in clay,
	Who shall then be youre son? (4/189-194)

The play of John the Baptist (Play 19) is another where the possibility of an older independent Towneley Cycle arises. It is placed at the beginning of the Passion, and its location there may be a significant adoption of a tradition in which the Baptism was seen as the first stage in the Passion sequence and one which omitted the Ministry.[47] The contents and wording of the play differ markedly from York, and it contains a notable iconic moment in the stage direction 'Here let him give to him the lamb of God' (19/212sd, translated). This must have been a stage property, perhaps a picture or a symbolic animal. Probably this device was imitated by John Bale in his version of the mystery cycles discussed below. The vision of the Lamb which takes away the sins of the world brings a lyrical passage of adoration from John. He ends this scene with a warning to the audience.

In one other respect there is a significant hint of the earlier cycle, but it is one which the Wakefield Master seems to have taken over and elaborated. It is apparent, from the plays which are written entirely in his stanza, and from those in which it appears in part, that he was especially interested in the presentation of tyrants and devils. This is managed in a number of ways: by boasts and threats, by oaths, by cruel actions and by overweening and selfish treatment of subordinates. However, the concept of these types of character can be found in parts of the cycle which do not bear his characteristic mark and which almost certainly pre-date his contribution. The Pharaoh Play (Play 8), for example, is one of the group borrowed from York, which it follows metrically. In the first stanza Pharaoh proclaims his authority:

> All Egypt is myne awne,
> To leede aftyr my law;
> I wold my myght were knowne
> And honoryd, as hyt awe.   (8/9-12)

The subsequent action shows his persecution of the Jews and the challenge by Moses, inspired by Deus. As Pharaoh responds to this he calls repeatedly on the evil powers, and occasionally upon 'Mahowne', as in:

> Heyf up youre hertys unto Mahowne!
> He will be nere us in oure nede.
> Help, the raggyd dwyll, we drowne! (8/410-2)[48]

Both these passages are in the York version and cannot therefore be the original work of the Wakefield Master (unless of course we suppose that York borrowed him before 1463).

The Towneley Cycle is the only one to have a complete play on Caesar Augustus (Play 9), another example of the preoccupation with tyrants. It bears no sign of the work of the Wakefield Master, and is not derived from York. He rants, in a different stanza from that used by Pharaoh, and seeks to dominate his subordinates:

> And looke ye grefe me noght,
> For if ye do, it shall be boght,
> I swere you by Mahowne!
> I wote well if ye knew me oght,
> To slo you all how lytyll I roght,
> Ston-styll ye wold syt downe. (9/7-12)

He repeats his call on Mahowne a number of times and, on hearing of a threat from a child, he orders a search and imposes a tax. In these actions he is an anticipation of Herod, just as the conflict between Pharaoh and Moses is an anticipation of the clash between Sathan and Christ in the Harrowing of Hell. The main point to note, however, is that it appears that the author was able to draw upon conventional ways of showing a tyrant who opposes Christ and good men, and that this dramatic motif could be seized upon by the Wakefield Master. The latter extensively develops evil tyrants in Herod and Pilate.

For Herod he may have drawn some ideas from the Play of the Magi (Play 14) where Herod rants in a six-line stanza and invokes Mahowne many times. The Play of Herod the Great (Play 16) is entirely the work of the Wakefield Master and it deals substantially with the Slaughter of the Innocents. The character of Herod was traditionally violent and a byword for wrath. In pictorial representations, such as a roof boss in Norwich cathedral, he is shown with his legs crossed to express his anger. This convention was followed in the drama, as in the famous stage direction in the Shearmen and Taylors' play at Coventry where he rages on the pageant and in the street also.[49] For the Wakefield Master he was a tyrannical figure and, instead of having Herod begin the play with a rant, he has Nuncius build up a picture of him in which his tyrannical behaviour is partly a parody of divine power:

> He is kyng of kyngys,
> Kyndly I knowe,
> Chefe lord of lordyngys
> Chefe leder of law. (16/53-6)

This is followed by an alliterated list of the countries he rules, a list which may be associated with Satan's temptation of Christ on the mountain top. Herod has power of life and death and when he hears about the Infant from the Magi he immediately begins to threaten. Taking advice from his Consultus, in an echo of the Caesar play, he orders a search for evidence. He readily agrees, when advised, to undertake the Slaughter of the Innocents. The killing is done onstage and a report is made to Herod, who rejoices that his heart is at ease because he has 'shed so mekyll blode' (16/679). He becomes a grotesque figure, celebrating an imaginary triumph:

> A, Mahowne,
> So light is my saull
> That all of sugar is my gall!
> I may do what I shall,
> And bere up my crowne. (16/685-9)

As with the quarrel over the imaginary sheep in the First Shepherds Play, the audience knew otherwise: for all his verbal fluency, the Wakefield Master was able to rely upon the silence of irony.

His interest in tyrants is also manifested in the development of Pilate which runs through several plays in the Passion sequence. Pilate follows Herod in his many references to Mahowne and to devils, and he is the central figure of a group of persecuting characters including Cayphas, Soldiers and Torturers. Arnold Williams in his pioneering study of the Towneley Pilate noted a shift of responsibility for the events of the Passion away from Sathan towards him, and showed that in contrast to a number of other versions of his character, as in York Play 33, he reveals no sympathy for Christ. He notes that whilst other versions show Pilate as inconsistent, Towneley portrays him as unwaveringly evil.[50] The Wakefield Master elaborated his presence by writing the initial boast in the Conspiracy (20/1-77), and in having him send Malchus and Soldiers to arrest Christ (20/624-75). The continuing cruelty is shown by the first part of the Scourging in which he builds up the threat to Christ:

> Syrs, looke ye take good hede
> His cloysse ye spoyll hym fro;
> Ye gar his body blede,
> And bett hym blak and bloo.   (22/157-60)

In the Crucifixion Play, Pilate plays but a small role, the main business being the cruelty of the Torturers and the laments of Christ, Mary and John, but it is significant that there is one stanza by the Wakefield Master given to Pilate in which he again threatens violence to those who disobey him (23/9-21). Expansions to the part of Pilate are also found in the Dicing (Play 24) where he begins the play with a thirteen-line stanza in Latin, followed by three macaronic ones. The effect of the Latin presumably was to recall familiar phrases of worship for a medieval audience, but that being so, it must also have been blasphemous:

> Myghty lord of all
> *Me Cesar magnificavit.*[51]
> Downe on knees ye fall!
> Greate god *me sanctificavit,*
> Me to obey over all
> *Regi reliquo quasi David.*   (24/40-5)

His self-identification with David is particularly sharp in the light of Christ's descent from him. At the end of this play there is another brief intervention in the Wakefield Master's stanza given to the Third Torturer who condemns dicing and vows to live a holy life. Pilate, who unusually has himself taken part in the game and pulled rank when he was losing to secure the seamless garment of Christ for himself, ends by blessing the Torturers. Pilate's last appearance in the cycle is in the Resurrection, which is one of the plays borrowed from York. In this case the opening sequence comprising Pilate's boast is not found in the York version as we now have it: nor is it in the thirteen-line stanza. However, the tone is so like Pilate's other boasts in Towneley that it is plausibly attributed to the Wakefield Master.[52]

Summing up Pilate's appearances in the Passion sequence it seems that his development as the major opponent of Christ is quite deliberate. The contrast with the mainly silent Christ is particularly striking, and indeed he is in some ways an Antichrist in that certain of his speeches show him as a parody which is typical for the Antichrist. His part was enlarged or pointed up in each of the Plays 20, 22, 23, 24 and 26, and his role is supported in its characteristic mixture of cruelty, blasphemy, magic, and legal distortion in a number of places, especially the Buffeting (Play 21) in which the leading roles are taken by Cayphas and Annas. This play is written entirely in the stanza of the Wakefield Master. There is little doubt that his interventions were made with a sense of the potential for reiteration which the cyclic form made possible. If the plays were ever performed in the text we now have, the effect of the recurrence of the evil characters, dominated by Pilate's frequent appearances, must have been overwhelming, and it seems clear that this was a strategy supported by the Wakefield Master.

The enlargement of evil characters is also to be found in other parts of the cycle, and it is identifiable with the devils, as well as with individual human characters in a more private sphere: Cain,

Noah's Wife, and Mak. We find the Wakefield Master's intervention palpable in all these. Though devils are referred to from time to time, their actual appearances in Towneley are confined to the Fall of Lucifer (Plat 1), the Harrowing of Hell (Play 25), and Judgement (Play 30). Lucifer is notable for the reversal of true values which is implied in his physically taking over God's seat: 'I am so semely, blode and bone, / My sete shall be theras was his' (1/102-3). He asks his followers to admire his worthiness to sit in the seat of the Trinity (1/104-5). The two other plays involving devils are both derived from the York counterparts. The changes to the Harrowing involve the development of a subordinate devil called Rybald, whose name is presumably anticipated in the York version (37/99), and the modifying of Sathan to make him more defiant (25/185-8) together with his mainly verbal confrontation with Christ once the gates of Hell are broken. The language recalls Lucifer, the boasting Herods, and Pilate. Because Sathan doubted the divinity of Christ he is led to question whether he was a man, and here his confusion makes it ironically clear that he is correct to stress Christ's humanity, since it was doctrinally important that this be established: 'Thy fader knew I well be syght / He was a wright his meett to wyn' (25/249-50). He tries to outwit Christ by claiming that Solomon and Job had said that no one could ever come out of hell, but Christ turns the argument against him, showing that he, Sathan, will prove the truth of it. The dramatic tension is well sustained for Sathan believes that he will now acquire more sinners and be free to roam the world to entrap them, and he tries to shake Christ by the hand as though he has negotiated a new agreement (25/353-4). Christ responds by insisting that he is to be sent down 'Into thi sete where thou shall syt' (25/368). His decline is enacted onstage and so recalls the Fall of Lucifer.

The adaptation of the York Judgement play by the Wakefield Master is chiefly interesting because of the incorporation of the devil Tutivillus, not found in the original. This character had an enormous and varied ancestry in dramatic and non-dramatic works.[53] His traditional role as a collector of minor sins and verbal fragments into sacks which would be unpacked at Judgement Day is given a much sharper edge by the Wakefield Master. Here he is made to present a satire upon legal and ecclesiastical graft, an area which is closely linked with the oppression of the poor graphically outlined in the Shepherds plays, and in the characters of Annas and Cayphas. This satirical activity gives him a moral function at the Judgement, and there are echoes of the Deadly Sins of Sloth and Avarice. It brings the reality of human sin into detailed portrayal, even where it is closely involved in the life of the church, and so helps in the process which is found in the Wakefield Master's preoccupations elsewhere in the cycle. Some criticism has been levelled at him for obscuring the clear dramatic lines of the York Judgement, which is a most successful and moving play in its own right. But the changes here seem designed to meet a different objective from those of the York authors. Though the dramatist uses and enlarges the devils' role here, it seems that he was also inclined to make human corruption a main theme in his work throughout the cycle, and this was done ultimately in preference to the use of devils as Christ's antagonists. This process can be seen also at work in the invention and treatment of the individual sinners mentioned above, Cain, Noah's Wife and Mak, the sheep stealer.

 The authorship of the Murder of Abel (Play 2) has been attributed to the Wakefield Master, though there are perhaps only two stanzas in his usual metre. A. C. Cawley has presented a number of verbal parallels between this text and others known to be of this authorship,[54] and the subject matter and dramatic style are close to the usual mode. There is the same use of demotic speech and the sense of the evil in human beings as well as a social framework of oppression and exploitation: these have to be set against very confused metrical arrangements which suggest a good deal of revision. Possibly it was the character of Cain which most attracted the Wakefield Master. Traditionally, and through the Scriptures, he had borne a curse, and the dramatisation here concentrates upon showing how he was utterly committed to evil, with many curses and references to the devil. Yet he is made so articulate and uncompromising that his indestructibility commands attention and his outrageous defiance of Deus makes him fascinating:

> Whi, who is that hob over the wall?
> We! who was that that piped so small?
> Com, go we hens, for parels all -
> God is out of hys wit! (2/299-302)

In this way he manifests an important feature of the cycle plays in that they tend to employ unredeemable evil characters who give expression to the need to contemplate the horror of damnation. Such are the Antichrist in Chester, the devil in York, Judas in many continental Passions, and in Towneley we find the sequence culminating in Pilate which so attracted the Wakefield Master.

Cain seeks to dominate Garcio, his boy, by verbal and physical attacks, and he has an abusive rivalry with Abel. At times his manic discourse suggests madness: Deus describes him as 'wode' (2/352). The dramatist uses the common motif of separating the sheaves to Cain's own advantage in such a way that it seems irrational, since no one could see this as an adequate response to his obligations to God. Yet there may be a cross-current here in that tithing was notoriously unpopular. Though Cain expects to go to hell, the curse pronounced by Deus preventing anyone from killing him isolates him even further. He is condemned to outlaw and exile. This is underlined by the grimly farcical comedy of his proclamation of his own pardon, while Garcio undercuts his speech line by line with irrelevant and contrary comment (2/420-41). His perversity is not lovable and the dramatist has exercised himself to cut out sympathy for him. Yet paradoxically he still draws our interest as a human being, and it may well be that to fail and be condemned is just as human a characteristic as to be saved.

Noah's Wife was often seen as a rebellious figure but here the dramatist has sharpened up the conflict between her and Noah, often resorting to farcical detail. This is achieved by modifications to both characters, and these may well be seen as part of the concentration on human failings found elsewhere in the cycle. Although Noah is here linked typologically with Christ, his link with Adam perhaps is more suggestive of fallibility.[55] Despite his being the means by which Deus preserves the human race, he is an irritable domestic tyrant: it is he who strikes the first blow (3/318), and he repeatedly threatens violence (3/314, 551-2, 559, 588-9). Noah's Wife, like Mak's, is made articulate about her many discomforts and she lives in fear of her husband:

> If he teyn, I must tary,
> Howsoever it standys,
> With seymland full sory,
> Wryngand both my handys
> For drede.   (3/304-8)

Their quarrel continues after she has reluctantly entered the ark, and Noah in disgust addresses the men in the audience, warning them to chastise the tongues of their wives. But things are not entirely on his side even though he reflects the divine purpose for the human race. There is a sense that the conflict between man and wife bears hard upon them both, and that their pain is caused by their own sinning. Peace is brought by their sons who urge reconciliation (3/599-604). It is so strong that at one point on the voyage Noah asks his wife to take the helm (3/625), and at another moment he pointedly asks her advice (3/683-9). At the end of the play the sense of redemption is powerful enough for Noah to think that even those who have been drowned might receive grace, and he prays that 'we' might have a place in heaven with the saints and angels.

The process by which human suffering is transformed by divine grace reappears emphatically in the Shepherds plays. The presence of the two versions here, both apparently the work of the Wakefield Master, has not been satisfactorily explained, and it may be that his decision to write a second version had nothing to do with the exigencies of performance. Its title in the manuscript, which may be translated as 'Another [Pageant] of the Same Men' (*Alia eorundem*), seen at its most direct, merely suggests that he decided to write another play about shepherds without giving a hint as to why. There are similarities, however, which may indicate that he was satisfied with some aspects of the first play and yet thought to try a different approach. Both present a period of discomfort and suffering by the Shepherds; both have some complex action involving folly and evil; both are brought to a climax by the angelic song which is discussed as music, and both involve a measure of transcendence from their struggling lives ('We mon all be restorde - / God graunt it be so!' 12/716-7) to the adoration of the child and the presentation of gifts. These gifts are themselves a reflection of the poverty of the Shepherds, but also of their devotion. Some of these features are conventional to Shepherds plays, and it is apparent that the author wished to use the conventions in his own ways. At the end of both plays the contrast with the Chester Shepherds play is quite striking. The latter shows the Shepherds transformed into new ways of life, but the Wakefield Shepherds seem to go back to their usual lives, even though they have seen what they have seen. If this is so it accords with the Wakefield Master's concern with the substance and the difficulty of human experience.

   In presenting these lives in the two plays he gives much detail. The Shepherds complain about the weather, their wives, the imposition of exploitative practices, the illnesses of their sheep. In both plays there is tension between them. In the First Shepherds Play resentment is directed against Jak Garcio, and in the Second against Mak who already has a reputation for thieving, and who has a number of traits which mark him as an outsider, including speech with southern characteristics. But the major development in both plays is the introduction of non-scriptural elements in the plot which had a previous existence in folklore. This move is not of course unique in the cyclic drama but the development here is particularly strong and persistent and it naturally raises curiosity about why it was done. On the one hand, for us in the modern world, it has been a success since these elements always attract attention and enjoyment when they are performed or considered. But perhaps the dramatist was moving beyond the purely orthodox, and if he was, it is quite difficult for us to gauge the impact of this in his own time. The most significant elements are the huge accumulation of food (which may be real or imaginary) assembled by the Shepherds for their supper, and the ridiculous episode of the quarrel over imaginary sheep in the first play, and the elaborate development of the story of Mak's theft and its concealment of a sheep in a cradle as a kind of parody of the Nativity in the second. These items existed separately and were incorporated into the plays with the effect of making clearer the folly and sin of the characters. They thus have a didactic aspect, and yet they have a compulsion of their own which also makes plainer the texture of these lives. Besides this the Wakefield Master's interest in paradox and irony prevents too simple a treatment of the nature of these people.

In the First Play two of the Shepherds fall to quarrelling over whether one shall drive his sheep past the other, the point being that the sheep are imaginary. The Third Shepherd intervenes, pointedly asking 'Where ar youre shepe, lo?' (12/195) and he sets about showing how foolish they are. To do this he unties his sack and pours the grain upon the ground, asking them to gather it up. Like the lost grain they have lost their wits: yet he has forgotten that he too has lost his grain in the process. His folly in turn is shown up by Jak Garcio:

> Of all the foles I can tell,
> From heven unto hell,
> Ye thre bere the bell. (12/266-8)

What is intriguing here is that Garcio is not likely to have the sympathy of the audience even though he is somewhat downtrodden by the others. The episode carries an ambivalence which sets up a different evaluation of humans from the purely didactic one noted above.

In the Second Shepherds Play the episode containing Mak functions in much the same way. His story of concealing the sheep is a folk tale and his part in the play shows him as crooked, with a thief's cunning. He is even given a kind of black magic in that he puts a spell upon the sleeping shepherds while he steals their sheep. His exchanges with his wife and his comments about her also show him in a bad light: like Cain, he is hardly a lovable rogue, and the suspicions of the Shepherds and their precautions against him are well-founded. To an extent his wife is articulate about the sufferings of women and the poet allows her to give a picture of labouring in the home which undermines in part the male discourse of Mak:

> Full wofull is the householde
> That wantys a woman. (13/606-7)

It is she who thinks of the plan to hide the sheep, and her initiative nearly works. The exposure of the crime comes through a simple act of kindness by the Third Shepherd, something anyone might do. It is an intensely dramatic moment since the audience knows all about the concealed sheep and is no doubt put on tenterhooks about a possible discovery by his change of direction. He calls the "baby" 'That lytyll day-starne', a tender phrase which is subsequently repeated for the Christ-child (13/834 and 1049). Going back to the cradle to give it sixpence, he finds the lost sheep. But even here a strongly moral line is avoided: instead there is emphasis upon grace. Rather than the punishment of the law, which might well have been capital, Mak is tossed in a canvass, and his shame is thus exposed. Here, at least the pains of hell are avoided.[56] It seems that with Cain, Noah's Wife and Mak the main impulse was to reveal the hard truth of the predicament of evil. This revelation would not necessarily mean pardon: it is not an amoral ignoring of evil in human beings, since the evil must inexorably be shown. Presumably the poet hoped that amelioration might be brought about more effectively in this way than by the conventional fear of the pains of hell. He is not soft about evil, but he does look very closely at it, and in some respects this is idiosyncratic and is a personal vision rather than one sanctioned by traditional aspects of belief. But one should be cautious about seeing this as necessarily heterodox.

The Wakefield Master's impact upon the Towneley Cycle is enormous. Several of the items with which he was concerned, especially the Shepherds Plays and the Buffeting, show a rich complexity of dramatic effects. The question of how they were performed, however, remains problematic. The very small amount of mid sixteenth-century external evidence does not rule out processional performance like that at York.[57] Many of the plays, and not only those which were borrowed, are quite compatible with this mode. However a few of the plays, including both the Shepherds Plays and the composite Conspiracy and Capture (Play 20) require a more complex stage setting. The Wakefield Master was concerned with these and it may well be that he did not have processional staging in mind. Besides the fields where the Shepherds fall asleep and Mak's cottage, the Second Shepherds Play has to have a place for Mary and the Child. There are a number of specific moves between these. Similarly the Conspiracy and Capture begins in Pilate's court; Christ is then welcomed to the chamber for the Last Supper; he moves to the Mount of Olives; Pilate orders the Soldiers to go to arrest Christ; they do so and take him back to Pilate. The absence of staging detail in the manuscript suggests that it was somewhat remote from any performance: it may indeed have been an assemblage of disparate items which were made to conform to the idea of a cycle without much direct consideration of how to perform the result. Thus the best that can be said about the question of performance is that although there are many remarkable dramatic effects in the cycle, the text leaves us with a number of possibilities and few certainties. But these of course do not militate against the attraction of the idea of a cycle.

The Cornish Cycles
Though there are considerable difficulties in evaluating the two Cornish cycles because the survival of but a small quantity of

Middle Cornish limits accessibility, they shed a good deal of light upon the main concern of this study, the nature and aesthetic possibilities of the cycle form. Access is made even more difficult because very few other Cornish dramatic texts are known, the history of the Cornish language and its decline is problematic, and it is quite hard to relate the two extant texts, the *Ordinalia* and the fragmentary *Creacion of the World*, to medieval performances in any particular place or places. Nevertheless there are strong internal indications that the *Ordinalia* was performed, and the nature of its text gives rise to some significant aspects of authorship and the concept of a cycle. Whilst information about other cycles in Cornwall is hard to come by, it is apparent that there was a vigorous dramatic tradition in the county, and in the case of the performances—of whatever kinds of plays—it was said by Richard Carew in connection with the traditional amphitheatres or *plen-an-gwaries* that 'the country people flock from all sides many miles off to see and hear [the play]'.[58] The recent volume in the REED series gives plenty of evidence for this vigorous dramatic life, but it does not add a great deal about the cycle drama in general. The records do however make clear that St. Ives and Bodmin might have been places where there was a large-scale commitment to drama. At St. Ives, for example, in 1571–2 there was a play which lasted for six days; and Bodmin seems to have been a town of sufficient size to support a large play.[59]

However rich this dramatic life may have been, the text of the *Ordinalia* gives us strong indications about authorship, and also about the possibilities of performance. It seems very likely, arguing from the homogeneity of the text and its structural integrity, that this text is substantially the work of one author. This puts it in a remarkable category since we have to consider that in several other English cycles and many continental ones there is a great deal of unevenness in the texts and that many of them bear the mark of several different writers, or even of compilation by accretion.

The text of the *Ordinalia*, recently dated between 1395 and 1419 and contemporary with early appearances of cycles elsewhere in England, is in three parts which were apparently performed on three successive days.[60] The *Origo Mundi* runs from the Creation, which is shown in some detail, through selective events in the lives of Noah, Abraham, Moses, David and Solomon to the Creation of the Temple in Jerusalem. The *Passio Domini* tells the story of the Temptations of Christ, some of the events of the Ministry, though these are concentrated upon Jerusalem, and the Arrest and Crucifixion. The third part, *Resurrexio Domini*, shows the Resurrection, followed by the Appearances and extensive treatment of the doubts of Thomas, the Death of Pilate and the Ascension, leading on to Christ's triumphal entry into heaven. From these items, the broadly conventional outline of the cycle is apparent, but there are a number of significant departures, including the absence of the Nativity and the Judgement, and the inclusion of some events which are not present in the other English cycles. Beneath the apparent conformity there also lie several distinctive features and it is in these that we can see most clearly the activity of a deliberately selecting intelligence pursuing specific structural arrangements, and, through them, doctrinal and aesthetic objectives.

There are several distinct structural preoccupations, but with a text as complex and subtle as the *Ordinalia* it is important not to oversimplify. A number of cohesive devices work intermittently alongside more persistent strategies, and beyond this, the three parts individually show distinctive aspects of design. The author —and it does seem reasonably safe to speak of one author here— has built into the *Origo Mundi* the Legend of the Cross which affects a significant number of incidents. In effect it connects the Tree of Knowledge in Paradise with the Cross, and it does so by a distinctive narrative structure.

In pursuance of God's promise at the Expulsion, Adam sends Seth, his son, back to Paradise, retracing the burnt footsteps of his mother and father, to seek the Oil of Mercy. Looking into Paradise, he sees a tree in which there appears a serpent, and then 'A little child newly born' (*Origo Mundi*, l. 805). Seth brings back three seeds of the fateful apple which he places under the tongue of his dead father. From these grow three rods which are later rediscovered by Moses, and which he buries on Mount Tabor. They are brought to Jerusalem by David where they grow miraculously into a single Holy Tree under which he expresses his penitence over his misconduct with Bathsheba. The tree is then used by Solomon's carpenters to make a beam for the Temple. It does not fit, but he puts it into the Temple where it is touched by Maximilla. When she does so, her clothes catch fire, and she anachronistically proclaims the coming of Christ. She is stoned for heresy and the wood, now thought to be accursed, is placed over the brook of Cedron. From there it is sought out by the Torturers to form the Cross. While the sequence from Fall to Crucifixion is not concerned only with this strong link touching so many Old Testament figures, it does remain a persistent interest and the audience is in a position to observe and anticipate the stages in the story. The legend is not original to the *Ordinalia*: it is found in three common sources for the mystery plays, the *South English Legendary*, the *Cursor Mundi* and the *Northern Passion*.[61] With this, as with a many other elements in the cycle, we can conclude that the author was thoroughly familiar with the conventional material: he was presumably an educated cleric. But the originality lies in the management of the cycle itself and the incorporation of this material in appropriate ways. This is made clearer during the Passion, and after it, when the cross is repeatedly referred to as the tree-cross, or some similar phrase (as *pren crous* in *Passio Domini*, l. 2374), so that the link between the Fall and the Crucifixion is thoroughly sustained. Even the Torturers use the phrase *crous pren* (*Passio Domini*, l. 2514).

While this concept is thus seen to persist in the *Passio Domini* the emphasis does shift notably away from it in this section. Instead there is now a priority in the form of a concern for the nature of Christ—who, though anticipated, had not appeared in the first part of the cycle—and there is special concentration on his role as God and man. We find this, for example, in the words of the two Doctors who are the unscriptural inventions of the dramatist. Summoned by Annas and Caiaphas to take part in the interrogation of Christ, they refer to Christ as half God and half man. This may be heretical, and they even mock him as a 'mermaid ... half fish and half man' (ll. 2403-4), but the perversion does draw attention paradoxically to Christ's special nature in a context when this is of paramount importance.[62] A range of other characters is used to bring out his divinity. Notably there are the Boys who welcome him into Jerusalem: one says 'Joy to thee, Lord of the world, / And heaven also!' (ll. 289-90). The Smith who refuses to make the nails, speaks correctly of his dual nature: 'To be God and man likewise, / Now I know well' (ll. 2704-5).

On the other hand there is a typological continuity running from the *Origo Mundi* to the *Passio* which draws attention to Christ as a new Adam and which emphasizes in a different way the link between the Fall and the Redemption. The one necessitated the other, yet at the same time the dramatist notes that the submission of Christ was a voluntary one. This act of will is fortunate for mankind, and yet it is also a thematic continuity because Christ, i.e. God, could have started again, but instead he chose to return to the ground and rise again, completing the Redemption.[63] This act of will counterbalances Adam's act of willful disobedience in eating the forbidden fruit. The omission of the Nativity may be explained in terms of this concentration upon the Redemption.[64]

In addition to this, the *Resurrexio Domini* contains another range of structural considerations. Here Christ is no longer quite a man: his divinity having been manifested, he comes to his full role as loving and triumphant ruler of the universe. This is a culmination of the interrelationship between Christ's divinity and his humanity. It is perhaps this which makes the absence of a Judgement sequence most significant. As in some other respects, the dramatist follows continental patterns, but the point seems to be that this Christ is less a Judge and more a Saviour. Thus the omission of Judgement is complementary to that of the Nativity.

One of the most effective devices in this third part of the cycle is the application of the myth of the Death of Pilate which is, in one form, attached to the apocryphal *Gospel of Nicodemus*.[65] This tells of the disastrous end of Pilate who is summoned by Caesar and arrested for killing Christ. He is tried, and despoiled of Christ's robe, acquired at the Crucifixion, and finally put into prison. There he kills himself, but his body proves impossible to dispose of, causing the death of others by poisoning the River Tiber. Finally it is taken far out to sea whence the devils carry it off to hell. The sequence is inserted between the final allaying of the doubts of Thomas and the scene of the Ascension, and its effect is parodic, since it mirrors and inverts many elements in the Passion. Its function here could be seen as a parallel to the management of the Antichrist passage at Chester. There seems little doubt that this episode is exciting theatre, and its presence is evidence of the highly sophisticated structural control of this cycle.

The last structural device, chronologically speaking, is the triumphal entry of Christ into heaven. This gives finality to his role in the Redemption, and it shows both the completion of his life on earth, in which he blesses the disciples and sends them out to preach, and his appearance as a lover knight in heaven. The latter part sets out the importance of his love for mankind, and it reasserts his divinity, which we have seen as a persistent dramatic motif through the Passion. Initially the Angels do not quite recognise him because he is clothed in red garments, which are scriptural and which suggest both the sacrifice of his blood (*Resurrexio Domini*, ll. 2622-3) and the triumph over the Devil (ll. 2574). Responding to the questions of the Angels, he recalls his Passion, especially the wounds he received (ll. 2579-94), and the souls he released from hell. In this way the dramatist has made use of the convention of retrospect, which we have observed in other cycles, but the function of it here is to sustain this last powerful image of Christ, the loving Redeemer. Once Christ is seated at the right hand of the Father, the play is concluded by the Emperor, who reminds the audience that 'To the sons of men he shewed, / Very truly, much love' (ll. 2637-8).

To this variety of structural devices, we can add two features which function intermittently, and yet which demonstrate the unifying interests of the author. These are the way human characters are used, and the function of the devils. Whilst the devils function at a supernatural level and reappear over a long period of history, the humans are used for specific roles which illuminate the structural devices we have been discussing. In the *Origo Mundi* the episodes are centred upon a succession of patriarchal figures who are included largely because of the historical process we have noted above. It is very striking that the author has stuck closely to the traditional Old Testament heroes, and it may well be that he had some version of the Ages of history in mind. Though the importance of the idea of the Ages of history has been somewhat over-emphasised, the concept is part of the process whereby the divine and the temporal aspects are made to interact.[66] Within each episode there is also a strictly limited selectivity at work. Thus from the huge range of possibilities for the story of David, the dramatist has selected enough of the Bathsheba affair, including the conspiracy against Uriah to bring out David's guilt. This then becomes a factor in not allowing him to complete the building of the temple, even though he is divinely led to the discovery of the rods. His unworthiness means that it has to be left to Solomon, his son.

Once the *Origo Mundi* is completed the human characters have to function differently, and yet there is a consistency between them. Of the closest of Christ's associates, Mary is treated circumspectly. She is made to function in her maternal role, even though the Nativity is omitted, and she commands Christ's attention during both the *Passio* and the *Resurrexio*. But her lamentations are restrained; there is no hint of her childhood as it appears in N-Town; and the role is presented in such a way as to avoid the affective piety seen elsewhere in the cycles and other art forms.

The treatment of Thomas is a notable feature of the *Resurrexio*, and makes for a vigorous theatrical episode. He follows the traditional role, but his arguments with the other disciples and with Mary Magdalene are much more extensive. At one point he leaves the upper room and descends to the playing area where his voluble dissociation from his colleagues is made more physical. Most probably the effects sought bear upon the important theme of Christ's divinity, and also upon him as a very palpable human being. In this last respect he fits in well with the repeated sense of the fallibility of human beings which is found through the cycle. In the end he is allowed to touch the heart of Christ through the wound (ll. 1531-2, 1539-41). A similar treatment occurs with Peter, but we shall consider him below in the discussion of staging. We might note, too, that there are virtually no characters who are like the monstrous villains found in some other cycles. This does not mean that there are no evil humans—the Torturers are a sufficient example—but the mode of grotesque satire found in the portrayal of boasting Pharaohs, Herods and Pilates elsewhere is absent.

The devils form a significant theatrical resource in the *Ordinalia* and they are given a location of their own, as is commonly the case. Probably their chief function is primarily to mark the progress of the long process of Redemption. It may well be significant of the Devil's status here that the Fall of Lucifer is not shown. The omission, assuming that it is deliberate, reduces the Devil's adversarial role. In accordance with the emphasis upon human freewill, the responsibility for the Fall of Man is placed squarely upon Adam and Eve in spite of the Devil's role as tempter. The devils do have some power however, and they take Adam's soul to hell when he dies. At the beginning of the *Passio* Satan fails to deceive Christ and he acknowledges his defeat and the loss of power (ll. 148-50), a significant prelude to what is to come. Though Judas plays his traditional part in the betrayal of

Christ, he is not specifically prompted by the Devil. But when Judas hangs himself, Satan is ready to take his soul, commenting that because Judas had kissed Christ, his soul could not leave through his mouth (ll. 1534-6). Unfortunately the text does not explain exactly how this is to be staged: the iconographical convention is that the exit of his soul caused his bowels to explode.

The knowledge of defeat and the awareness that Christ is the Son of God prompts the devils to try to prevent the Crucifixion. Beelzebub appears to Pilate's Wife and explains that there will be vengeance upon her and her children if Christ is slain (*Passio Domini*, ll. 1919-24). This is an anticipation of the *Mors Pilati* in the *Resurrexio*. The downward course of the devils is marked by the breaking of the gates of hell by *Spiritus Christi* and the leading out of the imprisoned souls. It appears that the devils were deceived in their aspiration to power. They still control the damned, but that is their limit. If they were deceived, it was more likely a matter of self-deception than of God deliberately deceiving them. In this way, like the sinful Adam, they are contributors to their own predicament.

The fragmentary *Creacion of the World* consists of 'the First Daie' and reveals different aspects of the idea of the cycle in Cornwall. As Paula Neuss has shown, it partly derives from the *Ordinalia*, though it covers the story only as far as the end of the Noah episode. Beyond this it promises the redemption 'tomorrow ... granted through the mercy of God the Father' (ll. 2544-5). This would naturally follow the greater elaboration of the Legend of the Cross, and Seth's part in it, which is apparent on the first day. Unfortunately there is no text for the second day, or any indication of how many days were required altogether.

The effect of the greater detail of the *Creacion* is to proliferate narrative elements, including the Creation of the Angels, the Fall of Lucifer, the Coming of Death (an allegorical figure) and the death of Cain, killed by Lamech, his blind descendant. There is also a larger variety of characters, most of whom are drawn with psychological realism. This text was written down in

1611 by William Jordan, who may have been its author or reviser. Whoever was responsible for the text at first apparently played the part of God in the *Ordinalia* and incorporated his part verbatim into the new text.[67]

Turning to the staging of the Cornish cycles, we find sufficient detail to show something of its method. In the text of the *Ordinalia* diagrams have survived for each day, apparently indicating a circular playing place. There are eight named stations around the circle. Many of these are changed from day to day, though heaven in the east (towards Jerusalem) remains the same, and the Torturers are always based in the north east. This emblematic significance is further extended by having Pilate succeed to Pharaoh's station in the north west, and the instruments of worldly power, David, Herod, and Tiberius are in the west. Bakere has pointed out that for the *Passio* there is no station called hell, as there is in the north for the other days, and that with the exception of heaven and the Centurion's, all the other stations are for evil characters, including one for the specially invented Doctors noted above.[68] Perhaps the significance of this distribution is that it increased the sense of Christ's isolation and his exposure to his destroyers, in an almost unrelieved evil ambience.

The action of the cycle can thus be played at the locations, which are called *tenta* (Lat.), and in the spaces between. The text is rich in stage directions, many of which are concerned with movement from place to place, and with movement up to and down from the stations, as in: *Hic descendit Pilatus, et iet in tentum Cayphas* (Here Pilate goes down, and Caiaphas shall go into his tent, *Passio Domini*, l. 1616sd). There was concern for visual display including flowers in Paradise, and in the use of the bank surrounding the performing area.[69] There are also details about costume, and a number of directions which indicate to actors the gestures which are to accompany their words.

Two kinds of recurring stage directions give scope to the actor to vary his performance as though the author leaves him to judge how far to carry out his action. In a number of places a direction is accompanied by the phrase *si placet* or *si voluerit* ('if he likes'). Sometimes this is linked to *pompabit*, a verb which suggests walking about, on occasions parading or showing off authority or status. However, the tone of such performances must have varied. When Lucifer bewails his loss of power as Christ is imprisoned by Pilate, making the Crucifixion inevitable, the stage direction has: *Pompabit Lucifer si placet* ('Here he shall walk about, if he pleases', *Passio Domini*, l. 1906sd). Perhaps the point partly is to allow the actor to give sufficient time to shift attention to a new place and time.

The particular strength of this method of staging can be illustrated by the episode containing Peter's three denials of Christ in accordance with the scriptures. As we have seen, he is important for his human fallibility. His three denials are separated in time, and while they are going on the play is successively concerned at another part of the acting area with the examination of Christ by Caiaphas, including a blow by the executioner, Caiaphas's tearing his garments, the blindfolding of Christ, the beating game and the spitting (*Passio Domini*, ll. 1237-1446).

The *Creacion* offers little evidence to suggest that the presentation was necessarily in a *plen-an-gwary*, though the balance of probability suggests that it was. If so, we can only be sure of three conventional stations, heaven, hell and Paradise (heaven probably with three levels and hell with two[70]). Some movement between them is designated in stage directions. Noah apparently builds the ark somewhere in the space, and Tubalcain mocks him as he does so fully in the sight of the audience (ll. 2295-9). On the other hand, many of the stage directions (which are all in English even though the text is mostly in Cornish) are concerned with advising the actors on how to speak or move. These might indicate that a more intimate setting was envisaged at some time. As in the *Ordinalia* there are many directions here which are intended to prompt the stage managers in advance to attend to properties, or to prepare for the next stage in the action. These are more numerous in the *Creacion*, and they argue strongly that someone went over the text with the needs of performance very much in mind.

There seems little doubt that the Cornish cycles were able to capitalize on the idea of a cycle and adapt it to local conditions but we might also note that even the revised date of 1391 to 1419 now proposed for the evolution of the *Ordinalia* text would still make it one of the earliest cycles for which we have an authenticated contemporary text. If this is so we must entertain the possibility that the Cornish text was not so much an imitation of a conventional model so much as a potential contributor to its development.

The N-Town Cycle

The N-Town Cycle plays a substantial role in this study because of a number of unique features. The most important is the eclectic nature of the manuscript which is discussed below. The absence of any supporting material or records, and the difficulty or indeed impossibility of attributing it to any particular urban context mean that it cannot be considered to follow some of the practices we have been observing in the other extant English cycles, as well as in those which have come down to us in fragments or only as records. This cycle does not appear to have been performed in a city; there is no evidence of pageant carts or guild ownership; and in some parts of this cycle the dramatic imagination revealed is in pursuance of other considerations and practices than those in common in the other cycles. There must indeed be considerable doubt as to whether we can assume that N-Town was ever produced in its entirety.

But the selection of incidents, by and large, follows that of the other English language cycles, even though we shall observe that there are some striking individual departures from this pattern. The date 1468 appears at the end of the Purification (Play 19). In itself, this does not necessarily mean that the whole manuscript was written by then: the more likely inference is that this individual episode of the Purification was complete in that year, and that it may be an indication that some or all of the rest followed after it. The evidence of the language and the handwriting points to the last quarter of the fifteenth century.[71] If this is so, the compilation of N-Town occurs when the tradition of English cycle plays, not to mention the continental analogues considered in Chapters Three and Four, was well established, and the presumed date occurs precisely in that period of the fifteenth century when the cycles were in a phase of rapid development here and on the continent. This suggests that the compiler would have had a number of precedents to inform his selection and arrangement of the material.

The fact that the whole of the codex is substantially the work of one scribe, who seems to have been simultaneously assembling the material into an apparent whole, would also make it likely that whatever individual or separable intentions he may have had or he may have taken over, he meant to produce a codex which would in appearance and in construction approximate to others already in existence. He certainly tried to make the codex look coherent and consistent by such devices as the general layout of pages, the rubrication of individual plays, and the provision of large, elaborate numbers at the head of each play. We should note too that the manuscript of the York Cycle is thought to have been copied at this time (*c*. 1463-77), though it reflected customs of performance as well as content which had been established at York over many years before. There is no doubt that the N-Town compiler had plenty of models to help to determine the shape of his work, and its manifestation at this time suggests that he was well aware of the cycle tradition he was now following. Because of the mode of staging in parts of the cycle it is also possible that he was aware of continental models of Passion plays which were reaching their most fruitful developments in the second half of this century, especially those in France where there was a widespread proliferation of performances and manuscripts after Gréban's *Passion* (*c*. 1450).

It is apparent, however, that the manuscript does not embody a simple act of compilation and transcription even though there is a consistent pursuit of cyclic form. The codex begins with a Proclamation which sets out to describe the contents of each of the plays. Its purpose was apparently to give notice of a performance of the whole cycle at a place whose name is left blank. However, its summary of episodes, here called 'pageants', does not coincide exactly with what has actually survived in the plays themselves, and the study of the relationship between the Proclamation, with its distinctive thirteen-line stanzas, and the plays has proved fruitful in revealing many different aspects of the evolution of this cycle as we now have it, and in suggesting the extent to which revision was undertaken before or during the process by which the scribe laid out the text.

Passion Play I, comprising plays 26-28 and covering events from the Conspiracy to the Arrest, had a physically separate existence before it was incorporated into the cycle, and the handwriting, though it is thought to be the same as that of the main scribe, is actually looser and more sprawling, suggesting that he completed this part of the codex at a different time. Passion Play II, consisting of plays 29-31 and parts of 32 and 34, appears to have been separate originally but the scribe may have transcribed it specially and blended it into the cycle alongside some older material.[72] There must be a distinct possibility that the composition of the Passion Plays was an independent concept from the idea of the cycle as a whole. An earlier version of the cycle was embodied in the Proclamation, however much it varies from the surviving text; but the substitution of the two-part Passion does not alter the principle of the original cycle. It is not feasible, however, to guess now by how much time the independent copying of Passion Play I preceded the compilation of the codex. In spite of the explicit intention expressed in the Proclamation that a performance of the whole cycle will be undertaken, Contemplacio, who introduces Passion Play II, makes it clear that at some stage this was a continuation: 'to procede the matere that we lefte the last yere' (29/6); and he follows this with a summary of the events in Passion Play I.

Another part of the cycle, which has been identified by Peter Meredith as the Mary Play, and so named by him, seems also to have had a separate existence.[73] For this the manuscript pages themselves are not distinctively separable, but the content of the individual episodes concerned is self-identified as distinct (8/10-13) and the sequence presents many details which are coherent and consistent within the limits of this apparently discrete part. The presence of Contemplacio, an expositor figure, is a characteristic of the Mary Play, and his contributions help to articulate the differences of approach. These have to do with the idea of the Virgin Mary and her birth and exemplary life before the Incarnation. The episodes from this separately conceived sequence have been fitted into the cycle together with other material about Mary, some of it pre-existing in the original scheme outlined in the Proclamation. Thus the Conception of Mary (Play 8), Mary in the Temple (Play 9), the Betrothal of Mary (Play 10), the Parliament of Heaven and the Annunciation (Play 11) and the Visit to Elizabeth (Play 13) are all in some measure derived from the separate play about Mary, but embedded in some of these plays are items from an early phase of the cycle. Much of Joseph's Doubts (Play 12), which is located within the Mary Play sequence, is also thought to have been present in the early state. It is of special interest, pointing to the somewhat fluid state of the cycle at this time, that in copying the Visit to Elizabeth the scribe allowed two endings to remain in the manuscript.[74] The Trial of Mary and Joseph (Play 14), which comes next, is not part of the Mary Play, and is partly represented in the Proclamation. There is the further insertion of material about Mary towards the end of the cycle of the Assumption of Mary (Play 41). This is quite separate from the Mary Play, and its dramatic mode is distinctive. It is also special in that it is not in the hand of the principal scribe even though he has made corrections on some of its pages and sought to integrate it with the rest of the plays in appearance by means of numbering and rubrication. It is written on paper which differs from that of the rest of the plays. Even more striking are its distinctive dramatic and liturgical style, its length, and the nature of the dramatic experiences it embodies. These factors all tend to suggest that once again we have an independent text whose transcription might have been separate in time from the assembling of the codex. The process of incorporation involved here is thus closer to that for Passion Play I than for Passion Play II. It would seem that the evidence of the inclusion of the Passion Plays, the Mary Play, and the Assumption points to a concern to put a cycle together, and in doing so to make use of a variety of materials which happened to be conveniently at the disposal of the compiler, whether they were of his own making or not.

Several scholars, especially Rosemary Woolf and Stephen Spector, have argued that in spite of the discrete nature of these individual items a measure of coherence is still achieved.[75] The evidence for this lies in a number of features of the cycle as it now stands, notably the use of angels and devils, the frequent references to the fact that the devils were for a long period in the narrative deceived over the true identity of Christ, and the prevalence of some important issues like the concepts of Wisdom, penance and obedience. There is also the repeated emphasis upon the role of the Virgin which we have noted in the added items, but which is also manifest in the cycle comprehensively. Some of these items are probably present because they represent a common theological outlook among those who were responsible for the generation of the cycle. Others, however, are more likely to be a matter of narrative or theatrical convenience. A common approach should thus be perceived to be somewhat variable. Such items are not to be found spread uniformly throughout the cycle, however: the cyclic form makes intermittent incorporation of such things acceptable. In any case, it can be logically supposed that even if the items assembled by the compiler did have different provenances and intentions originally, the act of selection, which implies both inclusion and rejection, was in itself a process by which coherent meaning might be approached and laid out.

But in contrast to these cohering items, some of which we shall examine in more detail shortly, it cannot be ignored that the cycle has some very different and indeed incompatible aspects to it. Recent critical theory has made us more aware of the unstable nature of literary texts and made it desirable to look at the many different influences which tend to produce inconsistencies and elements which pull against each other. One of the chief of these in N-Town is the matter of staging, especially as this reflects very different practice and also very different ways of thinking about how dramatic effects are to be achieved. We have found that there is a variety of theatrical styles in other cycles, including both York and Towneley, and we have noted it as a characteristic of cycle form that it accommodates a variety of approaches. But here there seems to be no way of reconciling the differences and it seems likely that the compiler was simply not able to propose or envisage a coherent performance style for his work. Once again the strong possibility arises that the text was not put together with a specific performance in mind, as the Proclamation envisages. If a performance, as implied in the Proclamation, ever took place, it was not one which is faithfully represented by the surviving codex. Instead we have a text with some indications of specific performance details, but these occur sporadically and in separate parts. That does not mean, however, that the work does not embody work by someone of distinguished and intensely practical stage imagination. This is most plainly seen in the two parts of the Passion sequence.

These episodes are distinguished by the adoption of a place and scaffold mode of presentation, similar in method to that of the Cornish cycle and to a large number of the continental analogues we have discussed, though there is nothing here to parallel the strong supposition that the Cornish performance was in the round. It is impossible to tell what made the author favour this mode for the Passion, especially as there does not seem to be any particular inclination in this direction elsewhere in the cycle. Here we are presented with an extraordinarily sophisticated grasp of how to use this kind of acting space. Essentially it involves both the theatrical potential of complex individual stations and the use of movement between them which can be made to register a range of dramatic effects. It appears that there are four such 'scaffolds' in Passion Play I and five in the second part. As the linguistic analysis of the cycle shows that the copyist probably originated in or near East Harling in south-west Norfolk, this form of staging may well be compared with that employed by other plays from East Anglia which used place and scaffold.[76] Besides the continental analogues referred to above, the Digby *Mary Magdalene* (*c.* 1500) and the early fifteenth-century morality, *The Castle of Perseverance*, both exhibit a dramaturgy based upon a series of locations and a good deal of toing and froing between them.[77] In configurations such as these the movements between the stations virtually become processions, and in doing so they take on their own dynamic of performance. Processions can, after all, embody a variety of moods, as they do indeed here, and the act of procession has semiotics and spectacle peculiar to it, including costumes and body language, and the order in which the items are arranged. These can be sustained whether the audience are arranged 'in the round', or the stage is linear or semi-circular with the audience looking substantially from one direction. Movements between locations are not simply a matter of taking characters around or across the acting area: they become a process of theatrical timing. The stage direction at the beginning of Play 31, which deals with Satan and Pilate's Wife and the Second Trial before Pilate, reads:

> *Here enteryth Satan into the place in the most orryble wyse. And qwyl that he pleyth, thei xal don on Jesus clothis and ouyrest a whyte clothe, and ledyn hym abowth the place, and than to Pylat be the tyme that hese wyf hath pleyd.* (31/1sd)

It is apparent from this that while Satan soliloquizes about his plans for the Crucifixion, and the Demon in hell summons him to change his intention for fearing of damaging the infernal empire, Christ is to be paraded around the large acting space in a white costume, as in mockery of a fool, and that he is to become the centre of attention again only when Satan has terrified Pilate's Wife about the effects of the Crucifixion. In the meantime the audience is aware of Christ's presence as it were peripherally. The stage direction reveals that the manipulation of space and timing was quite deliberate. At other times switching from one place to another is a much more direct change, but even then it would seem that while a scaffold is on hold with its occupants "frozen" within it, the audience may not forget them entirely. This occurs for the Last Supper where Christ enters the house for the meal and remains there while the Bishops, Priests and Judges prepare the conspiracy. When this is complete, attention returns to him.[78] Such manipulation of the stage spaces and the audience's attention to them reaches a high degree of sophistication in parts of the N-Town Cycle. This whole method of staging is especially remarkable because it manipulates time and space on separate but related axes. At its most effective it recalls the processes of anticipation and recollection we have noted in other cycles, especially York.

If we now turn to the kinds of staging implied or suggested by the other episodes in the cycle very little consistency is to be found, and it is extremely unlikely that most of the rest was written for place and scaffold. Even the Mary Play sequences do not have the interlocking of locations we have been discussing, though in the absence of detailed stage directions (of the kind we do find in the Passion Plays) it is difficult to be certain.[79]

In other episodes, whilst we cannot rule out the possibility of place and scaffold playing, the presentation is very much simpler, and, critically there is often no attempt to suggest that the action of the individual play involves the simultaneous activity found in the Passion Plays. Thus the Moses episode (Play 6) is very simply conceived: he asks for God's blessing, sees the burning bush and receives the Ten Commandments which he then rehearses to the audience. Deus speaks twenty of the 194 lines, and Moses has the rest. The physical moves are limited to Moses' seeing the burning bush, taking off his shoes to approach it and finding the tables from which he preaches. Many of the plays have fewer than 200 lines and their rehearsal of didactic material is the main function.

The Jesse Root (Play 7), which follows Moses, has significant material for the structure of the cycle since it fulfills the role of the prophetic anticipation of the Nativity by dwelling upon Christ's lineage, and it also celebrates Mary's triumph over the devil. Roboas Rex says:

> Of our kynrede yitt men xul se
> A clene mayde trede down foule Sathanas. (7/51-2)

But the action of this play is a kind of iconic procession. Ysaias begins the sequence with his prophecy and he is followed by Radix Jesse who describes how a branch will spring from him, 'The which by grace xal destroye deth' (7/23). For the rest of the play kings and prophets speak alternately, each explaining his significance for the grace to come. No doubt in a performance the costumes could be a striking feature and the play does also illustrate the importance of procession as a dramatic medium, especially in terms of the order of the components.

At the end of Passion Play I there follows another procession which is as simple in its dramaturgy as Jesse Root. It may well have been included as a kind of complement to it: the first for the Nativity and the second for the Crucifixion. This has only forty lines and it is not rubricated as an individual play or mentioned in the Proclamation. Bibliographically speaking it seems to be part of the Passion Play I section of the manuscript, but it does fit into the cycle appropriately since it celebrates the eleven apostles (i.e. not Judas Iscariot who has just betrayed Christ) and John the Baptist. The dialogue is spoken by two Doctors exclusively, who welcome each of the holy figures in turn. The analogues of this episode may well be found in Corpus Christi processions, but the appearance of this episode here adds remarkably to the structure of this cycle, and it is also a distinctive contribution to its dramaturgy.

The texts of the plays dramatising the Nativity indicate that there was some dislocation in the cycle at this point. The Shepherds play (Play 16) contains material which is found in the other English cycles, including the argument about the Angel's song, the references to the prophets of the Nativity such as Balaam and Moses, and the move to the stable to salute the Child. But the play is rather short and its action is simple. The motif of the homely gifts presented to Christ is absent. The text of the cycle does not have a play numbered 17, but as the Magi, the next play after the Shepherds, is numbered 18, it seems that another episode was envisaged. The Proclamation, however, gives no indication of what this missing play might have been, and we seem to have here some evidence that in assembling the codex the compiler was at a bit of a loss. Some difficulty follows after the Magi play since the Purification (Play 19) interrupts the order of events, separating the arrival of the Magi, and their visits to Herod and Christ (Play 18) from their departure avoiding Herod, and the Slaughter of the Innocents, as in scripture (Play 20). The Purification, which is very awkwardly placed here, is not mentioned in the Proclamation, but there is a clear reference to one of the most remarkable features of Play 20, the account of the Death of Herod. This grim event was much elaborated in the exegetical writings, including the *Legenda Aurea*.[80] The episode, unique to N-Town among the English cycles, shows how Mors kills Herod and his two Soldiers while they are feasting after the Slaughter of the Innocents. The rejoicing of Diabolus is followed by the warning of Death to all people. He is terrible to look upon:

> Thow I be nakyd and pore of array
> And wurmys knawe me al aboute,
> Yit loke ye drede me nyth and day.   (20/272-4)

The statement in the Proclamation that 'Deth xal thrylle his syde' (l. 240) suggests that to add to his conventional skeletal appearance he also carried a spear or dart.

The Assumption of Mary (Play 41) is a complex and lengthy play (529 lines) whose performance demanded a number of locations and may therefore have required a place and scaffold presentation. However there is no sign of the simultaneous action notable in the Passion Plays, and it may be that it originated in a church where the different levels required for the earth, the temple, the sepulchre, heaven and hell might have been accommodated, along with the organ which provided the many musical items. Rosemary Woolf suggested a church setting using a gallery. The possibility of church performance is enhanced by Richard Rastall's discussion of the burial liturgy in this play, and by his suggestion that if the play was done in a church environment the part of Mary could well be sung, where appropriate, by a choirboy.[81] Whatever the playing place there is a good deal of movement up and down, which implies that such movements must have been easily accomplished. Though the principal source is the *Legenda Aurea*, the dramatic flow of the piece is inventive. Initially a Doctor sets up the situation soberly and tells the audience that they are to see the Assumption. At line 27, however, he goes 'into character' and becomes a crabbed part of the ecclesiastical old guard anxious to preserve the Jewish Law. The Bishops see Mary as a threat and conspire against her. In response to her petition, Sapientia (Christ, in his role as Wisdom), sends a message by an angel to reassure her that she will come to him. The action that follows is marked by Latin stage directions and shows that the Apostles, who are well differentiated, are summoned to her death bed. After further heavenly intervention, her soul ascends to Christ, and her body is taken to the tomb. If the performance was in a church, an Easter sepulchre might well have been appropriate here. As her body is carried the Bishops intervene, having descended from their place with a view to stoning her (41/409sd). They insult the bier, but when one of them is stuck to it by his hand, a forced conversion is effected by Saint Peter. The converted Bishop seeks to convert his former allies, and those who resist are taken off to hell by Demons. In the last phase of the play Dominus wishes that Mary's body be brought to heaven. She returns to it and then ascends body and soul, with organs playing (41/521sd). Even though this play does not match neatly much else in the dramatic styles of N-Town the musical and stage awareness it shows is clearly the work of someone able to set up an elaborate play.

In turning to recurring and unifying elements in the cycle, we need to bear in mind the contrary indications noted in the manuscript. The question of unity is intriguing because the process of composition for any work may indeed be a matter of bringing together disparate elements. It is unquestionable that the compiler of N-Town was striving for unity at least in appearance, but given the dispersed nature of the materials available to him inconsistencies were inevitable. These do not however militate against the concept of the cycle, and the compiler's manipulation of his material supports the view of its strength and adaptability as a dramatic form. If we suppose, then, that he was working towards unity we may find in his selection indications of ideas as well as of dramatic techniques which tend towards unification. For convenience we can divide these items into broadly theological or didactic aspects and features which are manifest more in the dramaturgy, but the distinction is hardly exclusive. For example we find that in many plays in this cycle there are passages of prophecy and retrospect. These features we have already noted in other cycles, and they do seem to be fundamental to this dramatic form. They are spread widely through N-Town, and we may pick out the retrospect of Christ's suffering by Luke and Cleophas (38/8-88) and Christ's account of the origin of the world in the play of the Doctors (21/65-104). For his own purposes the Devil also gives a preview of the Passion (26/41-60).

Though some critics have suggested that N-Town is an especially theological cycle, it is hard to see that it is exceptionally so. Admittedly there are references to the Psalms, the *Legenda Aurea* and other religious works, which suggests that the author or authors needed support from authorities; but these are what might be expected. We have already indicated some of the preoccupations to be found in other cycles, such as the interest in the Trinity and the continuing concern with the revelation of the Son of God.

These also appear in N-Town where mention of the Trinity is commonplace. References can be noted in Plays 1, 8, 9, 10, 11, 12, 13, 29, and 41 (where a holy palm is sent from the Trinity, l. 466). In the Mary Play especially there is a strong sense of its influence and the loyalty it demanded. The play of Joachim and Anna (Play 8) shows the Trinity operating somewhat anachronistically in a pre-Christian world by the singing of 'Benedicta sit beata Trinitas' in the Jewish Temple, and by the commitment of the priest Ysakar 'To servyn God in Trinité' (8/97sd and 120).[82] In the Parliament of Heaven when, in response to the debate between the Four Daughters of God about mankind's fate, the Incarnation is decided upon, the three figures of the Trinity speak separately and their specific functions are made clear (11/189-212). The moment of impregnation, echoing iconographical conventions, is given a specifically visual and dramatic force in this stage direction:

> *Here the Holy Gost discendit with iij bemys to oure Lady, the Sone of the Godhed nest with iij bemys to the Holy Gost, the Fadyr godly with iij bemys to the Sone. And so entre all thre to here bosom.* (11/292sd)

At a climactic moment in the Visit to Elizabeth after Mary and Elizabeth have performed the *Magnificat* in Latin and English, for her meekness Mary is described as the 'trone and tabernakyl of the hygh Trinité' (13/138).

The identification of Christ as Son of God is another doctrinal aspect we have found of importance in other English cycles. In N-Town, besides the references to the Trinity, it comes up as a separate issue in Plays 23, 25, 26, 29, 32, and 34. It is intimately associated with the role of the Devil who appears under a number of names through this cycle and who is perhaps more prominent here than in the others. He is also referred to in a number of significant places, including the Last Supper (27/387-8) and the Assumption (41/153-61). It is likely that his importance is structural in as much as he is repeatedly seen as the enemy and in his activities he confronts Christ in a number of places. Contemplacio in his introduction to the Parliament of Heaven prays to the Lord to have compassion because the Devil has deceived mankind by his iniquity (11/24). His prayer is answered in this cycle in that it is followed directly by the Parliament and the Annunciation. At the corresponding Parliament of Hell (Play 23), Satan is anxious. His main difficulty is that he does not believe that Christ is the Son of God. He articulates his fear of losing power if Christ really is divine:

> If that he be Goddys childe
> And born of a mayd mylde,
> Then be we rygh sore begylde
> And short xal ben oure spede. (23/23-6)

The immediate consequence is the Temptation of Christ in which Christ's identity is still concealed and Satan despairs:

> What that he is I kannot se;
> Whethyr God or man, what that he be
> I kannot telle in no degré.
> For sorwe I lete a crakke. (23/192-5)[83]

The motif of the Devil's ignorance is well established in exegetical literature,[84] but the interest here lies in the way it is made to operate dramatically in the cycle. The articulate young Christ, who in N-Town gives a much more credible performance with the learned Doctors than he does in the other cycles, is quite specific. He says of the marriage of Mary and Joseph:

> That holy wedlok was grett stopage
> The devyl in dowte to do abyde. (21/247-8)

The Devil, however, remains in ignorance in his magnificent soliloquy at the beginning of Passion Play I. Here he reiterates that Christ claims to be God's Son, born of a maid for Man's salvation, and adds:

> Than xal the trewth be tryed, and no ferdere be delayd
> Whan the soule fro the body xal make separacyon. (26/ 43-4)

He encourages Judas to betray Christ to the Jews (27/466-73). The turning point comes later in the brilliantly managed Play 31 which exploits to the full the theatrical management of time and space discussed above.[85] Whilst Christ is led back to Pilate, Satan in soliloquy expresses his continuing anger at his rebuff over the Temptation of Christ and he plans the Crucifixion and subsequent welcome in hell. But a Demon, calling from hell, warns of their loss of power, and Satan immediately changes tack, trying to prevent the Crucifixion by terrifying Pilate's Wife over the consequences to her and her husband. In this he is unsuccessful and the consequences are dramatised in the Harrowing of Hell where Belyall knows that nothing may stand against Anima Christi (33/37), and he is bound in endless damnation in hell (35/55-6) before Anima Christi returns to his body in the tomb.

From this account it is apparent that the Devil plays a significant part in the structure of N-Town and it looks as though the compiler might have been aware of the effectiveness of his sequence of appearances. This may of course be a matter of chance since much of this material is present either in the Gospels, or in the apocryphal developments of them like *The Gospel of Nicodemus*. But his dramatic initiatives are several times portrayed, especially in Passion Play I, suggesting that it is as much a matter of dramatic judgement as of the exegetical background. We may compare his activities with that of the Angels who appear in a large number of individual plays.[86] They are frequently used in their traditional function as messengers between heaven and earth, but at times they bring comfort, as to Mary in the Assumption (41/117-65) and Christ on the Mount of Olives (28/53-64). Several times they are given music, but what they say can be functionally important as well. It seems that they weigh less structurally than the Devil, but their roles are still valuable doctrinally and in terms of the dramatic presentation.

Other recurring theological themes are to be found in the references to the Law, to the importance of Obedience, the doctrine of penance and the concept of Christ as the embodiment of Wisdom.[87] The Jews struggle to defend their Law and accuse both Mary and Christ of violating it. It is a significant aspect of the

Trial before Pilate, who is finally obliged to condemn Christ by the working of the laws. The condemnation itself is an elaborate legal ritual which includes the freeing of Barabas and the sentencing of the thieves as well as of Christ (31/169-210). The theme of obedience is notable in the treatment of Abraham and of the submissiveness of Mary in the Mary Play as well as in the Assumption.

The importance of penance is stressed by John the Baptist and by Christ. In other cases the audience is very much the target. Christ preaches about it before the events of the Woman taken in Adultery (24/1-40). It is not quite clear whether this is a direct address to the audience or whether there is a stage audience as well. John the Baptist, however, speaks of penance in his Prologue to the Conspiracy (26/125-64). Here there is no other witness, and the function of his speech is partly a rebuttal of the Devil who has just spoken. It may well be that direct address to the audience is a deliberate dramatic choice in many places in N-Town: it certainly has a strong bearing upon the didactic aspects of the cycle, but it should also be remembered that such sequences can be very exciting to perform.

John Bale's Mystery Cycle

Three surviving printed texts by John Bale (1495–1563) and his lists of his other works indicate that at some time in the 1530s he composed a sequence of plays comprising a prophets episode and a narrative of the life of Christ in ten titles, from the Baptism to the Resurrection. If this is so, it seems that, like the compiler of N-Town, he was aware of the concept of cyclic form and perceived that he could make use of it. While the former's reasons for adopting it still remain open to debate, Bale's interest can be focussed rather more sharply in view of what we know of his life and beliefs. Moreover there is no doubt, from the three plays that survive, that Bale was the author of this work *ab initio* and, to judge from the fact that he is named as the Prolocutor, and other circumstantial evidence from Cromwell's payments, it looks as though he also performed in them himself.[88]

Bale was brought up as a Carmelite in Norwich and at Cambridge. In these early years there were opportunities for him to come into contact with the English cycle play at Norwich, where one is known to have existed. In the 1520s, before his conversion, he travelled widely on the continent, visiting Carmelite houses in the Low Countries (1522–3) and in France as far south as Toulouse (1527). At this period the Dutch Rhetoricians' Plays were often concerned with biblical subjects, and there was an annual performance in Brussels of a part of the *Bliscapen*, the cycle on the joys of Mary which dealt with many episodes concerning Mary and Christ. It is also the time when there were many *Passions* in France, to the extent that the *Passion* of Arnoul Gréban, which was composed about 1450, was now widely adapted and performed, and indeed printed in Michel's version, and there were also performances of other independent texts. On his return to England Bale became Prior of the Carmelites at Ipswich where the order is known to have supported a Corpus Christi play (now lost). His move to a similar appointment at Doncaster by 1534 could hardly have been to a locality where he was more likely to have come into contact with cycles. Here he would have been in striking distance of York, Wakefield and Beverley, and there is now some reason to suppose that there was also a cycle at Doncaster itself.[89] Though this last is no longer extant, it is hard to imagine that Bale did not know of it, and there must be a possibility that he contributed in some way in this momentous decade. Up to this point Bale was a Catholic and he would have been trained to respond to the many aspects of doctrine and worship in the cycle plays he encountered. However, about half way through the 1530s he turned Protestant, and his published list of the plays in his own cycle were all based upon that significant change. Even so, he admits to one play, which he never catalogues, and he does it in such a way as to disown it because it was part of the old religion: it was on the subject of the Harrowing of Hell. His rejection of it is found in his manuscript

Answer to Certain Articles, a document he wrote in prison to vindicate his new Protestant beliefs.[90] The fact that he did not so reject all the other titles we are considering points to their being acceptable to his new stance in contrast, even though we cannot confirm this by an examination of all the texts.

Thus we can take account of one who, being brought up as a cleric in the old religion, thought it valuable and useful to adapt the cyclic form to the new. This argues both a belief in the efficacy of the form in itself, and an estimation that by adapting it he could make a positive contribution to the new cause. In this he almost certainly received strong support from Thomas Cromwell who was at this point actively engaged in the propaganda for Protestantism and the political means of furthering it.

Bale wrote bibliographies of his work at least four times. The most complete appeared in his *Summarium* (Wesel, 1548), and it was repeated in the *Catalogus* (Basle, 1558). The lists contain some anomalies, and there may be an overlap between some of the titles, but it is clear that he had composed plays about Christ at the Age of Twelve, the Passion (in two books) and the Resurrection (also in two books) in English by about 1536. It is about this time that he seems to have been supported by Cromwell, and it is very likely that he then had an acting company. By then he had also written a Life of John the Baptist in fourteen books, and this may well have been a cycle in itself. The Baptist had a special significance for the Carmelites and Bale would have been able to draw upon information gathered before his conversion. There is little doubt that these works were all plays as he labelled the list to that effect. He subsequently added the following episodes about the Ministry and the Passion by the time he wrote the list published in 1548, and most likely before 1540 when he left England to go into exile:

God's Promises
The Preaching of John the Baptist (including the Baptism)
The Temptation of Christ
The Raising of Lazarus

The Feast of Simon the Leper
The Conspiracy of the Priests
The Last Supper
The Burial and Resurrection

All these plays are now lost except for the three italicised, which were printed at Wesel in 1547 and 1548, each bearing on the title-page the date 1538 for its "compilation". It is not known whether any of the other titles were printed, but the format, decoration and layout of these texts were made to match by the printer, and the last two were printed with continuous quire signatures. Their publication came at the end of a series of non-dramatic polemical works written in exile, and it may have been predicated upon the expected death of Henry VIII and the accession of Edward VI, his more Protestant son (1547), which would allow Bale's return to England.

The anomalies mentioned above and the passage of time between the presumed time of performance and the publication at Wesel mean that we cannot be certain of what Bale actually wrote and acted in the 1530s, but it does seem that these plays were prepared for performance. They were written for very limited casts: *God's Promises* could be performed by two actors, and *The Temptation* and *John Baptist's Preaching* could be done substantially by two actors with a little help from extras.[91] There is a distinct possibility that Bale took these plays on tour at this time. The adaptability and simplicity of the implied style of performance suggest that this would have been practicable. Bale himself appeared in all three as the Prolocutor, and he may have doubled this with other roles. It is not clear that all the plays were ever performed in sequence, but there are interesting indications that the audience were invited to perceive links between the plays which have survived. Thus the last line of *God's Promises* suggests continuity: 'More of thys matter conclude hereafter we shall' (l. 982). The beginning of *John Baptist's Preaching* is a retrospect:

> The Lawe and Prophetes   draweth now fast to an ende,
> Which were but shaddowes   and fygures of hys commynge.   (ll. 8-9)

Such continuity is an essential advantage of cyclic form and it is further sustained at the beginning of *Temptation* where Baleus Prolocutor begins with another brief retrospect:

> After hys baptyme   Christ was Gods sonne declared   [*revealed*
> By the fathers voice   as ye before have hearde.   (ll. 1-2)

As well as suggesting continuity, this brings to mind the fundamentally important concept of a divine shaping of events.

Considering the three plays individually we find that there is a notable variety in their dramatic style. *God's Promises* is the most patterned, being divided into seven Acts in each of which a patriarchal figure has a dialogue with Pater Coelestis about mercy. There is practically no action: physical events like the Flood and the Burning Bush are avoided, and the climax of each Act is the promise of divine mercy. Bale did not eschew the Catholic lore entirely, however, because each Act ends with the singing of an anthem, accompanied on a portative organ, from the liturgy of Advent, and it is apparent that here and in the two other cycle plays, Bale was still prepared to use the Vulgate. The chief dramatic interest, apart from this, is the intensity of the dialogues with Pater Coelestis. These bring out the importance of symbols such as the creeping serpent, the rainbow and the descent of the dove (ll. 140-1, 264, 899), and an historical sense, which is undoubtedly Bale's adaptation of the understanding of divinely ordered historical periods. *God's Promises* certainly allows him to provide a retrospect into the Old Testament, but his concentration upon the Ministry and the Passion is an interesting adaptation of continental dramatic practice in the cycles. There is a summative view of salvation history: Bale speaks

> of man the first creacyon
> The abuse and fall   through hys first oversyght
> And the rayse agayne   through Gods hygh grace and myght.   (ll. 24-6)

The interest in periodisation can be detected elsewhere in Bale's non-dramatic writings, though he does not always use the same schemes.⁹²

This framing of the cyclic sense of history is essentially Protestant in approach, though in all these cycle plays Bale adopted a distinctly milder controversial stance than is apparent in most of his other writings including the morality plays, *King Johan* and *Three Laws*. The approach here is concerned with the individual conscience, the importance of the knowledge of the individual which is based upon an appreciation of scripture, and the cardinal Lutheran doctrine of *solus Christus*. The latter is seen in the conclusion by Baleus Prolocutor:

> For all the worldes synne   *alone Christ payed the pryce*
> In hys onlye deathe   was mannys lyfe always restynge
> And not in wyll workes,   nor yet in mennys deservynge.
>
> (ll. 971-3, my italics)

To be able to talk of the play in these terms suggests that Bale had set himself a distinctive intellectual and proselytising programme in his adaptation of cyclic form. There is no doubting his perception of the seriousness of the medium of drama and the necessity of the audience to respond to it:

> To waye soche matters   as wyll be uttered here,
> Of whome ye maye loke   to have no tryfelinge sporte
> In fantasyes fayned,   nor soche lyke gaudysh gere.   (ll. 16-8)

This also suggests that he had some suspicions about the work of others. It should be added that Bale's positive use of drama for polemical purposes can be supported by other Protestant examples.⁹³

Bale's handling of the scriptural material in *John Baptist's Preaching* and *The Temptation* is theatrically inventive and yet indicative of the importance he attributed to it. In the former he adapts three representative scriptural references from the Vulgate into characters, making Turba Vulgaris (Common Crowd), Publicanus (Tax Gatherer) and Miles Armatus (Armed Soldier) each receive baptism. In turn each is required, in parallel stage directions, to kneel before the Baptist. These submissive sinners are contrasted with the abusive and conspiratorial Sadduceus and Phariseus who are made to suggest the Catholic clergy Bale wished to attack. John makes a vituperative denunciation of their hypocrisy (ll. 255-72). His dialogue with Christ establishes the power of baptism even though John has to be persuaded to overcome his reluctance to baptize Christ himself. The descent of the dove is noted in a stage direction (l. 143sd) and the action ends with the singing of a hymn to the Trinity.

The Temptation is faithful to the biblical accounts, and gives special emphasis to the importance of the Word. It consists almost entirely of dialogue between Christ and Satan in which the latter's attempts to distort the scriptures for his own advantage are fully exposed. It is characteristic of Bale's Protestant views that his Christ should be much more concerned with argument than in many Catholic examples.[94] Satan pursues the traditional line of trying to discover whether Christ really is divine, but Bale allows him no answer. He retires from the scene trying to comfort himself with his belief that the Pope will continue to do his work and threatening Christ with death if he continues to preach God's Word. Bale's conclusion as Prolocutor brings out the theme of persecution to which he attached considerable importance, and which in all probability played a substantial part in the lost presentation of the Passion. He saw persecution as the inevitable lot of the faithful Christian, as the frontispiece of his autobiographical *Vocacyon* makes clear. This is seen within the framework of his faith in the power of scripture which has shown the wickedness in this episode.

Besides their publication there is one other circumstance which suggests that Bale thought of these plays as a coherent unit. He records in the *Vocacyon* that they were performed together at the Market Cross in Kilkenny on August 20, 1553. This was the day that Queen Mary was proclaimed in the town, and Bale seems to have promoted this performance against the renewal of Catholic ritual which he now perceived was being effected. Whether he also knew that mystery cycles were now likely to be revived along traditional lines is another matter. As to the lost plays, it seems from his other writings that through them Bale would have sustained his belief in the importance of Scripture, and that in the play about the Conspiracy of the Priests he would have found further scope for attacking the clergy. His handling of the Resurrection of Lazarus would have placed emphasis upon faith rather than upon miracles, which he considered to be clerical trickery. The Feast of Simon the Leper might well have involved Mary Magdalene, a character acceptable to Protestant revisionism as Lewis Wager's *Life and Repentance of Mary Magdalene* (1566) reveals.

Bale's adaptation of cycle drama comes at a time when there was still a great deal of vitality in this form. It is roughly contemporary with revisions at Coventry, Chester and Norwich, and there were regular performances of cyclic drama at York and elsewhere. At this point in its history English cycle drama was very much a going concern.

Notes

1. Alexandra F. Johnston & Margaret Rogerson [eds.], *REED: York*, 2 vols., Toronto, 1979, vol. I, pp. 112 (1477) and 119 (1478).
2. M. Dorrell, 'Two Studies of the York Corpus Christi Play', *LSE* n.s. 6 (1972), pp. 96-107.
3. Quotations are from Richard Beadle [ed.], *The York Plays*, London, 1982, with obsolete letters modernized.
4. Johnston & Rogerson [eds.], *REED: York*, vol. I, p. 21.
5. For John Clerke's annotation of the manuscript which points to modifications large and small see Peter Meredith, 'John Clerke's Hand in the York Register', *LSE* n.s. 12 (1981), pp. 245-71.
6. One of the possible exegetical sources for this intervention by the Devil, commenting upon Matthew 27:19, the scriptural basis for the episode, suggests that the Devil thought that just as he had used a woman to bring death into the world so he would use one to persuade the Jews to free Christ and so maintain the Devil's own kingdom; see Rosemary Woolf, *The English Mystery Plays*, London, 1972, p. 245, and *Glossa Ordi-*

naria, in: *PL* 114, col. 173.
7. For the controversy about the extent of playing off the waggons in medieval times, see Margaret Rogerson, 'Raging in the Streets of Medieval York', in: *The York Cycle Then and Now* (Special volume of *Early Theatre* 3 [2000]), pp. 105-25. See also Cami D. Agan, 'The Platea in the York and Wakefield Cycles: Avenues for Liminality and Salvation', *Studies in Philology* 94 (1997), pp. 344-67.
8. Peter Meredith, 'The City of York and its "Play of Pageants"', in: *The York Cycle Then and Now* (Special volume of *Early Theatre* 3 [2000]), 23-47; R. B. Dobson, 'Craft Guilds and City: The Historical Origins of the York Mystery Plays Reassessed', in: Alan E. Knight [ed.], *The Stage as Mirror: Civic Theatre in Late Medieval Europe*, Cambridge, 1997, pp. 91-105.
9. Beadle [ed.], *York Plays*, pp. 448-9.
10. Johnston & Rogerson [eds.], *York*, vol. I, p. 26, and Peter Meredith, 'The *Ordo Paginarum* and the Development of the York Tilemakers' Play', *LSE* n.s. 11 (1980), pp. 59-73.
11. Compare the discussion of Pilate in Towneley below, pp. 256-7.
12. Beadle [ed.], *York Plays*, p. 453.
13. Lynette R. Muir, *The Biblical Drama of Medieval Europe*, Cambridge, 1995, p. 138. Rosemary Woolf, *English Mystery Plays*, p. 272, notes that continental versions followed a different tradition in having the descent into hell after the Resurrection. For a possible source for the Harrowing see William Henry Hulme [ed.], *The Middle-English Harrowing of Hell and Gospel of Nicodemus*, London, 1907 [EETS OS 100], pp. 97-124.
14. V. A. Kolve, *The Play Called Corpus Christi*, London, 1966, pp. 195-6.
15. 47/217-28. However a passage of at least four lines is apparently missing, and interestingly the later annotations suggest that a new section of text was eventually played: see Beadle [ed.], *York Plays*, p. 411. The Towneley dramatist extended their role in this episode beyond his York source, see below, pp. 266-7.
16. Beadle [ed.], *York Plays*, pp. 459-60, notes that this group was suspended from performance between 1548 and 1554, and again from 1561, presumably out of Protestant sentiment.
17. Woolf, *English Mystery Plays*, p. 55.
18. Richard Beadle, 'Verbal Texture and Wordplay in the York Cycle', in: *The York Cycle Then and Now* (Special volume of *Early Theatre* 3 [2000]), pp. 167-84.
19. Alexandra F. Johnston, '"His langage is lorne": The Silent Centre of the

York Cycle', in: *The York Cycle Then and Now* (Special volume of *Early Theatre* 3 [2000]), pp. 185-95.
20. For other versions of the Transfiguration see Muir, *Biblical Drama*, p. 117.
21. Johnston & Rogerson [eds.], *REED: York*, vol. I, p. 55.
22. R. M. Lumiansky & David Mills [eds.], *The Chester Mystery Cycle: Essays and Documents*, Chapel Hill, 1983, pp. 187-8.
23. Lawrence M. Clopper [ed.], *REED: Chester*, Toronto, 1979, pp. liii-liv. In his paper, 'The History and Development of the Chester Cycle', *Modern Philology* 75 (1978), p. 231, he suggests that this earlier Corpus Christi play was limited to a Passion.
24. David Mills, *Recycling the Cycle: The City of Chester and its Whitsun Plays*, Toronto, 1998, p. 117.
25. Lumiansky & Mills [eds.], *Chester: Essays and Documents*, pp. 311-8, analyse the stanzas in the whole cycle and show that the forms aaa^{4}b^{3}ccc^{4}b^3 and the closely related aaa^{4}b^{3}aaa^{4}b^3 amount to 1117 out of 1476, there being a number of variations which would make the predominance even higher.
26. Frances A. Foster [ed.], *A Stanzaic Life of Christ Compiled from Higden's Polychronicon and the Legenda Aurea, edited from MS. Harley 3909*, London, 1926 [EETS OS 166], pp. xxix-xlii, indicates that the strongest influence is in Plays 6, 8, 9, 18, and 21.
27. Mills, *Recycling the Cycle*, p. 156, where there are other examples.
28. David Mills, 'Theories and Practices in the Editing of the Chester Play-Manuscripts', in: Derek Pearsall [ed.], *Manuscripts and Texts: Editorial Problems in Later Middle English Literature*, Cambridge, 1987, p. 115.
29. Lumiansky & Mills, *Chester: Essays and Documents*, pp. 35 and 195.
30. Albert C. Baugh, 'The Chester Plays and French Influence', in: Arthur Hobson Quin [ed.], *Schelling Anniversary Papers*, New York, 1923, p. 49.
31. In the majority of manuscripts this is followed by a comic episode concerning the devils' welcome for an ale-wife into hell, but one scribe perhaps thought it inappropriate and omitted it. There is, unfortunately, no way of knowing how often she appeared in the actual performances.
32. Mills, *Recycling the Cycle*, p. 158.
33. Printed as Appendix IB by R. M. Lumiansky & David Mills [eds.], *The Chester Mystery Cycle*, 2 vols., London, 1974-86 [EETS SS 3 and 9], vol. I, p. xxx.
34. Mills, *Recycling the Cycle*, p. 163.
35. Lumiansky & Mills [eds.], *Chester Mystery Cycle*, vol. II, p. 27.
36. As with Adam's vision (noted above) the material of this play is not

original: the dramatist has drawn upon Adso, *Libellus de Antichristo*. But again here the managing of the material within the cycle is dramatically noteworthy. For the dynamics of the dramatization of this episode here and elsewhere see my 'Staging God in Some Last Judgement Plays' (forthcoming).

37. Two further unifying strategies running through the cycle may be added. John J. McGavin, 'Sign and Tradition: The *Purification Play* in Chester', *LSE* n.s. 11 (1980), pp. 90-104, discusses the importance of signs and their misappropriation by a series of evil characters; and Kathleen M. Ashley, 'Divine Power in Chester Cycle and Late Medieval Thought', *Journal of the History of Ideas* 39 (1978), pp. 387-404, relates the theme of God's omnipotence to nominalist thought. The nominalist principles, especially the greatness of God, are discussed by Peter W. Travis, *Dramatic Design in the Chester Cycle*, Chicago, 1982, pp. 142-73.

38. When Benjamin Britten set the play for his *Noyes Fludde* (1958), he was particularly sensitive to the verbal rhythms and set them with marked differences. Indeed if one is familiar with his score, it is difficult to read the play without recalling his perception of them.

39. Lumiansky & Mills, *Chester Mystery Cycle*, vol. I, pp. 464-5, l. 15sd.

40. For comparative discussion of Shepherds plays see Woolf, *English Mystery Plays*, pp. 182-93; and Peter Happé, *English Drama before Shakespeare*, Harlow, 1999, pp. 68-74.

41. For comparison with corresponding episodes see my 'Staging God in Some Last Judgement Plays' (forthcoming).

42. Barbara D. Palmer, 'Recycling "The Wakefield Cycle": The Records', *RORD* 41 (2002), p. 96.

43. C. M. Gayley, *Plays of our Forefathers*, London, 1907, pp. 161-90.

44. Until the controversial decision by Stevens and Cawley to print them in thirteen lines, these stanzas had usually been set out in a nine-line form which combined the first eight lines into four, following the manuscript's usual but not entirely consistent layout. As their edition is likely to be the most used one for the foreseeable future, I follow their layout here, noting however that it means that the line-numbering of all previous editions and critical commentary has to be discounted: see Martin Stevens, *Four Middle English Mystery Cycles: Textual, Contextual, and Critical Interpretations*, Princeton, 1987, pp. 130-55, and Martin Stevens & A. C. Cawley [eds.], *The Towneley Plays*, 2 vols., London, 1994 [EETS SS 13], vol. I, pp. xxviii-xxxi.

45. See Stevens & Cawley [eds.], *Towneley Plays*, vol. I, p. xxviii, who

note the instance where the York Register has been corrected by John Clerke using the Towneley reading: cf. York 37/241-4 and Towneley 25/261-4.
46. *Ibidem*, vol. II, pp. 454-5.
47. *Ibidem*, vol. II, p. 540.
48. See M. Paull, 'The Figure of Mahomet in the Towneley Cycle', *CD* 6 (1972), pp. 197-200.
49. Hardin Craig [ed.], *Two Coventry Corpus Christi Plays [...] re-edited from the manuscript of Robert Croo, 1534*, London, 1957 [2nd ed.] [EETS ES 87], l. 783sd. Shakespeare remembered the ranting Herod (from Coventry?) in *Hamlet* 3.2.12.
50. Arnold Williams, *The Characterization of Pilate in the Towneley Plays*, East Lansing, 1950, pp. 16 and 74-5.
51. It is tempting, but only conjectural to relate *magnificavit* to the key word *magnificat* in Mary's scriptural submission at the Annunciation (Luke 1:46).
52. Stevens & Cawley [eds.], *Towneley Plays*, vol. II, p. 601.
53. Margaret Jennings, 'Tutivillus: The Literary Career of the Recording Demon', *Studies in Philology: Texts and Studies* 74 (1977), pp. 10-35.
54. A. C. Cawley [ed.], *The Wakefield Pageants in the Towneley Cycle*, Manchester, 1958, pp. xx-xxi.
55. Stevens & Cawley [eds.], *Towneley Plays*, vol. II, p. 447.
56. It may be a deliberate irony here in that tossing a pregnant woman in a canvass was a means of inducing labour.
57. The evidence is reported by Palmer, 'Recycling "The Wakefield Cycle"', pp. 120-1.
58. *Survey of Cornwall*, London, 1602, pp. 71-2, quoted in full by Paula Neuss [ed. and trans.], *The Creacion of the World: A Critical Edition and Translation*, New York-London, 1983, Appendix I, pp. 239-40.
59. Gloria J. Betcher, 'A Reassessment of the Date and Provenance of the Cornish *Ordinalia*', *CD* 29 (1995-96), pp. 447-9, and S. L. Joyce & Evelyn S. Newlyn [eds.], *REED: Cornwall*, Toronto, 1999, p. 513. For a list of thirty-seven *plen-an-gwaries* in Cornwall, compiled by Oliver Padel, see pp. 560-3.
60. Betcher, 'Reassessment', p. 436. References for the text of the *Ordinalia* are to Edwin Norris [ed.], *The Ancient Cornish Drama*, Oxford, 1859, 2 vols.
61. Robert Longsworth, *The Cornish Ordinalia: Religion and Dramaturgy*, Cambridge, Mass., 1967, p. 47, points out that there was a tradition of survivals of relics from the cross in Cornwall.
62. Gloria J. Betcher, 'A Tempting Theory: What Early Cornish Mermaid

Images Reveal about the First Doctor's Analogy in *Passio Domini'*, *EDAM Review* 18 (1996), pp. 65-76, brings out the ambivalent nature of mermaids in Cornish iconography.
63. See *Resurrexio Domini*, ll. 977-82, and Longsworth, *Cornish Ordinalia*, p. 92.
64. Longsworth, *Cornish Ordinalia*, p. 65, offers liturgical evidence in support of the omission.
65. Jane A. Bakere, *The Cornish 'Ordinalia': A Critical Study*, Cardiff, 1980, p. 96.
66. See Kolve, *The Play called Corpus Christi*, pp. 101-110, and Bakere, *Cornish 'Ordinalia'*, p. 112. John Bale used the idea in *God's Promises* and *Three Laws*: see below, p. 304.
67. Neuss [ed. and trans.], *Creacion of the World*, pp. xxxix-xlii.
68. Bakere, *Cornish 'Ordinalia'*, p. 155.
69. *Ibidem*, p. 167.
70. Neuss [ed. and trans.], *Creacion of the World*, pp. lii, liv.
71. Stephen Spector [ed.], *The N-Town Play: Cotton MS Vespasian D.8*, 2 vols., London, 1991 [EETS SS 11-12], vol. I, pp. xxiii, xxxviii-xl.
72. Stephen Spector, 'The Composition and Development of an Eclectic Manuscript: Cotton Vespasian D VIII', *LSE* n.s. 10 (1977), p. 75; and Peter Meredith [ed.], *The Passion Play from the N. town Manuscript*, Harlow, 1990, Appendix 4, pp. 245-50.
73. Peter Meredith [ed.], *The Mary Play from the N. town Manuscript*, Harlow, 1987, pp. 1-12.
74. See Spector [ed.], *N-Town Play*, vol. II, p. 466, and Meredith [ed.], *Mary Play*, pp. 134-7.
75. Woolf, *English Mystery Plays*, pp. 309-10; Spector [ed.], *N-Town Play*, vol. II, pp. 552-4.
76. Meredith [ed.], *Passion Play*, p. 9, notes that on the whole scribes tended to remain fairly close to their places of origin.
77. Mark Eccles [ed.], *The Macro Plays*, London, 1969 [EETS 262], pp. xxi-xxii; John McKinnell, 'Staging the Digby *Mary Magdalen*', *METh* 6 (1984), pp. 126-52. This version of *Mary Magdalene* has many attributes of cyclic form: see Donald C. Baker, John L. Murphy & Louis B. Hall jr. [eds.], *The Late Medieval Religious Plays of Bodleian MSS Digby 133 and e Museo 160*, Oxford-London, 1982 [EETS 283], p. xlvi.
78. See the stage directions at 27/76 and 348.
79. Meredith [ed.], *Mary Play*, p. 20, preserves a cautious neutrality about the *mis-en-scène* for the Mary Play, leaving open the possibilities of performing indoors or in the open air.
80. See Spector [ed.], *N-Town Play*, 21.179-80, note to 20/232sd.

311

81. Woolf, *English Mystery Plays*, pp. 288-9; Richard Rastall, *The Heaven Singing: Music in Early English Religious Drama*, Cambridge, 1996, vol. I, pp. 290-1, 328 n. 80.
82. The sequence *Benedicta sit beata Trinitas* is also sung for the marriage of Mary and Joseph (10/301sd), JoAnna Dutka, *Music in the English Mystery Plays*, Kalamazoo, 1980, p. 23.
83. This is the second devilish fart in N-Town, cf. after Diabolus is cursed at the Fall of Man, 2/273.
84. C. W. Marx, *The Devil's Rights and the Redemption in the Literature of Medieval England*, Cambridge, 1995.
85. See the quotation above, 31/01sd.
86. They appear in Plays 2, 5, 8, 10, 11, 12, 13, 16, 18, 20, 28, 36 and 41.
87. For the importance of Wisdom and the related issue of Man's Wit, see Kathleen M. Ashley, '"Wyt" and "Wysdam" in N-Town Cycle', *Philological Quarterly* 58 (1979), pp. 121-35.
88. For a fuller consideration of the evidence in this section see my 'John Bale's Lost Mystery Cycle', *Cahiers Elisabéthains* 60 (2001), pp. 1-12.
89. Barbara D. Palmer, 'Corpus Christi "Cycles" in Yorkshire: The Surviving Records', *CD* 27 (1993), pp. 218-31.
90 '...*descendit ad infernam*...lyke as my self had before tyme sett yt forth ... in a serten playe ... the sowle of Crist soch tyme as hys corse laye in the grave ded vysytt hell.' PRO, SP 1/111, f.182 (1537).
91. For possible doubling schemes, see Peter Happé [ed.], *The Complete Plays of John Bale*, 2 vols., Woodbridge, 1985-86, vol. I, pp. 154-5.
92. His play *Three Laws* depends upon a threefold division, see Peter Happé, *John Bale*, New York, 1996, pp. 31-2.
93. Paul Whitfield White, 'Reforming Mysteries' End: A New Look at Protestant Intervention in English Provincial Drama', *Journal of Medieval and Early Modern Studies* 29 (1999), pp. 121-47.
94. See my '"Erazed in the Book": The Mystery Cycles and Reform' (forthcoming).

Chapter Six
Cyclic Form (II)

In this Chapter we shall review historical, functional and structural aspects of cyclic form, whether dramatic or iconographic. Our primary purpose has been to show that the cyclic form, so markedly successful in the English mystery plays, was part of a much wider artistic and cultural enterprise in western Europe. The extant English plays, though famous, are few in number and yet they share much with the dramatic forms found elsewhere and reviewed in Chapters Three and Four, and with the variety of iconographic modes considered in Chapter Two. But it is also apparent that they were highly individual enterprises, and that their creators and those who realised them in performance were proceeding along individual lines which distinguished them from one another. This interplay between analogy and divergence seems to be one of the chief characteristics, and perhaps one of the chief attractions of cyclic form. In the case of the English cycles, several are distinctive in that they were performed on pageant waggons by craft guilds and they embodied a narrative from Creation to the Last Judgement. This pattern is not closely followed by all the known English examples—of the extant comprehensive texts only York and Chester conform incontestably—but it does seem to be one of the defining modes. By contrast, although some cycles on the continent presented a narrative from Creation to Doomsday, though some were processional, some were played on waggons and some were performed by trade guilds, the English combination is rarely found there in exactly the same form—if at all.

The historical position of the English cycles is intriguing. The *York Cycle*, first mentioned in 1376, seems to have been quite well established by the second decade of the fourteenth century.

The lists embodied in the *Ordo Paginarum* in the city's A/Y Memorandum Book indicate a substantial spread of plays by the year 1415, and it seems certain that by then the process and routines of performance were well in place.[1] The information about the individual pageants in these lists corresponds quite well with the manuscript of the plays written down half a century later. If the lists can be interpreted as embodying a complete cycle, we may conclude that the York Cycle occurs very early in the historical perspective. It certainly had some influence on English successors, notably on Towneley, but whether this influence spread to the continent is highly problematic. The earliest conjectural dates for the Cornish *Ordinalia* (*c.* 1375), the lost Beverley Corpus Christi pageants (1377) and the fragmentary Coventry Corpus Christi play (1392) bear comparison with that for York, though it is not ascertainable exactly how far these cycles had been developed by these dates.

There were, nevertheless, many anticipations of different kinds. Some of these are discernible in the theological background to the process of instruction and devotion, which the cycles were meant to promote. Here a balance is necessary, for paradoxically there was a long-standing ecclesiastical suspicion of dramatic activities which had many manifestations.[2] But the cycles themselves were the work of educated and, for the most part, orthodox clerics who sought to promote the Church's task of worship and instruction, and they drew extensively upon established theological writings for many details of narrative and explication which contributed to the texture of the cycles. They also had access to poetic reworkings of patristic and apocryphal writings such as the *Gospel of Nicodemus* and *The Northern Passion*.[3] That the cycles were a powerful resource is sustained by the fact that when dissent movements began to appear in the sixteenth century, cyclic form attracted new authors having new perspectives, who must have seen that it could be adapted to their own objectives. For example, besides John Bale's lost mystery cycle, there is also Jacob Rueff's Protestant Passion at Zurich (1545).[4] On the other hand a re-emphasis of traditional Catholic values is apparent in some later cycles, and indeed in some of the later iconography, as with Tintoretto. We have also noted, following the work of David Mills, how the Chester Cycle became part of the religious politics of the city in the late sixteenth century.

In terms of historical events, at the beginning of the period in which we find dramatic cycles, there was a range of processes functioning as a part of the growing intensity of late medieval piety, and we may propose here that the new feast of Corpus Christi, developed in the fourteenth century, as well as the growing influence of the Franciscan order both had significant influence. It seems entirely possible that the establishment of Corpus Christi played an important part in the evolution of dramatic cycles.[5] Its effect was a public demonstration of piety, which spread rapidly through Christendom and placed a premium upon outdoor celebration, especially in the form of processions. It brought God out into the streets, where he was carried for all to see and worship. The detail we have noted for the *Künzelsau Fronleichnamspiel*, for example, makes it quite clear that there the dramatic performance accompanied the Sacrament. The feast itself took place in the summer, when outdoor events could flourish on a grand scale, in such a way that municipal aspirations came to be satisfied alongside religious ones. The choice of subject matter incorporated within the processions often seems closely related to the narrative embodied or implied in the dramatic cycles. These events were part of the manipulation of time whereby the here and now of a summer day and a city *en fête* was interlinked with a cosmic design. The sense of divine intervention in human affairs was made manifest. In the case of the English processional performances, and this may also be true elsewhere when procession was a fundamental ingredient in the celebrations, as for the *Bliscapen* at Brussels and the cycle at Künzelsau, there must have been a sense that the town or city was transformed by the circumstances of the performance.[6] Such an impression is intensified by Memling's visual presentation of Jerusalem as a kind of Bruges.

Similarly one may ask whether Christ entering Jerusalem was also entering the city of York.

Though there was the reality and continuity of historical time in the procession, there was also a process of identification, often symbolic, located within the items of the procession which transcended the historical narrative and in doing so departed from a normal chronological sequence. This may have been achieved by types and antitypes, and also by the frequent re-appearance of individual characters such as Christ, Mary and the Apostles in different guises. The Corpus Christi celebration also facilitated a range of quasi-dramatic experiences, especially in Spain and the Low Countries where quasi-mimetic forms such as inanimate figures and miming, as well as *tableaux vivants* were used. But against all this we must not lose sight of the fact that many cycles developed entirely without direct reference to Corpus Christi, particularly in France. In view of the large size of the French achievement we must take into account other developments in worship, and, in the light of this, the influence of the Franciscans was of some import.

We have seen that the thrust of Franciscan spirituality was towards making religious experience part of everyday life, and along with this went a powerful exploitation of the quasi-mythical status of the founder. It is especially important for our purposes that the linking properties of cyclic form were explored in the decoration of the Basilica at Assisi, and that from there many of the existing characteristics of cyclic form could be further disseminated in Italy and beyond, by what we should now call the promotional activities of the order. This included the notion of Francis as an *alter Christus*. In imagery of this kind the double value of such symbolic elements as the stigmata carried by both Christ and St. Francis could be brought out, so as to make each narrative reflect upon the other. But the changes in spiritual dimensions were no doubt wider than this particular Franciscan mission. We can see these particularly in the development of religious art from the twelfth century onwards. The greater sense of the suffering of

Christ, and his portrayal as a Man of Sorrows is an important emotional shift, which had much effect upon the ways in which he was portrayed in cyclic forms, visual and dramatic. This gave opportunity for a more powerful effect upon the feelings of the observers, and it also required or implied a much greater attention to the detail of suffering. The iconographic aspect of this is discernible, for example, in the illustrations of Christ's sufferings in *The Holkham Bible Picture Book* early in the fourteenth century, well before the earliest reference to the York Cycle in 1376.

The presence of the Virgin in cycles is another resonant element. Her story is made a structural feature in the *Bliscapen* and in Memling's *Advent and Triumph*. As with St. Francis, parallels could be drawn between the narrative of her life, death and assumption with those of Christ himself: the example in Duccio's *Maestà* is particularly compelling. There could be an intense and complex interweaving of the two narratives. This happens in the Books of Hours, as well as in the many variations in the dramatic versions of her presence at the crucifixion. There is also the poignancy of her plea that some other way of atonement may be found than that of the suffering and death of her son. Cyclic form, with its exploitation of repetition and cross-reference was peculiarly well adapted to these processes. Looking back from the period of its greatest achievement, which may well be the latter half of the fifteenth century and the first half of the sixteenth, I suggest that these circumstances must have been significant factors in its development.

Anticipations of form may have been influential. The liturgical drama was performed in traditional ways before and during the period of cyclic drama, but before this developed it had shown interesting steps towards coalescing incidents, particularly in concentrations around the Nativity and the Passion. These were usually tied to the parts of the Church calendar to which they were related, whereas many dramatic cycles, with their comprehensive narratives, were performed at times separated from particular events in the Church year, probably under the influence of Corpus Christi. Hence it is necessary to distinguish the achievements such as the Benediktbeuern plays from the later cycles. Their setting was related to ecclesiastical rather than to civic ceremony and their location was, and almost certainly remained within a church building of some kind where the relationship between the congregation/audience and the ceremony would have been markedly different from that for the performance of the outdoor cycles. Richard Axton has also suggested that, although direct influence from the liturgical drama is problematic, the presence of ceremonial detail in some of the plays about the three Marys at the Tomb in the form of elaborate repetition, and the emphasis upon the *Magnificat* in the Salutation of Mary may well recall similar material in the liturgical drama.[7] The evidence given in Chapter Two about the dating of the evolution of pictorial cycles also seems relevant here: like them the liturgical drama had a much longer period of activity than we can assume for the dramatic cycles.

Another possibly influential feature from the liturgical drama would have been the availability of musical settings which could be developed within the cycles. In some cases this was done sparingly, and the main dramatic medium was the spoken word, the music being used at selected emphatic points or perhaps moments of resolution. In most dramatic cycles, however, there is considerable reliance upon musical elements drawn from the liturgy: indeed it is the chief musical resource. Richard Rastall has demonstrated that music in the English cycles had a range of dynamic functions related to things like movement, and entrances and exits. He has shown that its incorporation and performance was the work of trained musicians, and he has identified its role in presenting heavenly characters, and also the evilly disposed.[8]

In the German tradition, however, we have a much more concentrated mode of presentation and the music appears to have amounted to a rather more substantial component in the performances. We have found this in the Alsfeld *Passion,* and the same may be the case in some individual English episodes like the N-Town Assumption. Such variation emphasises that influence upon the development of cyclic form could be applied in differing ways. One may suspect that music helped significantly as a means of drawing episodes together. In some German cycles, it appears that musical Choruses may also have been used for similar purposes, as with the three at Lucerne.

Some of the anticipations or influences we have been discussing can also be seen as being important as structural devices. This is apparently the case with the Virgin, whose role we have noted in a number of cycles, the *Passion d'Auvergne* being one of the most remarkable. Her anxieties about Christ's death and her own also invite close comparison in both narrative and emotional effects, and in some cycles this is also present in the concern sometimes manifested by God the Father, as in Gréban (ll. 8816-8). The setting for this last is usually the Debate of the Four Daughters, which became one of the chief structural devices in the dramatic cycles since it provided a rationale for the Incarnation, as discernible in the cycles associated with Arras and Bologna, and in Gréban's *Passion*, the *Bliscapen* and N-Town. This is perhaps one of the most comprehensive devices, and its usefulness can be seen in the variation in the places in which the Debate, or instalments of it, are inserted into the narratives. One of these variations is God the Father's disgust at human wickedness and the oft-repeated motif of his regret at having created mankind at all, but this is usually played against his compassion, a conflict which is embodied in the intensity of the argument between the Daughters. It does seem, however, that the Debate was developed more within the continental cycles than in the English ones.[9] It certainly had a prior theological basis, but the dramatic initiative, making it a powerful rationale for the Incarnation, was probably French and the chief claimant seems to be the *Passion d'Arras* where it leads directly to the Annunciation (ll. 1-1076).

The devils, perhaps the obverse of the Debate, are also used structurally. Initially the sensational fall of Lucifer provides a remarkable spectacle, and the relationship between his fall and the creation of Adam is a starting point for much of what is to follow.

But the subsequent attempts to restore his position, to establish a rival hegemony or to exact revenge are used to sustain or restart the narrative. Both the visual cycles and the dramatic ones are rich with his later activities, right up to Judgement Day, though it appears that the latter featured more extensively in the visual representations than in the plays. One thematic aspect, which can be made to recur in several episodes, is the divine deception whereby the Devil is kept in the dark by not knowing of Christ's divinity. Though this does not appear in all versions, it has a pervasive effect in a number of cycles, especially N-Town, where his ignorance is much exploited by the dramatist or compiler.[10] The influence of the Devil is pervasive in another sense in that there are often proliferations of devils, especially in the French cycles. In spite of the fact that some French *Passions* do not begin with the Fall of Lucifer, the presence and influence of the Devil are persistent. This is sometimes used in such a way as to suggest a devilish superplot managed by Lucifer, who (unfortunately for him) is chained in hell, while Satan and others roam the world to implement his schemes. When disagreement breaks out, and Satan, returning to hell, is punished by his master, the confusion and incompetence of evil becomes a valuable dramatic theme.[11] The devilish human beings perhaps enhance it. There are often parallels with the Devil in the presentation of Pilate, Herod, Annas and Caiaphas, emphasised by the rhetoric of their boasting speeches, and their conspiracy and cruelty. In the case of Pilate, who can sometimes be rather more sympathetic or even vacillating, there is also the tradition from the *Acta Pilati* which shows his subsequent destruction and here the inversion of the story of Christ's resurrection is thematically effective and a marked structural feature. More rarely there is the story of Judas, which is in part an inversion of the story of Christ, as in the *Passion Catalane-Occitane*.

Besides these features, we have also noted the structural role played by the Trinity, as in the Chester Cycle, and there is also a didactic continuity provided by figures which are concerned with the instruction of the audience. This is notable in the parts of the Chester Cycle which are introduced by the Doctor or the Expositor, in the Contemplatio sections of N-Town, and even the *Rector Processionis* at Künzelsau. At times in this discussion we have noted the relationship between types and antitypes and this also informs the process by which different sections of a cycle may be made to interconnect. This feature is present in both the iconographic material, as in the windows of King's College Chapel in Cambridge, as well as the dramatic, as in the parallels between Isaac as boy and man with Christ.[12] These structural devices obviously act in different ways, and they are also intermittent at times, but they do evidence aspects of cyclic form which sought to increase the coherence of the diversity of episodes. However, we note especially that none of these devices can be regarded as universal, and the approach to a comprehensive design using them is somewhat spasmodic. This brings into question the idea that the cycles, dramatic or iconographic, are necessarily organised around unifying themes.[13] A certain looseness of structure seems to be endemic in cyclic form, and one of the functions of the structure is to provide opportunities for richness in individual episodes. A good example of this is the way the work of the Wakefield Master in the Towneley Cycle has been interpreted here. We have seen him developing particular episodes like the Shepherds (twice), but apparently leaving many others untouched.

Possibly the most striking part of this investigation does indeed lie in the artistic opportunity presented by cyclic form. In both the visual and dramatic cycles we can see the creators seeking ways in which a large body of material might be shown to advantage. Here it is worth recalling that our discussion of the variety of texts has shown that many cycles were not invented at one blow, but were developed over a lengthy period, and those authors who might have begun them might well have had no idea how they were going to end up. Even more, we can say that until the cycles were finally abandoned or destroyed, they probably never achieved a final or definitive stage, but carried within them the abiding possibility of change. This is even true of cycles attributable to a known author such as Gréban or Michel. Many cycles, then, never had one single state and their existence was a Protean one. Moreover the creation of cycles was often not the work of one author, but the result of the contributions of many, who modified the work of their predecessors. As time went on and the idea of dramatic cycles became more widespread, such developments may well have been based upon conventional precedents. In some cases we have reason to believe that the initiative of performers was a factor. Even in the iconographic cycles we have discussed, we have found that the principal artists have often shared the work with collaborators and pupils. In the dramatic cycles, especially in England, there was scope for a variety of different forms of dramatic writing, and we have noticed how often the style of individual episodes is subject to variation. Perhaps in the English form, indeed, with its peculiarly separated incidents, as determined by the separated pageant waggons, the scope for individual initiative was large. It may even have been encouraged as different guilds competed with one another in terms of dramatic achievement, and perhaps also in social terms. However, it seems inescapable that cycle form was distinguished by its capacity to accept revision and this flexibility must have attracted many contributors.

The existence of the cycles is also influenced by the question of literacy. We have assumed that they were composed by educated clerics because they contain so much that is in line with approved and tested theology, yet many of those performers or witnesses could not read, and thus the texts of the plays existed in a status largely unfamiliar to us today. The creation of a manuscript to embody existing practice, as seems to be the case with the York Register, implies that the cycle existed previously without ever being comprehensively written down for a considerable number of years. It only achieved its destined form when it was performed in the streets. In this respect, in other words, the cyclic form is a manifestation of a pre- or sub-literate culture. It did exist, but not in the form of a modern book. The study of the texts of the cycle plays therefore requires a peculiar discipline, one in which the ever-changing form requires special attention.

But there is another side to the question of whether these dramatic cycles were books. The N-Town play seems to be more of a paper compilation than a codification close to a cyclic performance like the York manuscript. Even if we allow for the strong possibility that some N-Town episodes were performed, it is hard to sustain the idea that the whole cycle ever really existed as a performance. Yet the compiler may very well have intended his book to be typical of a performance manuscript, but written down in such a way that it was accessible to readers even if it were never actually performed. The process of compilation can also be considered in the printed version, the only surviving early edition, of *Le Mistère du Viel Testament.* In this case it seems that different authors wrote individual plays which were then combined for publication. The plays at Lille were written out in a biblical sequence by the compiler in the 1480s. Of the seventy-two plays about ten or twelve were performed each year, though there was apparently no attempt to follow a historical sequence in performance.[14]

As the cycles unfold we can observe that there are a number of features which recur in many of them. One of the most important is the process of anticipation, and the complementary recapitulation. The foreshadowing may be employed for individual characters, as with Adam and Christ, or it may be a question of ways in which a particular episode may anticipate something which will occur later, as in Isaac's carrying the wood for the sacrifice foreshadowing Christ on the way to Calvary. Sometimes the cycles make use of sequences involving prophecy, and though these incidents are often not in themselves very dramatic in a realistic mode, they have an important function in providing a historical context for Advent. On the other hand, Adam's presence at the foot of the cross at the Crucifixion is a particularly pointed way of recalling his original sin, now redeemed. The perception of links of this kind may be facilitated by very explicit reference, but there is also a process whereby a rich texture of cross allusion is presented without being explicated.[15] Indeed, our later perspective upon the cycles is perhaps inhibited because we cannot always be sure of identifying the web of allusion which the two processes of anticipation and recollection provide. In some ways this is a matter of a traditional texture, and it is apparent that some episodes are much more susceptible to a wealth of cross reference than others. Such material is not only significant in narrative terms: it is also a matter of the emotional implications that may lie between two incidents or characters.

In certain circumstances the place of performance contributes much to the exploitation of cyclic form. We have noted how in the York Cycle the sequence of waggons, proceeding one after the other could bring to each station a sense of renewing and redirecting attention. It is a marked feature, apparent still in the performances given from time to time in the same streets in recent years, that each waggon has to arrive and the play has to begin, and these are features of the dramatic experience of the onlookers. Similarly the episode comes to an end and the waggon has to proceed down the street while another takes its place. By contrast, the place and scaffold mode, discernible in parts of N-Town, in the *Ordinalia*, and in most of the French and German cycles, emphasises cyclicity by ways which point up the simultaneity of episodes and incidents. The effects achieved by Memling in his two cyclic paintings parallel this panoramic effect. In this way cyclic form facilitates a multiplicity of narrative. There may be an overall historical continuity, which has much to contribute to the meaning of a cycle, but the creators could draw upon a wealth of different initiatives. To some extent this may even have been a matter of a main story and a number of related offshoots from it. Even in the continental *Passions*, which typically confine themselves to the narrative from the Entry into Jerusalem to the Ascension, there are many devices which force us to recall the Old Testament past and to anticipate the Judgement. Perhaps the most interesting iconographic example of the relationship between narratives is the ways in which the different narrative sequences are arranged for the bosses in Norwich cathedral. There the disposition of narrative allows a re-statement of part of the narrative. Indeed there are many places within individual cycles where repetition of theme and incident seems to be a salient feature. In both modes we should also be aware that there was much interaction between the cyclic practice of individual towns and cities in terms of both time and place. For the Towneley Cycle some episodes were borrowed from York, and we have recalled the extensive promulgation of the texts of the *Passions* by Gréban and Michel.

In their different ways both these styles of cyclic production can provide a continuity of narrative, and opportunities to depart from it. This now seems to have been a key feature of the cycles. In Chapter One we noted how they could be both centrifugal and centripetal. This capacity is undoubtedly a great advantage if one of the broader objectives is to sustain a sense that the whole of history, human and divine, is contained within the cyclic process. This is especially true for those cycles which turn again and again to the close detail of particular settings and events in specific incidents. We can see this operating in both the iconographic and the dramatic modes. For the former we might recall the detail of the scenes showing Peter's Denials in Duccio's *Maestà* and for the latter the marital frustrations of Mak and his wife in the Towneley Second Shepherds Play.

In this study of cyclic form we have tried to show that it had a historical reality and that it embodied aesthetic advantages which attracted many dramatists and artists. Even if we can no longer assume that the cycles were the commonest form of drama in the late middle ages, they were, in fact, distributed over a very large part of western Europe, and their work was successful and popular for a significant period of up to two centuries, in the case of the dramatic cycles, and for rather longer for the iconographic ones. Because of the ubiquity of medieval Catholicism for the main part of their historical existence, they transcended national, linguistic and cultural boundaries, in so far as we can define them for medieval times, but at the same time the strength of their local appeal was such that there was scope for many individual characteristics and aspirations. This double appeal they may have shared with many other artistic forms—they are certainly not unique in this respect—but it is one of their most abiding characteristics. The focus of our study has been the English mystery cycles. Though they were generated at the geographical margin of Europe, we should no longer regard them in isolation since they were integrated into wider dramatic and iconological perspectives. They were part of these cultural realities, and in the case of the York Cycle at least, because of its early date and powerful reputation, there may have been a significant contribution to their development. The cycles remain part of the European cultural inheritance, and it is a distinct possibility that the frequent attempts to revive their dramatic potential today in England and North America answer to the construction of a meaning for our contemporaries as well as to an interest in historical reconstruction.[16]

Notes

1. Alexandra F. Johnston & Margaret Rogerson [eds.], *REED: York*, 2 vols., Toronto, 1979, vol. I, p. 3 and 16-26.
2. This is documented in William Tydeman [ed.], *The Medieval European Stage, 500–1550*, Cambridge, 2001, pp. 113-7.
3. Lawrence M. Clopper, *Drama, Play, and Game: English Festive Culture in the Medieval and Early Modern Period*, Chicago-London, 2001, p. 210, has recently made a case for the principal Chester author as a layman
4. Tydeman [ed.], *The Medieval European Stage*, pp. 377-8. See Jacob Rueff, *Das Züricher Passionsspiel: Das lyden vnsers Herren Jesu Christi das man nempt den Passion, 1545*, [ed.] Barbara Thoran, Bochum, 1984, p. 5, who also notes Protestant Passions by Hans Sachs and Sebastian Wild. Paul Whitfield White, 'Reforming Mysteries' End: A New Look at Protestant Intervention in English Provincial Drama', *Journal of Medieval and Early Modern Studies* 29 (1999), pp. 121-47, has noted that there was widespread support for drama among Protestants.

5. V. A. Kolve, *The Play Called Corpus Christi*, London, 1966, p. 286 and note 26, observes, however, that it is difficult to establish a direct connection between the feast and the plays, and suggests that the procession itself had no direct papal authority. He also points out that the guilds were very quick to assume responsibility for the procession.
6. For a sense of the differing communities in which medieval plays were produced see Lynette Muir, 'European Communities and Medieval Drama', in: Alan Hindley [ed.], *Drama and Community: People and Plays in Medieval Europe*, Turnhout, 1999 [*Medieval Texts and Cultures of Northern Europe*, 1], pp. 1-17.
7. Richard Axton, *European Drama of the Early Middle Ages*, London, 1974, pp. 171-3.
8. Richard Rastall, *The Heaven Singing: Music in Early English Religious Drama*, Cambridge, 1996, vol. I, pp. 221-3, 176-215. JoAnna Dutka, *Music in the English Mystery Plays*, Kalamazoo, 1980, pp. 7-9, discussed music in relation to action and as a structural element.
9. See Peter Meredith and Lynette R. Muir, 'The Trial in Heaven in the *Eerste Bliscap* and Other European Plays', *Dutch Crossing* (1984), n° 22, pp. 84-92, and Hans-Jürgen Diller, 'From Synthesis to Compromise: The Four Daughters of God in Early English Drama', *EDAM Review* 18 (1996), pp. 88-103.
10. This idea was explored by T. Fry, 'The Unity of the *Ludus Coventriae*', *Studies in Philology* 48 (1951), pp. 527-70, and somewhat modified by C. W. Marx, *The Devil's Rights and the Redemption in the Literature of Medieval England*, Cambridge, 1995.
11. On the self-defeat of the devils in social terms, see John D. Cox, *The Devil and the Sacred in English Drama, 1350–1642*, Cambridge, 2000, pp. 29-30.
12. This role of Isaac is explored by Rosemary Woolf, *The English Mystery Plays*, London, 1972, pp. 147-52. See also plays 33A and 33B in Gustav Milchsack [ed.], *Heidelberger Passionsspiel*, Tübingen, 1880.
13. See Michel André Bossy, 'Afterword', in: Sara Sturm-Maddox & Donald Maddox [eds.], *Transtextualities: Of Cycles and Cyclicity in Medieval French Literature*, Binghamton, 1996, p. 201.
14. See Alan E. Knight, 'Cyclicity in Medieval French Drama', in Sturm-Maddox & Maddox [eds.], *Transtextualities*, pp. 192-4.
15. I have been struck by some interesting technical parallels between cyclic form and Samuel Beckett's *Waiting for Godot*. Even though there must be many objections to regarding this play as a cycle, which it is unnecessary to rehearse here, Beckett uses processes of anticipation, recollection and repetition for both language and events in ways which become central

to the dramatic texture of his play. Moreover the suspension of the normal procedure of narrative, even though we may search eagerly, but vainly for it, and the circularity which seems to encompass the succession of events, at least in part, may help to illuminate some of the essentials of cyclic form.

16. For modern reconstructions see John R. Elliott jr., *Playing God: Medieval Mysteries on the Modern Stage*, Toronto-Buffalo, 1989, pp. 141-3 (there is a Chronology for 1901-1980, pp. 145-8); Lynette R. Muir, 'Résurrection des Mystères: Medieval drama in Modern France', n.s. *LSE* 29 (1998), pp. 235-47; and *The York Cycle Then and Now* (Special volume of *Early Theatre* 3 [2000]), pp. 205-74, containing notes by eight directors at the complete performance of the York Cycle at Toronto in June 1998.

Bibliography

I. DRAMA
Primary Texts (Dramatic and other)

Baker, Donald C., John L. Murphy & Louis B. Hall jr. [eds.], *The Late Medieval Religious Plays of Bodleian MSS Digby 133 and e Museo 160*, Oxford & London, 1982 [EETS 283] for *Mary Magdalen*.
Beadle, Richard, [ed.], *The York Plays*, London, 1982.
Bédier, Jean, 'Fragment d'un ancien mystère', *Romania* 24 (1895), pp. 86-94.
Beuken, W. H., [ed.], *Die Eerste Bliscap van Maria en Die Sevenste Bliscap van Onser Vrouwen*, Culemborg, 1973.
Bevington, David, [ed.], *Medieval Drama*, Boston, 1975.
Bibolet, Jean-Claude, [ed.], *Le 'Mystère de la passion' de Troyes: Mistere de la passion Nostre Seigneur, Troyes, XVe siècle*, 2 vols., Genève, 1987.
Cawley, A. C., [ed.], *The Wakefield Pageants in the Towneley Cycle*, Manchester, 1958.
Cohen, Gustave, [ed.], *Le livre de conduite du régisseur et le compte des dépenses pour le mystère de la passion de Mons*, Paris, 1925.
Coigneau, Dirk, [ed.], *Mariken van Nieumeghen*, Den Haag, 1982.
Corbató, Hermenegildo, *Los misterios del corpus de Valencia*, Berkeley, 1932.
Cornagliotti, Anna, [ed.], *La passione di Revello: Sacra rappresentazione quattrocentesca*, Torino, 1976.
Craig, Hardin, [ed.], *Two Coventry Corpus Christi Plays [...] re-edited from the manuscript of Robert Croo, 1534*, London, 1957 [EETS ES 87] [2nd ed.].
D'Ancona, Alessandro, [ed.], *Sacre rappresentazioni dei secoli XIV, XV e XVI*, 3 vols., Firenzi, 1872.
De Bartholomaeis, Vincenzo, [ed.], *Il teatro abruzzese del medio evo*, Bologna, 1924 [rpt. 1979].
——, *Laude drammatiche e rappresentazioni sacre*, 3 vols., Firenze, 1942 [rpt. 1967].
De Estrella, Juan Christoval, *El Felicissimo Viaje d'el Muy Alto y Muy Poderoso Principe Don Phelippe*, [Antwerp], 1552.

De Rothschild, James, [ed.], *Le mistere du vieil testament*, 6 vols., Paris [*SATF*], 1878-91.
Durán i Sanpere, Agustí, & Eulàlia Durán [eds.], *La passió de Cervera, misteri del segle XVI*, Barcelona, 1984.
Durbin, P. T., & Lynette Muir [eds.], *The "Passion de Semur"*, Leeds, 1981 [*Leeds Medieval Studies*, 3].
Eccles, Mark, [ed.], *The Macro Plays*, London, 1969 [EETS 262].
Elliott, John R., jr., & Graham A. Runnalls [eds.], *The Baptism and Temptation of Christ: The First Day of a Medieval French Passion Play*, New Haven, 1978.
Erbe, Theodor, [ed.], *Mirk's Festial: A Collection of Homilies*, London, 1905 [EETS ES 96].
Foster, Frances A., [ed.], *A Stanzaic Life of Christ Compiled from Higden's Polychronicon and the Legenda Aurea, edited from MS. Harley 3909*, London, 1926 [EETS OS 166].
Francis, W. Nelson, [ed.], *The Book of Vices and Virtues: A Fourteenth-Century English Translation of the Somme le roi of Lorens d'Orleans*, London, 1942 [EETS 217].
Frank, Grace, [ed.], *La passion d'Autun*, Paris, 1934 [*SATF*].
———, [ed.], *La passion du Palatinus*, Paris, 1972.
Froning, Richard, [ed.], *Das Drama des Mittelalters: Die lateinischen Osterfeiern und ihre Entwicklung in Deutschland*, Darmstadt, 1964 [rpt.].
Furnivall, F. J., [ed.], *Robert of Brunne's 'Handlyng Synne'*, A. D. 1303, with those parts of the Anglo-French treatise on which it was founded from MSS. in the british Museum and Bodleian libraries, 2 vols., London, 1901-03 [EETS OS 119 and 123].
Happé, Peter, [ed.], *The Complete Plays of John Bale*, 2 vols., Woodbridge, 1985-86.
Hennig, Ursula, [ed.], *Das Wiener Passionsspiel: Cod. 12887 (Suppl. 561) der Österreichische Nationalbibliothek zu Wien*, Göppingen, 1986.
Hersart, Théodore, vicomte de La Villemarqué [ed. and trans.], *Le grand mystère de Jésus, passion et resurrection, drame breton du moyen âge, avec une étude sur le théatre chez les nations celtiques*, Paris, 1865.
Hulme, William Henry, [ed.], *The Middle-English Harrowing of Hell and Gospel of Nicodemus*, London, 1907 [EETS OS 100].
Janota, Johannes, [ed.], *Die hessische Passionsspielgruppe: Edition im Paralleldruck*, I: *Frankfurter Dirigierrolle—Frankfurter Passionsspiel*, Tübingen, 1997.
Jeanroy, Alfred, & H. Teulié, [eds.], *Mystères provençaux du quinzième siècle*, Toulouse, 1893.
Jodogne, Omer, [ed.], *Le 'Mystère de la passion' (Angers 1486)* [de] *Jean*

Michel, Gembloux, 1959.

——, [ed.], *Le mystère de la passion* [d'] *Arnoul Gréban*, 2 vols., Brussels, 1965-83.

King, Pamela M., & Clifford Davidson [eds.], *The Coventry Corpus Christi Plays*, Kalamazoo, 2000.

Klammer, Bruno, [ed.], *Bozner Passion 1495: Die Spielhandschriften A und B*, Berne-Frankfurt, 1986.

Knight, Alan E., [ed.], *Les mystères de la procession de Lille*, vol. I: *Le pentateuque*, Genève, 2001.

Koopmans, Jelle, [ed.], *Le mystère de Saint Remi*, Genève, 1997.

Le Verdier, Pierre, [ed.], *Mystère de l'incarnation et nativité de Notre Sauveur et Rédempteur Jésus-Christ répresenté à Rouen en 1474*, 3 vols., Rouen, 1884-6.

Leendertz, P., [ed.], *Middelnederlandsche dramatische poëzie*, Leiden, 1907.

Liebenow, Peter K., [ed.], *Das Künzelsauer Fronleichnamspiel*, Berlin, 1969.

Lumiansky, R. M. & David Mills [eds.], *The Chester Mystery Cycle*, 2 vols., London, 1974-86 [EETS SS 3 and 9].

Macdonald, Aileen Ann, [ed.], *Passion catalane-occitane*, Genève, 1999.

Meech, Sanford Brown, & Hope Emily Allen [eds.], *The Book of Margery Kempe*: The text from the unique MS. owned by Colonel W. Butler-Bowden, London, 1940 [EETS, 212].

Meredith, Peter, [ed.], *The Mary Play from the N. town Manuscript*, Harlow, 1987.

——, *The Passion Play from the N. town Manuscript*, Harlow, 1990.

Milchsack, Gustav, [ed.], *Heidelberger Passionsspiel*, Tübingen, 1880.

——, [ed.], *Egerer Fronleichnamsspiel*, Tübingen, 1881.

Mone, Franz Joseph, [ed.], *Altteutsche Schauspiele*, Quedlinburg-Leipzig, 1841.

Morris, Richard, [ed.], *Dan Michel's Ayenbite of Inwyt, or Remorse of Conscience*: in the Kentish dialect, 1340 AD, London, 1866 [EETS OS 23].

Neuss, Paula, [ed. and trans.], *The Creacion of the World: A Critical Edition and Translation*, New York-London, 1983.

Newbigin, Nerida, [ed.], *Nuovo corpus di sacre rappresentazioni fiorentine del quattrocento*: edite e inedite tratte da manoscritti coevi o ricontrollate su di essi, Bologna, 1983.

——, *Feste d'Oltrarno: Plays in Churches in Fifteenth-Century Florence*, 2 vols., Firenze, 1996.

Norris, Edwin, [ed.], *The Ancient Cornish Drama*, Oxford, 1859, 2 vols.

Paris, Gaston, & Gaston Raynaud [eds.], *Le mystère de la passion d'Arnoul*

Greban, Paris, 1878.

Peacock, Edward, [ed.], *Instructions for Parish Priests* [by] *John Myrc*, London, 1868 [EETS OS 31].

Perry, Anne J. A., [ed.], *La passion des jongleurs: Texte établi d'après la bible des sept estaz du monde de Geufroi de Paris*, Paris, 1981 [*Textes, dossiers, documents*, 4].

Powell, Lawrence F., [ed.], *The Mirrour of the Blessed Lyf of Jesu Christ ... made before the year 1410 by Nicholas Love*, Oxford, 1908.

Richard, Jules-Marie, [ed.], *Le mystère de la passion: Texte du manuscrit 697 de la Bibliothèque d'Arras*, Arras, 1891 [rpt. Genève, 1976].

Rouanet, Léo [ed.], *Collección de autos, farsas y coloquios del siglo XVI*, 4 vols., Madrid, 1901.

Rueff, Jacob, *Das Züricher Passionsspiel: Das lyden vnsers Herren Jesu Christi das man nempt den Passion, 1545*, [ed. by Barbara Thoran], Bochum, 1984.

Runnalls, Graham A., [ed.], *Le mystère de la passion Nostre Seigneur: du manuscrit 1131 de la Bibliothèque Sainte-Geneviève*, Genève, 1974.

——, [ed.], *La passion d'Auvergne: Une édition du manuscrit nouvelle acquisition française 462 de la Bibliothèque Nationale de Paris*, Genève, 1982.

Schützeichel, Rudolf, [ed.], *Das mittelrheinische Passionsspiel der St. Galler Handschrift 919*, Tübingen, 1978.

Servet, Pierre, [ed.], *Le mystère de la résurrection. Angers (1456)*, 2 vols., Genève, 1993.

Shephard, William P., [ed.], *La passion provençale du manuscrit Didot: Mystère du XIVe siècle*, Paris, 1928 [*SATF*].

Simmons, Thomas Frederick, & Henry Edward Nolloth [eds.], *The Lay Folk's Catechism or the English and Latin Versions of Archbishop Thoresby's Instruction for the People* [...], London, 1901 [EETS OS 118].

Spector, Stephen, [ed.], *The N-Town Play: Cotton MS Vespasian D.8*, 2 vols., London, 1991 [EETS SS 11-12].

Stevens, Martin & A. C. Cawley [eds.], *The Towneley Plays*, 2 vols., London, 1994 [EETS SS 13].

Surtz, Ronald E., [ed.], *Teatro castellano de la Edad Media*, Madrid, 1992.

Torroja Menéndez, Carmen, & María Rivas Palá [eds.], *Teatro en Toledo en el siglo XV: 'Auto de la pasión' de Alonso del Campo*, Madrid, 1977.

Touber, Antonius H., [ed.], *Das Donaueschinger Passionsspiel*, Stuttgart, 1985.

Treutwein, Cristoph, [ed.], *Das Alsfelder Passionsspiel: Untersuchungen zu Überlieferung und Sprache*, Heidelberg, 1987.

West, Larry E., [ed. and trans.], *The St Gall Passion Play*, Brookline, Mass., 1976 [*Medieval classics, texts and studies*, 6].

——, [ed. and trans.], *The Alsfeld Passion Play*, Lampeter, 1997.

Wright, Stephen K., *The Vengeance of Our Lord: Medieval Dramatizations of the Destruction of Jerusalem*, Toronto, 1989 [days 2 and 3 on microfiche].

Wyss, Heinz, [ed.], *Das Luzerner Osterspiel*, 3 vols., Berne, 1967.

Zacher, Julius, 'Mittelniederländisches Osterspiel', *Zeitschrift für deutsches Alterthum* 2 (1842), pp. 302-50.

Secondary Texts

Accarie, Maurice, *Le théâtre sacré de la fin du moyen âge: Etude sur le sens moral de la 'Passion' de Jean Michel*, Genève, 1979.

Aers, David, 'Humanity of Christ: Reflections on Orthodox Late Medieval Representations', in: David Aers & Lynn Staley, *The Powers of the Holy: Religion, Politics and Gender in Late Medieval English Culture*, University Park, 1996, pp. 15-43.

Agan, Cami D., 'The Platea in the York and Wakefield Cycles: Avenues for Liminality and Salvation', *Studies in Philology* 94 (1997), pp. 344-67.

Allegri, Luigi, *Teatro e spettacolo nel medioevo*, Bari, 1988.

Ashley, Kathleen M., 'Divine Power in Chester Cycle and Late Medieval Thought', *Journal of the History of Ideas* 39 (1978), pp. 387-404.

——, '"Wyt" and "Wysdam" in N Town Cycle', *Philological Quarterly* 58 (1979), pp. 121-35.

Axton, Richard, *European Drama of the Early Middle Ages*, London, 1974.

Bakere, Jane A., *The Cornish 'Ordinalia': A Critical Study*, Cardiff, 1980.

Baugh, Albert C., 'The Chester Plays and French Influence', in: Arthur Hobson Quin [ed.], *Schelling Anniversary Papers*, New York, 1923, pp. 35-63.

Beadle, Richard, [ed.], *The Cambridge Companion to Medieval English Theatre*, Cambridge, 1994.

——, 'Verbal Texture and Wordplay in the York Cycle', in: *The York Cycle Then and Now* (Special volume of *Early Theatre* 3 [2000]), pp. 167-84.

Beckwith, Sarah, 'Making the World in York and the York Cycle', in: Sarah Kay and Miri Rubin [eds.], *Framing Medieval Bodies*, Manchester, 1994, pp. 254-76.

——, 'The Present of Past Things: The York Cycle as Contemporary Theory of Memory', *Journal of Medieval and Early Modern Studies* 26 (1996), 355-79.

——, 'Sacrum Signum: Sacramentality and Dissent in York's Theatre of Corpus Christi', in: Rita Copeland [ed.], *Criticism and Dissent in the Middle Ages*, Cambridge, 1996, pp. 264-88.

——, 'Absent Presences: The Theatre of Resurrection in York', in: David Aers [ed.], *Medieval Literature and Historical Enquiry: Essays in Honor of Derek Pearsall*, Woodbridge-Rochester, 2000, pp. 185-205.

——, *Signifying God: Social Relation and Symbolic Act in the York Corpus Christi Plays*, Chicago, 2001.

Betcher, Gloria J., 'A Reassessment of the Date and Provenance of the Cornish *Ordinalia*', *CD* 29 (1995-96), pp. 436-53.

——, 'A Tempting Theory: What Early Cornish Mermaid Images Reveal about the First Doctor's Analogy in *Passio Domini*', *EDAM Review*, 18 (1996), pp. 65-76.

Billington, Sandra, 'Social Disorder, Festive Celebration, and Jean Michel's *Le Mistere da la Passion JesusCrist*', *CD* 29 (1995), pp. 216-74.

Bordier, Jean-Pierre, *Le jeu de la passion: Le message chrétien et le théâtre français (XIIIe–XVIe s.)*, Paris, 1998.

Bossy, Michel André, 'Afterword', in: Sturm-Maddox & Maddox [eds.], *Transtextualities*, pp. 195-203.

Braet, Herman, Johan Nowé & Gilbert Tournoy [eds.], *The Theatre in the Middle Ages*, Leuven, 1985.

Brooks, N. C., 'Processional Drama and Dramatic Procession in Germany in the Late Middle Ages', *JEGP* 32 (1933), pp. 141-71.

Chambers, E. K., *The Mediaeval Stage*, 2 vols., Oxford, 1903.

Chocheyras, Jacques, *Le théâtre religieux en Dauphiné du moyen âge au XVIIIe siècle (domaine français et provençal)*, Genève, 1975.

——, *Le théâtre religieux en Savoie au XVIe siècle: Avec des fragments inédits*, Genève, 1971.

Clopper, Lawrence M., 'The History and Development of the Chester Cycle', *Modern Philology* 75 (1978), pp. 219-46.

——, [ed.], *REED: Chester*, Toronto, 1979.

——, *Drama, Play, and Game: English Festive Culture in the Medieval and Early Modern Period*, Chicago & London, 2001.

Couturier, Marcel, & Graham A. Runnalls, *Compte du mystère de la passion: Châteaudun 1510*, Chartres, 1991.

Cox, John D., *The Devil and the Sacred in English Drama, 1350–1642*, Cambridge, 2000.

Craig, Hardin, *English Religious Drama of the Middle Ages*, Oxford, 1955.

Crouch, David J. F., *Piety, Fraternity, and Power: Religious Gilds in Late Medieval Yorkshire, 1389–1547*, Woodbridge-Rochester, NY, 2000.

Cruciani, Fabrizio, *Teatro nel rinascimento: Roma 1450–1550*, Roma, 1983.

D'Ancona, Alessandro, *Origini del teatro italiano: libri tre, con due appendice sulla rappresentazione dramatica del contado toscano e sul teatre mantovano nel sec. XVI*, 2 vols., Torino, 1891 [rpt. 1966-71].

De Bartholomaeis, Vincenzo, *Origini della poesia drammatica italiana*, Torino, 1952 [2nd ed.].

Diller, Hans-Jürgen, 'From Synthesis to Compromise: The Four Daughters of God in Early English Drama', *EDAM Review* 18 (1996), pp. 88-103.

Dobson, R. B., 'Craft Guilds and City: The Historical Origins of the York Mystery Plays Reassessed', in: Alan E. Knight [ed.], *The Stage as Mirror: Civic Theatre in Late Medieval Europe*, Cambridge, 1997, pp. 91-105.

Donovan, Richard B., *The Liturgical Drama in Mediaeval Spain*, Toronto, 1958.

Dorrell, Margaret, 'Two Studies of the York Corpus Christi Play', *LSE* n.s. 6 (1972), pp. 63-111.

Dreimüller, Karl, 'Die Musik im geistlichen Spiel des späten deutschen Mittelalters: Dargestellt am Alsfelder Passionsspiel', *Kirchenmusikalisches Jahrbuch* 34 (1950), pp. 27-34.

Duffy, Eamon, *The Stripping of the Altars: Traditional Religion in England, c. 1400 – c. 1580*, New Haven-London, 1992.

Dutka, JoAnna, *Music in the English Mystery Plays*, Kalamazoo, 1980.

Edwards, Robert, *The Montecassino Passion and the Poetics of Medieval Drama*, Berkeley, 1977.

Elliott, John R., jr., *Playing God: Medieval Mysteries on the Modern Stage*, Toronto-Buffalo, 1989.

Evans, Marshall Blakemore, *The Passion Play of Lucerne: An Historical and Critical Introduction*, New York, 1943.

Flanigan, C. Clifford, 'Liminality, Carvival and Social Structure: The Case of Late Medieval Biblical Drama', in: Kathleen M. Ashley [ed.], *Victor Turner and the Construction of Cultural Criticism: Between Literature and Anthropology*, Bloomington, 1990, pp. 42-63.

Frank, Grace, *The Medieval French Drama*, Oxford, 1954.

Fry, Timothy, 'The Unity of the *Ludus Coventriae*', *Studies in Philology* 48 (1951), pp. 527-70.

Gangler-Mundwiler, Dominique, 'Les diableries nécessaires. Le role des scènes diaboliques dans l'action des mystères de la passion', in: Marie-Jeanne Drury [ed.], *Mélanges de littérature: Du Moyen Age au XXe siècle, offerts à Mademoiselle Jeanne Lods*, 2 vols., Paris, 1978, vol. I, pp. 249-68.

Gayley, C. M., *Plays of our Forefathers*, London, 1907 [rpt. 1968].

Gibson, James M., '"Interludium Passionis Domini": Parish Drama in Medieval New Romney', in: Alexandra F. Johnston & Wim Hüsken [eds.], *English Parish Drama*, Amsterdam, 1996, pp. 137-48.

Goldberg, P. J., 'Craft Guilds in the Corpus Christi Play and Civic Government', in: *Society, Politics and Culture*, Cambridge, 1986, pp. 16-47.

Grundmann, Herbert, *Religious Movements in the Middle Ages: The Historical Links between Heresy, the Mendicant Orders, and the Women's Religious Movement in the Twelfth and Thirteenth Century, with the Historical Foundation of German Mysticism*, [trans.] Steven Rowan, Notre Dame, 1995.

Happé, Peter, *John Bale*, New York, 1996.

——, 'Devils' Languages in some Corpus Christi Plays', *Theta* 3 (1996), pp. 43-61.

——, 'Cycle Plays: The State of the Art', *European Medieval Drama* 2 (1998), pp. 63-84.

——, 'Devils in the York Cycle: Language and Dramatic Technique', *RORD* 37 (1998), pp. 79-98.

——, *English Drama before Shakespeare*, London, 1999.

——, 'Performing Passion Plays in France and England', *European Medieval Drama* 4 (2000), pp. 57-75.

——, 'Subversion in the *Towneley Cycle*: Strategies for Evil', in: Mike Pincombe [ed.], *The Anatomy of Tudor Literature*, Aldershot, 2001, pp. 11-23.

——, 'John Bale's Lost Mystery Cycle', *Cahiers Elisabéthains* 60 (2001), pp. 1-12.

——, [Review of:] *The York Cycle Then and Now* (Special volume of *Early Theatre* 3 [2000]), *EDAM Review* 23 (2001), pp. 130-3.

——, 'The Management of Narrative in the Performance of Cycle Plays: the Cornish *Ordinalia*, *La Passion d'Auvergne* and *N Town*', *EDAM Review* 24, (2002), pp. 105-121.

——, 'Procession and the Cycle Drama in England and Europe: Some Dramatic Possibilities', *European Medieval Drama* 6 (2002), pp. 31-47.

——, '"Erazed in the Booke": The Mystery Cycles and Reform' (forthcoming).

——, 'Staging God in some Last Judgement Plays' (forthcoming).

Henrard, Nadine, *Le théâtre religieux médiéval en langue d'oc*, Genève, 1998.

Hindley, Alan, [ed.], *Drama and Community: People and Plays in Medieval Europe*, Turnhout, 1999 [*Medieval Texts and Cultures of Northern Europe*, 1].

Jeffrey, David L., 'Franciscan Spirituality and the Rise of Early English Drama', *Mosaic* 8 (1975), pp. 17-46.

Jennings, Margaret, 'Tutivillus: The Literary Career of the Recording Demon', *Studies in Philology: Texts and Studies* 74 (1977), pp. 1-95.

Johnston, Alexandra F., 'The York Corpus Christi Play: A Dramatic Structure based upon Performance Practice', in: Braet, Nowé & Tournoy [eds.], *Theatre in the Middle Ages*, pp. 362-73.

———, '*The Word made Flesh*: Augustinian Elements in the York Cycle', in: Robert A. Taylor *et al.* [eds.], *The Centre and its Compass: Studies in Medieval Literature in Honor of Professor John Leyerle*, Kalamazoo, 1993, pp. 225-46.

———, '"His langage is lorne": The Silent Centre of the York Cycle', in: *The York Cycle Then and Now* (Special volume of *Early Theatre* 3 [2000]), pp. 185-95.

———, 'The York Cycle and the Libraries of York', in: Caroline M. Barron & Jenny Stratford [eds.], *The Church and Learning in Later Medieval Society: Essays in Honour of R. B. Dobson*, Donnington, 2002, pp. 355-70.

Johnston, Alexandra F., & Margaret Rogerson [eds.], *REED: York*, 2 vols., Toronto, 1979.

Joyce, S. L., & Evelyn S. Newlyn [eds.], *REED: Cornwall*, Toronto, 1999.

King, Pamela M., 'Corpus Christi, Valencia', *METh* 15 (1993), pp. 103-10.

———, 'The *Festa d'Elx*: Civic Devotion, Display and Identity', in: Twycross [ed.], *Festive Drama*, pp. 95-109.

———, 'Contemporary Cultural Models for the Trial Plays in the York Cycle', in: Hindley [ed.], *Drama and Community*, pp. 200-16.

———, 'Seeing and Hearing: Looking and Listening', in: *The York Cycle Then and Now* (Special volume of *Early Theatre* 3 [2000]), pp. 155-66.

Klausner, David, [ed.], *REED: Herefordshire, Worcestershire*, Toronto, 1996.

Knight, Alan E., 'Cyclicity in Medieval French Drama', in: Sturm-Maddox & Maddox [eds.], *Transtextualities*, pp. 179-94.

———, 'The Bishop of Fools and his Feasts in Lille', in: Twycross [ed.], *Festive Drama*, pp. 157-66.

———, [ed.], *The Stage as Mirror: Civic Theatre in Late Medieval Europe*, Cambridge, 1997.

———, 'Processional theatre and the rituals of social unity in Lille', in: Hindley [ed.], *Drama and Community*, pp. 99-109.

———, 'Guild pageants and Urban Stability in Lille', (forthcoming).

Hummelen, W. M. H., '"Pause" en "Selete" in de *Bliscapen*', in: Hans van Dijk, Bart Ramakers *et al.*, *Spel en spektakel: Middeleeuws toneel in de Lage Landen*, Amsterdam, 2001, pp. 133-53 and 339-44.

Kolve, V. A., *The Play Called Corpus Christi*, London, 1966.

Lebègue, Raymond, *Le mystère des actes des apôtres: Contribution à l'étude de l'humanisme et du protestantisme français au XVIe siècle*, Paris, 1929.

Linke, Hansjürgen, 'A Survey of Medieval Drama and Theater in Germany', *CD* 27 (1993), pp. 17-53.

Longsworth, Robert, *The Cornish Ordinalia: Religion and Dramaturgy*, Cambridge, Mass., 1967.

Lumiansky, R. M. & David Mills [eds.], *The Chester Mystery Cycle: Essays and Documents*, Chapel Hill, 1983.

McGavin, John J., 'Sign and Tradition: The *Purification Play* in Chester', *LSE* n.s. 11 (1980), pp. 90-104.

McKinnell, John, 'Staging the Digby *Mary Magdalen*', *METh* 6 (1984), pp. 126-52.

Martin, L. H., 'Comic Eschatology in the Chester *Coming of Antichrist*', *CD* 5 (1971), pp. 163-76.

Marx, C. W., *The Devil's Rights and the Redemption in the Literature of Medieval England*, Cambridge, 1995.

Massip, Francesc, [ed.], *Formes teatrals de la tradició medieval*, Barcelona, 1995.

Mazouer, Charles, *Le théâtre français du moyen âge*, Paris, 1998.

Meredith, Peter, 'The *Ordo Paginarum* and the Development of the York Tilemakers' Play', *LSE* n.s. 11 (1980), pp. 59-73.

——, 'John Clerke's Hand in the York Register', *LSE* n.s. 12 (1981), pp. 245-71.

Meredith, Peter, & John E. Tailby, *The Staging of Religious Drama in Europe in the Later Middle Ages: Texts and Documents in English Translation*, Kalamazoo, 1983 [*Early Drama, Art and Music Monograph Series*, 4].

——, 'The City of York and its "Play of Pageants"', in: *The York Cycle Then and Now* (Special volume of *Early Theatre* 3 [2000]), pp. 23-47.

Meredith, Peter, & Lynette R. Muir, 'The Trial in Heaven in the *Eerste Bliscap* and Other European Plays', *Dutch Crossing* (1984), n° 22, pp. 84-92.

Mills, David, 'Theories and Practices in the Editing of the Chester Play-Manuscripts', in: Derek Pearsall [ed.], *Manuscripts and Texts: Editorial Problems in Later Middle English Literature*, Cambridge, 1987, pp. 110-21.

——, *Recycling the Cycle: The City of Chester and its Whitsun Plays*, Toronto, 1998.

Muir, Lynette R., *The Biblical Drama of Medieval Europe*, Cambridge, 1995.

——, 'European Communities and Medieval Drama', in: Hindley [ed.],

Drama and Community, pp. 1-17.
——, 'Résurrection des Mystères: Medieval Drama in Modern France', *LSE* n.s. 29 (1998), pp. 235-47.
Neri, Fernando, 'La "Passione"', *Pallante* 8 (1929), 9-73.
Neumann, Bernd, *Geistliches Schauspiel im Zeugnis der Zeit*, München-Zürich, 1987.
Nowé, Johan, *Von Gottesdienst zum Menschenspiel: Eine Einführung zum biblischen Dramas des deutschen Mittelalters*, Leuven-Amersfoort, 1987.
Palmer, Barbara D., 'Corpus Christi "Cycles" in Yorkshire: The Surviving Records', *CD* 27 (1993), pp. 218-31.
——, 'Recycling "The Wakefield Cycle": The Records', *RORD* 41 (2002), pp. 88-130.
Pantin, W. A., *The English Church in the Fourteenth Century*, Cambridge, 1955.
Paull, M., 'The Figure of Mahomet in the Towneley Cycle', *CD* 6 (1972), pp. 197-200.
Paxson, James J., Lawrence M. Clopper & Sylvia Tomasch [eds.], *The Performance of Medieval Culture: Essays on Chaucer and the Drama in Honor of Martin Stevens*, Cambridge, 1998.
Petit de Julleville, [Louis], *Les Mystères*, 2 vols., Paris, 1880.
Piccat, Marco, *Rappresentazioni popolari e feste in Revello nella metà del XV secolo*, Torino, 1986.
Plesch, Véronique, '*Etalage complaisant?* The Torments of Christ in the French Passion Plays', *CD* 28 (1994-95), pp. 458-85.
——, '*Ludus Sabaudiae*: Observations on Late Medieval Theater in the Duchy of Savoy', *EDAM Review* 21 (1996), pp. 1-21.
Portillo, Rafael, & Manuel J. Gomez Lara, 'Holy Week Performances of the Passion in Spain: Connections with Medieval European Drama', in: Twycross [ed.], *Festive Drama*, pp. 88-94.
Prosser, Eleanor, *Drama and Religion in the English Mystery Plays: A Re-Evaluation*, Stanford, 1961.
Ramakers, B. A. M., 'The Oudenaarde Corpus Christi Tableaux and Late Medieval Drama', in: Massip [ed.], *Formes teatrals de la tradició medieval*, pp. 195-207.
——, *Spelen en figuren: Toneelkunst en processiecultuur in Oudenaarde tussen Middeleeuwen en Moderne Tijd*, Amsterdam, 1996.
Rastall, Richard, *The Heaven Singing: Music in Early English Religious Drama*, vol. I, Cambridge, 1996.
Rogerson, Margaret, 'Raging in the Streets of Medieval York', in: *The York Cycle Then and Now* (Special volume of *Early Theatre* 3 [2000]), pp.

105-25.
Rubin, Miri, *Corpus Christi: The Eucharist in Late Medieval Culture*, Cambridge, 1991.
Runnalls, Graham A., 'The Evolution of a Passion Play: *La Passion de Semur*', *Le Moyen Français* 19 (1986), pp. 163-202.
——, 'Un mystère de la passion inconnu? Les fragments du MS BN, N. A. F. 10660', *Romania* 111 (1990), pp. 514-41.
——, 'Were They Listening or Watching? Text and Spectacle at the 1510 Châteaudun Passion Play', *METh* 16 (1994), pp. 25-36.
——, 'Les mystères de la passion en langue française: Tentative de classement', *Romania* 114 (1996), pp. 468-516.
——, *Les mystères français imprimés: Une étude sur les rapports entre le théâtre religieux et l'imprimerie à la fin du moyen âge français, suivi d'un répertoire complet des mystères français imprimés (ouvrages, éditions, exemplaires), 1484–1630*, Paris, 1999.
——, 'Le Livre de Raison de Jacques Le Gros et *Le Mystère de la Passion* joué à Paris en 1539', *Romania* 118 (2000), pp. 138-93.
——, *Les mystères dans les provinces françaises: En Savoie et en Poitou, à Amiens et à Reims*, Paris, 2003.
Sentaurens, Jean, *Séville et le théâtre de la fin du moyen âge à la fin du XVIIe siècle*, 2 vols., Talence-Lille, 1984.
Shergold, N. D., *A History of the Spanish Stage: From Medieval Times until the End of the Seventeenth Century*, Oxford, 1967.
Simon, Eckehard, [ed.], *The Theatre of Medieval Europe: New Research in Early Drama*, Cambridge, 1991.
Simpson, James, *The Oxford English Literary History*, vol. II: *1350-1547, Reform and Cultural Revolution*, Oxford, 2002.
Spector, Stephen, 'The Composition and Development of an Eclectic Manuscript: Cotton Vespasian D VIII', *LSE* n.s. 10 (1977), pp. 62-83.
Sponsler, Claire, *Drama and Resistance: Bodies, Goods, and Theatricality in Late Medieval England*, Minneapolis, 1997.
Staines, David, 'The Medieval Cycle: Mapping a Trope', in: Sturm-Maddox & Maddox [eds.], *Transtextualities*, pp. 15-37.
Stern, Charlotte, *The Medieval Theater in Castile*, Binghamton, 1996.
Stevens, Martin, *Four Middle English Mystery Cycles: Textual, Contextual, and Critical Interpretations*, Princeton, 1987.
Strietman, Elsa, 'The Low Countries', in: Simon [ed.], *Theatre of Medieval Europe*, pp. 225-52.
Sturm-Maddox, Sara, & David Maddox [eds.], *Transtextualities: Of Cycles and Cyclicity in Medieval French Literature*, Binghampton, 1996.
Surtz, Ronald E., *The Birth of a Theater: Dramatic Convention in the*

Spanish Theater from Juan del Encina to Lope de Vega, Princeton, 1979.
——, 'The Franciscan Connection in the Early Castilian Theater', *Bulletin of the Comediantes* 35 (1983), pp. 141-52.
——, 'Spain: Catalan and Castilian Drama', in: Simon [ed.], *Theatre in Medieval Europe*, pp. 189-206.
Swanson, R. N., 'Passion and Practice: The Social and Ecclesiastical Implications of Passion Devotion in the Late Middle Ages', in: A[lasdair] A. MacDonald, H. N. B. Ridderbos & R. M. Schlusemann [eds.], *The Broken Body: Passion Devotion in Late Medieval Culture*, Groningen, 1998 [*Mediaevalia groningana*, 21].
Tailby, John E., 'Die Luzerner Passionsspielaufführung des Jahres 1583: zur Deutung der Bühnenpläne Renward Cysats', in: Braet, Nowé & Tournoy [eds.], *Theatre in the Middle Ages*, pp. 352-61.
——, 'The Role of the Director in the Lucerne Passion Play', *METh* 9 (1987), pp. 80-92.
——, 'Lucerne Revisited: Facts and Questions', *LSE* n.s. 29 (1998), pp. 347-58.
——, 'Drama and Community in South Tyrol', in: Hindley [ed.], *Drama and Community*, pp. 148-60.
Thiry, Claude, 'Une avocate inspirée? Procula dans quelques passions françaises', *Le Moyen Français* 11 (1982), pp. 54-88.
Travis, Peter W., *Dramatic Design in the Chester Cycle*, Chicago, 1982.
Twycross, Meg, [ed.], *Festive Drama*, Cambridge, 1996.
Tydeman, William, [ed.], *The Medieval European Stage, 500–1550*, Cambridge, 2001.
White, E., 'Places to Hear the Play in York', in: *The York Cycle Then and Now* (Special volume of *Early Theatre* 3 [2000]), pp. 49-78.
White, Hayden, *Metahistory: The Historical Imagination in Nineteenth-Century Europe*, Baltimore, 1973.
White, Paul Whitfield, 'Reforming Mysteries' End: A New Look at Protestant Intervention in English Provincial Drama', *Journal of Medieval and Early Modern Studies* 29 (1999), pp. 121-47.
Williams, Arnold, *The Characterization of Pilate in the Towneley Plays*, East Lansing, 1950.
Woolf, Rosemary, *The English Mystery Plays*, London, 1972.
Worp, J. A., *Geschiedenis van het Drama en van het Tooneel in Nederland*, 2 vols., Groningen, 1904.
Wright, Stephen K., '*The Destruction of Jerusalem*: An Annotated Checklist of Plays and Performances, *c*. 1350-1620', *RORD* 41 (2002), pp. 131-56.
Wyatt, Diana, 'The Pageant Waggon: Beverley', *METh* 2 (1979), pp. 55-60.
York Cycle Then and Now, The (Special volume of *Early Theatre* 3

[2000)].
Young, Karl, *The Drama of the Medieval Church*, 2 vols., Oxford, 1933.
Zeeman, Elizabeth, 'Nicholas Love — A Fifteenth-Century Translator', *Review of English Studies* n. s. 6 (1955), pp. 113-27.

II. ICONOGRAPHY

Alpatoff, Michel, 'The Parallelism of Giotto's Paduan Frescoes', *The Art Bulletin* 29 (1947), pp. 148-54.
Anderson, Mary Désirée, *Drama and Imagery in English Mediaeval Churches*, Cambridge, 1963.
Backhouse, Janet, *Books of Hours*, London, 1985.
Baxandall, Michael, *Giotto and the Orators: Humanist Observers of Painting and the Discovery of Pictorial Composition, 1350-1450*, Oxford, 1971.
Bellosi, Luciano, *Giotto: The Complete Works*, Florence, 1981.
——, *Duccio: La Maestà*, Milano, 1998.
Belting, Hans, 'The New Role of Narrative in Public Painting of the Trecento', in: Kessler & Simpson [eds.], *Pictorial Narrative*, pp. 151-68.
——, *The Image and Its Public in the Middle Ages: Form and Fashion of Early Paintings of the Passion*, [trans.] M. Bartusis and Raymond Meyer, New Rochelle, N.Y., 1990.
Bernari, Carlo, & Piero De Vecchi, *L'opera completa del Tintoretto*, Milano, 1970.
Bevington, David, *et al.*, *Homo Memento Finis:The Iconography of Just Judgment in Medieval Art and Drama*, Kalamazoo, 1985.
Bologna, Ferdinando, *Early Italian Painting: Romanesque and Early Medieval Art*, London, 1964.
Borsook, Eve, *The Mural Painters of Tuscany: From Cimabue to Andrea del Sarto*, London, 1960.
Brooks, N. C., 'An Ingolstadt Corpus Christi Procession and the *Biblia Pauperum*', *JEGP* 35 (1936), pp. 1-16.
Brown, Patricia Fortini, *Venetian Narrative Painting in the Age of Carpaccio*, New Haven-London, 1988.
Caiger-Smith, A., *English Medieval Mural Paintings*, Oxford, 1963.
Cave, Charles J. P., *Roof Bosses in Medieval Churches: An Aspect of Gothic Sculpture*, Cambridge, 1948.
Chiellini, Maria, *Cimabue*, Firenze, 1988.
Collins, Patrick J., *The N-town Plays and Medieval Picture Cycles*, Kalamazoo, 1979.

———, 'Narrative Bible Cycles in Medieval Art and Drama', *CD* 9 (1975), pp. 125-46.

Davidson, Clifford, & David E. O'Connor, *York Art: A Subject List of Extant and Lost Art, Including Items Relevant to Early Drama*, Kalamazoo, 1978.

De Laborde, A., *Bible moralisé conservé à Oxford, Paris et Londrès*, Paris, 1911-27.

De Vos, Dirk, *Hans Memling: The Complete Works*, London, 1994.

Derbes, Anne, *Picturing the Passion in Late Medieval Italy: Narrative Painting, Franciscan Ideologies, and the Levant*, Cambridge, 1996.

Donovan, Claire, *The de Brailes Hours: Shaping the Book of Hours in Thirteenth-Century Oxford*, Toronto-Buffalo, 1991.

Frank, Grace, 'Popular Iconography of the Passion', *PMLA* 46 (1931), 333-40.

Garrison, Edward B., *Italian Romanesque Panel Painting: An Illustrated Index*, Florence, 1949.

Guest, Gerald B., *Bible moralisée: Codex Vindobonensis 2554, Vienna, Österreichische Nationalbibliotek*, London, 1995.

Haney, Kristine Edmondson, *The Winchester Psalter: An Iconographic Study*, Leicester, 1986.

Harrison, Charles, 'Giotto and "the rise of painting"', in: Norman [ed.], *Siena, Florence, and Padua*, vol. I, pp. 73-95.

———, 'The Arena Chapel: Patronage and Authorship', in: Norman [ed.], *Siena, Florence, and Padua*, vol. II, pp. 82-103.

Hassall, W. O., [ed.], *The Holkham Bible Picture Book*, London, 1954.

Henry, Avril, [ed.], *The Mirour of Mans Saluacioun[e]: A Middle English Translation of Speculum Humanae Salvationis, a critical edition of the fifteenth-century manuscript illustrated from Der Spiegel der Menschen Behältnis*, Speyer, Drach, c. 1475, Aldershot, 1986.

———, [ed.], *Biblia Pauperum*, Aldershot, 1987.

Katzenellenbogen, Adolf E. M., *The Sculptural Programs of Chartres Cathedral: Christ, Mary, Ecclesia*, New York, 1959.

Kemp, Wolfgang, *The Narratives of Gothic Stained Glass*, [trans.] Caroline Dobson Saltzwedel, Cambridge, 1997.

Kessler, Herbert L., & Marianna Shreve Simpson [eds.], *Pictorial Narrative in Antiquity and the Middle Ages*, Washington, D.C., 1985 [*Studies in the History of Art*, 16].

Kupfer, Marcia, *Romanesque Wall Painting in Central France: The Politics of Narrative*, New Haven & London, 1993.

Lavin, Marilyn Aronberg, *The Place of Narrative: Mural Decoration in Italian Churches, 431-1600*, Chicago-London, 1990.

Mâle, Emile, *The Gothic Image: Religious Art in France of the Thirteenth*

Century, [trans.] Dora Nussey, New York, 1972 [rpt. from the 1913 ed.].

James H. Marrow, *Passion Iconography in Northern European Art of the Late Middle Ages and Early Renaissance: A Study of the Transformation of Sacred Metaphor into Descriptive Narrative*, Kortrijk, 1979 [*Ars Neerlandica*, 1].

Mocanu, Virgil, *Tintoretto*, [trans.] Carlos Kormos, London, 1977.

Nepi Sciré, Giovanna, *The Accademia Galleries in Venice*, Milan, 1998.

Newlyn, Evelyn S., 'Between the Pit and the Pedestal: Images of Eve and Mary in Medieval Cornish Drama', in: Edelgard DuBruck [ed.], *New Images of Medieval Women: Essays towards a Cultural Anthropology*, Lewiston, 1989, pp. 121-64.

Newton, Eric, *Tintoretto*, London, 1952.

Norman, Diana, [ed.], *Siena, Florence, and Padua: Art, Society, and Religion, 1280-1400*, 2 vols., New Haven-London, 1995.

——, 'Duccio: the recovery of a reputation', in: Norman [ed.], *Siena, Florence, and Padua*, vol. I, pp. 49-71.

——, '"A noble panel": Duccio's *Maestà*', in: Norman [ed.], *Siena, Florence, and Padua*, vol. II, pp. 455-83.

O'Connell, Michael, 'The Civic Theatre of Suffering: Hans Memling's Passion and Late Medieval Drama', in: György E. Szonyi [ed.], *European Iconography East and West*, Leiden, 1996, pp. 22-34.

——, *The Idolatrous Eye: Iconoclasm and Theater in Early- Modern England*, Oxford, 2000.

Pächt, Otto, *The Rise of Pictorial Narrative in Twelfth-Century England*, Oxford, 1962.

Pickering, F. P., *Literature and Art in the Middle Ages*, London, 1970.

——, 'The Gothic Image of Christ: The Sources of Medieval Representations of the Crucifixion', in: *Essays on Medieval German Literature and Iconography*, Cambridge, 1980, pp. 3-30.

——, 'Trinitas Creator: Word and Image', in: *Essays on Medieval German Literature and Iconography*, Cambridge, 1980, pp. 46-58.

Plesch, Véronique, 'Walls and Scaffolds: Pictorial and Dramatic Cycles in the Duchy of Savoy', *CD* 32 (1998), pp. 252-90.

Queen Mary's Psalter: Miniatures and Drawings by an English Artist of the 14th Century, Reproduced from Royal MS. 2 B VII in the British Museum, [intro.] George Warner, London, 1912.

Réau, Louis, *Iconographie de l'art chrétien*, 6 vols., Paris, 1955-59.

Robb, Bruce, 'Tintoretto's San Rocco *Crucifixion*', in: C. Weight [ed.], *Painters on Paintings*, London, 1969, pp. 3-31.

Romanelli, Giandomenico, *Tintoretto: La Scuola Grande di San Rocco*, Milano, 1994.

Romanini, A. M., 'Bible Cycles in Art', *New Catholic Encyclopaedia*, New York, 1967, vol. II, pp. 524-32.
Rose, Martial, *The Norwich Apocalypse: The Cycle of Vault Carvings in the Cloisters of Norwich Cathedral*, Norwich, 1999.
Rose, Martial, & Julia Hedgecoe, *Stories in Stone: The Medieval Roof Carvings of Norwich Cathedral*, London, 1997.
Ross, Ellen M., *The Grief of God: Images of the Suffering Jesus in Late Medieval England*, Oxford, 1997.
Ross, Lawrence J., 'Art and the Study of Early English Drama', *RORD* 6 (1963) 35-46.
Royer, E., *Nouveau guide des calvaires bretons*, Rennes, 1985.
Sandler, Lucy Freeman, *The Psalter of Robert De Lisle in the British Library*, London, 1983.
Schiller, Gertrud, *Iconography of Christian Art*, [trans.] J. Seligman, 2 vols., London, 1971-72.
Sheingorn, Pamela, 'On using Medieval Art in the Study of Medieval Drama', *RORD* 22 (1979), pp. 101-9.
The St. Albans Psalter (Albani Psalter), [intro.] Otto Pächt, C. R. Dodwell & Francis Wormald, London, 1960.
St. John, Michael, *Chaucer's Dream Visions: Courtliness and Individual Identity*, Aldershot, 2000.
Stubblebine, James H., [ed.], *Giotto: The Arena Chapel Frescoes: Illustrations, Introductory Essay, Backgrounds and Sources, Criticism*, London, 1969.
Tietze, Hans, *Tintoretto: The Paintings and Drawings*, New York, 1948.
Tintori, Leonetto, & Millard Meiss, *The Painting of the Life of St. Francis in Assisi, with Notes on the Arena Chapel*, New York, 1962.
Tristram, Ernest W., *English Medieval Wall Painting*, London, 1950.
——, *English Wall Painting of the Fourteenth Century*, London, 1955.
Tronzo, William, 'The Prestige of Saint Peter's: Observations on the Function of Monumental Narrative Cycles in Italy', in: Kessler & Simpson [eds.], *Pictorial Narrative*, pp. 93-112.
Wayment, Hilary, *The Windows of King's College Chapel, Cambridge: A Description and Commentary*, London, 1972 [*Corpus Vitrearum Medii Aevi: Great Britain*. Supplementary Volume 1].
——, *The Stained Glass of the Church of St. Mary, Fairford, Gloucestershire*, London, 1984.
White, John, *Duccio: Tuscan Art and the Medieval Workshop*, London, 1979.
Wieck, Roger S., *Time Sanctified: The Book of Hours in Medieval Art and Life*, New York & Baltimore, 2001 [rpt. from the 1988 ed.].
Wormald, Francis, *The Winchester Psalter*, London, 1973.

Index

Actes des Apôtres, Mystère des
  34, 43, 143, 167
actors 32, 149, 185, 199, 230, 302
Alsfelder Passionsspiel 45, 48-9,
  169-78, 318
Amiens 42, 142
angels 173-5, 179, 211-2, 239, 288
Antichrist 245, 247, 250-1
anticipation 18, 23, 26, 70, 104,
  113, 235-6, 249-50, 291, 314,
  319, 323-4, 327-8
Aristotle 15
audience 67, 15-3, 160, 229, 291, 299
authorship 19, 274
Axton, Richard 318
Bale, John 35, 299-306
  God's Promises 301-3
  Preaching of John the Baptist
    301-4
  Temptation of Christ 301, 303-4
  Vocacyon 305-6
Beckett, Samuel 327-8
Benediktbeuern 21, 44, 318
Beverley Cycle 21, 26, 35, 300, 314
Biblia Pauperum 26, 82-3, 86, 103-5
Bliscapen 55-7, 206-12, 215, 300,
  315, 317, 319
Bologna Cycle 53, 196-8, 319
Books of Hours 68, 86, 92-5, 317
Bordier, Jean-Pierre 40, 146
Breton Passion 60, 147
Brinay 70, 71
Britten, Benjamin 309
Brooks, N. C. 180
Burgundy 40, 143-4
Cambridge
  King's College Chapel 82-3, 321
Carew, Richard 274
Catalan Plays 58, 147, 214, 216-8
Cawley, A. C. 36, 267
Cervera 215-6, 218

Chalivoy-Milon 70-1
Charlemagne 15-6
Chartres cathedral 75-6
Châteaudun 146
Chester Cycle 36-7, 223, 240-55
  Noah (3) 242, 251-3
  Moses (5) 248
  Shepherds (7) 246, 253-4
  Judgement (24) 254-5
Chocheyras, Jacques 149
civic authorities 21, 32, 80, 124
Cividale Plays 51
Clerke, John 227, 230, 232
Codice de los autos viejo
  216, 218
comedy 172, 253, 268, 308
Confrérie de la Passion
  –Paris 142,164
  –Rouen 166, 167
Cornish Plays
  Ordinalia 39, 223, 273-82, 314
  Creacion of the World 39, 281-2
Corpus Christi, Feast of 20, 28-33,
  57-8, 137, 178-9, 214-5, 222-3,
  243, 315-6, 317-18, 327
costumes 111, 121, 157-8, 239, 290
Coventry Cycle 35, 241, 247, 263,
  306, 310, 314
Cromwell, Thomas 300, 301
Cysart, Renward 47, 185-9, 190
dance of death 254
Dauphiné 149
De Estrella, Juan Christoval Calvete 56, 207
De Lisle Psalter 89-91, 92
devils 49, 91, 140, 149, 154, 156,
  163, 171-4, 177, 179, 202, 204,
  224-5, 233-5, 246-7, 255, 266-7,
  279-81, 296-8, 305, 306, 319-20,
  327
Devotio Moderna 107

dialogue 30, 161, 178-9, 183, 188-9, 200, 205, 216, 252, 260-1
Donaueschingen Play 47, 195
dossals 84
Duccio 84, 108-14, 317, 325
Elliott, John R. 158, 328
emotion 67, 75, 79, 107, 128-30, 151, 161, 200, 205, 225-6, 260-1
Evans, M. Blakemore 187
Fairford, St. Mary's church 80-2
figuration 26, 49, 72, 74, 82-3, 92, 103-4, 114-5, 121, 233-4, 277, 316, 321, 324
flagellanti 51-2
Florence Plays 51-3
fools 120-1, 271
Four Daughters, Debate of the, see: *Procès de Paradis*
Franciscans, see: St. Francis
Frankfurt Cycle 45-6, 50, 169
Garrison, Edward B. 85
Gayley, C. M. 256
Giotto 18, 74-5, 109, 114-8, 203
Gréban, Arnoul 26, 40-2, 68, 116, 139-40, 150-8, 202, 285, 300, 319
guilds 29, 35, 54, 60, 62, 80, 214, 228, 284, 313, 322, 327
Hainault 146
Haney, Kristine Edmondson 88
Harrison, Charles 116
Hedgecoe, Julia 76, 78, 79
Heidelberger Passionsspiel 49
Hereford Pageants 19, 35
historiated cross 85-6
history 17, 26, 106, 279, 304, 326
Holkham Bible Picture Book 105-8, 317
Homer 15
Incarnation et Nativité (Rouen) 165
Innocent III 23
John the Baptist 162, 236, 261, 299

Johnston, Alexandra 28, 237
Jordan, William 282
Kemp, Margery 27
Künzelsau Fronleichnamspiel 47, 170, 176, 178-84, 315, 321
Kupfer, Marcia 70-1
language 43, 143-4, 237, 258, 290
laudesi 50
Lavin, Marilyn Aronberg 72
Leicester Play 35
Lille Plays 194-5, 323
liturgical drama 21-2, 50, 317-8
Love, Nicholas 28
Lucerne Cycle 44-5, 47, 169, 184-90, 319
Lumiansky, R. M. 249
Maastricht Passion 54, 212
manuscripts 14, 37-8, 41, 103, 133, 148, 159, 184-5, 191, 192, 194, 206, 212, 217-8, 224, 240, 242, 255-6, 281, 284-8, 300-1, 322-3
Mariken van Nieumeghen 55
Mary the Virgin 70, 122-3, 147, 148-9, 152-4, 159-62, 205, 208, 219, 279, 287-8, 294, 317, 319
Memling, Hans 18, 109, 118-24, 158, 208, 315, 317, 324
Meredith, Peter 287
Michel, Jean 40-3, 68, 140-3, 192-3
Mills, David 244, 249, 315
Mirk, John 25
Mistère du Viel Testament 34, 42, 140, 143, 164-5, 323
modern performances 220, 324, 328
Mons 42-3, 142, 143
Montecassino Plays 51
music 45-6, 160, 173-6, 189-90, 199-200, 203, 210, 213, 217, 234, 238, 293-5, 303, 318-20
Mysteri de Rampans, Lou 149
Mystère de la Résurrection

347

–Angers 166
Mystères Rouergats 147-8
mysticism 27-8
Newcastle Plays 35
New Romney 35
Norwich Plays 35, 80, 247, 300, 306
N-Town Cycle 38-9, 223, 284-99, 323
  Passion Play I, II 286-8, 292
  Moses (6) 291-2
  Jesse Root (7) 292
  Shepherds (16) 293
  Death of Herod (20) 293
  Assumption of Mary (41) 287, 293-5, 318
oil of mercy 164-5, 260, 275-6
Oudenaarde 31, 55
overlap 67, 185-6, 235, 325
Passion, Mistère de la (Arnoul Gréban), see: Gréban
Passion, Mystère de la (Jean Michel), see: Michel
Passion Catalane-Occitane 147, 217, 320
Passion Cyclique 42, 142, 149
Passion d'Arras (Eustache Mercadé) 41, 138, 319
  see: *Vengeance*
Passion d'Autun 41, 143-5
Passion d'Auvergne 43, 143, 158-9, 162-3, 215, 319
Passion de Mons 42, 43
Passion de Nostre Seigneur (Sainte Geneviève) 43, 137-8
Passion de Palatinus 40-1, 144-5
Passion de Semur 41, 143, 145-6
Passion de Troyes 42, 164
Passion des Jongleurs 22, 41, 136, 143-5
Passion en Rime Franchoise (Valenciennes) 43
Passione de Revello 53-4, 201-5

Pecham, Archbishop 24, 25
place and scaffold 48-9, 171, 182, 185-6, 197, 199, 203, 206, 216-7, 282, 289-91, 324
plen-an-gwary 274, 283
politics 20, 29, 70, 202, 219, 223
printing 19, 42, 44, 68, 93, 142, 166, 302
Procès de Paradis 138, 150-1, 165
processions 29-31, 50, 119, 139, 154-5, 169, 170, 173-5, 178-81, 186-8, 194-5, 207-8, 212, 215-6, 224, 244, 290, 292
psalters 76, 87-9
Queen Mary's Psalter 87, 91-2
Ramakers, Bart 55
Rastall, Richard 294, 318
recapitulation 18, 139, 141, 229, 235-6, 237-8, 249, 256, 277, 295, 302, 323-4
REED 19, 274
Reformation 14, 23, 31, 33, 247, 300, 305, 314, 326
Romanelli, Giandomenico 124
Rome Plays 53, 198-201
Rome – St. Maria Maggiore 68-70
roof bosses 76-80, 95, 263, 325
Rose, Martial 76-9
Rueff, Joseph 314
Runnalls, Graham A. 40, 137, 145, 146, 158, 192
St. Anselm 23, 27, 138
St. Francis, and Franciscans 23, 24, 50, 84, 107, 131, 315-6, 317
  – Assisi 24, 74-5, 109, 131, 316
St. Gall Passion 44
St. Thomas Aquinas 26, 232
Savoie 149
Schubert, Franz 16
Seville 31, 57-8, 170, 214-6
silete 170, 179-80, 210

sources 144, 232-3, 241, 249, 254, 276-8, 293-5, 298, 308, 309, 314
Spector, Stephen 288
stage directions 148, 160, 178, 181, 200-1, 203-4, 252, 255, 282-3, 290-1, 296
stained glass 80-3
tableaux vivants 30, 55, 214, 216, 316
Tailby, John 186
theology 20, 24-8, 69, 134, 295, 309
time 17
Tintoretto 109, 124-30, 315
Toledo 58, 215, 216
Towneley Cycle 35, 37-8, 223, 237, 255-73, 289, 314, 325
  Murder of Abel (2) 267-8
  Noah (3) 268-9
  Pharaoh (8) 261-2
  Caesar Augutus (9) 262
  First Shepherds (12) 270-1
  Second Shepherds (13) 270-3
  Herod (16) 262-3
  John the Baptist (19) 261
  Judgement (30) 266-7
Trinity 244-6, 254, 295-6, 320-1
Valencia 31, 215, 216, 218

Vengeance Jhesuchrist, Mystère de la (Mercadé) 34, 41, 138-9, 166-7
Venice, St. Mark's 72-3
Venetian painters 85
versification 158, 160, 163, 193, 197, 210, 225, 226, 238, 251-2, 257, 260, 262, 286, 308, 309
violence 107, 157, 167, 161, 193
Wakefield Cycle, see: Towneley Cycle
Wakefield Master 37, 223, 256-8, 261-73, 321
Wiener Passionsspiel 46
Williams, Arnold 264
Winchester Psalter 87-9, 91
Woolf, Rosemary 236-7, 288, 294
worship 68, 93-4, 239, 248, 314
Wycliffe, John 23
York Cycle 33, 36, 37, 223-39, 255, 285, 313-4, 316-7, 324, 326
  Dream of Pilate's Wife (30) 226-30
  Remorse of Judas (32) 230-2
  Harrowing of Hell (37) 232-5
Zacher, Julius 212